ALSO BY ESTHER SCHOR

Emma Lazarus

Hills of Holland: Poems

Strange Nursery: New & Selected Poems

Bearing the Dead:
The British Culture of Mourning from
the Enlightenment to Victoria

Cambridge Companion to Mary Shelley (editor)

The Other Mary Shelley: Beyond "Frankenstein" (coeditor)

Women's Voices: Visions and Perspectives (coeditor)

BRIDGE

OF

WORDS

BRIDGE

OF

WORDS

———◦⦿◦———

ESPERANTO AND
THE DREAM OF
A UNIVERSAL LANGUAGE

ESTHER SCHOR

METROPOLITAN BOOKS
HENRY HOLT AND COMPANY
NEW YORK

Metropolitan Books
Henry Holt and Company
Publishers since 1866
175 Fifth Avenue
New York, New York 10010
www.henryholt.com

Metropolitan Books® and m® are registered trademarks
of Macmillan Publishing Group, LLC.

Library of Congress Cataloging-in-Publication Data

Names: Schor, Esther H., author.
Title: Bridge of words : Esperanto and the dream of a universal language / Esther Schor.
Description: New York : Metropolitan Books, [2016]
Identifiers: LCCN 2015018907 | ISBN 9780805090796 (hardback) |
    ISBN 9781429943413 (e-book)
Subjects: LCSH: Esperanto—History. | BISAC: LANGUAGE ARTS & DISCIPLINES /
    Linguistics / General. | HISTORY / Europe / General. | HISTORY / Social History.
Classification: LCC PM8209 .S36 2016 | DDC 499/.99209—dc23
LC record available at https://lccn.loc.gov/2015018907

Our books may be purchased in bulk for promotional, educational,
or business use. Please contact your local bookseller or the Macmillan
Corporate and Premium Sales Department at (800) 221-7945, extension 5442,
or by e-mail at MacmillanSpecialMarkets@macmillan.com.

First Edition 2016
Designed by Meryl Sussman Levavi
Printed in the United States of America

1   3   5   7   9   10   8   6   4   2

al samideanoj pasintaj kaj nuntempaj,
KORAN, VERDAN DANKON

to Esperantists past and present,
GREEN AND HEARTFELT THANKS

It is not down in any map; true places never are.

HERMAN MELVILLE, *Moby-Dick*

Contents

═══════

Part II. Doktoro Esperanto and the Shadow People

Samideanoj II: Iznik to Białystok, or *unu granda rondo familia*

IZNIK

BIAŁYSTOK

Part III. The Heretic, the Priestess, and the Invisible Empire

Samideanoj IV: Bona Espero, or Androids

Author's Note

Because I have used pseudonyms for most of the Esperantists mentioned, I have reversed the usual practice of using asterisks to indicate pseudonyms. Thus pseudonyms appear without asterisks, and asterisks are reserved for actual names (at first mention). Historical figures and cited authors are referred to by their actual names, without asterisks.

All translations from Esperanto are my own, except where otherwise indicated in the notes.

BRIDGE

OF

WORDS

Introduction

On the muggy July afternoon when I visited the Okopowa Street Cemetery, the dead Jews who'd slept on while the Nazis packed their descendants into cattle cars bound for Treblinka were still asleep. After hours tracking the contours of the Ghetto behind a detachment of Israeli soldiers, I was relieved to be among the lush ferns, rusted grilles, and mossy stones. Here and there, tipped and broken monuments had settled where they'd fallen among yellow wallflowers. In other sections, weeded, swept, and immaculately tended, huge monuments incised with Hebrew characters bore a heavy load of sculpted fruits, animals, priestly hands, and the tools of trades. The stones were cool to the touch, amid a musky odor of rotting leaves.

Among the largest monuments in the cemetery—the baroque monument to the actor Ester Rachel Kamińska; the porphyry stone of writer I. L. Peretz; the ponderous granite tomb of Adam Czerniaków, who after pleading in vain for the lives of the Ghetto's orphans took his own—was a large sarcophagus. On top rested a stone sphere the size of a bowling ball. Below a ledge of marble chips planted with plastic begonias was a large mosaic, a sea-green star with a white letter *E* at the center. Rays of blue, red, and white flared out in all directions. It was gaudy and amateurish, awkward in execution. The inscription read:

DOKTORO LAZARO LVDOVIKO ZAMENHOF
KREINTO DE ESPERANTO
NASKITA 15. XII. 1859. MORTIS 14. IV. 1917

Esperanto: I recalled one glancing encounter with it when I was twenty-three, an American in self-imposed exile, living in a chilly flat in London. The reign of Sid Vicious was about to be usurped by Margaret Thatcher, and the pittance I earned in publishing was just enough to buy standing room at Friday matinees and an occasional splurge on mascara. My boyfriend, Leo, and I found a rock-bottom price for a week in the Soviet Union; the only catch was that January, the cheapest time of the year to go, was also the coldest: in Moscow, 28 degrees Fahrenheit below; in Leningrad, a balmy zero. Leo took his parka out of storage; I borrowed warm boots, a fake-fur coat, and a real fur hat, and off we went. (In fact, I found it much warmer in the Soviet Union than in London, at least inside—chalk that up to central heating, which I could not afford.)

At the Hermitage, I wandered over to a large, amber-hued painting labeled Рембрандт. *Pembrandt?—no, Rembrandt.* A prodigal myself, I recognized it as a painting of the Prodigal Son, a young man kneeling in the embrace of a red-caped patriarch. As I drew closer to the supplicant, I noticed he had an admirer besides me: a tall, slender woman about my age with wispy bangs, stylish boots, and a brown wool coat. The previous day, a well-coiffed Intourist guide had explained to me that there were three kinds of women in Russia: women with fur hats, women with fur collars, and—she paused for effect—women with no fur at all. Here was one of the latter, and while I noted her furlessness, she greeted me in Russian. "Привет."

"*Preevyet.* Hello," I said.

She smiled. "My name is Ekaterina, I am from Alma Ata. Where are you from?" She seemed to be rummaging for more English words, but after "Do you speak Esperanto?" the pantry was bare.

Laughing, I asked, "*Français?*" but she wasn't joking.

"*Ne, ne,*" she said deliberately, her gray eyes narrowing, "Es-per-AN-to." One of us, I was sure, was ridiculous, but who? She, speaking to me in a pretend language? I, ignorant of Russian, Kazakh, and Esperanto, in my red Wellingtons, got up as Paddington Bear? Even as we shook hands and parted ways, the conversation was swiftly becoming an anecdote, a story to tell next week at the Swan over a pint of bitter.

Twenty-five years later, with prodigal sons of my own, I stood at what might have been, for all I knew, the grave of Esperanto itself, and thought of Ekaterina. She'd be in her late forties now, her forehead lined, her hair graying or, more likely, rinsed flame-red. Still furless, she'd be stuck in a concrete high-rise in Alma Ata (now Almaty), where years pass slowly, heaving their burdens of debt and illness and worry. I wondered how Esperanto had journeyed from Poland to Kazakhstan, how long it had endured, and who had erected this monument. Who laid out this mosaic, chip by tiny chip—men? women? both? Jews? Poles? Kazakhs? Where had they come from, and when? And why such devotion to a failed cause, to the quixotic dream of a universal language?

I didn't know it then, but I would spend most of a decade trying to find out.

* * *

The man who called himself Doktoro Esperanto (Doctor Hopeful) was a modern Jew, a child of emancipation adrift between the Scylla of anti-Semitism and the Charybdis of assimilation. Ludovik Lazarus Zamenhof was born in 1859 in multiethnic Białystok under the Russian Empire, the son and grandson of Russian-speaking language teachers. For a time, as a medical student in Moscow in the 1870s, he had dreamed among Zionists, but dreams are fickle things. His did not lead him to found a Jewish settlement in the malarial swamps and rocky fields of Palestine. In fact, they led him to dream of a Judaism purged of chosenness and nationalism; a modern Judaism in which Jews would embrace—and, in turn, be embraced by—like-minded others bent on forging a new monotheistic ethical cult. He believed that a shared past was not necessary for those determined to remake the world, only a shared future—and the effort of his life was to forge a community that would realize his vision.

Had Zamenhof been one of the great God-arguers, he'd have taken God back to the ruins of Babel for a good harangue. God had been rash (not to mention self-defeating) to ruin the human capacity to understand, and foolish to choose one nation on which to lavish his blessings and curses, his love and his jealousy. But Zamenhof was not an arguer. Benign and optimistic, he entreated his contemporaries, Jews and non-Jews alike, to become a people of the future. And to help them to cross the gulfs among ethnicities, religions, and cultures, he threw a plank across the abyss. As he wrote in *The Essence and Future of an International Language* (1903):

Ludovik Lazarus Zamenhof, Doktoro Esperanto
[Österreichische Nationalbibliothek]

> If two groups of people are separated by a stream and know that
> it would be very useful to communicate, and they see that planks
> for connecting the two banks lie right at hand, then one doesn't
> need to be a prophet to foresee with certainty that sooner or later
> a plank will be thrown over the stream and communication will
> be arranged. It's true that some time is ordinarily spent in waver-
> ing and this wavering is ordinarily caused by the most senseless
> pretexts: wise people say that the goal of arranging communi-
> cation is childish, since no one is busy putting planks across
> the stream . . . ; experienced people say that their progenitors
> didn't put planks across the stream and therefore, it is utopian;
> learned people prove that communication can only be a natural
> matter and the human organism can't move itself over planks etc.
> Nonetheless, sooner or later, the plank is thrown across.

In time, he hoped—and, against strong evidence, believed—that this
simple plank laid down by one man would become a bridge of words.

With the tools of modernity—reason, efficiency, pragmatism—he
sanded down the plank till it was smooth; people would cross over without getting splinters from irregular verbs or knotty idioms. Then, unlike
most language inventors, Zamenhof renounced the privileges of a creator,
without reneging on a creator's duties to his progeny. He is the only
language inventor on record ever to cede his language to its users, inviting them to take his rudimentary list of roots, combine them with a
handful of affixes, and invent words for new things, new occasions. And
where roots were not to hand, Esperantists were *by fiat* free to invent new
ones. It didn't matter whether the plank was thrown across a stream or
an ocean; if one were determined to cross, it would reach.

The "international language," as Zamenhof initially called it, was
designed not to replace national languages but to be a second language
for the world. While earlier lingua francas, such as Greek, Latin, and
French, had issued from empires, Zamenhof invented a language that
would commit its users to transcend nationalism. Free of imperial or national identity, Esperanto would serve neither dogma nor nationalism
nor arms nor money but the conscience and reason of its users, who
had determined to become a better people of the future. Perhaps no dream
of the century was more quixotic, except for Zamenhof's other dream:
that human beings would, decade after decade, choose this inheritance,

treasure it, and expand its expressive reach. And yet, for well more than a century and on six continents, people have done, and still do.

Esperantists, even in their most practical moments, have always dreamed of change, but they have not always shared the same dream. Zamenhof's "international language" has been used by anarchists, socialists, pacifists, theosophists, Bahá'ís, feminists, Stalinists, and even McCarthyites; as sociologist Roberto Garvía puts it, "Esperantists ended up speaking the same language, but not dancing to the same music."[1] Ironically, while Esperantists were often vague about what united them, totalitarians, fascists, and Nazis were not; sooner or later, Esperanto would always be reviled as a cosmopolitan, subversive movement inimical to nationalism and tainted by its Jewish origins. As we shall see, a few Esperantists made strange bedfellows with imperial powers, but sooner or later, they were forsaken. And being forsaken by an empire, for Esperantists, usually meant being banned, imprisoned, or shot. When Esperantists confronted the dreams of Hitler and of two latter-day Josephs—Stalin and McCarthy—the results were at best perilous, at worst murderous.

But the story of Esperanto is also a story of fantastic resilience, adaptation, and renovation. The early concept of the *fina venko*—the final triumph of Esperanto as a world language—has died a thousand deaths, most notably in 1922, when the League of Nations remanded a proposal to teach Esperanto in schools to a marginal committee on intellectual cooperation. Since then the ranks of the *finavenkistoj* have steadily dwindled. During the Cold War era, in place of the *fina venko*, Esperantists raised the banners of human rights, pacifism, and nuclear disarmament. In 1980, a later generation of Esperantists would officially renounce the *fina venko,* declaring themselves to be an autonomous, diasporic culture. With the Raumists, as they were called (after the Finnish town where they convened), Esperanto's universalist ideology was recast in a late-twentieth-century sensibility, askew, decentered, and skeptical of grand narratives altogether. Instead, the Raumists addressed themselves to the well-being, culture, and development of the Esperanto community, devoting time and attention to Esperanto in exchange for all manner of satisfactions: social, psychologial, ethical, political, aesthetic, intellectual, sexual—everything, that is, except political power and financial gain.

When I mention my work on Esperanto, I'm often asked, "How many people speak it?" I too, have asked this question, to which some Esperantists have offered answers. Amanda, ex-president of the Australian Esperanto Association, replies, "How many people collect stamps? How long is a piece of string?" Others point me to the website of the Universal Esperanto Association, which records "hundreds of thousands, possibly millions," in seventy countries. The only estimate with academic prestige is that of the late psycholinguist Sidney Culbert, who in 1989 put the number at between one and two million. Still, as Culbert conceded, "the tendency to overestimate the number of speakers of one's own language is not uncommon";[2] this particular psycholinguist spoke only Esperanto at home and drove a Honda bearing plates with the greeting "SALUTON"—Esperanto for "hello."[3]

The internet has augmented the number of learners, if not speakers. The online lernu! course, between 2004 and 2016, chalked up nearly twenty million visits to the site, and the Esperanto Duolingo website, launched in 2015, boasted 333,000 members after only ten months. How many Esperanto learners actually learn it well enough to participate in the community, online or off, is impossible to say; no doubt many take it up for the sheer fun of it, with no thought to the community at all.

My favorite answer to the question "How many?" was offered by Adél, a wry Hungarian teenager: "*Sufiĉe!*" she joked, meaning enough to comprise a vibrant worldwide community—and enough asking how many.

Esperantists may be hard to count, but they're not hard to find. On a recent bus tour of Central Asia, I had a free day in Samarkand. It was late at night when a minute or two of web surfing revealed an Esperantist within range: *Anatoly Ionesov, Director of the International Museum of Peace and Solidarity, whom I had never met. At 11:00 p.m., I emailed him; at 11:05 he invited me to meet him the following morning. That day I spent sitting in the parlor beside Anatoly and his wife, Irina, drinking tea at a table laden with enough cakes, cookies, dried apricots, sweets, rolls, and marmalade to feed a multitude. Anatoly oriented me to the museum: here were forty years of disarmament posters; there, autographed photos with peace greetings from Whoopi Goldberg, John Travolta, and Phil Collins. He told me about learning Esperanto in the Russian army, in Siberia; I told him about my travels in Cuba and Brazil. We admired photos of each other's children, and all the while, he was fashioning tiny origami swans, which he gave me when we parted. Strangers hours earlier, we embraced warmly, bona fide members of what Zamenhof called *la granda rondo familia*—the great family circle—of Esperantists.

When I returned to the group that evening, my companions all asked the same question: "Did you speak in Esperanto?"

"If we hadn't," I said, "it would have been a very quiet afternoon."

"Then . . . it works?"

It works.

To convince them further, I could share a long email I just received from a friend, tenderly announcing his new grandchild. He wrote, in Esperanto, about how eager he was for his son to finish his tour in the army; a spiritual crisis that happened while he was reading the Book of Numbers; his ninety-five-year-old father, shuttled back and forth from nursing home to hospital to rehab; a nasty gust of wind that slammed a screen door on his finger; the X-ray results (not definitive); the chances of receiving workers' comp (not good); and the prospect of missing days of work (a mixed blessing). Only a vibrant, living language could be equal to rendering the nitty-gritty of a life, replete with aging parents, children, and grandchildren; jobs and sick days; everyday fear and everyday hope.

To make a census of Esperantists, even in the days when one had to enroll or subscribe rather than simply click a mouse, was always a fool's errand. Today's Esperantists are eastern and western; northern and southern; men and women; students and retirees; moderates and leftists; activists and homemakers; gay, straight, and transgender. They come in more colors than the children on the UNICEF box—who, if memory serves, are only peach, brown, gold, and red.

Adél is right; enough asking "how many." I spent seven years among Esperantists not to count them but to listen to them. I wanted to get beyond the pieties and the utopianism and find out why real people choose this language, over others, to say what they have to say. What I heard sometimes sounded like a cacophony of voices, talking about ordinary, everyday things; universal harmony is not the first idea that comes to mind. But listening over time, and in so many places, I became convinced that these voices speak to our moment.

Multiculturalism, which is the lifeblood of Esperanto, has acquired prestige in our day as the last, best challenge to militaristic nationalism and violent sectarianism. We live, as never before, in the interstices between cultures, plying among a repertoire of people and places. What do we know when we are multicultural? That we may have different words for things; that there are ways and ways of life; but that we all have bodies. We were all born; we all will die. We make love, and some of us make children. How difficult should it be, then, to remember we are all human? In many parts of the world, it is very difficult, and since we live amid global networks, with access to images and sounds occurring at the ends of the earth, we live in those places, too. As I write these words, schoolgirls in sub-Saharan Africa are being kidnapped and enslaved; in the Middle East, the children of Abraham are lobbing rockets at one another; ISIS is breaking the heart of Syria by cracking its breastbone. Esperanto was invented not to teach us humanity, but to allow us to practice it freely, as, where, and when we choose. And where humanity is concerned it is hard to imagine a world more in need of practice than ours.

"Only connect," wrote E. M. Forster; ah, if it were just that easy. But even now, in the Internet age, Esperanto is about connection, not connectivity; about social life, not social networks. Esperanto has no passwords. It is a homemade, open-access affair invented by one man—an amateur in every sense of the word—and made available to all. The Internet may point Esperanto toward a future rather different from its past. But Esperanto reminds us why we strove to make communication easier, faster, cheaper, and ubiquitous. The Department of Defense may have wanted the Internet for security; what the rest of us wanted was one another.

* * *

The monument in Warsaw, commissioned in 1921, is the work of many hands. The winning design was submitted by Mieczysław Jan Ireneusz Lubelski, a Polish sculptor, and the Scottish granite was donated by the Esperantists of Aberdeen. Transport of the monument from Scotland to Poland was paid for by the Warsaw Monument Committee, with help from the Polish government, the Jewish community of Warsaw, and the laborers, who worked for a nominal fee. It was erected and dedicated in 1926; the mosaic followed, but only after 97 percent of Warsaw's 350,000 Jews had been destroyed, Zamenhof's two daughters and son among them. The Esperantists returned to his tomb and did precisely what Jews do at graves: place stones.

This book, however, is not a memorial. I did not write it to elegize a bygone hope, to portray a quirky cult, or to roam a neglected byway of modernity. I wrote this book to discover why Esperanto has, unbelievably, beaten all the odds: competition from rival language projects, two world wars, totalitarian regimes, genocidal death factories, the nuclear arms race, and the emergence of fundamentalist sectarianism—not to mention the juggernaut of global English. The language-movement of Esperanto survives because it addresses a particularly modern predicament: to negotiate the competing claims of free individuals on the one hand, and on the other, communities bound by values and traditions. Esperantists reconcile liberalism and communitarianism *by freely choosing a tradition of ideals*.

But as much as I respect Esperantists for making this choice, and for the gorgeous language and culture they have made, they are also the victims of their own mythology. Specifically, they uphold the myth that Esperanto's vaunted political neutrality (which has its own unhandsome history) removes it from the arena of politics. On the contrary, Esperanto is *essentially* political, as I have argued to roomfuls of disconcerted Esperantists; it was created to enable diverse peoples to talk not only past their differences but also about them. Zamenhof envisioned multiethnic cities, states, and continents—indeed, a multiethnic world—using Esperanto for the sake of reconciliation and harmony. I want to honor the achievement and longevity of Esperanto, but even more to herald its untapped potential to bring us closer to political justice. Esperanto's greatest power of all is to be powerless and yet to compel us to move from bafflement to understanding, from conflict to resolution.

Bridge of Words began as a biography of Zamenhof, who, like the subject of my biography *Emma Lazarus*, was a modern Jew of the pogrom-ridden 1880s, trying to steer a course between universalism and particularism. But because Zamenhof gave his universal language to its users, Esperanto is their creation, too. Hence this book is a biography of Esperanto's collective creators, the Esperanto community, and a report from its trenches. And like the universal language, a hybrid of several tongues, this book is a hybrid of cultural history and memoir. Each of the four parts pairs a historical narrative with a memoir of my sojourns, visits, on five continents, among *samideanoj*—which is how Esperantists refer to one another, invoking the commonality of vague "same-idea-ness."

The Esperanto world is a place where minds are changed, and mine was no exception. As the memoirs in this book will show, encountering hundreds of Esperantists in far-flung places was also an encounter with myself. What I realized, during the seven years I spent speaking the language of "the hoping one," was how keenly I needed to infuse my life with hope. And living in the universal language, among people from distant countries, I realized that I had failed to understand—and make myself understood by—those closest to me. Esperanto brought me to a reckoning with the choices I had made and those I had yet to make. Had I predicted, when I began this project, the course my future would take, I'd have been very wrong. Regarding the future of Esperanto I am no prophet either, but of one thing I am sure: there will be no *fina venko*, when the whole world is speaking Esperanto. But Esperanto does not need to succeed in the future. It has already done so in the present, a human creation that is rare and valuable, and the intimation of a better world.

PART ONE

THE DREAM OF A UNIVERSAL LANGUAGE

1. Zamenhof's Babel

My friend Michael was reading galleys of his new book when an email arrived.

> Dear Sir,
>
> I am the proud translator of your book into Swedish. I have two questions (there will be more, I promise!):
>
> 1) "She had as much success reading *The Cat in the Hat* as she would a CAT scan." The book *The Cat in the Hat* is translated into Swedish, so far so good, with the title *"Katten i Hatten"* which is almost the same. A CAT scan however is a *"datortomografi"* or *"skiktröntgen"*—no cats in sight. I thought of exchanging the CAT scan for *"hattiska hieroglyfer"*—"Hatti hieroglyphs"—they should be pretty hard to read! But then we have to shift the resemblance from "CAT-Cat scan" to *"Hat-Hatti."* Or would you prefer something more technical and CAT scanny?
>
> 2) When you come home and find the knives "behind a set of rarely used dishes," are these some kind of plates or more like bowls?
>
> Best wishes,
> Anders

The email made Michael anxious. He imagined his Swedish readers coming upon "Hatti hieroglyphs," lowering the book, and staring into the middle distance, where they would find, as Anders put it, "no cats in sight." With cats become hats, scans become hieroglyphs, and dishes become plates or even bowls, was this still his book? "If only," Michael said wistfully, "I had written the book in Esperanto."

His assumption, of course, was that Esperanto was invented to be a universal language that would put us all beyond translation, and I can see why he thought so: it's an ancient dream, the dream of reversing the curse of Babel and restoring us to some lost capacity to understand language perfectly. But to put us "beyond translation" is decidedly not the project of Esperanto. Instead of deeming language to be compromised by its humanity, Zamenhof placed his confidence in human beings: both in their will toward understanding and in their recognition that understanding, at the best of times, is a fraught endeavor. A language of collective invention, he believed, would be far more likely to succeed than a language closely held, meted out, or even ostentatiously bestowed by its inventor. In fact, the more users coined new words, the more likely the language was to be widely used and cherished, for each new word traced a crossing from one language to another. Esperanto was invented not to transcend translation, *but to transact it.*

By aligning universal understanding with the future rather than the past, Zamenhof broke with the West's central myth of linguistic difference: the story of the Tower of Babel. Though biographers René Centassi and Henri Masson dubbed Zamenhof "the man who defied Babel," Zamenhof knew that to defy Babel was folly. For Zamenhof, Babel was not a curse to be reversed, but the mythic elaboration of an epistemological problem: how can we know the meaning of another person's utterance, whatever language they happen to speak?

Zamenhof was not only an acute reader of Genesis; he also spent most of a decade translating the entire Hebrew Bible into Esperanto, completing it only three years before his death. If Zamenhof doubted that there existed a unitary world language before Babel, he would have found the biblical evidence on his side. I don't simply mean the long chapter on human diversity—the "table of nations" (Genesis 10)—that immediately precedes the story of Babel. I want to suggest that even in the Garden of Eden story, the notion of an original, universal language is at best dubious.

Chapter 1 of Genesis represents both divine and human speech, and while God and Adam seem to understand one another—no one asks for translation or expresses befuddlement—what each does with language is clearly different. God creates with it, Adam names with it, and their languages differ as much as "Let there be light" differs from "You're a lemur." Even the appearance of mutual understanding may be deceptive; after all, God uses the word "die" in a deathless world without bothering about being understood. And while the biblical redactor is noncommittal about whether the humans understood their God, the poet John Milton in *Paradise Lost* was unequivocal: they did not because . . . how could they?

This occlusion of understanding may be why there is only a modicum of conversation in Eden, very little of it quoted. For example, whether Eve actually speaks to Adam is anyone's guess, since she is never directly quoted in conversation with him. After Eve eats the fruit, the doings that follow—sharing the fruit, donning leaves, hiding out—occur speechlessly, in a quick dumbshow of shame that ends in the first rhetorical question: "Where are you?" God asks, and the ensuing duet of inquisition and blame isn't much of a conversation either. In the cascade of divine curses—on man, on woman, on serpent—speech travels in one direction, from power to powerlessness, and after Adam renames "the woman" Eve (Genesis 3:20), he will never name anything again, ceding the naming of his sons to their mother. At best, Edenic conversation is a lopsided affair; at worst, it's sabotaged, whether by divine commandment or serpentine deception.

By the time we reach the story of Babel in Genesis 11, whether God and humans speak the same language is almost beside the point; they barely speak to one another. After the flood, when the smoke from Noah's sacrifice rises, God, for the first time, can be heard muttering to himself: "for the imagination of man's heart is evil from his youth" (Genesis 8:21). What takes God by surprise, in the Babel story, is that humans have connived to do something in concert and on their own initiative. After the fiasco in the garden and the fratricide in the field, after all the quotidian murders, rapes, and betrayals, one wouldn't have thought so: "And they said, Go to, let us build us a city and a tower, whose top may reach unto heaven; and let us make us a name, lest we be scattered abroad upon the face of the whole earth" (Genesis 11:4). Their project—manifold and complex, like so many human undertakings—was hotly debated by the rabbis of the Talmud. Some apologized for Babel's builders, whose aim, they reasoned, was to climb up and slit the tent of heaven where another unjust flood awaited innocent and guilty alike. Other rabbis staunchly defended God. For them, the builders were a concatenation of sinners with various motives: to colonize heaven, to worship idols, to lay siege to the kingdom of God. And accordingly, they argued, God meted out fierce punishments to the builders, some of whom were turned to apes and others to phantoms.

But perhaps the rabbis overlooked a different provocation:

> And the LORD came down to see the city and the tower, which the children of men builded. And the LORD said, Behold, the people is one, and they have all one language; and this they begin to do: and now nothing will be restrained from them, which they have imagined to do. Go to, let us go down, and there confound their language, that they may not understand one another's speech. (Gen. 11:5-7)

What exactly was their offense? This was not the first time human beings "imagined" evil plans repugnant to God. In Genesis 6, when the "sons of God came in unto the daughters of men," he'd conceded that "the wickedness of man was great in the earth, and . . . every imagination of the thoughts of his heart was only evil continually" (Genesis 6:5). What was new to Babel was the builders' plan to "make us a name," for to name oneself is to usurp a divine prerogative. And since the punishment at Babel was to avenge the human will to "make . . . a name" for oneself, God doomed each of the builders to speak *only unto himself*—to speak without being understood by another. God might have punished the builders of Babel by constraining the power to build, to rule, or to go to war, but he did not. Nor did God ram unintelligible phonemes into their mouths. Instead, having direly misestimated the power of human conversation, God blunted the human capacity to understand others and to elicit understanding.

In fact, the biblical narrative says nothing about the multiplication and dispersal of languages. The proverbial name for the story, from the Middle Ages on, is "the confusion of tongues" (*confusio linguarum*), not "the diffusion of tongues." In fact, the Hebrew word for "language" (*safah*, a lip rather than a tongue) is always singular in the story, as it is in the Latin Vulgate and the English King James Version. The "curse of Babel" renders all language as opaque *as if* it were what we call "foreign" language, and though "the same language and the same words" spoken at the beginning are spoken after the tower falls, translation has become necessary, even for speakers of the same tongue. If mortality is what it is like to live after Eden, misunderstanding—to speak perpetually in need of translation—is what it is like to live after Babel.

But the ruin of understanding was only one consequence of Babel. After destroying the tower, the builders' hedge against being "scattered abroad," God scattered them throughout the world. What better way to punish their arrogation of peoplehood for themselves, their choice to be a people? To give God his due here, we can imagine God's weariness, his exasperation with humanity. "I will never understand them," God might have thought. "I made them Eden, they sinned; I dried up the flood and they sinned again. Twice I filled their lungs with heaven and twice they spent my breath in evil. I have tried twice, twice, to make humans.

"Now I will make Israel."

When God renamed Abram *Abraham*, the curse of Babel was complete; with one carefully interpolated syllable, an idolator's son became the first Israelite. God's crowning revenge on the builders of Babel was the choice of Israel, and there, on Israel, God's attention rested, leaving the rabbis of the Talmud to finish off the builders of Babel. Which they most certainly did, declaring "the generation of the scattered" personae non gratae in the world to come.

The Tower of Babel story is not only a myth of misunderstanding; it is also a myth of the diaspora as an existential condition. From the Babel myth, Zamenhof intuited that the perpetual impulse of humans to stake "a name for themselves" on a piece of territory only compounded the problem of misunderstanding. And while Zamenhof accepted misunderstanding as part of the human condition, he refused to accept its human costs: lives lost to tribalism, anti-Semitism, and racism; pogroms just yesterday and perhaps a war of empires tomorrow. Instead, he set about to convince misunderstood and scattered human beings that they had the capacity, without divine intervention, to understand one another better by joining together not over land, not over a tower, but over language. (Even the people Israel, he pointed out on numerous occasions, were now among the scattered, and if they were going to claim any authentic, modern identity, they, too, needed to take the matter of language into their own hands.) Perhaps the language of Adam was given by God, but the language that would rescue Adam's and Eve's heirs from their worst impulses would be a very human thing.

2. West of Babel

Zamenhof's radically humanist revision of the "curse" of Babel sets him apart from the history of language invention in Western Europe, where Babel's curse was taken to be the doom of linguistic difference. To reverse this "curse" was not only to dream of language which was divine and perfect; it was also to dream of human beings capable of perfect understanding—beings who are different from us.

The most audacious of those who sought to reverse the "curse" of Babel yearned for God's own language, for words empowered to speak the universe into being. Others imagined secret, esoteric languages that were the preserve of initiates: kabbalistic acrostics, numerology, and anagrams; the gnostic "magic languages" of Paracelsus and the Rosicrucians; the divine "signatures" perceived in nature by the seventeenth-century German mystic Jacob Boehme. Still others invented devices, symbols, and meta-languages designed to mediate between human beings and the words they failed to grasp. Umberto Eco's *The Search for the Perfect Language* surveys a millennium of such inventions, among them that of Ramon Llull (ca. 1230–1315), a Franciscan who asked himself what language might best propound the truth of Scripture to infidels.[1] Starting with logical propositions rather than glyphs and words, Llull selected nine letters and four figures, combined them into questions, compounded questions into subjects, and multiplied subjects into propositions. Using only these elements and the engine of combination, Llull's *Ars Magna* purported to generate 1,680 logical propositions, a repertoire from which one might choose a few key points to which an infidel would, without translation, *necessarily* consent. Such propositions would have a kind of liquidity from culture to culture, on which the truth could skip like a stone. By "truth," of course, Llull meant *his* truth, not the infidel's. That Llull died at the hands of the Saracens may suggest that something more than revelation was lost in translation.

In the early modern period, language needed to do more than propound truths; it needed to translate a host of others to European interlopers in Asia, Africa, and the Americas—merchants and governors as well as missionaries. Llull's Saracen "infidel" was displaced by the Chinese, Hindus, Native Americans, and Africans. Polyglot Bibles became the model for massive polyglot dictionaries called polygraphies. The frontispiece of Cave Beck's *Universal Character* of 1657 features a table around which three men in various national costumes are seated: a Dutch burgher, a mustachioed and turbaned Indian, and an African in a toga. On the right stands a native of the New World in a grass skirt and a Carmen Miranda–esque headpiece, who salutes in the universal sign for "Hey, no problem!" His long spear, its tip resting idly on the floor, is conspicuously flaccid, to assure us that he's checked his aggression at the door.

Meanwhile, the printing press, less than a century after its invention, scattered projects and programs for language reform all over Europe, many of which had germinated in newly emerging scientific societies. After the restoration of the British monarchy in 1660, several members of the new "Royal Society of London for the Improvement of Natural Knowledge" were spurred to invention by the legacy of Sir Francis Bacon (1561–1626). Bacon's profound intuition, as he put it in *The Advancement and Proficience of Learning* (1605), was that "words are the footsteps of reason"—*written*, not spoken, words. Bacon held that written words could do more than simply refer to speech; they could refer directly to thought itself. Though Zamenhof was an autodidact when it came to philosophy and linguistics, his invention of roots that referred to ideas rather than words is remarkably consonant with Bacon's call for the invention of "real characters."

Thus with Bacon, philosophical rather than divine truth became the desideratum of language projects. Invoking Chinese ideograms, arbitrary signs that "expresse neither Letters, nor Words, but Things, and Notions," Bacon imagined characters that would represent thoughts with a philosophical rigor *exceeding that of words*. Moreover, Bacon believed Chinese characters to be universally legible among the peoples of Asia. Not only would "real characters" mean the same thing to one Briton and her neighbor; they would also be legible to people speaking different tongues—in fact, to all peoples and nations. The use of "real characters," in short, would grant Europe what Bacon believed Asia already had: a way of communicating without resort to translation, with characters that could be entrusted to convey thought itself. What Bacon didn't realize was that legibility across cultures did not imply that characters were understood identically among cultures. As soon as characters were interpreted as words, their philosophical purity was compromised.

Such was the problem with the boldest attempt to answer Bacon's call, that of John Wilkins (1614–1672), the first secretary of the Royal Society (and Oliver Cromwell's brother-in-law). Wilkins was a man of large

ambitions, undertaking to develop a comprehensive, "pansophic" system
of knowledge. Devoting five years to his pansophic obsession, Wilkins
tried to tabulate all knowledge in the form of concept trees split by distinctions based on sensory data. In the case of animals, his taxonomies
are recondite but effective; but to define tickling via rigorous concept
trees was another story. Tickling, in Wilkins's view, was a titillation
(rather than a piercing) entailing "dissipation of the spirits in the softer
parts by a light touch" (as opposed to "distention or compression of
parts" or "obstruction in nerves or muscles"), and which while light is
nonetheless painful (unlike actions that "satisfy appetites"), and which is a
corporeal action addressed to "sensitive bodies" (as opposed to "vegeta-
tive" or "rational" ones), an action absolute (rather than relative) and peculiar to living creatures (as opposed to an action imitative of the gestures of
creatures).

In Wilkins's *Essay Towards a Real Character and a Philosophical Language*—a tome measuring two feet by one foot—"real characters" finally
appear in Section III. Here Wilkins rendered in strange glyphs each of
the ultimate terms in his branching tables. To rocket language beyond
ambiguity, he invented a script that looked like squadrons of tiny anten-
naed spaceships. The problem was that there were 2,030 distinct characters, so that to use them would require prodigious feats of memory. As a
work-around, Wilkins then represented each glyph by combinations
of letters. "For instance," he wrote, "If (De) signifie *Element* then (Deb)
must signifie the first difference; which (according to the Tables) is *fire*:
and (Debá) will denote the first Species, which is *Flame*. (Det) will be the
first difference under that Genus, which is *Appearing Meteor*; (Detá)
the first Species, viz. *Rainbow*; (Deta) the second, viz. *Halo*." But loading
each letter with such a huge burden of information was dangerous; stuff
happens, including misprints. For example, if my son writes to me about
his "psythology" instead of "psychology" paper, chances are I'll chalk it
up to a late night out, but if Wilkins's "Deb" appears in lieu of "Det," we're
dealing with a meteor instead of a fire.

The pitfall of Wilkins's *Essay* is not the multiplicity of characters; it's
the multiplicity of words. Heaping up terms to make precise categories
and heaping up categories to make precise distinctions, Wilkins delivered
heaps and heaps of words, not universal ideas. Moreover, tall stacks of
words were left off the tables; an appendix includes a dictionary of some
fifteen thousand English words keyed to the tables by synonyms and

periphrases. In Wilkins's system, there was even a metaphor particle that magically transformed any word into a figure of speech—"dark," for example, into "mystical."[2] Figures within characters, characters within universes, wheels within wheels.

Wilkins's very public failure to invent a language purely of ideas provoked extreme responses. On one hand, the German philosopher and mathematician Gottfried Wilhelm Leibniz (1646–1716) sought a method for producing knowledge rather than organizing, defining, and representing it. His *caracteristica* were designed to reckon with truths as one would with numbers, to conduct ratiocination by means of numerical ratios. And with such a calculus, blind to the particular propositions being manipulated, Leibniz claimed the power to put truths to the test, and even to discover new ones. On the other hand, Jonathan Swift (1667–1745), in *Gulliver's Travels* (1726), skewered the idea of a "Universal Language to be understood in all civilized Nations." In the Academy of Lagado, Gulliver encounters "a Scheme for entirely abolishing all Words whatsoever; . . . that since Words are only Names for *Things*, it would be more convenient for all Men to carry about them, such *Things* as were necessary to express the particular Business they are to discourse on." "I have often," continues the empiricist Gulliver, "beheld two of those Sages almost sinking under the Weight of their Packs, like Pedlars among us; who, when they met in the Streets, would lay down their Loads, open their Sacks, and hold Conversation for an Hour together; then put up their Implements, help each other to resume their Burthens, and take their Leave."

Leibniz envisioned a shining steel language of logic beyond the stain of things; Swift satirized a bulky language of things beyond the trammels of logic. At the end of the dream of a universal language without misunderstanding lies a language without words.

3. A World of Words

By the end of the seventeenth century, the British philosopher John Locke (1632–1704) delivered a death blow to philosophical language projects. For Locke, the notion of words (or characters) with transparent, universal meanings was worse than a fantasy: "It is a perverting the use of words," Locke wrote, "and brings unavoidably obscurity and confusion into their signification, whenever we make them stand for anything but those ideas we have in our minds." Locke's stark, uncompromising theory of language in his *Essay Concerning Human Understanding* (1690) sapped words of all their power: the power to infallibly represent and refer, the power to convey one person's ideas to another, above all, their power to propound and compound knowledge.

Wilkins and Locke are divided by the watershed between ancient and modern views of language. Where Wilkins had been invested in the notion of a divine "curse" of Babel, Locke grounded the human capacity to understand (or misunderstand) language in God-given liberty. "Every man has so inviolable a liberty to make words stand for what ideas he pleases,"[3] wrote Locke, that no one could possibly evoke his own ideas in another's mind. In Locke's view, such mental "liberty" is rarely disruptive of communication when dealing with simple ideas; but when it came to moral ideas "concerning honour, faith, grace, religion, church &c.,"[4] one was as likely to misunderstand a term in one's own tongue as in a foreign one: "If the sounds they applied to one idea were such as by the hearer were applied to another . . . [there would be] two languages."[5]

Locke approached this predicament as a trial for society rather than as a conundrum for consciousness. Human beings, he observed empirically, were willing to forgo the radical liberty of language in favor of convention and conformity, entering into a sort of linguistic social contract. Speakers of a language were to avoid abusing words (especially as metaphor, which he libeled, famously, a "perfect cheat"); otherwise "men's language will be like that of Babel, and every man's words, being intelligible *only to himself,* would no longer serve to conversation and the ordinary affairs of life" (my italics). It was for a novelist, Laurence Sterne, to reveal both the darkness and the comedy in Locke's vision, suspending his characters in *Tristram Shandy* (1759–1767) between "hobby-horse" solipsism and dire miscommunication. When the amorous, anxious Widow Wadman asks Uncle Toby where he was injured during the Siege of Namur, Uncle Toby does not point to his mauled groin. Instead, he builds her a scale model of the battlefield and points to a bridge.

Where? . . . There.

After Locke, the era of the a priori language project—a philosophically rigorous language created from whole cloth—gave way to reformist a posteriori projects, which involved rationalizing existing languages. Such projects were abetted by a new interest in discovering a "universal grammar," residing deep within existing languages; this, in turn, prompted the development of "laconic," pared-down, grammars of European languages. By 1784, a rationalized, regularized French was disseminated in Count Antoine de Rivarol's "On the Universality of the French Language." In the glare of the French Enlightenment, language became the spear of reason, renovation, and revolution, and the ensuing revolutionary-Napoleonic period became a crucible for the power of language to remake the social order. Not only were monuments, streets, towns, and playing cards renamed; so were the seasons, the months, and the days of the week. Those named for kings—the Louises and Lerois—took the names of Roman liberators.[6]

But whereas in France language was coopted for reason and revolution, German thinkers of the Counter-Enlightenment regarded language as an inherited armor against reason's ruthlessness. Language, since it evolved in tandem with historical, environmental, and racial factors, was culturally particular. Yet, as Giambattista Vico had argued in the *New Science* of 1725, language was also universal, insofar as it evolved in all cultures according to universal patterns. Wilhelm von Humboldt (1767–1835) believed that language shaped the entire worldview of particular cultures; while Johann Gottfried Herder (1744–1803) held language as the means by which the *Volk* would shape its destiny. That language and culture were utterly enmeshed suggested to Humboldt a pair of looming dangers: language could not only estrange us from one another; it could also be used to injure people and damage whatever they held dear.[7]

4. A "Vexed Question of Paternity"

The late eighteenth and early nineteenth centuries saw the rise of nationalist language movements in Italy, Hungary, and Poland. Such projects inspired Zamenhof's sense that language could be assigned a moral mission, though, as Garvía has noted, his interethnic purpose was diametrically opposed to nationalism.[8] In fact, proponents of these movements of national revival viewed the notion of an international language with suspicion and distaste. As the Italian poet Giacomo Leopardi (1798–1837) put it, a universal language would be "the most enslaved, impoverished, timid, monotonous, uniform, arid and ugly language ever . . . incapable of beauty of any type, totally uncongenial to imagination."[9] In France, Antoine

Destutt de Tracy (1754–1836) warned against the desire for a universal language, conjuring a jejune, homogeneous intellectual life centered on an ossified authority.[10] Behind all these misgivings is the menacing specter of a universal language driven by the exigencies of imperial power.

By the middle decades of the nineteenth century, Napoleon's imperial adventure, having laid new networks of communication and transportation, had given rise to new international bodies and protocols for international trade and research. The *Encyclopédistes'* efforts to make language more effective and efficient now took root in France and spread to Germany, Scandinavia, and Italy. Not since the seventeenth century had so much time and energy been spent on language building. The first scholarly study of invented languages, published in Paris in 1903, surveys thirty-eight projects, almost all of them a posteriori "improvements" on existing European languages.

In the spring of 1879, a night of insomnia gave rise to Volapük, the first invented language to capture the imagination of thousands; perhaps tens of thousands. Volapük's inventor, a German Catholic priest named Johann Martin Schleyer (1831–1912), claimed he'd received the language in a vision from God. Schleyer's claim notwithstanding, the design of Volapük was anything but divine; in fact, designed for and embraced by an elite, it was effete, feeble, and very difficult to master. The first problem was phonetic. Aiming for a universally pronounceable alphabet, Schleyer changed the letter *r* to *l*, ostensibly to benefit the Chinese, yet it soon emerged that Japanese speakers had problems pronouncing *l*. Deformations of familiar phonemes soon became fodder for satire. In 1887, a skeptical commentator for the *New York Times* wrote:

> It may startle the reader . . . to learn that he is a *melopel* [American] who is perusing his morning *pöp* [paper] unaware of the true state of his case. . . . He may have come across the Atlantic from *Yulop* [Europe] or have smuggled himself and his pigtail into California after a month's voyage from *Sinän* [China]. . . . In any case, his *daduk* [education] is sure to be incomplete, since he is not proficient in Volapük.[11]

But Schleyer's phonetics were only one problem; another was that his words were inflected with a myriad of endings. With its endlessly morphing verbs, whose endings indicated tense (including six conditional

*Johann Schleyer, the inventor of
Volapük
[Österreichische Nationalbibliothek]*

tenses), number, mood, voice, and sometimes gender, Volapük entered the realm of absurdity. That a single verb might take 505,440 different forms[12] became, for Volapük's detractors, proof of its lunacy. As the late Donald Harlow, former president of the Esperanto League of North America, once put it, the problem with Volapük was that it had "more verb forms than speakers."[13]

As Garvía has shown, Volapük clubs sprang up within a narrow demographic of male, educated, German-speaking Catholics, and its membership never diversified.[14] Attaining any fluency in the language seems to have been optional; German, not Volapük, was the lingua franca of the congresses of 1884 and 1887. Within a decade of its inception, the movement foundered while Schleyer bickered with reformists in his ersatz academy, contesting the notion that Volapük might be used in commercial settings.[15] The dissonance between Schleyer's account of passively receiving the language from God and his harshly proprietary behavior did not go unremarked. In 1907, the historian W. J. Clark mused on the debacle as a "vexed question of paternity": "This child . . . was it a son domiciled in its father's house . . . ? Or a ward in the guardianship of its chief promoters? Or an orphan foundling, to be boarded out on the scattered-home system at the public expense?"[16]

5. *Lingvo Internacia*

Meanwhile, in Warsaw, a young man about to father his own language was watching the rise and fall of Volapük closely. The son of emancipated Jews who retained strong ties to the Jewish community, Ludovik Lazarus Zamenhof hailed from Białystok, a "Babel of languages," in which Russians jostled Poles; Poles, Germans; and everyone, Jews, since they made up about 70 percent of the population. Multilingualism was not the preserve of the educated; it was the way one bought eggs, greeted policemen, prayed, and gossiped with coreligionists. At the same time, Zamenhof grew up convinced that linguistic difference lay at the root of interethnic animosity, and before he was out of his teens he had set out to fashion an auxiliary language for peoples crammed together in multiethnic cities, for ethnically diverse nation-states, and for the growing number of organizations designed to modernize commercial relations among countries.

An 1896 letter from Zamenhof to his friend Nikolai Borovko is Esperanto's own Book of Genesis; it tells a story not of making but of unmaking. Like the proverbial Indian wood carver who sculpted elephants by "removing everything that is not elephant," Zamenhof crafted Esperanto by turning language over in his hand and then paring it away to an austere simplicity. In a bid for rigor and economy, he at first tried out a conceptual grid much like that of John Wilkins, denoting concepts by letters and combining them in easily pronounced phonemes. To express the eleven-letter *interparoli* (to speak one to another), he ventured the two-letter syllable "pa": "Therefore, I simply wrote the mathematical series of the shortest, but easily-pronounced combinations of letters, and to each gave the meaning of a definite word (for example, a, ab, ac, ad,—ba, ca, et cetera)." But unlike Wilkins, Zamenhof tested the scheme on himself and, finding that it made prolific demands on the memory, aborted it.

His watchwords were simplicity and flexibility. He had already rejected the idea of reviving Greek or Latin, convinced that a truly international language had to be neutral, nonethnic, and nonimperial; in other words, a language that did not yet exist. While he was inventing conjugations, he encountered the comparative simplicity of English grammar:

"I noticed then that the plenitude of grammatical forms is only a random historical incident, and isn't linguistic necessity."[17] In short order, Zamenhof simplified his grammar-in-progress to a brief document of a few pages. For verbs in the present indicative, he used a single ending: *Mi kuras, li kuras*—simpler, in fact, than English (I run; he run*s*)—avoiding Volapük's overinflection of verbs. There would be no distinction between singular and plural verbs: *mi kuras* (I run) and *ili kuras* (they run)— simpler than French (*je cours* but *ils courent*). Except in reference to persons, personal pronouns, and professions, there would be no distinction between masculine and feminine subjects.

Zamenhof collated his lexicon of nine hundred roots mainly from Romance languages, German, English, and Russian; conjunctions and particles he culled from Latin and Greek. When in doubt, he favored Latin roots: "house" was *dom-*; "tree," *arb-*; "night," *nokt-*. To attain wordhood, a root simply donned a final vowel, a sort of team jersey identifying it as a specific part of speech. *Nokt-* with an *-o* ending joined the noun team: "night." With an *-a* ending it joined the adjective team: *nokta*, as in "night-hour"; and with an *-e* ending, the adverb team: *nokte*, meaning "by night," et cetera. It could even join the ranks of verbs, as in the compound *tranokti* (to sleep over). Like Schleyer, Zamenhof relied on a system of affixes for word building, though he attributed this element to an epiphany he'd had about commercial signs: the suffix *-skaja* was used on both a porter's lodge and a candy shop. In Esperanto, for instance, the prefix *ek-* (begin, or start), added to the verb *lerni* (to learn), gives us *eklerni*, "to begin to learn," as in *Kiam vi eklernis Esperanton?* (When did you start to learn Esperanto?) Suffixes, like cabooses, also extend the reach of words: the suffix *-aĵo* (a thing), added to *manĝi* (to eat), gives us *manĝaĵo* (food); the suffix *-ejo, manĝejo* (dining hall). Some affixes, taking noun, adjective, or adverb endings, can become free-standing words: *ilo*, a tool or device; or *male*, "on the contrary." Strung together, affixes sometimes offer gains in concision, but at the same time create clunky polysyllabic words. The early poets in the language regarded the prefix *mal*, meaning "the opposite of," as the verbal equivalent of ankle-weights, and over time many *mal-* words—such as *malsanulejo*, literally, "a place-for-unwell-people"—have been bested by lithe competitors, such as *hospitalo*. Yet many affix clusters have survived, incurring affection and loyalty precisely because their Esperantic origins are so obvious.

Despite the prestige of Esperantism in the construction of new words,

Zamenhof placed a premium on the internationalism of his lexicon. A century and a half before digital algorithms emerged to assess the internationalism of a word,[18] Zamenhof used his own multilingualism and a stack of dictionaries to accomplish the task. To combine words from distinct European languages must have seemed natural, too, to a speaker of Yiddish. It was not Volapük but Yiddish, a mongrel of Germanic, Semitic, and Slavic words, on which Zamenhof modeled his international language. (Apart from the interrogative *Nu* and the exclamatory *Ho ve!*, however, there are few overt borrowings from Yiddish; some speculate that *edzino*—"wife"—derives from the Yiddish *rebbetzin*, a rabbi's wife.)

What had happened to Yiddish over a millennium, in mass migrations of Jews from Western to Eastern Europe and back, Zamenhof would try to recapitulate within his new, international language. The percentage of Slavic words in Esperanto and Yiddish is similar (15 percent). But whereas the ratio of Germanic to Romance words in Yiddish is more than three to one, this relationship is reversed in Esperanto. Zamenhof had already spent several years trying to modernize Yiddish, but with Esperanto, he found another, better way to recast Yiddish as a modern language. It was as if he wrapped Yiddish in a chrysalis, where its medieval German metamorphosed into French modernity. When it emerged, it would have shed forever its ancient Hebraicism. And as we shall see, it was Esperanto, rather than his romanized Yiddish, that Zamenhof would offer up as a modern language for emancipated Jews.

Still, the early practice of cobbling words together instead of borrowing them inoculated the infant language from the antibodies of the world's dominant languages. These days, when so-called "international" words are invariably drawn from English, the Akademio de Esperanto has rigorously resisted the anglicization of Esperanto. The Internet, for example, is not *interneto* but *interreto*, using the Esperanto word for "net" (*reto*); a computer is a *komputilo,* using the Esperantic suffix for a tool or device; a website is a *retejo,* a "net-place"; and to browse or surf is *retumi,* which means "to do something on the net." Several words are now in use for a flash drive: *memorbastoneto* (memory stick), *poŝmemorilo* (pocket memory device), *memorstango* (memory rod), and most simply, *storilo* (storage device). And there is another reason for preferring Esperantic coinages to international borrowings: such coinages do for Esperanto what idiomatic phrases do for national languages—turn a language into a sociolect, which fosters community. No wonder, then, that Esperantists get a charge out of decoding these clumsy, agglutinative words, such as *polvosuĉilo* (a "dust sucker," aka vacuum cleaner) or *scivolemo* ("the inclination to want to know," aka curiosity), or *akvoprenilo* ("a device for taking out water," aka hydrant). The bulb that flicks on when an Esperantist encounters or generates an unfamiliar word yields both light and warmth.

What leaves many novices to Esperanto cold, however, is Zamenhof's system of correlatives, also known as *tabelvortoj* (table words). The correlatives are a highly elaborated version of correlative systems Zamenhof knew in Romance, Germanic, and Slavic languages. In English, for example, if we want to ask a question about place, we start with *wh-*, add *-ere* and get "where." Similarly, if we want to make a demonstrative statement about place, we start with *th-* and add *-ere* to get "there." Esperanto has five groups of such word beginnings, not only for interrogation and demonstration but also for indefinites, universals, and negatives. It also has nine groups of word endings, not only for place but also for time, quantity, manner, possession, entity, etc. Now imagine a grid in which the five word beginnings are arranged horizontally across the top, and the nine word endings are arranged in a column at the far left. Combining beginnings and endings creates the forty-five correlatives in the table.

Zamenhof never expected his readers to memorize the lists of correlatives, and no tables appear in the inaugural pamphlet of 1887. Only a fraction of correlatives are in frequent use; many are used routinely, and some are rarely used. Some can be used as pronouns, for instance, *ĉiuj*, which means "everybody," or as adverbs—*tiel*, meaning "in this manner." And they are essential for word building: for instance, *tiusense*, meaning "in this sense," or *ĉiutage*, meaning "everyday." When novices find a correlative leaping into their conversation, it's the first intuition they have of their competence. And the casual, comfortable use of correlatives—in conversation and as building blocks—is a good indicator of fluency.

* * *

Given that Esperanto was forged in Europe, designed for Europeans, and built from European languages, the charge of Eurocentrism is hard to deny. As we shall see in Part III, however, far from barricading it against non-Europeans, the Eurocentrism of Esperanto was largely responsible for its initial forays into China and Japan. That said, not all Esperantists

		Question ("What")	Indication ("This/ that")	Indefinite ("Some")	Universal ("Each, every")	Negative ("No")
		ki-	ti-	i-	ĉi-	neni-
Quality	-a	kia (what a)	tia (such a)	ia (some kind/sort/ type of)	ĉia (every kind/sort/ type of)	nenia (no kind/ sort/type of)
Reason	-al	kial (why)	tial (therefore)	ial (for some reason)	ĉial (for all reasons)	nenial (for no reason)
Time	-am	kiam (when)	tiam (then)	iam (sometime)	ĉiam (always)	neniam (never)
Place	-e	kie (where)	tie (there)	ie (some- where)	ĉie (every- where)	nenie (nowhere)
Manner	-el	kiel (how, as)	tiel (thus, as)	iel (somehow)	ĉiel (in every way)	neniel (no how, in no way)
Associa- tion	-es	kies (whose)	ties (this/that one's)	ies (someone's)	ĉies (every- one's)	nenies (no one's)
Thing	-o	kio (what)	tio (this/that)	io (some- thing)	ĉio (every- thing)	nenio (nothing)
Amount	-om	kiom (how much)	tiom (that much)	iom (some, a bit)	ĉiom (all of it)	neniom (none)
Individual	-u	kiu (who, which one; which [horse])	tiu (that one; that [horse])	iu (someone; some [horse])	ĉiu (everyone; each [horse], all [horses])	neniu (no one; no [horse])

Esperanto Table

agree that the language, even from a linguistic perspective, *is* Eurocentric; some, citing Zamenhof's earliest accounts of creating the language, say that it is not Indo-European at all. Zamenhof hinted at this when he confessed that he'd created Esperanto in "the *spirit* of European languages" (my italics). In the spirit—but not in the flesh? Apparently not, since Esperanto's morphology, the rules by which words change according to tense, mood, number, and gender, is signally different from that of Indo-European languages. Esperanto roots, unlike words in Indo-European languages, *never* alter their internal constituents when they take different endings. In English, today I *swim*, and yesterday I *swam*; but in Esperanto the root for swimming—*naĝ*—is always the same, no matter when I dive into the pool. Zamenhof's aim was to rationalize morphology, making roots instantly recognizable and easy to look up in a dictionary. His term for the division of words into "immutable syllables" (morphemes) was "dismemberment":

> I introduced a complete dismemberment of ideas into independent words, so that the whole language consists, not of words in different states of grammatical inflexion, but of unchangeable words [roots]. [The reader] . . . will perceive that each word [root] always retains its original unalterable form—namely, that under which it appears in the vocabulary.[19]

Thus, insofar as Esperanto glues together immutable roots, endings, and affixes, it is an agglutinative language, like Japanese, Hungarian, and Navajo.

But though this morphology would have been alien to most Europeans, Zamenhof counted on his European-derived lexicon to make Esperanto seem natural and familiar to his European readers: "I have adapted this principle of dismemberment to the spirit of the European languages, in such a manner that anyone learning my tongue from grammar alone . . . will never perceive that the structure of the language differs in any respect from that of his mother-tongue." Like Bacon and Wilkins, Zamenhof demoted words to secondary status; Esperanto was not a "world of words," after all, but a world of roots, concepts, structures that became a language when humans actively and ingeniously turned them into words. And though Zamenhof's roots recall Bacon's and Wilkins's "real characters," there is a crucial difference. "Real characters" were an end in themselves, inscribing a pristine and unique knowledge of the world; but Zamenhof's roots were destined for the rough and tumble of endings, juxtapositions, and linkages, for conversation and debate. Even Esperanto words are little dialogues between roots and their affixes.

Esperanto was invented to bring conversation to a world of misunderstanding. It was designed so that we should not always speak "only unto ourselves," but to others, despite difference of nationality, creed, class, or race. But what Zamenhof discovered, having created a language "in the spirit of European languages," is that it was more than a *tradukilo*—"a translation device." By using Esperanto, he came to think in Esperanto, which had a spirit all its own. As he wrote to Borovko in 1896:

> Practice, however, more and more convinced me that the language still needed an elusive something, a connecting element, giving the language life and a definite, fully formed spirit. . . . I then began to avoid word for word translations of this or the other tongue and tried to think directly in the neutral language. Then I noticed that the language in my hands was already ceasing to be a . . . shadow of this or that other language . . . [that it] received its own spirit, its own life, its own definite and clearly expressed physiognomy, independent of any influences. The words flowed all by themselves, flexibly, gracefully, and utterly freely, like a living, native tongue.[20]

Like Mary Shelley's Doctor Frankenstein, who took lifeless body parts and turned them into a creature, Doktoro Esperanto took the "dismembered" parts of other languages and created a new being entirely. It must have been a lonely venture, being the sole speaker of a language yet to be put before the world. But whereas Doctor Frankenstein fled the laboratory on seeing his creature, Zamenhof engaged his in conversation. And then it happened: entrusted with his own thoughts, the *lingvo internacia* suddenly spoke in its own voice, from its own spirit, spontaneous, animated, free. By 1887, there was no longer any question: a child of his own brain, this "clumsy and lifeless collection of words" had become a living language. If there is a note of wonder in his recognition that the language had a life apart from his own, there was also apprehension about the life it would live in other minds, on other tongues.

Samideanoj I
NASK, or Total Immersion

=====

1. *Ĉu vi lernas ĝin?*

Ĉu vi lernas ĝin? asks my green-and-white T-shirt with the Esperanto insignia. "Are you learning it?"

Apart from online learning, to study Esperanto in the United States is not a simple matter. Aside from a few classes taught in university towns or major cities, courses are few and far between, but this was not always the case; in the 1950s, seven towns in New Jersey alone offered weekly classes. Since 1970, however, the foremost course in the country has been the North American Summer Esperanto Institute, or NASK, which also happens to be the most intensive Esperanto immersion course in the world. Residing for three decades at San Francisco State University, it moved for a few years to Vermont, then to the University of California at San Diego, where I enrolled for the three-week program. (Since then, to boost enrollment, NASK has been scaled back to eight days; enrollment skyrocketed.)

I signed up for the intermediate level and started to prepare by studying on my own. On Amazon I found a hardcover book, published in the 1980s, called *Esperanto: Learning and Using the International Language*. It's a ten-lesson program written by an American, David Richardson, for Americans—people who live in New York and drive cross-country to California, who measure out their lives in miles, pounds, and dollars. The dialogues feature a bumbling father, part absent-minded professor, part Homer Simpson; a bossy, know-it-all mother; two eye-rolling teenagers. No one has time for Dad's endearing foibles, everyone talks over everyone else, the kids leave the table before dinner is over—a typical American family. Except that around the dinner table they speak Esperanto.

In search of a more interactive method of learning, I clicked on a few links from the Esperanto-USA homepage and arrived at the bright green, user-friendly website called lernu! ("learn!"; lernu.net). A section of the site is designed specifically for English speakers, English being one of forty-odd languages made available by the "lernu! team." A variety of online courses are available, at various levels, the most famous of which is *Gerda Malaperis* (Gerda Disappeared), a mystery novel scientifically designed by Claude Piron to teach words in descending order of frequency. But the audio of *Gerda* was dauntingly rapid, so I opted for a basic course called *Mi estas komencanto* (I am a beginner). Lesson one got off to a nice, slow start: *Kio estas via nomo?* (What is your name?); *De kie vi estas?* (Where are you from?). The next couple of lessons enabled me to ask if someone were a student and if not, what "labor" he or she did; whether that person had come on a bus or a train; and to confess that I was nervous. I wasn't—until lesson six, when it emerged that the course was designed to prepare me for an Esperanto congress.

> *Ĉu vi volas loĝi en amasloĝejo aŭ en ĉambro?*
> *Kio estas amasloĝejo?*
> *Amas-loĝ-ejo estas granda ejo kie multaj loĝas surplanke.*

> Do you want to stay in an *amasloĝejo* or in a room?
> What's an *amasloĝejo?*
> *Amas-loĝ-ejo* is a big place where many people sleep on the floor.

It sounded like a youth hostel for Carmelites, but the point was to show how Esperanto builds words from the ground up. *Amas-* is a root meaning "mass"; *loĝ-*, a root meaning "stay" or "dwell"; and *-ejo,* a suffix (or stand-alone word) meaning "a place where." There was also the issue of the *ĉapeloj*—diacritical marks called "hats" in Esperanto. The Esperanto alphabet has twenty-eight letters, five of which are *c, g, h, j,* and *s* wearing tiny "hats"—*ĉ, ĝ, ĥ, ĵ, ŝ*—that alter their pronunciation. The letter *c* is pronounced "ts," but when topped by a *ĉapelo,* it becomes "ch." Also *u,* when preceded by *a,* usually puts on a crescent to become *ŭ.*

Once I registered for lernu!, I immediately began receiving emails, entirely in Esperanto, with the lernu! "word of the day." Most days, thanks to my experience with French and Italian, I could decode the word easily: *kurta*, like the Italian *corto*, meant "short"; *trista* (in French, *triste*) meant "sad"; *tosto*, of course, meant "toast"—a champagne toast, not toaster toast, which is *toasto* (toe-AHS-toe). The words I couldn't spontaneously decode I had to interpret from context: "*ĈERKO: Kesto, en kiun oni metas la korpon de mortinto.*" Decoding: "*ĈERKO:* a chest in which one puts a dead body"—i.e., a coffin. Then there was "*PUM: Pum! la viro falis en la riveron.*" "The man falls in the river," I managed, noting that *pum* could be redoubled to evoke a nuisance. And with the ending *-adoj*, it could be turned into a relentless, repetitive cacophony. Where Americans hear "boom-boom-boom," Esperantists hear *pumpumadoj* (poom-poom-ah-doy).

With a modicum of Googling, I discovered an alternative to lernu!: an online phrasebook designed for English-speaking congress-goers with more than one type of congress in mind. Unlike the wholesome, patient lernu!, where one repeated, repeated, repeated, here things were said only once.

> *Mi ŝatas renkonti novajn homojn.* (I like meeting new people.)
> *Mi ŝatas vin.* (I like you.)
> *Mi amas vin.* (I love you.)

At this point one chose one's own adventure. For the amorous, there was *Mi volas vin* (I want you), and *Mi ne povas vivi sen vi* (I can't live without you). And just in case, there was *Mi estas graveda* (I'm pregnant) and *Kiel vi povas fari tion al mi?* (How could you do this to me?). For the less venturesome, there was *Mi sentas la mankon de vi* (I miss you) and *Samideane* (Regards—"used only for a fellow Esperantist"). Knowing I was more likely to say *amasloĝejo* than *graveda*, I returned to lernu!, and two weeks later, found that I was capable of a halting reading—in Esperanto—of the NASK website.

2. Affixed

There are twenty-four students at NASK, ranging in age from seventeen to eighty-two, plus the instructors, Greta, Benedikt, and Wayne; Nell, an administrator; and an assistant with the unlikely name of Slim Alizadeh, a thirtyish Iranian-American IT guy. Slim's role is various: he edits and produces the daily newsletter, solicits presenters for the evening programs, and leads the optional afternoon excursions—which begin today, Slim announces, with a hike to the *glisilejo*. I can't find it in my dictionary, so I try to decode it: *glisi*, "to glide"; *-ejo*, "place." A gliding place? A place for gliding? Life at NASK often seems to be about finding opportunities to teach affixes, and our afternoon excursion to the Torrey Pines Gliderport is clearly one of them.

Assigned to suites in a dorm, we learn the difference between a roommate (*samĉambrano*, "same-room member") and a suitemate (*samĉambrarano*, "member of the same cluster of rooms"). We're roughly grouped by gender and age. In my suite are three middle-aged women and myself, while the seven or eight college students room downstairs in suites whose doors are always propped open. All the female students are science majors and all the male students are humanities majors—data point? In practice, it only means that the women are quicker with advice for a frozen MacBook: "Just take the battery out." Residing in the next entryway are students in a Stanley Kaplan SAT intensive, who are referred to affixedly as *Kaplanuloj*—Kaplaners. It is Slim who refers to non-Esperantists in general as *mugloj*; muggles. Our dorm is hardly Hogwarts, but stocked with twenty-nine Esperantists, it is a place apart.

There are no pledges to sign, no vows to take, but it goes without saying that we're to speak only Esperanto, morning, noon, and night; on campus and off (assuming the company of other NASKers). And almost without exception, we do. Had there been an explicit rule, it would have been simple: *Neniam krokodilu!* (Never crocodile!). *Krokodili* is the first slang word any Esperantist learns; it means "to speak one's native language at an Esperanto gathering." But Esperantists, a great many of whom are polyglots, are given to fine distinctions: *aligatori* (to alligator) means to speak one's first language to someone else speaking it as a second language; *kajmani* (to cayman) means to carry on a conversation in a language that is neither speaker's native tongue.

Only Esperanto could have brought together the four women in my suite. There is Marcy, a travel agent who arranges Esperanto-language package tours each July and the producer of a goofy instructional video series called *Esperanto: Pasporto al la Tuta Mondo* (Esperanto: Passport to the Whole World). Across the hall is Kalindi, a jolly forty-six-year-old secretary from Kathmandu. She has long, shining black hair and applies peppermint-pink lipstick as soon as she finishes a meal. On hot days, she favors cotton saris; on cool ones, track suits in mint green and fuschia. She has come the farthest of any participant, and after NASK she'll continue on to the Universal Congress in Rotterdam and then travel around Europe for a month with *samideanoj*. Kalindi hosts every Esperantist who passes through Kathmandu in her home, where one bedroom is designated the *Esperanta Ĉambro* (Esperanto Room).

The fourth member of the ensemble is a heavyset woman in her sixties who sits on the landing beside a heavy-set bearded man; perched on folding chairs, they could be a couple escaping a stifling Bronx apartment for a gulp of fresh air. Greeting me, she says in flatly American Esperanto, *"Mi estas Tero, jen mia edzo, Karlo"* (I'm Earth; this is my husband, Charles), handing me a shiny green cardboard star. Outside of NASK, he is David, a computer programmer, but she is harder to nail down. She was born Angela Woodman, the daughter of a trombonist with the Detroit Symphony who'd also played with Artie Shaw: "Look him up on the International Tuba Euphonium Association oral history website," she urges. Every afternoon she can be found writing the words of Esperanto pop songs in indelible marker on a huge lined, easeled pad, kindergarten style. One day it is *"Ĉu vi, ĉu vi, ĉu vi, ĉu vi volas dansi"* ("Do You Wanna Dance?"), another, *"Kamparanino"* ("Guantanamera"). When we walk through the leafy campus to class in the morning, Tero picks up pieces of eucalyptus bark and turns them into eerie gray masks. She tells me she spent many years on a Hare Krishna ashram but one day left with the ashram's mandolin in tow and never looked back. ("I knew I could use it in my clown act.") At home in Northern California, she is a part-time Berlitz teacher, but mostly, she and Karlo work as sound engineers for . . . she pauses, not to find the word, but to coin it.

"Filkfestoj."

"Kio ĝi estas?" I asked. (What is that?)

She explains, in what will become a familiar resort to paraphrase and circumlocution, that "filkfests" are musical jam sessions that occur at science fiction conventions. I add the word to my glossary.

3. Greta's World

The intermediate class comprises three sleepy college students—George, Meja, and Christy—and three middle-aged women: Tero, Kalindi, and myself. Promptly at 9:00 a.m., Greta Neumann enters the room and asks, "How do you greet people in your culture? With a handshake?" (shaking her left hand with her right); "A hug?" (hugging herself ardently); "A kiss on the hand?" (grasping her right hand in her left and bringing it tenderly to her lips).

Greta is by far the most fluent Esperanto speaker I have ever heard; not surprising, since she and her Swedish husband, Benedikt (the teacher of the advanced class), met in Esperanto, romanced in Esperanto, and now live their married life in Esperanto. A German woman in her early thirties, she has close-cropped strawberry-blond hair, limpid blue eyes, and a plastic face that, to convey new vocabulary, knows no limits. It can delight in an imaginary glass of champagne, show the weariness of a great-grandmother, or crinkle and pout like a bawling infant. Her teaching methods are vaudevillian; she mimes the word *skotaduŝo*—"Scottish shower"—by taking an invisible shower that runs *very* hot; then *very* cold; then *very* hot.

Sudden shifts from ludic to tragic are a daily occurrence in Greta's class. Strong, expressed emotions, it seems, are par for the course in *Esperantujo*, where trust runs high and emotions run large. Laughing one moment, weeping the next, we resemble a bipolar support group. Today, Greta starts class with a game called *Onklo Federiko Sidas en la Banujo* (Uncle Frederick's Sitting in the Bathtub). Greta calls out a word in that sentence, and we scrawl a substitute in the same part of speech, then fold down the paper and pass it to the left. At the end of the round, we read out the sheets before us, one by one, to reveal what odd escapades our fellow *NASKanoj* are up to:

> *Spiono Bernardo pensas pri io sur la kafejo.*
> (Bernard the spy thinks about something on top of the café.)
> *Bestkuracisto Wayne vicas malantaŭ la ratonesto.*
> (Veterinarian Wayne lines up in back of the rats' nest.)

The room is inundated by belly laughs, cresting in giddy shrieks; Greta herself laughs uncontrollably, dabbing at tears.

When we reconvene after a coffee break, Greta passes out a purple sheet and reads the poem printed on it; the poem is narrated by a German man, a devout Christian, who passively watches a Jewish neighbor being dragged out of his apartment. By the end, Tero is crying silently, amid a general hush. Then Greta asks each of us in turn a simple question: Who is speaking? When is this taking place? When it comes to Kalindi, she's bewildered; she can't identify the setting. Greta begins, tentatively, to assess Kalindi's ignorance. Does she know who Adolf Hitler was? Yes, she's heard of him, it is a familiar name, but . . . So Greta explains to our Nepalese *samideano* about the rise of Hitler, the Nazi regime, the Final Solution, the wagons of Jews sent to death camps; about the murder of Jews, communists, gypsies, and gays. (She might have added Zamenhof's three adult children, all executed by the Nazis.) Suddenly she turns to the three college students: "What do you learn about genocide in your schools—I mean, about the treatment of Native Americans?" Carl, Meja, and Christy snap to attention; with Greta's coaching, they scrape together the words: *traktatoj* (treaties), *teritorioj rezervataj* (reservations), *spuro de larmoj* (trail of tears).

I ask Greta for some one-on-one time to find out more about her; I'm half hoping she'll switch to English when we're alone, but she sticks to Esperanto, paced between a trot and a canter. I'm following without too much difficulty, though fashioning questions and follow-ups is taxing. As we walk through the eucalyptus groves, she tells me she was raised in East Germany. "Before eighty-nine. I'd always been *civitema*"—community minded—"and interested in other cultures, and there were very few opportunities to travel," she said. "When I was eighteen, my girlfriend was doing Esperanto and it became a way to get out of my own place and connect to people in other places, cities, countries." After she earned her master's degree in Korean, Greta and Benedikt moved to Seoul, where she now teaches at a foreign language institute. Greta lives in the interstices between cultures, speaking German with her students, English with her colleagues, Korean with her neighbors, and Esperanto with her husband.

I ask her what she understands by the phrase *interna ideo*—the vaguely defined "inner idea" of Esperanto. "When I come home from a congress," she says, "and I look at my photos and I see Germans and Nepalis and Indians and Japanese and Americans all together—all *speaking* together— I think, this is really an amazing thing. I guess the central idea is friendship among peoples." She pauses to consider. "But it's different for me than for a lot of Esperantists. They meet another Esperantist and they think, 'Ah! My automatic friend!' But there are plenty of Esperantists I don't like; I choose my friends. I have Esperantist friends and German friends and Korean friends. For me, Esperanto is a private language—the language I speak with my husband, the language in which I live my private life—so I don't primarily think of it as something belonging to the whole world."

Benedikt, a quiet, slouchy Swede, dorky-cool in his habitual red T-shirt, is by profession a programmer. In *Esperantujo,* however, he's a rock star, a founding member of the band Persone; the name is a pun, meaning both "personally" and "via sound." He's written many of their songs, all bearing diffident titles such as *"Mi ne scias"* (I don't know) and *"Kaj tiel plu"* (And so forth). Even within *Esperantujo,* Benedikt leads a double life; he is not only a rock star but also a grammarian, the author of *PMEG* (Complete Manual of Esperanto Grammar), a hardcover book four inches thick in a taxicab-yellow dustjacket. (Word on the street is that the *P* in *PMEG* stands for *Peza*—"Heavy.") Around NASK, he's known as the *homavortaro*—the human dictionary—and deservedly so; he's even a member of the Akademio de Esperanto. No question about it: Greta and Benedikt, strolling into the dining hall in shorts, T-shirts, backpacks, and sandals, are an Esperanto power couple.

Wayne Cooper, who teaches the beginner class, is a professional American Sign Language interpreter from Missouri. Tall and lanky, with the pale blue eyes of a Siberian Husky, he always wears ironed button-down shirts and white khakis, and he speaks as crisply as he dresses. After lunch, he and Benedikt are discussing *signolingvo*—sign language—and Benedikt knows enough Swedish sign language to compare notes with Wayne, their four hands flying, tapping, slicing the air. Suddenly Wayne stands up and shakes two imaginary pom-poms over each shoulder; Benedikt laughs, shakes his head, and says, "No, there's no word in Swedish sign language for *huraistino."* That's Esperanto for "cheerleader," literally, "female hurrah specialist."

During a lull in their conversation, I ask Wayne and Benedikt whether they have a favorite Esperanto word. They look at one another with the shy smiles of twelve-year-old boys asked to reveal a crush. *"Mirmekofago,"* says Benedikt, and before I can start to decode (*mir-,* "a wonder"? *meko-,* "a bleat"?), he says in English "anteater," and, in Esperanto, "based on the

Latin name, *Myrmecophaga tridactyla*." (Later that evening, I look up the word in Wells's English-Esperanto dictionary, which defines *mirmekofago* as a giant anteater, *ekidno* as a spiny one, and *maniso* as a scaly one. An Esperanto lexicographer's work is never done.)

Wayne's turn: "*Vazistaso*—a transom. *Poefago*—a yak . . ."

"I have a new word for you," I say, and they exchange a glance that says, *How unlikely.*

I'd coined it the previous afternoon, walking through the San Diego County Fair with Kalindi. When we visited the 4H show, she taught me the word for llama (*lamao*, not *jamo*), and I taught her the word for goat (*kapro*). Back in Nepal, she said, her family eats *kapro* and *porko* and . . . she searched for the word in Esperanto, then declared, in English, "beaver!" I let it go. Kalindi didn't want to join the screaming teens on rides, so we wandered about, watching the roller coasters and sampling the greasy fare.

"Ready?" I say to Benedikt and Wayne: "*Profundefrititaj-tvinkoj.*" Now it's their turn to decode. Benedikt's lips move and he looks puzzled, but Wayne laughs: "Deep-fried Twinkies," he says in English, then, with ironic nostalgia, "*Ahh . . . la provinca foiro!*"

Ah . . . the county fair.

4. "A Stay-at-Home, Midwestern Guy"

At sixteen, Wayne found a teach-yourself guide to Esperanto. He taught himself, but since he knew no other Esperantists, he used it only as a written language. One day he answered the phone and a woman's voice said "*Saluton!*"—the customary Esperanto greeting. It was a Croatian Esperantist, visiting his town, eager for conversation. "When you haven't spoken the language," Wayne says, "it's hard, at first. Well, in fact, Esperanto isn't really easy, though that's the sell: it's easy and the people are fun. There are four things that make it difficult: the accusative, the reflexive, the table of correlatives, and the causative." In keeping with NASK protocols—if you're going to crocodile, spare the other *NASKanoj*—Wayne and I have gone to another room to speak English.

In college in his native Missouri, Wayne studied two years of classical Greek and planned to major in French, but a mix of prudence and midwestern practicality led him to nursing. He had worked in the Veterans' Administration as an administrator for decades, grabbing an early retirement when it was offered, then training for his second career as a sign-language interpreter. His son is a physician in the Army—"It skipped a generation," he says wryly; his daughter, adopted from India, is a social worker. (Interracial and interethnic adoption is more common in the Esperanto world than in the general population; it literally transforms a world of peoples into a *familia rondo*, a family circle.) But Wayne's not much of a traveler; "I'm a stay-at-home, midwestern guy." Not once in our conversation does he bring up the movement; the Universal Congress, which he does not attend; nor the *interna ideo*.

"Esperantists imagine enormous projects—great ideas—and then: who's going to do this? And they look at one another and then at their feet. They feel they have to spread the ideals and the language, but I don't. It's the same with my religion. It's mine; I don't need to convince anyone else. If Esperanto brings me together with two or three interesting people here and there, great. It usually does. Esperanto may be a moveable feast, but NASK is Brigadoon—a magical town that comes into being once a year, then just as mysteriously disappears."

One afternoon, Wayne presents me with a yellowed, dog-eared copy of the famous 1952 *Kvaropo* (Quartet), a breakthrough debut for the "Scottish school" of Esperanto poets: William Auld, Reto Rossetti, John Sharp Dinwoodie, and John Francis. This copy has been sitting for decades in the traveling NASK library, but Wayne tells me to keep it, as a kind of therapy—for the book, that is. "The best thing for it," he says, handing me the book, "is to be read." We read a few poems aloud. Wayne points out that Esperanto poetics frowns upon rhyming suffixes (including rhymed verb endings, a staple for Italian sonneteers) as third-rate technique. In fact, there is a name for it—*adasismo*—a word coined by one of the earliest Esperanto poets, Antoni Grabowski, from the chief offense: rhyming -*adas* endings (*kuradas*, "continues to run"; *staradas*, "continues to stand"). The term *adasismo* appears in the 1932 *Parnasa Gvidlibro* (Parnassian Guidebook), the first handbook of Esperanto poetics. Co-authored by the two preeminent men of Esperanto letters, the Hungarian poet Kálmán Kalocsay and the French grammarian and lexicographer Gaston Waringhien, the *Gvidlibro* is famous for its witty rhyming satires of bad poetic practice.

Also on the NASK bookshelf is the *Esperanta Antologio*, a classic anthology first published in 1958, edited by William Auld. I'd been introduced to it a few months earlier by *Humphrey Tonkin, an eminent man of letters in the Esperanto world and a professor emeritus of English Renaissance literature. When I met him at his home in Hartford, Connecticut, he greeted me in white khakis, a blue seersucker shirt, and moccasins. With a pink complexion and bushy white brows, he looks like an actor playing a university president, which is what he was, from 1989 to 1998, at the University of Hartford.

An Esperantist for more than half a century, Tonkin explained that Esperanto's system of word building offers poets a fantastic degree of flexibility. Sometimes these constructions are clunky; moreover, since almost all Esperanto words are accented on the penultimate syllable, they are hard to scan in poetic meter, which generally alternates strong and weak beats. Sometimes neologisms are coined to avoid them, but poets have another arrow in their quiver: eliding the "o" ending of singular nouns, which shifts the accent to the final syllable. But even without neologisms, agglutination is a small price to pay for turning Clark Kent roots into superwords, garbing the most everyday vocabulary with a dark cape of metaphor.

Before I ever uttered a sentence in Esperanto, Tonkin walked me through one of his favorite poems, a tiny gem by Victor Sadler:

> *Mi*
> *(kiam en la kuniklejo de via sako*
> *Vi furioze fosas pro bileto, kiu*
> *Tre verŝajne jam eskapis)*
> *Amas vin.*
>
> *(Kien, cetere, vi metis*
> *Mian koron?)*

A literal rendering in English would go something like this:

> I
> (when in the rabbit-hole of your bag
> You furiously dig for a ticket
> Which probably already escaped)
> Love you.
>
> (Where, by the way, did you put
> My heart?)

In English, a hybrid of Anglo-Saxon and French, we are spoiled for lexical choice; *kuniklejo* might be translated "rabbit-hole," "warren," or "hutch." Esperanto's scarcer resources, however, turn out to be a great boon. Calling the handbag a *kuniklejo* magically turns it into a rabbity place instead of comparing it to a "hole" or "warren" or "hutch." In the first stanza, the subject "I" is trailed by a long parenthetical modifier which provides the atmosphere in which the declarative statement "I love you" lives and breathes. Even after the delayed verb and adjective appear, the image of the woman furiously digging in her bag arrives whole and indelibly, the raison d'être of the poet's love.

The importance of the adverbial phrase in Sadler's poem points to a truth about adverbs: they are the Esperantist poet's most coveted super-power. Because any root has the potential to become an adverb by taking an -*e* ending, adverbs can propel Esperanto poems into elliptical orbits, making them hard to translate. The "adverb thing," as one of the NASK students calls it, has made its way like a termite into the lumber of collo-quial Esperanto. Where an English speaker might look out on a brilliant day and exclaim, "It's sunny!" an Esperanto speaker would say simply "*Sune!*" (Sunnily!) or "*Brile!*" (Brilliantly!). One night, after a few beers, a student named Bernard walks into a party to find all the folding chairs in disarray. He pauses to take it in: "*Seĝe!*" is all he says—"Chairily!"— and all he needs to say. "*Kiel vivi vegane*" ("How to Live Veganly") is the name of a leaflet Slim distributes the night he gives his gruesome Power-Point presentation about agribusiness. After showing a clip of little chicks being poured into a macerating machine, he ends with a picture of a *hundo manĝata telere;* a dog being eaten on bone china "platedly."

5. Filipo and Nini

Three days into the program, a new student arrives. He's a pudgy, florid man with white hair and a sparse, floury beard, around fifty, introducing himself as Filipo Vinbergo de Los-anĝeloso. An Esperanto first name is not uncommon at Esperanto gatherings, but a surname? *Okay, Philip Weinberg from LA, have it your way.* On both hands he wears compres-sion bandages, from which protrude ten swollen fingers. I introduce my-self and ask him the old standby: "*Pri kio vi laboras*?" (What work do you do?) Amid the ensuing avalanche of expression, I can't catch his job.

I'd later discover that he doesn't have one, and who or what supports him—a pension? family? disability insurance?—is a subject he never broaches, nor do I.

At dinner, Filipo tells me he's an amateur lexicographer: "My friend Charles, from Nigeria, and I have written an Ibo-Esperanto dictionary," he says breathlessly. "We noted the usage codes in the big dictionaries and transposed each of them into colors to be used to teach Ibo children Esperanto." I'm not sure who's teaching Ibo children Esperanto, or who Charles is, or even what a "usage code" is (or how one might be transposed), but Filipo has moved on to another subject. His words tend to leap ahead of his sentences, which pant in pursuit. Every so often, I stop him mid-sentence and summon him back to the task at hand: communicating *something*. He is always appreciative, Cowardly-Lionly, as if to say, "Thanks, I needed that."

Filipo is a NASK veteran, and he has a lot of credibility among the regulars, enough to mimic the earnest litany of questions Esperantists ask one another. "*Samideanoj!*" he says, in a mincing voice: "*When* did you first learn Esperanto? *Why* did you first learn it? *How* did you first learn it? *Where* did you first learn it? . . ." When Filipo makes a mock phone call—"*Ĉu . . . Ĉu— . . . Ĉu! . . . Ĉu? . . . ĈU!!!*"—I learn the many uses of the ubiquitous particle "*ĉu*": "I hear you," "Whether," "You said it!" "Really?" and "NOOO!" One afternoon, after a visit to the Birch Aquarium, we find ourselves with an hour to kill before the next bus. Filipo whips out a copy of *Reĝo Lear,* taking the part of Lear for himself and asking me to read the part of Cordelia. But not without a prefatory warning: "In Esperanto she's called Kor-de-*lee*-o," he says precisely. "*Rimarku!*" I take note.

* * *

The oldest student, Nini Martin-Sanders, is a petite, grandmotherly woman from northern California with a lilting voice and sapphire eyes. She wears a white visor and nursey white shoes; in between are sweatpants and a T-shirt advertising a folk festival from years ago. Except for one summer when she had surgery, Nini has attended every NASK since 1970. She seems happy to see any of us at any moment at all, greeting us all alike: "*Kara!*" (Dear!) Remembering names isn't easy these days. Nini walks slowly and her hands shake when she lifts a cup of tea, but she doesn't miss a class, an excursion, or an evening program, not even a meeting of the dormant U.S. Esperanto Youth Association, which Bernard is trying to revive. All gatherings at Esperanto conferences (except meetings of the executive and the academy) are open to everyone, but in the face of all these youth, we oldsters decorously sit on the periphery. Lost in thought, Nini suddenly asks, with some urgency, "Was Jeremy Bentham . . . a Unitarian?"

"No," says Slim, gifting Nini with a rare smile, "a *utilitarian*."

This summer, Nini's thirty-eighth year at NASK, the dining hall has instituted a no-tray policy to save money, power, and water. Most of us have no trouble balancing cups and saucers on salad bowls with one hand, toting plates of pizza and hummus in the other, but Nini can't, and this regime of frugality could well cost her a hip. Assisting Nini at meals is the collective task of all. Nini's favorite assistant, by far, is Wayne, and she makes no secret of adoring him. Every time he helps to seat her at the table, she catches the eye of whoever is near, points to Wayne, and says *"Bonkora, Ĉu?"* (Goodhearted, isn't he?) Wayne busses her plates, cuts her meat, brings her tea.

One day Nini arrives at lunch rattled, confused, distressed, babbling about her bad memory. Wayne sits down beside her, towering over her small frame, then lays his hands gently on her forearms. "What's wrong?" She can't remember the name of a song, and she needs it for an essay Benedikt assigned. While most of the advanced students are busy researching Esperanto history or culture, Nini has decided to write about Glendale, California, the town where she and her husband lived for twenty-two happy years.

"My second husband, the better one," she says suddenly. Turning to me, she asks whether I have a husband.

"One," I say, and Wayne adds, "One is enough."

"Yes!" Nini declares. "Especially if it's a bad husband! One is definitely enough." Before I can protest that mine is a good husband, Wayne tells her to breathe deeply. "I'm so impressed by your quietness," he says, as she closes her eyes and calms down. Then he asks softly, "Now, what are you trying to remember?" She opens her eyes and smiles; she still can't remember, she says, but she feels much better.

"Thank you, *Kara*," she tells Wayne. "Do you have a twin for me, my own age?"

Wayne says, "If I had a twin, he would be my age."

"Yes, of course, *Kara*," Nini sighs. "I mean someone with a heart like yours."

6. Total Immersion

Zamenhof told us we could, so we're inventing new words. Our weird coinages are like motors stuck together with duct tape, but they get us around. What to dub the NASK lounge—the *umejo*? (messing-around place) or the *diboĉejo* (locus of debauchery)? Definitely *diboĉejo*, is the consensus. Meja, a chemistry major from UCSD, introduces the verb *jutubumi* for "messing around on YouTube" and *Vizaĝlibro* for Facebook, though others prefer *Fejsbuk*. Karlo gets a kick out of inventing nouns— *truilo* (a hole-making implement)—then verbing them: "*La pafilo truilas la homon*" (the rifle beholes the person). Slim, constantly referring to his smartphone for schedules and plans, calls it his *kromcerbo*, "spare brain." Word invention is more play than task; we toss our word-birdies across an invisible badminton net, back and forth, not bothering to keep score. Tonight we'll gather for Esperanto Scrabble, which is played with roots, not words.

I'm starting to get jokes—for instance, Bernard's nightly signoff, "*Bonegedormu*," a pun that means both "sleep excellently" and "sleep together well." Throughout the day, I add to my word list.

tekokomputil/o—laptop
surgenu/i—to be on one's knees
perfort/o—violence
bildrakont/o—comic book
maĉgum/o—chewing gum
tondil/o—scissors
malfald/i—unfold

On a crowded city bus coming back from the July 4 fireworks— *piroteknikaĵoj*—surrounded by English for the first time in weeks, Steĉjo says in Esperanto, "Speaking English is like speaking in water; speaking Esperanto is like speaking in wine." Agreed; this would explain how tipsy I feel when conversation begins to flow freely. Some days I'm light as a glider at the *glisilejo*, unencumbered except for a backpack, a lanyard with my room key, and a UCSD Tritons water bottle. Other days, total immersion leaves me sodden, slow, language-logged.

The weather in San Diego has two settings (perhaps Slim has programmed it): gloomy, gray, and damp every morning; dry, clear, and sunny every afternoon, when I hike to the east campus to swim. Doing laps, I dimly remember my sadness of the late spring, when I turned fifty, like a coat long ago given to Goodwill. What *was* that all about? Is NASK balm or cure? Afterward, I lounge in the Jacuzzi, taking the sun full on my face, making a mental list of all the things I do not have to do—

> file health insurance claims
> send in a deposit for tennis lessons
> write a tenure review
> make fall checkup appointments for three kids
> reserve a table for our anniversary
> pick up the dry cleaning
> call Uncle Bert
> submit poems to *Southwest Review*
> bake a casserole for the food pantry
> schedule college interviews
> walk the dog
> feed the dog
> get the dog her shots
> book a DJ for the next bar mitzvah

—at least for another week.

* * *

One afternoon, Kalindi asks whether she can walk with me to the pool. "Not to swim," she says, "just for the walk." When we reach the complex, she gazes through the fence at the huge Olympic pool with eight black tines at the bottom, then at the practice lanes, then at the Jacuzzi. She seems awed, and I expect her to tell me she's never seen such a place in Nepal. Instead, she says in a low voice, "I have no *bankostumo*"— swimsuit—"because I don't swim in public. Women don't do that in my country."

"Oh, too bad," I say breezily, "but if you change your mind, let me know."

What a stupid thing to say, I think, swiping my card through the turn-stile as she heads back to the dorm.

The next day after lunch, Kalindi comes to my room with a bag from the UCSD bookstore and pulls out a blue-and-gold Triton swim-suit, a black swim cap, and goggles. I gasp, she beams, and we head to the pool.

It's a giddy venture for both of us, and we emerge from the locker room in high hilarity. But before I can put on my goggles, she hands me her cell phone. Taking her swimming means taking her picture: Kalindi in the Jacuzzi, Kalindi with the lifeguard, a long video of Kalindi doing the breaststroke the entire length of the pool, turning and waving cheer-ily from the other end. Who is going to watch this? Her daughter? Her husband? The *samideanoj* of Nepal?

Kalindi will, on her laptop, again and again. When she does the back-stroke, her pink smile is visible at fifty meters.

7. Brigadoon Out

Three weeks speed by, a blur of classes, meals, sing-alongs, field trips. My mood oscillates. I feel euphoric when my sentences flow, my ear catches the drift, and my coinages work; deeply frustrated when I sense that Esperanto isn't able to deliver the kind of nuance I want to convey—at least, that I *think* I want to convey. For what happens as I speak is chang-ing. I'm no longer searching a toolbox of adjectives for just the right one. Is the flycatcher I saw nesting outside the dining hall "little"? "Small"? "Tiny"? "Puny"? "Minuscule"? "Dainty"? "Lilliputian"? Instead, I grasp for the essence of a thing and eke it out by concepts. I don't have to decide whether a bird is "dainty" or "petite" because nouns can be made smaller or larger after they are uttered with a simple suffix: *-eta* means "smaller," *-ega*, "larger." Contempt can also be expressed by a suffix, since *-aĉa* hand-ily converts any noun to an execrable specimen. *Mal-*, a prefix that transforms a word into its antonym, doesn't simply negate; it tends to lap at words with nostalgia or regret. The aged are deeply, irrevocably *maljuna* (the opposite of young); the poor *malriĉa* (the opposite of rich); the hungry *malsata* (the opposite of sated). Whatever's just been said, you can counter by starting the next sentence, "*Male . . .*" (conversely, or opposite-ly).

To learn Esperanto is to find out how Esperantists before me have spoken all the things in their world into being. It's both heady and humbling. A cell phone is a *poŝtelefono,* "a pocket phone." An attitude is *sinteno,* "self-holding." A generous person is *donema,* "inclined to give." "As you wish" is the adverb *laŭvole,* "will-accordingly." Something full to bursting is *plenplena,* "full-full." A gay person is *geja* (hence *gejradaro,* meaning "gaydar") and a lesbian is a *lesbanino,* but a homosexual is a *samseksemulo,* "a person inclined toward the same sex." One British Esperantist observed to me that "we speak Esperanto from the inside out far more than we speak English from the inside out" because we create the language as we speak it.

Greta has promised a quiz in the last class, so I've studied my vocabulary list, reviewed reflexives and causatives, and drilled through the table of correlatives. Promptly at nine, she passes out a sheet of green paper headed "*Ĉu vi memoras?*" (Do you remember?) Below are two dozen questions. A handful pertain to grammar, a few to vocabulary, several to the words of poems or songs we've learned. But most quiz us on some ephemeral moment during the forty-five hours we've spent in class:

What did Meja name the wife of the fisherman in prison?
What is the first thing Kalindi does when she wakes up?
Where does George's great-grandfather live?
Who owns a zebra?

I was there, I know I was, but on most of them, I draw a blank.

When time is up, Greta reviews the quiz. After each answer, Meja yells "*Yesssss!*" as if she'd just bowled a strike, and it's clear that the other college students have virtually nailed them all. But for us three middle-aged women, whether we work in a bank, a filkfest, or a university, the story is different. Our scores are abysmal, as if we'd been slumped in the back, texting, all through the course. The students find it amusing; Tero, comically exasperating. "*How did you remember all that?*" she asks. I chuckle weakly, but after three weeks of laughter and blather, three weeks in which two dozen strangers have morphed into close friends, three weeks on my own, feeling increasingly sound and self-sufficient, it is a bruising moment.

In my family, I'm the one who remembers phone numbers from houses that have been razed, the birthdays of dead aunts, the names of all the exes. And besides, remembering is my profession: I'm an English professor, and it's my job to know how many fragments comprise the *Canterbury Tales* and where Byron's *Sardanapalus* takes place. True, it's sometimes hard to remember the name of a student I taught six months ago. But ever since my father's diagnosis with Alzheimer's disease I've had a talisman against dementia, and it seems to be working. That day the neurologist asked my father to count backward from one hundred by sevens and he tried—"One hundred, ninety . . . five, eighty . . . four"—and failed. My father—the spontaneous calculator of compound interest; the man who carried a plastic slide rule in his pocket to barbecues— failed. Since then, I've been putting myself to sleep at night by doing what he could not: counting backward by sevens. This makes it all the more startling to sit among twenty-two-year-olds and learn how much I have forgotten. I will bring this home, too, *this* knowledge, along with the tables of correlatives and the vocabulary lists.

* * *

For the final evening, I've promised Slim I'd organize a poetry reading—a *deklamado.* I put out a call for readers and, a few hours later, have a full roster of volunteers. Wayne lets me into the linguistics office to use the photocopier, and I begin leafing through the *Esperanta Antologio* to find a poem that suits each reader. "Not many women in here, are there?" I say.

Wayne picks up the anthology and pages through it. "Here's one by a woman," he says, handing the book back. "The only American in the volume."

The poem is called *"La Kialo Estas"* (The Reason Is) and the poet is none other than Nini Martin-Sanders. She wrote it forty years ago, in memory of D. E. Parrish, a fifty-year mainstay of the U.S. Esperanto movement. In 1969, Parrish was mowing his lawn in Los Angeles with a power mower when suddenly his next-door neighbor pulled out a rifle and shot him dead. The noise, she said afterward, had been bothering her.

In Nini's poem, the neighbor is not simply an insane woman; she is a *freneza nigrulino* ("crazy Negress") and her violent act is motivated not by delusions, per se, but by racial hatred.

Ial . . .

> *Ial ni malamas la alian*
> *Ial ni trancâs for*
> *Ial ni rigardas nur*
>> *Niajn haŭtojn . . . niajn eksterajojn*
> *Ial ni batalas*
>> *Fratoj kontraŭ fratoj.*

(For some reason . . . .

> For some reason, we hate one another
> For some reason, we slice away
> For some reason we only
>> Look at our skin—our exterior
> For some reason we battle
>> Brothers against brothers.)

It's full of compassion and outrage, but as a poem, amateurish, vapid, left over from the heydey of National Brotherhood Week. Why racism, why violence, why are we humans so inhuman to one another? Why, why, why? The answer, Nini's poem seems to say, is that the heart, on this summer afternoon in Los Angeles, has its reasons, however murderous and racist.

When Nini reads her poem at our final gathering, in a feathery voice, the event of forty years ago suddenly seems to have happened just moments ago. When she's finished, a brief silence, then a ripple of applause that grows louder and more rhythmic. Standing at the podium pleased and slightly baffled, Nini finally shuffles back to her seat.

There's been no rehearsal, but all the readers have practiced, reciting with vigor and clarity, several from memory. Puckish Sonja from Mexico reads a self-mocking Esperanto standby, "*Mi estas Esperantisto,*" and Meja, Sadler's little poem about a woman rummaging in her rabbit-warren purse. Filipo comes out as the anonymous poet of the daily newsletter, reading a poem for his brother. Tero reads a poem about Lady Godiva, and Stecĵo chants the "Siberian Lullaby" of Julio Baghy—more a spell than a poem: "*Hirte flirte flugas haroj / Siblas vintra vent'/Morde torde ŝiras koron /Larmoj kaj la sent' . . .*" To cap off the reading, Bernard recites Auld's famous poem "*Ebrio*" (Drunkenness), which mimics the slushy diction of inebriation: "*Ŝuvi puvi povi-povaŝ . . .*" Bernard has it by heart, lurching and swaying until finally, emitting the last word, *naŭzo* (nausea), he runs offstage, retching, to wild applause.

Diplomas are presented and each of us, even the *komencantoj* (beginners), make off-the-cuff remarks, thank-yous strung like cranberries. The college students say the last three weeks have been a blast, a hoot, an incredible party; the older students talk about the NASK family and how they will miss it until next summer. Greta plays flute to Benedikt's Spanish guitar, and the evening closes with a song written and performed by ponytailed Roberto, an aspiring animator, currently a clerk in a health food store. He takes the stage, lifts his guitar, and in a fine tenor takes us deep into a honeyed sadness that seems to last weeks, years, eons; his voice rises and falls, from peaks to valleys, cliffs to caves. For such a journey, for such sweetness, applause seems rather beside the point. When Roberto's voice fades to silence, people simply go up, one by one, and throw their arms around him.

* * *

The morning of our departure, we assemble in a large classroom for an evaluation session. Professor *Grant Goodall, a primo Esperantist and our liaison in the UCSD Department of Linguistics, says (in English) that he wants to hear from *all* of us; for the benefit of beginners, he welcomes our candid responses in English. Though it's ironic that English, not Esperanto, promises the most egalitarian discussion, it is a deeply Esperantist gesture.

It is the first time I've heard any of the *NASKanoj* speak English. One by one, we strip off our fantastical eucalyptus masks. Christy, from Raleigh, has a soft Carolina twang that makes her sound even younger than seventeen; Filipo sounds like he's still in New York on West Seventy-second Street, eating blintzes. Nini sounds like a kindergarten teacher, which is what she was for decades, decades ago. Stecĵo turns out to be a kid from Long Island; Meja sounds like the UCSD students skateboarding near the bookstore; and Bernard, the future academic, speaks a sophisticated CompLitese. Karlo's vowels as well as his passport are Canadian; and, to my surprise, Tero, who seems so West Coast, has a strong Minnesota accent, as though headed home to Lake Wobegon. The conversation is slow to get rolling, but then one of the older women complains that the classrooms are too far from the dorms; another chimes in that the shuttles are unreliable. Our "evaluation" swiftly turns into a

gripe session. "The food—it's not great, and the salad bar closes too early."
"The *Kaplanuloj* are too loud!" "The *diboĉejo* is too small." "The painters
entered my room while I was in there!" "The field trips . . ." someone says,
rolling his eyes. I look at Slim; *ouch*. Only Greta and Benedikt speak in
Esperanto, but they say little; Kalindi is silent. Brigadoon is dissolving
before my eyes, leaving a room full of irritated, underslept people remembering that they have planes to catch, emails to answer, jobs to resume.

When we walk back to the dorm to pack, most of us switch into Esperanto; it's more . . . comfortable? More in keeping with this place, this
time? A way to prolong, for a few more moments, something akin to
happiness? As we walk, Wayne says, "I make a standing offer to all my
students to write to me; some do. I ask each of them to set a goal—a goal
for two weeks from now, a month from now, for the next six months. For
the coming year. If you don't set a goal, nothing happens." I ask him how
often he speaks Esperanto when he's at home. "Well, once a month when
I can get to a meeting in St. Louis—but I'm often too busy to drive down
there."

He considers; when he resumes, his tone is confessional. "So, basi-
cally, only with my dogs. I tell my *pomerhundo*"—Pomeranian—"'*bona
hundo!*' and he gets it. I call my evil *ĉivavo*"—chihuahua—"'*Hundaĉo!*'
and he gets it." He shrugs, as if to dismiss the forty-nine weeks until he is
back in San Diego. "You just have to keep it going, and you do."

PART TWO

DOKTORO ESPERANTO AND THE SHADOW PEOPLE

1. Jewish Questions

In a letter of 1905 to the French Esperantist Alfred Michaux, Zamenhof wrote: "My Jewishness has been the main reason why, from earliest childhood, I gave myself completely to one crucial idea, one dream—the dream of the unity of humankind."[1] It's an unlikely claim for a man who, by his own account, "crossed the Rubicon"[2] from Jewish particularism to universalism, dismissed the claims of both Yiddish and Hebrew as modern Jewish languages, and invented, single-handedly, a new international language. But the man who deemed the Jews a "shadow people" lived always in the shadow of his Jewishness.

Zamenhof came to maturity in a world beset with Jewish questions. There were questions posed from without, by governments and non-Jewish elites: In an age of Jewish emancipation, to what extent would Jews be relieved of legal disabilities? Enfranchised as citizens? Assimilated into prestigious social circles, universities, and the higher echelons of commercial and professional power? Then there were the myriad of questions Jews posed to one another: How would Jews make the transition between life in the *kahal* (semi-autonomous Jewish community) and citizenship in a nation-state? Even with broadening civil rights, how were Jews to deal with entrenched anti-Semitism and intolerance in the private sphere? What new institutions and social forms would evolve within the Jewish community, and by the same token, what might be lost to assimilation? By the time Zamenhof entered his twenties, anti-Semitic violence in the Pale of Settlement had raised a most urgent question: What sort of future, if any, could Jews expect under the Russian Empire, and how were they to take their fate in hand?

In his letter to Michaux, Zamenhof made it clear that Esperanto had been motivated by his experience of anti-Semitism in the Russian Empire; but at the same time, he insisted that anti-Semitism was part of the larger, human problem of interethnic intolerance. What he did not disclose is that Esperanto, by 1901, had become part of a larger project to renovate Jewish religious experience, build a modern Jewish community, and gradually expand it to include people of other faiths and nationalities. Esperanto was a part of his answer to the Jewish question from within—the question of Jewish continuity in modernity. Paradoxically, this invented language would also promote Jewish authenticity, which Zamenhof found to be severely undermined by modernity. And if Esperanto could be an answer to the Jewish question, the Jews of Russia just might be the answer to sustaining Esperanto.

* * *

The man who devoted his life to a dream of untrammeled communication was the son of a censor. Markus (Motl, Mordka) Zamenhof, born in 1837 in Suwalki in what is now northeast Poland, was a child of the *haskalah*, the Jewish enlightenment. While most of his fellow Jews in the Pale of Settlement eked out a living as merchants and small-scale entrepreneurs, Markus, like his father before him, was a schoolteacher whose passion for foreign languages had widened his world.[3] Having settled in Białystok, Markus married Liba Rahel (Rosa) Sofer in 1858. A photograph taken twenty years later shows her carefully coiffed, in a dark winter dress, her left thumb hooked over a closed book that is more prop than pursuit. On December 3, 1859, Markus and Rosa welcomed their first child, Ludovik (Lazar). For nearly a decade, he had his parents' full attention, until 1868, when the first of his seven siblings was born.

Punctilious in his habits and driven to succeed, Markus moved the family to Warsaw where, in addition to his license to teach in Jewish state-run schools, he earned a second imperial certification to teach German in non-Jewish gymnasiums.[4] His performance was outstanding; for "perfect and diligent service," he received a third-rank appointment to the Order of St. Stanisłav.[5] His command of Russian, Polish, French, German, and Hebrew brought him to the attention of the Warsaw Censorial Committee, which in 1883 appointed him censor for all German materials received by post in Warsaw. Two years later, he took on the additional duties of censor for Hebrew and Yiddish materials, at a combined salary that doubled his pay as a teacher. To be an unconverted Jewish censor for the czar was both a point of pride and a warrant for rigorous self-containment. He reported to a baptized Jew in St. Petersburg, and his colleagues were most likely members of the Polish gentry, which had been hit hard by the emancipation of the serfs in 1865 and the agricultural depressions of the 1870s and 1880s.[6] His contemporary, Nahum Sokolov, editor of the Hebrew-language journal *HaTzefirah*, described him as "wise, pedantic and reserved; he measured his steps, sifted his words, an accurate chronometer, always equilibrated . . . [He was] buttoned-up to the collar, speaking in a monotone, with unvarying pronunciation."[7] A photograph taken in his early sixties shows a bald, gray-bearded, scholarly Markus in the regalia of St. Stanislav, his medals shining on his breast.

For most ambitious Jewish men in Markus's position, assimilation and conversion beckoned; otherwise, the choices were few, the horizons low. For a time, Markus seemed to have outstripped his options. He was both a decorated civil servant and a respected member of the Jewish community, called on to speak at a building dedication and much in demand as a Torah chanter. He wore the uniform of his office to synagogue but left his sword at home on the Sabbath and on holidays.[8] But his failure to censor a controversial *HaTzefirah* article on a union of Jewish merchants

Markus (Motl) Zamenhof, 1898
[Österreichische Nationalbibliothek]

Liba Rahel (Rosa) Zamenhof, née Sofer

appears to have led to his dismissal, first as German censor (which reduced his salary by more than half) and, a few months later, as censor of Hebrew and Yiddish books. When his abject plea for reinstatement was ignored, he returned to teaching at a gymnasium (secondary school).[9] The authorities left him his imperial decorations, which had always meant far more to him than to the czar.

Like most upwardly mobile Jews from greater Lithuania (which included present-day Lithuania, Belarus, and Ukraine), the Zamenhof family were multilingual. They spoke Russian in their Warsaw home, Polish and German in commercial transactions, and Yiddish in their dealings with relatives and Jewish neighbors; they chanted in Hebrew in the synagogue. Both Ludovik's father and grandfather had staked out identities as emancipated Jews by mastering and teaching the languages of Western Europe; no surprise, then, that when Ludovik began his studies at the prestigious #2 Men's Gymnasium in Warsaw, languages were his forte. A student of both Latin and Greek, he was commended for his excellence in the latter, also earning top grades in German, French, and mathematics.

Together, Markus and Rosa Zamenhof had raised their children to the emancipated Jewish life described by the poet Judah Leib Gordon: "a Jew

*Zamenhof's home in Białystok
[Österreichische
Nationalbibliothek]*

at home, a man on the street." But on the streets of Białystok, Ludovik
Zamenhof recalled finding no men at all:

> In Białystok, the population consisted of four diverse elements:
> Russians, Poles, Germans and Jew; each spoke a different
> language and was hostile to the other elements. . . . I was brought
> up as an idealist; I was taught that all men were brothers, and,
> meanwhile, in the street, in the square, everything at every
> step made me feel that men did not exist, only Russians, Poles,
> Germans, Jews and so on.[10]

The converse of his conviction that language wrought profound divi-
sions among people was another, just as deeply held: that language had
the power to transform people of various ethnicities into "men." If
Zamenhof needed evidence that language could unify human beings
and transform their aspirations, it was all around him. As Ivan Berend
has shown, "from the 1770s to the 1840s, with few exceptions, all the
Central and Eastern European languages"—Polish, Czech, Hungarian,
Rumanian, Serbian, and Croatian—"were modernized and standardized

literary languages were created . . . [that] provided a vehicle for the creation of national literatures and scholarship, education, journalism and legislation."[11]

Such developments were rooted in Herder's Romantic conviction that a common language was the spiritual essence of a people, indivisible from and essential to it: "Has a nation anything more precious," asked Herder, "than the language of its fathers?"[12] Zamenhof absorbed Herder's insight, but used it as an Archimedean lever through which to move diverse peoples with no "fathers" in common to conceive of themselves as a community. He had also absorbed Humboldt's notion of language as a "third universe" between the empirical world and cognition—as a mediator for the entirety of human experience.[13] From the legacies of both Herder and Humboldt, Zamenhof drew the guiding intuition of his life: that not only social relations but human beings themselves could be transformed by language.

In the autumn of 1878, about to turn nineteen, Zamenhof drafted a language expressly designed to turn "Russians, Poles, Germans, [and] Jews" into "men." That December, at a small birthday party for close friends, he formally launched—or in his words, "consecrated"— his *Lingwe Universala*. Presenting his friends with both a grammar and a lexicon (neither of which survives), he made a speech in the new tongue and together, the group sang a universalist hymn in the *Lingwe Universala*.

> *Malamikete de las nacjes*
> *Kadó, kadó, jam temp'está!*
> *La tot' homoze in familje*
> *Konunigare so debá.*

> Let the hatred of the nations
> Fall, fall! The time is already here;
> All humanity must unite
> In one family.

But as soon as the party was over, the new language became a lonely venture. None of the would-be "apostles of the language" was willing to sustain it, and Zamenhof would later rue the fact that only one of them eventually embraced Esperanto.[14] His early effort to found a new international language-collective was a failure. And before he would succeed in founding the community of Esperanto, he would fail again, but this time in the service of nationalism, not internationalism.

* * *

In one portrait from his teen years, Zamenhof looks studious in large round spectacles, his hair slicked and parted in the middle along the same axis as a sparse mustache. But a second photograph, taken in his early twenties, shows a far more romantic figure, free of glasses and mustache, sporting a brass-buttoned coat, black hair swept back over a wide brow, and a poet's melancholy gaze. This is the Ludovik who, in 1879, was sent to Moscow University to study medicine. Perhaps his parents meant him to pursue a more prestigious, less precarious career than that of a teacher or bureaucrat (other siblings followed him into medicine, as would two of his three children). Or perhaps they sought to redirect his quixotic aspiration to build a universalist language-community toward the more concrete matter of acquiring a profession. Zamenhof seemed to understand that he was to keep his aspirations under wraps while in Moscow, and conceal them he did—an unhappy choice, as it turned out: "The secrecy tormented me. Being obliged to hide my thoughts and plans, I hardly went anywhere or took part in anything, and the most beautiful time of life—the years of a student—for me passed most sadly."[15]

But soon his aspirations took another form, for the journey to Moscow took him closer to the pulse of Russian-Jewish intellectual life, which was centered in St. Petersburg. During the 1860s, the Jews of Russia, having endured segregation in the Pale of Settlement (1795), enforced conscription (1820s–), and compulsory enrollment at special Jewish "Crown" schools, had begun to take up the question of their future. Zamenhof arrived in Moscow twenty years later to heated debates between assimilationists and proto-Zionists (bent on "auto-emancipation"); within a brief time, four new Russian-language Jewish journals sprang up, and a fifth in Hebrew.

In a retrospective interview published in London's *Jewish Chronicle*, Zamenhof placed himself at the center of the controversy. Less than three years after drafting his *Lingwe Universala*, Zamenhof was becoming an ardent Jewish nationalist:

> Already, in the year 1881, when I was studying at the University
> of Moscow, I convened a meeting of fifteen of my fellow-students,
> and unfolded to them a plan which I had conceived of founding
> a Jewish colony in some unoccupied portion of the globe which
> would be the commencement, and become the center of an in-
> dependent Jewish State. I succeeded in impressing my views
> on my colleagues, and we formed what I believe was the first
> politico-Jewish organization in Russia.[16]

It was a fateful year for Jews, and for Zamenhof himself. In
March 1881, the assassination of Czar Alexander II (following two previous attempts) gave rise to pogroms against Jews in the Pale of Settlement. During the wave of murders, rapes, arson, and looting, the
complicity of police and government officials, scrupulously documented
by observers, created a sensation as far afield as Paris, London, and New
York. Zamenhof was galvanized by a need to address the most difficult
Jewish question of all: what was to become of the Jews of the Russian
Empire? Amid crackdowns in university discipline and whispers of con-
spiracy, he managed to complete his second year of studies, but with a
marked decline in grades.[17] An internal transfer record, gleaned from a
Moscow archive by Zamenhof's biographer, Aleksander Korĵenkov, declared him "well behaved and not under suspicion."[18] By autumn he had
decamped for Warsaw, attributing the move to his father's financial
straits; more likely, his activism had left him distracted, exposed, and
endangered.

Four months later, on Christmas Day, 1881, a pogrom broke out in
Warsaw, which occupied the western edge of the Pale of Settlement; in
its wake, the harsh May Laws of 1882 lashed Jews with new restrictions,
requiring all Jews living in Russia's major cities to relocate to the Pale.
Zamenhof, now studying medicine in Warsaw, threw himself into planning a future elsewhere for Eastern European Jews. His first Zionist
article, "What, Finally, to Do?" appeared serially in several numbers of
the Russian-Jewish journal *Rasyet* (Dawn) in 1882 under the anagram-
matic pseudonym G(H)AMZEFON. A Jewish homeland, he argued, was
a necessity, but it need not—in fact, *should* not—be located in Palestine,
also sacred to Christians and Muslims. A place where religious belief ran
high would place Jews in danger, sapping the resources with which they

were to build a state. Zamenhof did not expect the pious Jews in Palestine to welcome young Zionists; he seems to have believed their vows to rebuild the Temple and return Judaism to a purified religion of sacrifice and ritual. In short, Palestine was an alien, inhospitable, and primitive place that promised hostility rather than peaceful coexistence; a few years later, he would call it a "volcano."[19]

Zamenhof's considered proposal was for Jews to purchase a tract of unoccupied land—about sixty square miles—on the banks of the Mississippi River. There, he imagined, Jews would be free to enjoy the bounty of nature and to live unmolested. All their energy could be devoted to farming and building a Jewish state—as in Utah, he wrote, hardly suspecting that the Mormon struggle for Utah's statehood would last nearly fifty years. When Zamenhof's dream of an American Jewish colony met with ridicule, he swiftly recognized that the dream of a homeland in Palestine carried far more historical and cultural prestige. In his next article, he shifted gears, imagining Jews coming to Palestine "like bees . . . each from his own leaf and flower."[20] It was a romantic image that harbored a harsh truth: if there was to be any honey in the land of milk and honey, the Jews would be making it themselves.

Having been active in Moscow's Hibbat Zion (Lovers of Zion) movement, he now co-founded a chapter in Warsaw. He and his fellow Zionists called the organization Shearith Israel (Remnant of Israel) and developed a network of youths committed to raising funds for settlement in Palestine. Seeking the support of more powerful members of the Jewish community, he convinced the eminent advocate Israel Jasinowski to serve as president, perhaps an honorary title, since Zamenhof himself headed up "the Executive." By day he studied medicine: by night, he was the go-to man among Warsaw's young Zionists, coordinating the activities of three separate Zionist circles in Warsaw. And, at great personal risk, he illegally channeled funds for settlement in Palestine to a rabbi in Bavaria. At the home of a colleague in Hibbat Zion he met his future wife, the plain, square-jawed Klara Zilbernick, daughter of a successful soap manufacturer from Kovno (Kaunas).

Later, he would recall the unremitting duties of his Zionist days: "I drew up the rules, hektographed them myself, and distributed them, arranged meetings, concerts and balls, enlisted recruits, and established a patriotic Jewish library."[21] Among Zionists in Moscow, and during his period of Zionist activism in Warsaw, Zamenhof kept silent about his universal language. It was the same impulse that led him to tell an Esperanto magazine, years later, the story of his Moscow days without any mention whatsoever of his Zionist period. The skills he had acquired as a "Jew at home, a man on the street," had made him, like so many emancipated Jews of the Russian Empire, a chameleon, adept at surviving in diverse milieus by shaping his self-presentation to his audience.

Though he'd shelved the universalist language project, Zamenhof sooner or later homed back to his conviction that language was essential for fellowship and solidarity. Unlike his Yeshiva-educated contemporary, Eliezer Ben-Yehuda, the founder of modern Hebrew, Zamenhof decided that "ancient Hebrew," as he put it, could never serve the Zionist dream. Instead, he devoted more than two years to updating Yiddish for use in a Jewish state. In the early 1880s, a modernized Yiddish must have seemed far more practicable than Hebrew; after all, fully two-thirds of the world's ten million Jews were Yiddish speakers. While most Russian-speaking Jews still referred to it as a "jargon," Yiddish was slowly earning the respect of the most self-respecting Jews—writers, such as Mendele Mocher Sforim (Sholem Yankel Abramovitch); journalists, such as Alexander Zederbaum, who in 1863 had inaugurated a weekly Yiddish supplement to his Hebrew-language paper;[22] and Russified Jewish socialists, who chose Yiddish to take their message to the masses. Instead of using Hebrew characters, Zamenhof used Latin characters, inventing a new, rationalized orthography that would free Yiddish from German-influenced spellings. His innovations anticipated both Sovietized Yiddish, "liberated" from Hebraicisms in the 1920s,[23] and the enduring transliteration conventions developed the same decade by the Yiddish Scientific Institute (YIVO). To avoid homonyms, Zamenhof spelled homophonic twins, such as *nehmen* (to take) and *nemen* (names), differently. And just as he had composed an anthem to showcase his universal language in 1878, he now composed a Zionist ballad that doubled as a practicum in metered verse.

It is hard to say when he put aside the Yiddish project. Only in 1909 did he publish a portion of it in the Yiddish journal *Lebn un Visnshaft*; the whole manuscript of his modernized Yiddish did not appear until 1982, in Russian and Esperanto. But Zamenhof's disillusionment with Zionism can be dated to the final months of his medical studies in

Klara Zamenhof, née Zilbernick
[Österreichische Nationalbibliothek]

1883. To a group of settlers he had been funding in Palestine, Zamenhof wrote: "You left already a year and a half ago, but your affair stands
as it did in the start; no, worse, much worse." Comparing them unfa-
vorably to David, Bar Kokhba, Mucius Scaevola, and the Maccabees,
he calls them "Don Quixotes": "And now [the German-language journal *Kolonist*] regards you as wandering nihilists (not socialists). . . .
Lost, lost are your shining young strengths, which seemed the dawn of
salvation."[24]

Disappointed and disillusioned by the Zionist dream, he became
a wandering Jew. After receiving his medical degree in 1884, he spent the
next three years in a professional vagrancy. Still single, his life became
increasingly chaotic as he wandered from region to region, practicing
medicine briefly in the town of Veisiejai, 150 miles northeast of Warsaw,
and then in Płock, 60 miles west of Warsaw. Intent on more professional
security, he went to Vienna for training in ophthalmology. Returning to
Warsaw in 1885, he finally opened an ophthalmology practice and in 1887
married Klara Silbernick. Within two years, he would be the father of a
son and a daughter, Adam and Zofia. But it was as the father of Esperanto, which saw the light in 1887, that he would be better known. And
because of Esperanto, his most demanding child, he would continue to
wander, young family in tow.

Zamenhof family: (left to right) *Lidia, Klara, Adam, Ludovik*

2. Ten Million Promises

In 1887, when he published Esperanto's inaugural Russian-language pamphlet, Zamenhof was nearing thirty. He was a slight, bespectacled man given to chain-smoking, with piercing, faintly Asian-looking eyes that seemed out of place in his implausibly bulbous head. His boxy beard still black, he could have passed for a younger, less self-important brother of Sigmund Freud. After months of fruitlessly shopping around his new "international language," Zamenhof self-published the pamphlet with a Jewish printer in Warsaw under a pseudonym: "Doktoro Esperanto." He referred to it as the *lingvo internacia*, or simply as *internacia*, but within two years, as an Esperanto-German dictionary of 1889 reveals, it would become known by the name of its pseudonymous author: Esperanto.

The pamphlet, known today as the *Unua Libro* (First Book), wore some of the trappings of other European language projects: a lengthy foreword, a pronouncing alphabet, a dictionary, a list of sixteen gram-

Lingvo Internacia (Unua Libro)

matical rules, and, as a specimen translation, the requisite Lord's Prayer. But it contained other, more idiosyncratic items: an excerpt from the Hebrew Bible (Gen 1:1–10); a translation of a poem by the baptized German-Jewish poet Heine; and a jocular letter to a friend ("I'm picturing . . . the face you'll make after receiving my letter!"). Even more unusual was an exhibition of two original poems in the *lingvo internacia*, both melancholic effusions written in rhymed stanzas. One would call them conventional, were they not the sole poems in the language.

Making no reference to his high-minded ambition to break down barriers of ethnicity and nation, Zamenhof pitched the language as "an official and commercial dialect" that would yield economies of time and money. He was writing not for heirs to an ancient community of believers, but for secular moderns. To acquire "this rich, mellifluous, universally comprehensible language," he boasted, "is not a matter of years of laborious study, but the mere light amusement of a few days."[25] Hence, inspired by "the so-called secret alphabets," he proposed the language simply as a gamelike code, complete with a key, slender enough to "carry in one's note-book, or the waistcoat-pocket." Beyond the air of progress, functionality, and efficiency, there was another signal difference from earlier constructed languages. The *lingvo internacia* was presented as provisional and unfinished, and the reader was entreated to help bring it to completion. It was as if God had stopped the Creation on the fifth day, trusting the animals to make the people.

Toward the end of the brochure appeared eight coupons, printed on a single page:

> Promise
> I, the undersigned, promise to learn the proposed international language of Doctor Esperanto, if it will be shown that 10 million people publicly give the same promise.
> Signed:
> Name:
> Address:

The scheme was in equal measure canny and grandiose. Zamenhof knew that people would be more likely to commit to learning a new language if they could be assured of a community; but ten million promises? The combined populations of Warsaw and Paris numbered under four million. While waiting for the phantasmal ten million promises to materialize, Zamenhof invited criticism, vowing to maintain a one-year comment period, at the end of which he would tally the "votes" and publish "an abstract of the proposed changes." Only then would the language receive its "final form" from an unspecified "academy of the tongue."

Fortuitously, the emergence of Esperanto coincided with the fall of Volapük to ferocious infighting over linguistic issues. By 1887, many Volapükist circles had lost faith in the cause; some, like the Nuremberg circle, were only too glad to defect to Esperanto, a far easier language to learn, and one that seemed to promise more in the way of real-world applications, especially commerce. In the wake of Volapük's definitive collapse, Esperanto swiftly gained ground and within two years, the *Unua Libro* had been published throughout Europe in German, Hebrew, Yiddish, Swedish, Latvian, Danish, Bulgarian, Italian, Spanish, French, and Czech. There were two English editions, the first so faulty—and so much in demand—that it had to be redone a year later.[26]

Perhaps because he had received only a thousand coupons, mostly from Russia and Germany[27] (about 20 percent of them from Jews), Zamenhof decided to stimulate interest in Esperanto with a new publication. In 1888, he published the *Dua Libro* (Second Book), not in Russian but in the *lingvo internacia* itself, suggesting that there was now a substantial readership conversant with the language. Above all, Zamenhof wrote, readers should use the language in correspondence, coining new words as necessary, and he promised to supply them with a directory, which he did in 1889. But he did not want to retain the privileged role of "author" of the language, as he avowed in the *Dua Libro*:

> This brochure is the last word that I will utter in the role of author. From this day the future of the international language is no longer more in my hands than in the hands of any other friend of this sacred idea. We must now work together in equality, each, according to one's own strength. . . . Let us work and hope![28]

It was the first of many inventions of farewell, most of them forgotten as soon as Zamenhof perceived Esperanto to be under threat, from within or without. It was well and good to cede the language to its users, but as a practical matter, the disappointing influx of coupons rankled. News that the American Philosophical Society in Philadelphia was debating the question of an international language tempted Zamenhof with the hope that Esperanto might be adopted by a prestigious body, its well-being taken into their hands. But Zamenhof's dream was also his worst nightmare: that "experts" would "improve" a language meant to belong to its users.

When the proposed APS congress was scrapped, there was not a sufficient infrastructure for Esperanto to gain momentum. Still stung by his disappointment over the coupons, Zamenhof focused on building a community, proposing a new "League of Esperantists" comprising clubs rather than individual members. After twenty-five clubs had joined, the league would elect a ten-member Language Committee. Though he had forfeited ownership of the language, Zamenhof attempted single-handedly to draft rules of governance, which led to a falling-out with his two German co-editors on *La Esperantisto* (The Esperantist), a magazine based in Nuremberg. It was Zamenhof's fate, having renounced power over the movement, to be always at the mercy of the most powerful forces within the movement, whether this meant influential clubs, prestigious leaders or, early in the new century, strong national Esperanto organizations. With the magazine about to go under, Zamenhof contemplated selling stock in the movement to raise cash,[29] but the affair was saved by an infusion of cash from a well-to-do surveyor named Wilhelm Heinrich Trompeter, who in 1891 assumed financial responsibility for the movement. He even paid Zamenhof a one-hundred-mark monthly salary (about $600 USD in today's currency) for editing the journal.

Despite Trompeter's timely intervention, for Zamenhof the dozen years after the publication of the *Unua Libro* were an ordeal of poverty, professional stumbles, and dislocation fueled by a bitter elixir of determination, shame, and despair. He found himself in a bare-knuckle struggle to keep Esperanto alive, even as he struggled to do the same for both his family and his career. The impact on both family and career of his labor for Esperanto was disastrous. His publications had been largely funded by Klara's dowry, backed up by emoluments from her indulgent but increasingly frustrated father. In the late 1880s, Zamenhof sent his pregnant wife and young son, Adam, born in 1888, to stay with Klara's father in Kovno, and scouted for a town that met his two requirements: a dearth of oculists and a Jewish community. His 1889 attempt to establish a practice in the Ukrainian town of Kherson (which was one-third Jewish)[30] was a fiasco. As he later wrote, "I simply and literally, often, didn't even have anything to eat . . . neither my wife, nor my in-laws knew anything about this."[31]

During the hungry, lonely months in Kherson, Zamenhof somehow found the time to write articles, translate a story by Hans Christian Andersen, and edit *La Esperantisto*. As Korĵenkov notes, Zamenhof wrote for the magazine "in his real name, under pseudonyms, and anonymously,"[32] lest it seem that the entire issue was the work of one person. His translation of "The Little Mermaid," for example, was written under the pseudonym "Anna R." Perhaps he chose the name to attract women to the language; perhaps he identified with the trials of the mermaid, who paid for her desire to enter a larger, wider world by surrendering her tongue.

When Zamenhof's second child, Zofia, arrived in 1889, he reluctantly accepted a bailout from his "miraculous father-in-law" (as Esperantists refer to him) on the condition that he return to Warsaw. But when pressure mounted on Zamenhof's friable career, he sought a less expensive place to live in Grodno, a predominantly Jewish town not far from Białystok. As he later put it in a letter to Alfred Michaux:

> My income was larger than in Warsaw and life was less expensive. Although in Grodno, my income still didn't entirely cover my expenses and I had to continue to take support from my

father-in law, nonetheless, I patiently stayed in place there for a period of four years.[33]

Fleeting glimpses of Zamenhof's four "patient" years in Grodno have recently been brought to light by Korjenkov: Zamenhof sitting as a juror, attending meetings of the medical society, collaborating on public health research on the eyesight of schoolchildren, and volunteering to become an army medical doctor (which unlike his sister, he never became).[34] Surrounded by his wife and two children, he became much better integrated into the community than he had been in Kherson.

* * *

In January 1894, his hopes for both a league and a language committee dashed, Zamenhof proposed a radical overhaul of the *Unua Libro* and *Dua Libro*. After seven years of urging the users of the language to complete his work, he was impatient. He'd both hoped for and feared the embrace of Esperanto by a learned academy; now he knew that Esperanto's enthusiasts would be too weak to forestall "expert" intervention. Hence, he proposed a raft of reforms to alter pronunciation, numbers, and personal pronouns; the definite article was sent packing and adjectival agreement was suspended. Not only adjectives, but the "fundamental" endings of verbs and adverbs were altered. The accusative, which had enabled speakers of different languages to order words as they would in their own language, he excised, recommending subject-verb-object word order (which has historically predominated, according to the Dutch linguist Wim Jansen).[35] Taking his lexical inversion of Yiddish to an extreme, he now advised coiners of new words "to avoid German and Slavic words, and take, whenever possible, only from Romance languages"; he even recommended doing away with the tiny *ĉapeloj* over letters, which had posed typographical difficulties and which, he later learned, were an impediment to the visually impaired. Of the sixteen fundamental rules, only four stood unchanged.[36] The reforms were, in Korjenkov's phrase, "drastic,"[37] and the chief casualty was the vaunted simplicity and transparency of the language.

To adopt a raft of reforms would have returned Esperanto to infancy; moreover, it would have required all of Esperanto's enthusiasts to retrain and retool, and this the rank and file of the Esperantists (a body constituted by the subscribers to *La Esperantisto*) were not prepared to do. The rejection of Zamenhof's 1894 reforms led to a crisis of confidence in him, his movement, and his journal. Defections began, especially among former Volapükists in Nuremberg. Meanwhile, the number of subscribers to *La Esperantisto* plummeted, from 889 in 1893, to 596 in 1894, to 425 in 1895.[38] When even his patron, Trompeter, withdrew support, Zamenhof briefly collaborated with Tolstoy's publisher, Posrednik, publishing an Esperanto translation of an excerpt from Tolstoy's essay "Reason or Faith." But Tolstoy's essay and others condoning civil disobedience provoked the banning of *La Esperantisto* in Russia, and with two-thirds of its subscribers gone, the journal soon collapsed. In May 1895, an appeal to the censor from Tolstoy himself, describing Zamenhof as a man "passionately dedicated to his invention and having already lost by his enterprise,"[39] reversed the ban, but for *La Esperantisto,* it was too late.

Zamenhof must have known the reforms would be defeated, for even as he was developing them, he was translating *Hamlet* into the original 1887 version of Esperanto. With *Hamleto, Reĝido de Danujo,* Zamenhof launched a new international Library of Esperanto, which had been envisioned in the inaugural pamphlet of 1887: "Were there but an international language, all translations would be made into it alone, as into a tongue intelligible to all." [40] As Tonkin has observed, Shakespeare, revered by Goethe, Schiller, Pushkin, and Turgenev, was the playwright on whom litterateurs in the newly revived national languages (Polish, Czech, and Hungarian) had cut their teeth in the 1790s.[41] And in these European milieus, the brooding figure of Hamlet towered over the rest of Shakespeare's characters, representing intellect, philosophical independence, a dialectical relation to truth, and a challenge to corrupt anciens regimes.

But unlike Polish, Czech, and Hungarian, Esperanto was not the language of an ancient folk; in 1894, it was barely past teeth-cutting. In effect, Zamenhof was asking a seven-year-old to perform *Hamlet*—and perform it did, furnishing him not only with syllables for fluent blank verse, but also with a lexicon that, but for some three dozen new roots he coined for the occasion, was almost entirely sufficient for his needs. Thus, ambitious to build both a library and a community, Zamenhof produced a playable *Hamlet,*[42] his shaky command of English notwithstanding. With the aid of a German translation and probably a Russian one, too, he gave Esperanto its first Shakespeare play.

For Zamenhof, the final years of the century were years of despair and disaffection. When his father-in-law refused him funds to launch yet another journal, the Zamenhofs returned to Warsaw, where he set up his ophthalmalogical practice among the city's poorest Jews. He would remain in his house-clinic at 9 Dzika Street from 1897 until the final months of his life, depending on these Jews for his livelihood.

Meanwhile, Esperanto was buoyed by a new wave of enthusiasts in France. Until 1900, Russians constituted the single largest constituency in the movement, and the majority came from the heavily Jewish Pale of Settlement.[43] But in the final years of the century, Esperanto had been steadily gaining ground among an erudite group of French intellectuals—philosophers, mathematicians, a minister of state, and a university rector—which brought the movement to a crossroads: for the first time, the French overtook the Russians in the membership rolls.[44] In 1900 we find Zamenhof, Janus-faced, looking in two directions: toward Russia, where the Jewish intelligentsia were still debating, with more at stake than ever, their future and their tongue; and toward Paris, where Esperanto's future appeared to lie. But even with this new constituency in France, how was Esperanto, with virtually no one speaking it from birth and no institutions endorsing it, to survive into a new century? Perhaps France's leading intellects would use their influence to recommend Esperanto to the whole world, but if not, Zamenhof had another plan: to spread Esperanto among Russia's Jews—but this time, as a modern Jewish language.

3. A Shadow People

Having lost faith in Zionism as an answer to anti-Semitism, Zamenhof announced that he had "crossed the Rubicon" to universalism. He rarely revisited his Zionist period in his essays, letters, and interviews, though he never denied his Jewishness. "I want to work only for absolute justice among people," he later wrote. "I'm profoundly convinced that I'll bring my unhappy people much more good this way, than by a nationalist goal."[45] In fact, his striving for "absolute justice" entailed an audacious attempt to renovate Jewish religious experience, build a modern and authentic Jewish community, and gradually include people of other faiths and nationalities. It was in this imagined community that he hoped to root Esperanto, securing it as a hereditary language.

He was not the only Russian Jew of his generation to decry a moral hollowness among modern, assimilated Jews. In 1897, Asher Hirsch

Ginsberg, better known as Ahad Ha'am (One of the People), admonished the First Zionist Congress for failing to ground nationalism in the ethics of Judaism. Statehood, if not founded in moral vision and ethical commitment, was "idolatrous"; redemption, if equated with political sovereignty, merely a phantasm. "The deliverance of Israel," wrote Ahad Ha'am, lay neither in territorial covenant nor in diplomacy, but in the legacy of the prophets, "envisioning the reign of justice in the world at the end of days."[46]

Zamenhof's *Hillelism: A Project in Response to the Jewish Question* (1901), a Russian-language tract four times as long as the 1887 proposal for Esperanto, was his answer to this longing for prophecy. Its original title, *Call to the Jewish Intellectuals of Russia*, invokes earlier appeals to the Jews to assume responsibility for their fate, such as Leo Pinsker's 1882 *Auto-Emancipation* (which used an epigraph from Hillel), Emma Lazarus's 1881–82 *Epistle to the Hebrews*, and Theodor Herzl's *The Jewish State* (1896). In *Hillelism*, which he published under the Latin pseudonym "Homo Sum" (I Am a Man), he excoriated the false consciousness of emancipated, assimilated Jews who identified themselves as "Russians of Mosaic religion," the legal term for Jews in the Russian Empire:

> The Jewish people for a long time now haven't existed. . . . The expression "the Jewish people" . . . is only the consequence of an illusion, a deep-rooted metaphor, similar to the way in which we say about a portrait of a person, customarily, "There is that person" while nevertheless this person is already long dead and what remains to us in the portrait is only its shadow.[47]

To Zamenhof, these Russian Jews were wrong about two things: how Jewish they were and how Russian they were. First, no matter how many generations they had lived in Russia or how fluently they spoke the language, they would always be Jews to their Russian neighbors. Second, to invoke the "Mosaic religion" was doubly hypocritical, since these Jews neither showed respect for religious authority—divine, Mosaic, or otherwise— nor observed any religious or spiritual practices. To Zamenhof, the emancipated Russian Jews failed every possible test of being a people: they were scattered, irreligious, and immersed in the culture in which they lived, and they lacked ethnic homogeneity. "In whose name do we suffer and condemn our children to suffering? In the name of a phantom, an empty phantom."[48] The clincher, for Zamenhof, was that they "had no language," "since language is rightly that link which makes this or that group of human beings, a people."[49] Yiddish, although "rich in forms . . . and possessed of a rigorous grammar,"[50] was a "jargon," and Hebrew was embedded in the ancient observances and liturgy such modern Jews had forsworn. (Zamenhof was not above hedging his bets: only a decade earlier, he had issued the *Unua Libro* in both Hebrew [1888] and Yiddish [1889].)

For Zamenhof, the Jewish intelligentsia were culpable for clinging tightly to the image of the dead ancestor, to a world that could never again be theirs:

> We are simply chained to a cadaver. The regional-racial form of the Jewish religion now is not only a philosophical-religious absurdity, but also the fullest possible anachronism; and until such time as this form will exist, the suffering of the Jews will never, never cease, neither because of [ethnic] liberalism, nor because of Zionism, and after one hundred and after one thousand years, will Heine's prophetic words still pertain with the same strength: *Das Judentum is keine religion, es ist ein Ungluck.* [Judaism is not a religion, it is a misfortune].[51]

For the "absurdity" of nationalism, Zamenhof squarely placed the blame on those who "uttered the unhappy words, 'God made with us a covenant,'" thereby confounding monotheism with nationality and turning a philosophical, ethical world-concept into an ethnically homogeneous nation.

If the ancestors were mistaken, so was the Scripture that sanctioned the Abrahamic covenant. Hence, the God who despaired of humanity after the outrage at Babel, choosing to favor the people Israel, had to be reimagined. Only by dislodging the concept of a covenanting God—only through a *"change to the Hebrew religion"*—could the "inner system" of exile be altered. He was urging Jews who had already released themselves from Mosaic law to shed their allegiance to the Abrahamic covenant. What he proposed was a "purified" Judaism, unbound from Mosaic law and purged of nationalism.

The conundrum Zamenhof faced was the one that had faced the apostle Paul two millennia earlier: how to create a unified spiritual community after Mosaic law had been abandoned, especially if that community was no longer defined by ethnicity. Whereas Paul sought to instill discipline in the churches, Zamenhof developed a credo around the ethical teaching of the first-century B.C.E. rabbi Hillel: "Do not do unto others what is hateful to you." *Hilelismo*, as he called it, entailed three essential precepts:

1. We feel and recognize the existence of the highest Power, who rules the world, and this Power we call God.
2. God puts his laws inside the heart of each person in the form of conscience; for this reason, at all times obey the voice of your conscience, since it is the voice of God, and never silent.
3. Love your neighbor and act with others in such a way that you would wish them to act with you, and never do anything, openly or in secret, which your internal voice tells you does not please God. All other instructions . . . are only human commentaries.[52]

This third point was, in so many words, Hillel's famed response to the gentile who asked the rabbi to teach him Torah standing on one foot, except that Zamenhof omitted Hillel's coda: "[And now] go study." He was seeking to instill a motive for communal cohesion in what he perceived as a radically disintegrated Jewish people, writing in a mode that Andrew Wernick has called "socio-theology."[53]

If we look to Hillelism for the blueprint of a functioning community, we won't find it. Having lodged the "laws" of God "in the heart in the form of conscience," Zamenhof left authority, moral standards, judgment, and sanction entirely unaddressed. His guiding intuition in doing so was canny and pragmatic: the best way to transform Jews into Hillelists was by allowing them to live and act out what remained of their culture. Hillelism would wear, so to speak,

> an outer dress of present-day Judaism. But this clothing will be
> complete, definite and pure, and not full of holes and patches, as
> it is with present-day Jewish intellectuals, who randomly pick
> at their own rags here and take off the final remnants there, and
> all the while feel the complete abnormality and unhappiness of
> their nudity.[54]

Hillelism would garb modern Judaism in integrity rather than a patchwork of laws, but if it were to gain traction among the Jews of Russia, it had to be recognizably, culturally Jewish.

Thus, Zamenhof retained all religious observances and customs that could be adapted to Hillelist precepts. The Hebrew Bible, for instance, as long as it was regarded as a "human" book, would be retained as a treasury of legends and devotional poetry for the Jewish people. The Sabbath, purged of the punctilious observance of prescriptions, would remain a sacred day of rest, Judaism's best defense against materialism. And so on with the High Holidays and the Jewish festivals. Zamenhof even retained Hanukkah, not as a nationalist festival but as an "historical commemoration." (The fact that he was born during Hanukkah may have entrenched its appeal.)

Hebrew, however, was too suffused with nationhood to be amenable to Hillelism's "liberal conscience, and sincere expression of thought and prayer":

> [Yet] a group of people, desiring to call itself a people, must above all possess their *language*, otherwise, it is only the shadow of a people . . . a people only in a negative sense; that is to say, all existing peoples will not accept them as [if they were] something foreign; [this people] will not have its own identity.[55]

Only a "neutral, invented" language—one "unlimitedly rich, flexible, full of every 'bagatelle' which gives life to language, beautiful-sounding and extraordinarily easy"—could unify and authenticate a renovated, Hillelist people. As it happened, such a language—which Zamenof left unnamed— was already to hand: "The labors of the last decades show that this language not only can exist and satisfy the most refined followers, but that . . . it is so simple that even the most uneducated person can learn it very well in one week (and children can make it their own from birth)."[56] Clearly Zamenhof believed that Hilellists would pass this language on to their children, as peoples will. And over time, it would become "specially adapted to the spirit, life, manner of thought and expression, specifics and customs of these people who founded the initial contingent of Hillelists." Hillelism would transform a "fictive," shadow people into a real one, and Esperanto would be the means of transformation.

> In the same way that Hillelism will not exist without a neutral language, thus, the idea of the neutral language can never truly come into being without Hillelism. . . . The international

language will become strengthened in perpetuity only in the
event that there will exist some group of people who accept it as
a familial, *hereditary* language.[57]

In isolation, Esperanto was a code, Hillelism a cult. But together, they
constituted an ethical calling that looked to the future, not the past, for
the spirit of community.

As he later told the *Jewish Chronicle*, Hillelism promised the "normalization" of Jewishness.

> We ought to create in Judaism a normal sect, and strive to bring
> it about that that sect may come, in the course of time—say after
> 100 or 150 years—to include the whole Jewish people. We should
> then become a powerful group. Nay, more, we should be in a
> position to conquer the civilized world with our ideas, as the
> Christians have hitherto succeeded in doing, though they only
> commenced by being a small Jewish body. Instead of being ab
> sorbed by the Christian world, we shall absorb them; for that is
> our mission, to spread among humanity the truth of monothe
> ism and the principles of justice and fraternity.[58]

What readers of the *Jewish Chronicle* might have called "assimilation,"
Zamenhof imagined as Jewish salience and empowerment. His concept
of "normalization"—uniting Jews and then "conquer[ing] the civilized
world"—was, to say the least, idiosyncratic. And precisely at the moment
when he planned to usher Hillelism into the Esperanto world, his dreams
collided with a bitter reality: the prestigious Esperantists of France intended to hold the future of Esperanto hostage until Zamenhof agreed to
cut Hillelism loose. They told him that the problem was his religious
utopianism; he did not need to be told that in France, during the era of
Dreyfus, the problem was his Jewishness.

4. Mysterious Phantoms

Louis de Beaufront—who would come to be known as Esperanto's Judas—
was the man who single-handedly oversaw the blossoming of the French
Esperanto movement. Zamenhof's biographers have not been kind to

him, describing him as a "sham marquis," a "mythomaniac," and a "hypocrite" with a "tormented craving for importance" couched in "jesuitical humility." [59] He was born Louis Eugène Albert Chevreux in 1855 in Seine-et-Marne, near Paris. A multilingual private tutor, Chevreux let it be known that he was delicate in health following a bout of typhus, and he dropped hints of youthful indiscretions in India. In 1887, the year Zamenhof became "Doktoro Esperanto," Chevreux took the aristocratic patronym "de Beaufront," under which he appeared in the first directory of Esperantists (1888). From these obscure beginnings, Beaufront had an outsized—and dire—impact on the movement.

In 1892, when Beaufront published an Esperanto textbook for French speakers, there were only ten French subscribers to *La Esperantisto*. Beaufront changed that by rendering Esperanto palatable to the French bourgeoisie.[60] To that end, he emphasized the practical benefits of Esperanto in his promotional material, and in 1898, founded the Societé pour la propagation de l'Espéranto, which transposed the pedagogical practices of the French education system onto the *lingvo internacia*. Graded examinations modeled on those given to French students were administered to certify proficient Esperantists as "adepts," but membership was also available to those who gave financial support.[61] Not only did Beaufront accommodate Esperanto to the French bourgeoisie by invoking familiar institutions and procedures; he also presented the case for Esperanto to the French Association for the Advancement of Science at the 1900 Exposition Universelle. At Beaufront's urging, Zamenhof prepared a lengthy address called "Essence and Future of the Idea of an International Language," which he wrote under the pseudonym "M. Unuel" (meaning "Monsieur One of," perhaps an homage to Ahad Ha'am). Given unprecedented access to intellectuals, Zamenhof seized his chance to convince the eminent francophones who dominated the spheres of science and diplomacy just how urgently they needed Esperanto.

Hyperbolical, polemical, at times bombastic, the address was not finely calibrated to its audience, and it fell to Beaufront to edit and translate it for the academicians. Beaufront trimmed away some polemical passages but left intact Zamenhof's vaunting comparison of Esperanto to "the discovery of America, the use of steam engines and the introduction of the alphabet."[62] Massaged by Beaufront, Zamenhof's appeal was sufficient to attract a handful of prestigious adherents who soon became the movement's leaders: retired general Hippolyte Sebert, a ballistics expert

and reformer of library classification; Émile Boirac, the philosopher and
rector of the University of Grenoble; and the mathematician-philosopher
Louis Couturat, formerly of the University of Caen.

Beaufront's most influential convert, the worldly mathematician Carlo
Bourlet, persuaded the president of the eight-thousand-member cycling
organization Touring Club de France[63] that Esperanto would be invalu-
able to its members. Through the TCF, Esperanto attracted the linguist
Théophile Cart, who in 1904 cofounded the first Esperanto press (Presa
Esperantista Societo). Another important adherent was the French Jew
Louis Émile Javal, an innovator in the field of physiological optics, who
went blind from glaucoma in 1900. Javal believed that Esperanto, re-
formed and rendered in Braille, could help to bring literature to the blind;
he inspired more than a century of activism for Esperanto on the part of
blind *samideanoj*. Zamenhof's only Jewish counterpart among the French
leaders, Javal became a trusted intimate, and Jewish terms and references
make frequent appearances in their correspondence. In a letter to Javal,
Zamenhof quoted the "rule given to the ancient Palestinian sages: 'It is
not your duty to finish the work, but you don't have the right to distance
yourself from it.' "[64]

Bourlet's other signal contribution was to convince the firm of
Hachette to publish Zamenhof's long dreamed-of "Esperanto library of
world literature and philosophy." Thanks to Esperanto's newfound legit-
imacy in France, never again would Zamenhof need to self-publish. But
even with his financial stress alleviated, Zamenhof's late hours and incessant smoking told on his health, which was never robust. As he wrote
in a letter of 1905, "I'm not even 46 years old [and] I feel like a 60-year-old."[65]
He had already begun to suffer angina and shortness of breath, symptoms
of the heart disease that would eventually take his life. By day, he provided eye care to the Jewish poor of Warsaw, living among them and
operating a clinic in his home. By night, he devoted himself to Esperanto,
editing and translating for the Hachette series and writing articles and
letters. And in the moments between waking and sleeping, between cases
of cataract and of trachoma, he set his hopes on Beaufront's advocacy in
France.

On the face of it, Beaufront was making remarkable progress. The Association for the Promotion of Esperanto (soon renamed the French Association for the Promotion of Esperanto) more than doubled its membership

between 1902 and 1905, when its rolls showed 4,052 members.[66] Behind the scenes, though, Beaufront was embroiled in squabbles with Bourlet, while Cart, an antireformist, was squabbling with various proponents of reforming the language.

During the summer of 1904, seventeen years after Esperanto was first brought before the public, the inaugural international congress took place at Calais, jointly hosted by the English and French Esperantists from Calais and Dover, respectively. The congress drew nearly two hundred participants, and all sessions and activities were conducted entirely in Esperanto. Flushed with the success at Calais, Michaux, an influential lawyer (whom Korĵenkov identifies as Jewish)[67] offered his city, Boulogne-sur-Mer, as the host for a full-scale "Universal" Congress, to be held the following summer. Zamenhof's hope was that the Universal Congress would become an annual event, providing the movement with "a heart-warming religious center."[68] In fact, as he would later remark at the 1907 Universal Congress in Cambridge, England, he conceived of congresses on the model of the thrice-yearly Jewish pilgrimage festivals.[69]

By 1905, four years after he had offered Hillelism to the Jews of Russia, they had still not heeded his call; as he would later tell the *Jewish Chronicle*, "Many persons confessed to me that in their hearts they agreed with me, but they had not the courage to say so openly. I could not find a single person willing to help me."[70] His call to the Jews of Russia was, after all, paradoxical: He had appealed to them as a community, yet his tract denied that they were a functioning community. Having failed to persuade the Jews of Russia to become Hillelists, he saw the Boulogne Universal Congress as an opportunity to introduce Hillelism to Esperantists as an interethnic movement and, from this ingathering, build outward.

Hence, the now-famous letter to Michaux, in which he described Hillelism as a "moral bridge by which all peoples and religions could unite in brotherhood without the creation of any new dogmas and without the need for people to throw away their own religion, up to this point. . . ."[71] Warming to his theme, Zamenhof made his claim that his Jewishness was his chief motive for creating a language of interethnic understanding. As a Jew committed to universalism rather than to Zionism, he wrote, he had lived a "tormented" and "embattled life." On the other hand, he insisted that he had never concealed (and clearly did not intend to conceal) his Judaism. To send home the point that he had sacrificed for his vision—as a Jew, a doctor, a husband, and a father—the letter included a lengthy narrative of his failures and wanderings of the 1880s and 1890s.

Michaux, receiving the letter, warned the other French members of the Congress Committee that Zamenhof was liable to discourse about "mysticism." In response, the Congress Committee requested that Zamenhof submit the text of his inaugural speech. It was a remarkable document, tempering rapturous, millenarian optimism with chastened, homespun humility.

> The present day is sacred. Our meeting is humble; the outside world knows little about it and the words spoken here will not be telegraphed to all the towns and villages of the world; heads of state and cabinet ministers are not meeting here to change the political map of the world; this hall is not resplendent with luxurious clothes and impressive decorations; no cannon are firing salutes outside the modest building in which we are assembled; but through the air of our hall mysterious sounds are travelling, very low sounds, not perceptible by the ear, but audible to every sensitive soul: the sound of something great that is now being born. Mysterious phantoms are floating in the air . . . the image of a time to come, of a new era. [They] will fly into the world, will be made flesh, will assume power.[72]

Just as the Jews were a "shadow people" who had yet to realize themselves in modernity, the Esperantists were as yet "phantoms" of the just and harmonious people they would help to bring into being. The draft of Zamenhof's speech ended by invoking "a high moral force" with a hymn of his own composition, called "Prayer under the Green Standard."

> To thee, O powerful incorporeal mystery
> Great force, ruling the world,
> To thee, great source of love and trust,
> And everlasting source of life,
> To thee, whom all men present differently,
> Yet sense alike in their hearts
> To thee, who createst, to thee, who rulest,
> We pray today.

When the Congress Committee met in closed session to review the speech, the result was explosive. In Michaux's words (as quoted by Gaston Waringhien):

> One can hardly grasp the wonderment and scandal of these French intellectuals, with their Cartesian and rational[ist] spirit, representatives of lay universities and supporters of secular government, accustomed to and identified with freethinking and atheism, when they heard this flaming prayer to "the high moral Power."[73]

Though Zamenhof's address had not mentioned his Jewishness explicitly, it didn't seem to matter; he was framed by the French as a Jewish outsider:

> "But he's a Jewish prophet," cried Bourlet, and Cart for his part: "That Slav! Michaux will never be able to control this crazy man!"— and Sebert lamented: "We'll be ruined and a laughingstock."[74]

On the eve of the congress, Zamenhof came before the organizing committee, who pressured him to amend his speech and jettison the prayer. Tearful, isolated, apprehensive, he refused to change the speech, but agreed to drop the final stanza of the prayer, which declared that "Christians, Jews or Mahometans, /We are all children of God."

To most of the nearly seven hundred participants, who were unaware of the tension between Zamenhof and the organizing committee, the Boulogne congress was a phenomenal success. Arriving in Paris en route to the congress, Zamenhof found himself an instant celebrity. He was banqueted at the Hôtel de Ville, feted at the Eiffel Tower, named a Knight of the Legion of Honor, and given a VIP tour of the Esperanto Printing Society. And in Boulogne, he was greeted by cheers in the language he had invented. Esperanto proved itself equal to any occasion: meetings, concerts, a performance of Molière's *The Forced Marriage*, a mass, readings, banquets, balls, and excursions to Folkestone and Dover. On display were the green-and-white Esperanto flag, newly created by the Esperantists of Boulogne; books and magazines in Esperanto; and various souvenirs: "pencils, pens, erasers, plates, liqueurs ["Esperantine"],

The First Universal Congress, Boulogne-sur-Mer, 1905
[Österreichische Nationalbibliothek]

biscuits, soaps and even a completely fresh modern invention: an electric board that lit up when endings were in grammatical agreement."[75]

Delivering his contested speech the next day, Zamenhof hewed to his hard bargain. Exhausted by his ordeal before the Congress Committee, he was stunned to receive a long and thundering ovation. It was the first time, but not the last, that he would be revered by a throng of Esperantists as the godlike *Kreinto*—Esperanto's beloved creator. It thrilled him; it also embarrassed him. Whereas Schleyer had referred to himself as Volapük's "supreme leader,"[76] Zamenhof rejected the title *majstro* (master) whenever he was addressed as such.

Javal, a Jew, attributed Zamenhof's warm reception to the committee's efforts to conceal his Jewishness, especially from the French press. Of seven hundred articles about the congress, Javal noted, only one referred to Zamenhof as a Jew: "We needed admirable discipline to hide your origins from the public," Javal wrote. That anti-Semitism lay beneath the committee's "handling" of Zamenhof, Javal was in no doubt. But in the great tradition of Jewish self-deception, Javal ascribed anti-Semitism to the French public at large, commending the committee for protecting Zamenhof—and Esperanto.

In the era of Alfred Dreyfus, the Jewish army captain who had been convicted on trumped-up treason charges, and whose case had unleashed a wave of French anti-Semitism, Jewishness was at the very least a liability. But there was more at stake for the Congress Committee than managing public relations. Just as Dreyfus had polarized the French populace, his fate had riven the French leadership of the Esperanto movement. As Marjorie Boulton, Zamenhof's biographer, writes, "General Sebert and Javal were pro-Dreyfus, de Beaufront and Bourlet, anti-Dreyfus."[77] Neither Javal nor Zamenhof was willing to confront the fact that the Congress Committee, rather than deal with its potentially embarrassing disunity, had preferred to divorce Esperanto from Hillelism and occlude Zamenhof's own Jewishness. Even for the pro-Dreyfusards, saving the good name of Esperanto was a greater cause than defending Zamenhof's Jewishness. As Javal wrote to Zamenhof, "On this point all friends of Esperanto agree, that we must continue to hide the matter, as long as the great battle is not yet won."[78] By the time of Javal's death, two years later, the "great battle" for Esperanto—the *fina venko*—was no closer to triumph. As for the battle against French anti-Semitism, even thirty years after Javal's death, it was far from over: four of Javal's five children would perish in the Holocaust.

* * *

During these early years, the governing structure of the Esperanto movement was decidedly unstable. With French elites dominating the movement, pressure to accord national movements such as France and Germany an administrative role increased. During the run-up to the Boulogne Congress, Zamenhof proposed that the twenty member countries should be represented proportionally on a Central Committee, their delegates elected annually from a collective of local clubs.[79] And the Central Committee, in turn, would elect its own president. In addition, Zamenhof envisioned a suite of working groups overseeing administration, congresses, examinations, and the authorization of manuscripts (the Censor's Committee). A Language Committee could recommend changes to the Central Committee which, if approved, would still require ratification by the congress.

In July 1905, the Boulogne Congress defeated Zamenhof's proposal. In its place, they passed a toothless resolution, authored by Cart, declaring that "national Esperanto groups [should] strive for closer relations among them."[80] Rather than hash out the details and draw up a constitution—rather than take on the burden of self-government—the congress simply postponed the matter of governance to the next congress. As a sop to Zamenhof, he was licensed to name the members of the Language Committee. Indeed, he named ninety-eight members, but their prerogatives were nominal and their number would prove unwieldy. Relations between national units, local clubs, and individual members remained vague and unspecified; no mechanisms were in place to facilitate relations among them or to resolve disputes. Zamenhof had invented the *lingvo internacia* with ethnicities, not nation-states, in mind; but national organizations had become, and would long remain, powers to be reckoned with.

In lieu of a constitution of bylaws, Zamenhof wrote a seven-point Declaration on the Essence of Esperantism that, in its final form, came to be known as the Declaration of Boulogne. Before approving it, the Congress Committee excised two provisions: one for a central governing committee, and another which gave Esperantists of the future permission to abandon Esperanto if a superior auxiliary language were available for adoption. (And Zamenhof left it to them—not experts—to judge.) Instead of a framework by which Esperantists could deliberate over their future, the Declaration of Boulogne designated an immutable *linguistic* constitution: the famous *Fundamento,* which comprised the rules of grammar and usage in the inaugural pamphlet of 1887.

There were other, notable changes, all designed to scrape away the high polish of Zamenhof's ethical ideals. Whereas the *Unua Libro* of 1887 asserted that Esperanto belonged to "society," the Declaration of Boulogne now asserted that it was "no one's property, neither in material matters nor in moral matters." If Esperanto had no "owner," it would instead have "masters": "The spiritual masters of the language shall be . . . the most talented writers in this language." Thus, in place of a Hillelist spirituality, the declaration enshrined the "spirituality" of aesthetic style.

In its revised form, the document also declared ethical and moral commitments to have no bearing on Esperantism, which was now defined as "the endeavor to spread throughout the entire world the use of this neutral, human language. . . . All other ideals or hopes tied with Esperantism by any Esperantist is his or her purely private affair, for which Esperantism is not responsible." Esperantism, thus defined, had no moral motive, no ideology, no rationale; "ideas or hopes" were relegated to the private realm. In its final form, purged of any hint of Hillelism—

any reference to God, Jews, cadavers, or conscience—and disabled as a framework for deliberation and policy making, the document was so innocuous that the Congress Committee published it even before ratification.

According to a letter Zamenhof sent to Javal soon after the Boulogne Congress, he had agreed to privatize Esperantic ideals in the declaration with an ulterior motive. In fact, he disclosed, he intended to introduce Hillelism at the second Universal Congress in Geneva (1906) for those Esperantists who were ready, freely and on their own account, to affirm Hillelism as the "inner idea" of Esperanto. The emphasis would now be on building an interethnic monotheistic community, radiating from Esperantists outward. Ironically, it was a Jewish catastrophe that sharpened his resolve to broaden the appeal of Hillelism: during the revolutionary year 1905, in more than six hundred towns in the Pale of Settlement, anti-Semitic pogroms murdered Jews and ruined their towns, property, and livelihoods. From these bloody events, from these rent lives, the ghost of Hillelism was to rise again.

5. Homaranismo

Six months before the Geneva Congress of 1906, Zamenhof published, in *Ruslanda Esperantisto,* the twelve-point *Dogmoj de Hilelismo* (Dogmas of Hillelism). Like his earlier Hillelist pamphlet, published under the pseudonym "Homo Sum," this one also appeared pseudonymously, signed by a fictitious "Circle of Hillelists." In this iteration, Hillelism was to function as a community-based, ethical quality control on religion, transacted in Esperanto, with a few key social institutions attached: Hillelist temples, religious schools, and elder-care programs. The spread of Hillelism was to be nonviolent, a quiet, gradual cultural transformation that left Hillelists free to speak "family" languages at home. The *Dogmoj* entitled all Hillelists to their chosen or inherited religions, but bound them to reject religious principles that failed to meet the severe ethical standards of Hillelism, including nationalistic ideals; national, racial, and religious chauvinism; and "doctrines offensive to reason." Hence, Zamenhof exhorted Esperantists of all faiths and ethnicities to adopt a hyphenated Hillelist identity: not "I am Swiss" but "I am Swiss-Hillelist." In fact, since nations belonged to all their inhabitants, of whatever ethnicity, Hillelists were to reject country names based on ethnicity. For such countries, new names were to be fashioned by combining the word *lando* (a country) or *regno* (a sovereign state) and the name of the capital. Thus Russians would call themselves, after their capital, Peterburgregnaj-Hilelistoj; Poles, after theirs, Varsovilandaj-Hilelistoj.

By March 1906, Zamenhof had come to realize that what was true for Esperanto in France was also true for Hillelism: Jewishness, even the mere perception of it, was too great a liability. He would do to Hillelism what the French had done to him: rebrand and dejudaize the *Dogmoj* as a "philosophically pure monotheism." He now called it *Homaranismo*—a hard-to-translate term meaning, roughly, Humanity-ism.

Criticism was swift and harsh. Although Zamenhof had tried to obscure its Jewish origins, *Homaranismo* openly espoused a spiritual mission; even without invoking the Jewish rabbi Hillel, the doctrine was distasteful to the rationalist French elite. Beaufront savaged the project: "While we await the opening of the temples (Homaranist temples!) . . . we could perform the rites beneath the green of the forests, in green robes covered in gold or silver stars. Very poetic, isn't it?"[81] Another influential critic was the Lithuanian priest Alexander Dombrovski, who charged Zamenhof with passing off the central dogmas of Christianity as Homaranist. And Zamenhof's stated intention to present *Homaranismo* in Geneva met with a fierce backlash from the movement's Western European leaders. In the months leading up to the Geneva Congress, as mathematician and Esperanto historian Christer Kiselman has shown, he began backpedaling.[82] *Homaranismo* was liable to be perceived as a religion, he feared, not a "neutral bridge"; non-Esperantists would quail at having to learn a new language. It was all too utopian. Zamenhof consulted Javal, who warned him to avoid even mentioning *Homaranismo*. Anxious letters flew back and forth between Warsaw and Paris until Javal, worried about Zamenhof's health, advised him to forgo Geneva. He refused.

That June, after a ferocious pogrom in his native Białystok took some two hundred Jewish lives,[83] Zamenhof began to write his speech for the Geneva Congress. The message was urgent, and stripped of obfuscation: in the end, it was neither about *Homaranismo* nor about *Hilelismo*, but about Jews. In graphic and unsparing terms, he decried the violence:

> In the streets of my unhappy birthplace, savages with axes and iron
> stakes have flung themselves, like the fiercest beasts, against the

quiet villagers, whose sole crime ... was that they spoke another language and had another people's religion than that of the savages. For this reason they smashed the skulls and poked out the eyes of men and women, of broken old men and helpless infants![84]

The Geneva speech was a watershed; in it, Zamenhof consecrated Esperanto to the *interna ideo*, the "inner idea." "According to your advice," he told Javal, "I threw out of my congress speech the last part touching on *Homaranismo*—and speak only of the *interna ideo* of Esperantism."[85] The Declaration of Boulogne meant that the "inner idea" could not be specified, since all ideological commitments were the private affair of Esperantists. But by invoking the "inner idea" in Geneva, Zamenhof identified it not only with interethnic harmony but also with a mission to uproot anti-Semitism. *Homaranismo* would wear the "inner idea" as a mask that enabled his Jewish outrage, as well as his Jewish-based ethics, to pass in a wider world.

At Geneva, the "inner idea" had yet another use: Zamenhof used it as a tool for marginalizing those who had opposed him at Boulogne, portraying them as soulless individuals who regarded Esperanto merely as a language. In his Geneva speech, Zamenhof exhorted Esperantists to "break down, break down the walls" between peoples, defying and mocking those—Beaufront chief among them—who insisted that "Esperanto is only a language." He called for resistance from the "first fighters for Esperanto," refusing to let secularists and pragmatists "tear out of our hearts that part of Esperantism which is the most important, the most sacred." And a year later, at the 1907 congress in Cambridge, England, he used the "inner idea" to avenge the Boulogne Congress's failure to specify a democratic constitution for the Esperanto community. The Esperantists, he claimed, were "citizens of an ideal democracy," a parapeople, a quasi-nation, under its own green flag. He called this entity *Esperantujo*:

> Many people join Esperantism through mere curiosity, for a hobby or possibly even for some hoped-for profit; but from the moment when they make their first visit to *Esperantujo*, in spite of their own wishes, they are more and more drawn to and submit to the laws of this country. Little by little *Esperantujo* will become a school for future brotherly humanity.[86]

Homaranismo, he believed, would school the diverse and voluntary citizens of *Esperantujo* to become a people of the future.

The "inner idea" was an ancient prophetic strategy—those who had "ears to hear" would understand—designed for modern individuals of conscience: "I am leaving each person to clarify for himself the essence of the idea, as he wishes." There is pathos here, the inventor of the language resorting to circumlocution to tell his truth; but heroism too, for just as he had licensed the Esperantists to become builders of the language, Zamenhof was entrusting to them the invention, and perpetual reinvention, of its ideology. And as Garvía has shown, so they did. In the years leading up to World War I, a wide variety of ideologies found Esperanto consonant with their goals: theosophists and spiritists; women's suffragists and scouts; vegetarians and pacifists; and youthful "seekers" of various stripes.[87] What these groups had in common was not a particular ideology, but rather the understanding that ideology was more central to Esperanto than the language itself. Not one of them was invested in linguistic reform, the issue that had doomed Volapük, and which, in 1907, seemed poised to ruin Esperanto as well.

6. Idiots

During the Geneva Congress, Javal and Charles Lemaire, editor of the Esperanto magazine *Belga Sonorilo* (Belgian Bell) secretly offered Zamenhof the handsome sum of 250,000 francs to devote himself to a comprehensive reform of the language.[88] Javal had long felt that diacritical marks, or supersigns, were an unnecessary encumbrance, particularly for the visually impaired. And he found a particularly Jewish phrase with which to goad Zamenhof into reform:

> In my opinion it is a great misfortune that your reforms of 1894 were not adopted at that time, and, even at the risk of displeasing you, I shall say that it was your fault, *tua maxima culpa*, that it happened. Put that on the top line of the *al chet* [confessional] so that you can beat your chest next Yom Kippur.[89]

The offer was arguably more an emolument than a bribe; as a practical matter, the money would have freed Zamenhof from his medical practice for a year or more to revise the language. But even though he hoped, eventually, that "final" reforms would be put in place, Zamenhof felt he was being bought, and turned down the offer.

In early 1907, Zamenhof found himself on the threshold of the event he both yearned for and feared: a prestigious body of academicians were about to take up the fate of Esperanto. From the Exposition Universelle of 1900 had emerged a new academy called the Délégation pour l'Adoption d'une Langue Auxiliaire Internationale (Delegation for the Adoption of an International Auxiliary Language). At the helm was the Leibnizian philosopher-mathematician Louis Couturat, who with Léopold Leau had coauthored the first history of universal languages (1903). Couturat's scholarship had convinced him that Esperanto was currently the most promising entry in the field, but that it would need some key revisions if it were to meet the delegation's three requirements: internationalism, monosemy (the avoidance of identically spelled words), and the "principle of reversibility," which sociologist Peter Forster explains as follows:

> [Couturat] pointed out that . . . there were no fixed rules about how to derive verbs, for instance from nouns. . . . Thus *kroni* means "to crown," but does *krono* mean "crown" or "the act of crowning," "coronation"?[90]

In a rational grammar, Couturat argued, one could derive nouns from verbs and vice versa, without difficulty. But if Esperanto lacked the "principle of reversibility," it had something better—a proven track record of sustained use—and it emerged from the delegation's discussions as the leading entry.

The delegation set up a committee comprising a dozen luminaries, among them the chemist Wilhelm Ostwald (the committee chair); the linguist Jan Baudouin de Courtenay; the philologist Otto Jespersen; Boirac, rector of the Université de Grenoble; two anglophone men of letters—George Harvey, editor of the *North American Review*; and W. T. Stead, publisher of the *Review of Reviews*; Italian mathematician Giuseppe Peano; Couturat, Leau, and others.[91] From the start, the delegation's procedures were compromised: many of the more illustrious delegates did not appear for the Paris meetings, and some didn't even bother to send deputies. Inventors of languages were not to represent their own languages, a rule that Zamenhof observed and Peano ignored. In his stead, Zamenhof sent Beaufront, despite Beaufront's public contempt for *Homaranismo*. Though relations between them were shaky, Zamenhof had two good reasons to send him to Paris. First, Beaufront was deeply conservative vis-à-vis reform of the language; second, he would ensure that the delegation, whatever its suggestions, would yield to the will and authority of the Esperantists. Or so Zamenhof thought.

In May, the committee received a new entry, anonymously submitted over the name "Ido," the Esperanto word for "offspring." Indeed, the new entry resembled Esperanto, but an Esperanto purged of adjectival agreement, accusative endings, supersigns, and correlatives.[92] And there was another, signal change: anyone familiar with the delegation's three criteria would have quickly realized that Ido was Esperanto redesigned to satisfy Couturat's requirement of reversibility.

Beaufront publicly expressed his satisfaction that a rationalized, "improved" Esperanto was now available, and assured the delegation that the Esperantists would endorse it. While Ido, as the language came to be called, looked different, sounded different, *was* different from Esperanto, it was far *less* different than some of the more extreme reforms that Zamenhof himself had proposed. Like those who alter their surnames to assimilate, Ido had turned its back on its father's interethnic matrix—Slavic, Germanic, Jewish—to adopt (primarily) French word endings. That the delegation officially regarded the new proposal as "simplified"

Louis de Beaufront, Esperanto's "Judas"
[Österreichische Nationalbibliothek]

Esperanto was just fine with Beaufront, since it buttressed his assertion that the Esperantists would endorse the changes. And once Ido became the darling of the delegation, the Frenchification of Esperanto would be complete.

In a letter to Zamenhof, Beaufront made it plain that Ido was the favorite, which would inevitably mean the demise of Esperanto. Back in Warsaw, Zamenhof was insulted, outraged, and bewildered. To Sebert he fumed:

> I know nothing about the person of "Ido" and have never seen his grammar. . . . The behavior of M. De Beaufront seems to me very suspicious; to show my trust in him, I chose him as my representative before the delegation, and he, not asking me at all, suddenly and too startlingly went over to the reformers and wrote a letter to me, saying that Esperanto must certainly die, that, after five years, only the memory of Esperanto will remain.[93]

Between October 1907 and January of 1908, Zamenhof took every conceivable stance concerning the delegation. Tight-lipped and circumspect, he told the committee that he had received the Ido project and would consult with the Esperantists. To the Esperantists, he sometimes endorsed the delegation's authority but more often demanded that the delegation defer to the Esperantists—but to whom exactly? On this point he wavered, demanding variously that it be accountable to himself, to the Esperanto Language Committee, and to the next Universal Congress. Sometimes he denounced the delegation committee's members as "a few persons who perhaps have a very imposing exterior and very glorious names, but who have no right or competence to give orders in matters of international language."[94] Since the committee's charge was to select one or another auxiliary language, a "Permanent Commission" (including Beaufront) was set up to decide on specific features of the chosen auxiliary language. At one point, Zamenhof invited this commission to work under the aegis of the Esperanto Language Committee; when it refused, he demanded that Esperantists disavow the entire delegation, or else become "traitors" to the cause. His letters became increasingly shrill and erratic; then, just as he was in danger of losing his own "beloved child," he lost his father, Markus Zamenhof, who died in Warsaw on November 29.

In January 1908, when Ido was put forward as a "Simplified Esperanto," the Esperanto Language Committee would have none of it.
Zamenhof tendered a weak counterproposal, ignoring the pivotal issue
of reversibility. He was not simply being stubborn; by refusing to regu-
larize derivation, he was honoring the quirks and irregularities of what
was clearly, by contrast to Ido, a living language. And in snubbing the
scienculoj—the academic experts whose influence he had long feared—
he insisted that Esperanto was not, and would never be, the prerogative
of an elite. When his counterproposal was dismissed, Zamenhof issued a
scathing circular about the delegation's endorsement of Ido as a "Simplified Esperanto."

> As far as we're concerned, the Delegation committee no longer
> exists. . . . [T]here remain only some private individuals who—
> according to their own words—have now become Esperantists.
> But when these new Esperantists who joined Esperanto just a
> few weeks back begin to dictate rules to the Esperantist people,
> who have already worked more than twenty years . . . then we
> simply cast them aside.[95]

At moments of schism (as at all other moments), Esperantists are hard to
count, but it is estimated that one quarter of the movement's leaders de-
fected to the cause of Ido.[96] Still, the Ido schism was more palace coup
than proletarian revolution; only 3 to 4 percent of rank-and-file Esperantists transferred their allegiance to Ido.[97]

It was only a matter of time before the identity of Ido's anonymous
creator was revealed. In June 1908, *L'Esperantiste* featured a "Declaration
by Ido," signed by one Louis de Beaufront. But all along, it appears, Beaufront had merely been a surrogate for Couturat, who, as a member of the
delegation committee, had been disallowed from presenting his own proposal. Why Beaufront performed this role, we can only speculate. Perhaps it was a way of augmenting his own importance in a movement that
was to be the linchpin of intellectual exchange—or so the early Idists
thought. On the other hand, so many suspected Beaufront of inventing
Ido that his "Declaration of Ido" was a relatively painless way of heroically
protecting Couturat, with whom he had cast his fate.

As the Esperantists have told it ever since, the secession of the

Idists purged the movement of its logicians and tinkerers, of the language-fetishists who would have no truck with the *interna ideo*. Esperantists like to cite Bertrand Russell, who wrote of Couturat: "According to his conversation, no human beings in the whole previous history of the human race had ever been quite so depraved as the Esperantists. He lamented that the word Ido did not lend itself to the formation of a word similar to Esperantist. I suggested 'idiot' but he was not quite pleased."[98]

The Idists began to refer to Zamenhof's language as "primitive Esperanto," as though it were a "primitive church" that had been decisively superseded. As historian of science Michael Gordin has shown, Wilhelm Ostwald, the committee chair, played an important role in advocating for Ido among scientists in Europe and Russia. Expressing contempt for the Esperantists' reverence for their book of language rules, the *Fundamento*—"Ido 'does not have a holy book'"[99]—Ostwald characterized Ido as a triumph of scientific progress. But movements born in schism are usually destined for schisms of their own, and such was the case with Ido. Its most illustrious followers—including Ostwald—forsook it to invent Weltdeutsch (Ostwald), Novial (Jespersen), Occidental (educator Edgar de Wahl), and Romand (Michaux); Peano started his own Interlingua academy to promote his neo-Latin language. None of these inventions has become what Esperanto is: a living language with a worldwide community.

But for those most affected by the schism, including Zamenhof, it destroyed the ideal of *Esperantujo* as a unified, harmonious community. As Zamenhof defensively noted in 1908, the ax had not damaged the tree, which, in spite of "a great cracking noise," had "kept all its strength and lost only a few leaves."[100] Once the great cracking noise died down, Beaufront was forced out of his post as president of the Société Française pour la Propagation de l'Espéranto. Whatever illnesses, heroic achievements, or scandals Beaufront could boast in his remaining years (apart from a grammar of Ido, which he published in 1925), they are lost to us. He died, fittingly, in a village called La Folie in 1935, according to Boulton, "so much alone that the first news of his death came from the post-office stamp on a returned letter."[101] For the Judas of Esperanto, not even a potter's field.

7. The Sword of Damocles

In 1908, an important institution emerged to bridge the fault lines left by the Ido schism: the Universala Esperanto Asocio (Universal Esperanto Association), founded by a young Genevan named Hector Hodler. Son of the painter Ferdinand Hodler, Hector appears in his father's dreamlike paintings as an infant, a toddler with a Dutch-boy haircut, a boy in white linen, and a slim, nude diver; in all, like a ghostly visitant from a world of eternal youth.

Born in 1887, the same year Esperanto entered the world, Hodler learned the language at sixteen along with his charismatic schoolmate Edmond Privat, who became Zamenhof's first biographer. Together, Hodler and Privat founded a club as well as a journal, *Juna Esperantisto* (Young Esperantist); in 1907, Hodler acquired *Esperanto*, a magazine founded by the French anarchist Paul Berthelot. (Now called *Esperanto Revuo*, it remains the organ of the UEA.) Hodler's vision of a worldwide network of Esperantists dovetailed with two ideas floated at the 1906 Universal Congress: first, a network of Esperantist "consuls," who would provide services to traveling *samideanoj;* and second, a network of local offices devoted to running year-long programs and courses.[102]

Within two years after Hodler assumed the post of director, the UEA acquired over eight thousand members and a network of 850 consuls, later called delegates.[103] When in 1909 Zamenhof publicly endorsed the UEA as a realization of the *interna ideo*—"UEA unites . . . not all Esperantists, but all Esperantism"[104]—he seemed to be anointing Hodler as heir apparent. And with good reason: in the pages of *Esperanto,* Hodler had passionately elaborated his vision of an organization devoid of nationalism and chauvinism. For Hodler, the *interna ideo* was supranationalism; he envisioned an organization comprising individuals rather than national associations. Hodler was apparently indifferent to Zamenhof's Judaism-infused cult of *Homaranismo*, and without ever repudiating it, made it redundant to the *interna ideo* of the UEA.

Meanwhile, the movement's day-to-day operations were run out of the Central Office in Paris, financed and overseen by a committee elected by national units. In 1911, amid tensions between the UEA's network of individual delegates and the international network of national societies, an invidious distinction between "privileged" and "nonprivileged" consuls paralyzed the Universal Congress, which failed to approve yet another proposed system of governance. Michaux was among those who lobbied hard for a "democratically elected parliament"; rebuffed and outraged, he disbanded the 850-member Boulogne group which, six years earlier, had hosted the first international congress. By 1912, it had become impossible for Zamenhof both to propound the *interna ideo*, and to preside, even ceremonially, over what he called the *interna milito* (internal war), so he announced that he would resign his honorary post at the upcoming Universal Congress in Kraków.

Not by coincidence did he step down in Poland. After a rash of anti-Esperanto articles in the Polish press, he acknowledged that, as a Jew, he himself had cast a shadow over the movement. He told the Congress Committee in Kraków that, outside of Poland, Esperanto had its critics; but "among us [in Poland]," criticism was "based only on a more or less disguised hatred of me personally. It's a fact that I did ill to no one but I am a Jew born in Lithuania."[105] Asking the committee to refer to him not as a Pole, but as a "son of Poland," he clarified his identity as follows: "According to my religio-politcal convictions, I am neither a Pole nor a Russian, nor a Jew, but I'm a partisan of '*Homaranismo*' (don't confuse this with 'cosmopolitanism'); as far as my origins go, I count myself among the Jewish people." To this day, the term "Jewish-origin" (*judadivena*) is preferred to "Jewish" by many Esperantists, both Jewish and non-Jewish.

There were repercussions at Kraków about Zamenhof's Judaism, but from an unexpected quarter. When a Jew named Kvitner requested to salute the congress in the name of the Jewish people, the congress secretary, a lawyer named Leon Rosenstock, turned him down. Kvitner appealed to Zamenhof for a hearing, and it was rumored that Zamenhof responded, "Don't touch the Jewish problem during the Universal Congress, because the movement will suffer." (Zamenhof did not deny the episode, but later said he had urged Kvitner not to use the term "Jewish people," but rather "Yiddish speakers" or "those Jews who consider themselves a separate people.") Diatribes ensued from two leading Yiddish papers in New York, *Tageblatt* and *Die Wahrheit*. To the latter, Zamenhof retorted:

Every Esperantist in the world knows very well that I am a Jew. . . . The Esperantists know that I translated works from the Yiddish language; they know that already [for] more than three

years I devoted all my free time to translating the Bible from the
Hebrew original; they know that I always live in the strictly Jewish part of Warsaw (in which many Jews are ashamed to live),
and I continue to publish my works at a Jewish Press, etc. Is this
how a person acts who is ashamed about his origins and strives
to hide his Jewishness?[106]

But among all these claims that he was unashamed of his Judaism, the
creator of the universal language did not disclose that he had been among
Warsaw's leading Zionists in the 1880s.

The issue of Zamenhof's Jewish identity raised at Kraków did not go
away. Two years later, he was asked by William Heller, president of the
Litomierc Esperanto group, to join a new World Jewish Esperanto Association (TEHA). Zamenhof's response was to wish the organization well,
suggest that they publish a bilingual (Yiddish-Esperanto) journal, and
promise to attend a meeting. But he refused to join; he would counte-
nance neither nationalism "from above," in Michael Walzer's phrase, nor
from below, as he wrote to Heller:

> Every nationalism presents for humanity only the greatest un-
> happiness. . . . It is true that nationalism of a repressed people—as
> a natural defensive reaction—is much more forgivable, than na-
> tionalism of oppressing people; but if nationalism of the strong is
> ignoble, nationalism of the weak is imprudent; both . . . present an
> erring cycle of unhappiness, from which humanity never escapes.[107]

*   *   *

The marketplace of ideas put a negligible value on *Homaranismo*, just as
it had on *Hilelismo*—and, in the early days, on Esperanto. But Zamenhof
responded to indifference and rejection not by discarding his tattered
cause, but by taking it to new audiences, mended and patched. In 1913, he
published, for the first time under his own name, a revision of *Homaranismo*, referring to the sect as a "neutral-human religion." Despite the
name, the emphasis on universalist "religion" decisively gave way to that
of a "neutral-human" community. He was addressing not only ethical
monotheists among the Esperantists, but also atheists. He was also tar-
geting, for the first time, citizens of states with a continuous history of

interethnic conflict. In such polities, he argued, a neutral language, supported and sustained by the state, could promote the participation of linguistic minorities, ensuring inclusive and more equitable representation and a fairer distribution of goods. Moreover, equipped with a neutral-human language, citizens of various states could use their common tongue to discuss issues of common interest. He framed the issue not in terms of "language rights," as we would now say, but in terms of the ethical obligations of states toward their citizens.

For the first time, Zamenhof was glimpsing a role for Esperanto in politics: Esperanto, equally accessible to all and easy to learn, would be a method by which citizens of a multicultural state could equitably and jointly determine their future, deliberate on policy, adjudicate disputes, and educate its citizens of the future. Esperanto itself might be politically neutral, but Zamenhof was convinced that its value to political life in a state such as Belgium or Switzerland—or, someday, to an international federation of states—was potentially vast. As usual, Zamenhof lacked the influence, infrastructure, and funding to be an effective advocate for the use of Esperanto in such polities, but these were precisely the arguments that would be revived after Zamenhof's death by those seeking to bring Esperanto to the attention of the nascent League of Nations.

Just as Zamenhof was glimpsing, with his characteristic grandiosity, a wider role for Esperanto on the world stage, he became aware of more anti-Semitic attacks. This time, to his astonishment, they were written by and for Esperantists. "I had the illusion," he wrote, "that among Esperantists [this] was not possible, at least publicly. But in the May number of *Pola Esperantisto* appeared an article that banished my illusion."[108] A journalist named Andrzej Niemojewski published a farrago of slurs against putative Jewish customs, which included circumcision with a stone and the mutilation of corpses. In a preface, the editor praised Niemojewski as a "pioneer of liberal thought," who had done "deep research . . . in the Hebrew talmud, that frightful book of superstitions and hatred of everything non-Jewish."[109] In a searing letter to the editor, Zamenhof pointed to the hatred expressed in the Polish press "written in the civilized twentieth century . . . The present population . . . persecutes Jews in a most cruel manner, while the entire sin of the Jews consists only in this, that Jews also want to live and have human rights."[110] Instead of publishing the letter, the editor ridiculed protests from unnamed Jews which "clearly showed us the uncultured quality of the talmud-defenders." It was time to declare open war on the Talmud, wrote the editor, an "ignoble spot on our brightness, human ethics and dogmas."[111]

Zamenhof pressed on with his proposal for a "neutral-human religion." Within two years of stepping down at Kraków, he told Bourlet and Sebert that under the aegis of the upcoming Universal Congress in Paris, he planned to convene the first congress for what he now called a "Neutral-Human Religion." Bourlet and Sebert sensed an attempt to avoid the obstacles Zamenhof had faced in Boulogne. This Universal Congress was to be the largest ever—nearly four thousand had registered—and to avoid controversy, Bourlet and Sebert urged Zamenhof to hold his congress in Switzerland following the gathering in Paris.[112] He agreed, but in early August, war broke out. The Paris Congress opened and was immediately closed, but Ludovik and Klara Zamenhof, stranded in Cologne en route to Paris, were not on hand. Instead, they were forced to make a circuitous, two-week journey home to Warsaw, by way of Denmark, Sweden, and Finland. According to Boulton, this "was the beginning of his long dying."[113]

In fact, Zamenhof's "long dying" had begun some time before. A heavy smoker, he had had symptoms of heart disease for at least a decade: shortness of breath and chest pain. In the early months of the war, his condition worsened. By November, an "attack," probably angina rather than a heart attack, forced him to reduce his work regime severely. His son, Adam, also an eye doctor, took over his morning clinic and Zamenhof confined his medical practice to two afternoon hours daily. The family was more comfortable financially, and the following summer, while Warsaw was occupied by German troops, the Zamenhofs left Dzika Street in the Jewish quarter for a more spacious, seven-room abode at 41 Królewska Street, with a view of the Saski Park. There he went for daily outings: sometimes a ride, sometimes a stroll. There he entertained important Esperantist visitors—the poet and translator Antoni Grabowski, the pacifist Leo Belmont, and his future biographer Edmond Privat, to whom he confided his dimmed hopes for the future of human relations.

While Esperantists all over Europe fought for their national and imperial armies, Hodler's UEA, operating from neutral Switzerland, implemented a service ensuring the safe passage of an estimated two hundred thousand letters among enemy countries.[114] In 1916, again thanks to the

Hector Hodler, heir apparent

UEA, Esperantist POWs received a Christmas gift of food, tobacco, and Esperanto books and magazines.[115] Hodler, a pacifist in a time of war, looked ahead, exhorting Esperantists to take the lead in rebuilding postwar Europe:

> It is now the cannon's turn to speak, but it will not sound for eternity. . . . If we wish to build a new house on the present ruins, we need those workers who are not frightened away by the difficulties of reconstruction. Such workers are the elites of various countries, who, without prejudice and in a spirit of mutual toleration, will cast their gaze above the horizon of national frontiers, and will become conscious of a harmonious civilisation, broad enough to include all national cultures, tolerant enough to consider their diversity as a beneficial necessity. . . . Let Esperantists be the embryo of those future elites.[116]

For Zamenhof, despite the hopes he placed in the generation of Hodler and Privat, it was a grim time. He was ill and weak, reluctant to get enough rest and unwilling to stop smoking. His beloved daughter Zofia was in the Ukraine, unable to return to occupied Warsaw, and in 1916, his brother, Alexander, who had tried and failed to start a Jewish agricultural colony in Brazil,[117] committed suicide rather than fight in the Russian army.

All his business seemed unfinished; perversely, Zamenhof seemed to need it that way. No sooner had he completed his translation of the Hebrew Bible (1907–1914) than he added the Koran and the "holy books of Buddhism" to his list of world literature in need of translation.[118] And even with the Language Committee in place to anchor the living language to the *Fundamento*, he brooded on language reform in the fear that someday, the work of reforming Esperanto would be given over to "people with famous names, but absolutely no experience in our affair . . . We must solve this unhappy question, which constantly hangs over our language like the sword of Damocles."[119]

As the war groaned on, frontiers shifting as armies shuffled a few miles north, then a few south, Europe itself came to seem unfinished. Like Hodler, Zamenhof envisioned postwar rebuilding as an opportunity for social transformation. But whereas Hodler had addressed himself to the Esperantists, Zamenhof audaciously turned to the diplomats of Europe. His 1915 open letter, "After the Great War," dares the diplomats at the peace table to do more than move borders on a map: "Proclaim loudly . . . the following elementary, natural, but thus far, unfortunately unobserved principle: *Every land morally and materially belongs of equal right to all its sons.*" He called for a "United States of Europe," which required that minorities be guaranteed freedom of language (or dialect) and religion, and he urged that a permanent pan-European tribunal be set up to remediate injustice and adjudicate conflicts.

No longer was he trying to secure the survival of Esperanto. In fact, the more urgently he tried to propound Homaranism (by whatever name), the more he found himself detaching it from Esperanto. In Boulogne in 1905, he had been willing to sacrifice Homaranism to give Esperanto a fighting chance in Western Europe; now he was willing to cleave Esperanto from Homaranism, that his precious, beleaguered creed might survive him. He was ready to underwrite, at his own expense, a printed prospectus to be sent to five thousand world newspapers and five thousand "of the most important people in the world of knowledge."[120] In 1915, he told his friend Marie Henkel, an Esperanto poet from Dresden, that he wanted his pamphlet *Homaranismo* to be translated into four national languages and published in "every influential newspaper in the world." He had once asked Esperantists to translate masterworks of all European literatures into Esperanto; now he wanted his Esperanto tract rendered in the most powerful national languages of Europe.

The war put paid to Zamenhof's dreams of both congress and campaign, but it did not stop him entirely. He had realized a hard fact: that the *interna ideo,* once he'd nobly handed it over to the conscience of each Esperantist, had irretrievably fallen out of his grasp. In the early weeks of 1917, revising Homaranism once again, he took pains to distinguish between the *interna ideo* of Esperanto and Homaranism. As it stood, he now wrote, the *interna ideo* was an "undefined feeling or hope," which each Esperantist was free to embrace or reject, but in time, he hoped, individuals of conscience would embrace *Homaranismo,* "a special and completely defined political-religious program."[121] Esperanto on its own was not enough to repair the world; only a community that embraced the values of Homaranism could advance the common good.

Zamenhof's hope had dimmed, perhaps, but it was never entirely eclipsed. His final version of *Homaranismo,* like the *Unua Libro* of 1887, contained coupons for those willing to endorse and sign on to a new way of thinking, speaking, and acting. But it was too late for coupons and pledges. *Homaranismo* was to be Zamenhof's letter to Babel, but it never appeared, as he'd hoped, in foreign languages; only six decades later was it finally published, in Esperanto, in Zamenhof's collected works.

When Zamenhof made this final visit to the temple of Homaranism shortly before his death in 1917, he found himself alone, as he had after his call to the Jews of Russia. A photograph taken at that time is the only portrait extant in which he does not meet the camera's gaze. Instead, he gazes off with the serenity of a bespectacled bodhisattva. When he died of heart failure, in April 1917, he had been trying for thirty years to create a people worthy of the coming, better world. He had seen the Esperantists through schism and betrayal, through defection and disaffection. But in the end, he knew that they would never become the people he'd tried to create, who would share a future but not a past; who would cherish their creed, pass it to their children, and bring others into the fold.

What Zamenhof could not know was that Esperanto would survive the brutal twentieth century because women and men in each generation reinvented it—at times, during the century's most bloody decades, at risk of their lives. The shadowy "inner idea" in which Zamenhof had wanted

to lodge his ideal of community turned out to harbor many other contradictory ideals, some frankly incompatible with Zamenhof's. Sometimes
it would seem that there were as many "inner ideas" as Esperantists. But it
was the Esperantists after all, flawed, bickering, merely human, who
would shadow forth the people of a more just, harmonious world.

Samideanoj II
Iznik to Białystok, or *unu granda rondo familia*

═══════

IZNIK

1. Revenants

A few years ago, at the Institute for Advanced Study in Princeton, New Jersey, the philosopher Avishai Margalit asked whatever became of the third member of the revolutionary trinity of liberty, equality, fraternity. Having just returned from an Esperanto congress, I wanted to tell him that he wasn't looking in the right place; fraternity, the runt of the litter, was being fed on royal jelly in *Esperantujo*. During gatherings such as the annual Middle Eastern Conference (Mezorienta Kunveno), dislocated, sped-up, and 24–7ed, *samideanoj* form bonds quickly. Just speaking the language, with its railroad-flat compounds and exotic adverbs, makes them tipsy with pleasure. Strangers just yesterday, they're now as familiar with one another as college roommates, army buddies, colleagues denied tenure the same day. They're more than friends; they're family.

As Margalit argues in his essay "Fraternity" (2005), the ideal of fraternalism dismantled the ancien regime of paternalism, in which a figurative, ruling "father" decides what is good for his figurative, "subjected" children. So it's no accident that fraternity flourishes in *Esperantujo*, since Zamenhof, by ceding his paternal authority over Esperanto to its users from the start, freed Esperanto from the "dead hand" of its founding father. Instead he created, in the words of his inaugural anthem, "La Espero," *unu granda rondo familia*—one great family circle.

On the ground, however, Esperantist fraternalism does not evoke a lot of family resemblances; that's what happens when people share a future but not a past. Esperantists are as mixed as Esperantic phonemes, thrown together from many languages. They are multilingual and multicultural, and many are multinational and multiethnic as well. When you ask where they're from, they draw invisible maps with a finger on the table, then trace their trajectory. It takes about five minutes of conversation to learn that Dora Patel from Copenhagen is an Englishwoman raised in St. Albans, England; Mateo, an Israeli computer scientist, is a Turinese Catholic; Ambrus is a Hungarian living in Luxembourg. During a coffee break on an excursion in Turkey, Miguel, a Spaniard, and a German named Albert tell me their surnames are *judadivena*—of Jewish origin. (Albert tries out his English on me with a Scottish brogue, the residue of a sojourn in Aberdeen.)

Like Jews, Esperantists navigate among multiple identities at once, moving fluidly from their nuclear families to Esperantic circles to the workplace, and on to a world indifferent to matters of fraternity and harmony. I'll confess that at Esperanto gatherings, I sometimes feel that I'm among meta-Jews; after all, Esperanto was invented by a Jew who renounced peoplehood, but couldn't imagine a world without it. And although in *Hilelismo* and *Homaranismo* Zamenhof conceived of a widening gyre of meta-Jewish people, his experience at Boulogne warned him that he must not speak of them this way. After Boulogne, he would always speak of Esperantists as the para-people of *Esperantujo*, and the germ of the "great family circle" of all humanity.

* * *

In the spring of 2009, I flew to Turkey for the Second Middle Eastern Conference of Esperantists. As it happened, the gathering coincided precisely with a meeting of the G20 in London. Just as the movers, shakers, makers, and breakers of the world's twenty richest nations convened in London, I arrived in Iznik, a sleepy lakeside town three hours east of Istanbul. At this ingathering of nations, thirty-five citizens of seventeen countries talked about finances, dined at long communal tables, and assembled, like our counterparts in London, for a group photo. My Esperanto was far from fluent, but it had progressed beyond novice level, and it improved once I'd had a few conversations and recovered from jetlag; a glass or two of wine improved it further. Which was all to the good: here, unlike London, no interpreters were in evidence; none was needed, since our four-day summit of talks and tours, cabaret and chit-chat all took place in *la bela lingvo,* Esperanto.

Eran Regev, a young Israeli computer scientist, was one of three organizers of the gathering. The previous year, while the Israeli government was building a separation barrier twenty-five feet high between Israel and the West Bank, Eran decided it was time to talk through walls. To this end, along with UEA ex-President *Renato Corsetti and a Jordanian, Eran convened the First Middle Eastern Conference in Amman. Most of the twenty-five attendees were Israelis; also on hand were three Turks and a few venturesome Europeans. That only a handful of Arabs attended, all but one Jordanian, disappointed Eran, but didn't surprise him.

But, as I was surprised to learn from another Israeli Esperantist, the composer *Doron Modan, this was actually *not* the first Middle Eastern Esperanto Conference. Between 1934 and 1948, there was a series of encounters—conferences, excursions, informal visits, and joint educational ventures—between Jewish Esperantists living in Mandate-era Palestine and the Egipta Esperanto-Asocio (EEA), a contingent of Arabs, Britons, and others who convened in Cairo. Esperanto had had an erratic presence in Jersualem since 1908, when the (non-Jewish) director of the German Hospital founded the first Esperanto group. By 1925, sustained activity led to a congress in Jerusalem; the second congress, a joint effort of Paco kaj Frateco (Peace and Brotherhood), the Jerusalem Esperanto circle, and Konkordo (Concord) was held in May 1934, during a three-day "Oriental Fair" in Tel Aviv. It drew more than one hundred participants, including several Egyptians; a street in Tel Aviv, still called Zamenhof Street, was solemnly dedicated to the memory of Doktoro Esperanto. During the next decade, Jews and Arabs in Palestine collaborated on Esperanto instructional materials, published both in Hebrew and Arabic. Meanwhile, in Egypt, a Coptic Esperantist named Tadros Megalli had begun teaching Esperanto to small groups of Egyptians, soldiers from Britain and New Zealand, and a class of young girls.

In April 1944, Megalli went to Palestine with his student, Nassif Isaac, to attend the first congress of the Palestine Esperanto League (PEL), founded in 1941. While there, he visited a couple of Jewish agricultural settlements. Megalli's post-congress effusions, in the Arabic-language magazine *Asyut,* were worthy of a Jewish Agency propaganda newsreel: "We truly admired the magnificent labors undertaken by the Jews, who

created, from the rocks and desert soil, fecund and fruit-bearing earth."
An invitation to PEL members to attend the first Egyptian national
congress, an eight-day extravaganza to include visits to mosques and
synagogues, as well as a train trip to the pyramids, elicited 110 enthusiastic pledges. A failure to obtain visas for PEL members spurred one
Jewish Esperantist to propose a new umbrella organization, the Near
Eastern Esperanto League (PROEL), to be based in Cairo. A counterproposal emerged from another Jewish member of PEL: a series of coordinated joint ventures for the EEA and the PEL, including a shared
headquarters that would alternate between Tel Aviv and Cairo, a committee to entreat the UEA to hold an upcoming annual congress in the Near
East, and a jointly edited bulletin. As Jews, they were building a Jewish
state; as *samideanoj*, they were transforming the Near East into an Esperantist utopia.

But when the PEL next convened in Jerusalem two weeks before the
liberation of Buchenwald, neither the Egyptians nor the local Arabs
attended. Between the end of World War II and 1948, there were only
sporadic visits between EEA and PEL and occasional gestures of goodwill. When the grapeshot of scattered Arab-Jewish conflicts became artil-
lery rounds, relations between the PEL and EEA ceased and their fortunes
diverged. The PEL, now the Esperanto League of Israel (ELI), licked its
wounds and welcomed a new influx of *samideanoj* from among the Jewish refugees. By 1951 the EEA collapsed, most of its foreign membership
having dispersed. Nassif Isaac, photographed in 1944 on a Jerusalem
street, arm in arm with his Egyptian mentor and Jewish *samideanoj,* went
on to write books about spiritualism and reincarnation. He himself became a revenant, year after year, the sole Arab delegate to the Universal
Congress.

2. "The Blackened Gull"

The road from Istanbul to Iznik winds past high-rises, sport stadiums,
and blacktops, bumps up against the ferry port at the Sea of Marmara,
and resumes, on the far shore, in countryside. We drive past olive
groves and fields of anemones studded with beehives; their honeycombs
are tangy, as if the bees went out for curry the night before.

The conference organizer, *Murat Ozdizdar, is a compact, smooth-shaven high school chemistry teacher in his mid-forties. In an olive-green Timberland fleece, he looks game and prepared, like a hiker heading into the backwoods. Murat is the sort of affable and plucky traveler who totes Lonely Planet guidebooks, except that he spends most of his off hours organizing Esperanto events, for both Turks and visitors. In fluent, expressive Esperanto, he tells me about his travels overland in Nepal and Cambodia, and itemizes on his fingers (in euros) the fantastic economies he discovered there. When he visited America, the generosity of American acquaintances—the in-laws of a cousin's friend, the friend of a cousin's in-laws—had proved a perfect complement, in dollars, for his own stunning feats of thrift.

Murat, with an eye to the future of the Turkish movement, has in tow three of his star chemistry students. Someday they might be star Esperanto students, but just now they've barely finished a two-week crash course taught by a teacher Murat had flown in from Serbia. Still in their school uniforms, the boys are chatting in Turkish, sprawled over comic books, dozing over their iPhones. From time to time, a tinny voice begins to sing "In the towowown where I was born" and one of them answers his phone with a sleepy, *"Alo?"* Also on the bus are Branko, a Serbian actor and Esperanto broadcaster, formerly in aeronautics ("times were okay on earth," he tells me, "but not so good in the sky"), and Adrian, an affable, ruddy retired public-health professor from Maastricht. His mother, he tells me, was Anne Frank's third-grade teacher.

"What was Anne Frank like?" I ask. He shrugs, as if to say, *No man is a hero to his valet.*

Adrian now runs a B&B called Esperanto Domo, where Esperantists stay gratis. When we disembark in Iznik, he peers at a city map, swiftly decodes the iconic beer steins ringing the lake, and heads off.

As one Turkish conferee puts it, "Iznik is seismologically interesting." Located near a fault line where a 1999 earthquake killed an estimated forty thousand people, Iznik is an unlikely site for a ceramics industry, but those brilliant aqua and persimmon tiles that line the walls of Topkapi Palace are all made here. Murat's nose for a bargain has sniffed out a dormitory for seismologists on a dusty road a mile from town, where shared rooms go for twelve euros per night. Across the road are a bakery that runs out of bread around eight a.m., and next to it, a bar that closes by nine p.m. In the dimly lit reception area, there is no registration table, no written program; when we assemble, there is no *solena malfermito* (official opening) at which the Esperanto anthem, Zamenhof's hymn "La Espero," is customarily sung. Nor do I see the numbered nametags Esperantists always wear to identify themselves. (Names can be hard to catch by ear, but a number can quickly be looked up in the program.) With ingenuity in long supply in *Esperantujo*, participants soon improvise them from luggage tags.

If you go to a Middle Eastern Esperanto conference expecting panels on Turkish-Israeli tensions, Iranian armaments, or civilian casualties in Gaza, you will be disappointed. As far as programming goes, smaller Esperanto conferences resemble high school student council meetings, where the agenda is dominated by the student council itself. The program, scrawled in the lobby on a whiteboard, indeed revolves around Esperanto—the movement and, as a secondary matter, the language. This afternoon there will be sessions on the movement in Israel and Turkey; this morning, to open the conference, a session on Iran. Nader, a voluble pediatric cardiologist from Tehran, is busily setting up his PowerPoint presentation.

I know Nader only through correspondence. A few weeks earlier, I had sent out a call for Esperanto poems, hoping to set up a *deklamado* (reading) in Iznik. Within ten minutes Nader had emailed me the manuscript of an entire volume of original Esperanto poems by Iranians, edited by himself. Among dozens of odes to springtime, friends, and lovers, Nader's own 2003 poem "The Blackened Gull" stood out. The gull, begrimed with naphtha from oilfields burned in Operation Desert Storm, bears witness:

> *Ligo inter ŝtatoj,*
> *Plene armitaj soldatoj,*
> *Bombo-riĉaj Virkatoj,*
> *Malfeliĉaj atakatoj.*

> (A league among states,
> Heavily armed soldiers,
> Bomb-brimming Tomcats,
> Unfortunate victims.)

I was surprised to find verse about my own belligerent country since, except for antifascist satires about fascism, Esperanto poetry generally falls into line with the movement's revered tradition of political neutrality. Did it make a difference that this was a gull, not an Iraqi, croaking defiance—and in Esperanto? Maybe not; but maybe. Now, as his bullet points flash on the screen, Nader makes no mention of Tomcats, nor of Desert Storm, nor of any of the things Americans talk about when we talk about Iran: nuclear arsenals, anti-Semitism, homophobia; smiles and guns for Hezbollah. Instead, it shows Iranian Esperantists, young and old, men and women—some head-scarved, some not—dancing at a Norouz party, trekking in Azerbaijan, and teaching the *lingvo de paco* (language of peace) to Afghan refugees.

Nader sits down to polite applause, and Gabi goes to the podium. She's a hip, black-clad Sephardic Israeli wearing clunky pewter beads shaped in stars of David, crosses, and crescents. Here's her update about the Tel Aviv, Jerusalem, and Haifa clubs: as in Iran, so in Israel—dancing, trekking, teaching.

Next comes a lecture on *landnomoj,* the Esperanto names of countries, a landmine of a topic. The lecturer is *Anna Löwenstein, a slim, no-nonsense Briton in corduroys and sensible shoes. Anna's a leading woman of letters in the Esperanto world; she's written two Esperanto-language historical novels set in Rome, where she and her husband Renato Corsetti live. She's also one of a handful of women members of the academy and, as I would later learn, the founding editor of the feminist journal *Sekso kaj Egaleco* (Sex and Equality).

Anna promises to dispel, once and for all, the confusion around country names. One only needs to understand the rationale, she insists. Countries based on nationalities are formed from the name of the people. "*Italoj* live in *Italujo,*" she says, motioning to us to repeat after her, using the "container" suffix, *ujo,* to denote "the place containing Italians." Conversely, she continues, the names of certain countries, especially multiethnic ones, are the basis for naming their citizens. Instead of naming the country after the people, one names the citizens after the country using the "member" suffix, *ano*: *Israelo, Israelanoj.* What Anna doesn't say is that the "rationale" has all the rationality of Europe's borders since 1887, which have shaped and reshaped themselves around empires, nations, colonies, and treaties. To complicate matters, there's a "tomayto-tomahto" factor caused by a tendency to drop the *ujo* ending for the more internationalized *io.* Anna advises us to avoid the latter practice, since it leads to confusion when the root itself ends in *i.*

"For instance, a Burundian—" she continues.

"But why not ask the Burundians?" demands Agnes, a gravel-voiced, pugnacious Fleming who, during breaks on the dorm patio, is the lone smoker among us. "For example, Esperanto for 'Flanders' is Flandrio— but that's a romanization; a more natural, Germanic ending would be Flandren. So why should the Academy dictate to the Burundians what to call themselves?"

"We're not doing that," replies Miguel, whose Spanish accent slices through his Esperanto. "Anyway, why should the international language honor tribal practices? No nation's calling itself by a natural name; language is a cultural convention." Last night, he directed me to his website, where I found an mp3 of his Esperanto poem about a shamed samurai, recited to a doleful accompaniment of shakuhachi flutes. "It's crucial for academics like you to get the word out about the movement," he added, urgently. "Chomsky, you remember, says it isn't really a language." Miguel's a full-time Esperanto teacher, one of the few people in *Esperantujo* who makes a living (or most of one) from his expertise in the *lingvo internacia*. To be told it "isn't really a language" cuts deeply into his self-esteem; between him and Chomsky, it's personal.

At the end of the morning session, Renato raises the question of where to hold the Third Annual Middle Eastern Conference, since not every country in the region would be as welcoming to Israelis as Turkey. Egypt would be great, he says, but the Iranians would not be able to get visas. Kuwait would be great, too, but here the Israelis would be odd man out. So, Tunisia? Not exactly a thriving movement, but it could be done on the cheap, and Renato happens to know someone there in a Berber village; Renato happens to know someone everywhere. Murmurs of enthusiasm from the Turks, the Europeans, the Iranians, the lone American (myself), and the Israelis, who will head for Jerusalem in a few days to prepare for Passover. It's resolved: next year in Tunisia.

But because the Turkish movement wanted to keep up momentum, the Third Annual Middle Eastern Conference again took place in Turkey, not Tunisia. A year later, in 2011, the fourth conference was planned for Karaj, Iran, to the consternation of the Israelis, who knew they could not attend on an Israeli passport. In the event, a season of tumult, which quickly acquired the pastoral name of "Arab Spring," scotched the plan. Renato and Murat (Eran had since joined the twenty thousand Israelis living in Berlin) held out as long as they could before canceling. And al-

though word travels fast in *Esperantujo*, a Swiss family apparently entered Iran unaware that the conference had been canceled. "*Ho ve!*"
wrote a friend from France, Esperanto for "Oy vey!" For Renato, there
was nothing to be done but post a notice that any Esperantist who wanted
to visit Iran anyway would be warmly welcomed by *samideanoj* there. For
several days, the Swiss were incommunicado, until they finally emerged
from Iran to blog their adventures. "*Hura!*" wrote my French friend, as
universal sighs of relief were heard from Istanbul to New Jersey. It wasn't
until 2015 that the Middle Eastern Conference took place in Tunisia,
ten days after a massacre of twenty-one visitors to the National Bardo
Museum in Tunis, seventeen of them tourists. Before Renato could contemplate canceling the conference, there came a torrent of emails from
Esperantists vowing to go to Tunis anyway, "to show Esperantic solidarity with the people of Tunisia."

* * *

On the second day of the gathering in Iznik, I met Cemal, a light-eyed,
lanky Turk with a dancer's grace. For Cemal, Esperanto has pushed open
a heavy door. At twenty, while working on the floor of an electronics fac-
tory, he taught himself Esperanto from a book and promptly signed on
with the Esperanto hosting service, *Pasporta Servo*. Thirty years and hundreds of guests—"friends," as he prefers to say—later, he's visited New
York, Detroit, Europe, Iran, and Israel and he's aiming next for South
America; he's passionate about Argentine history. He's divorced, he says,
making a gesture even more universal than Esperanto: two index fingers
paralleled, then skewed apart. He sees his ten-year-old-son, who lives on
the other side of Istanbul, regularly, he says, but not how regularly. When
the fizzy talk about hosting and guesting washes down, there's an air of
sadness about him. As we drive past a graveyard, I ask whether Turks visit
cemeteries. "Well," he answers, "it depends on the imam. If the imam says
go, they'll go, otherwise . . . " His voice trails off. "But me, I like to go in
the winter"—pause—"to clear the snow off the names."

On the way back from Bursa, a city famed for mausolea, mosques, and
Fiat factories, we stop and pile out at an obelisk defaced with the logo of a
football team. The Turks milling about all seem embarrassed, even the
teens, who are "crocodiling"—speaking Turkish instead of Esperanto—
with a tall man in an oversized gray sweater and a shaved head. He looks
like Kojak on the weekend. Switching back to Esperanto, he tells me he's

a clown who performs in theaters, in hospitals, and on the street, though to make ends meet, he also acts and does voice-overs. "In a big country like America," he says, gesturing toward me, "there's so much work, a person can specialize. But Turkish clowns, well, we have to do it all."

On the bus, I sit with the three young chemistry students, who speak a smooth, slangless English. I teach them the phrase "take a chill pill"; in exchange, they dish about their favorite English author (Dan Brown), what websites are blocked in Turkey (Richard Dawkins, for his atheism), and in what situations you have to wash twice before entering a mosque (if you curse or fart). They want to know, since I'm a professor at Princeton, what kind of SAT scores will get them in. At lunch, over the local specialty of kebabs smothered in tomato sauce and melted butter, I ask them each to predict what the kid next to him will be doing in ten years. Three sly, mischievous smiles break out, and they all search one another's eyes, as if looking at tea leaves. "Him?" says Turhan, pointing to slender, serious Altan. "Working for NASA." Altan points to heavy-lidded Serkan and says in English: "Business. *Big* business." And Serkan slowly surveys Turhan, who's forgotten to pack jeans and has been wearing rolled-up versions of his school uniform since we left the city. "He'll be a presenter on television." Then, to guffaws: "A weatherman."

3. The Turk's Head

By some miracle, the final morning of the conference, Murat has scrounged up some loaves and fishes: four boxes of *maizflokoj* (cornflakes) and three liters of milk. While others crunch away, Murat and Cemal explain to two Poles, Tadeusz and Marta, how to catch a bus to the ferry. "You get on the bus," Murat says, "and when it's full it leaves."

"But when does it leave?" asks Tadeusz.

Cemal, like a good doubles partner, swings at this one: "You get on the bus," he says, "and when it's full it leaves."

Tadeusz shrugs, tosses it to Marta, who asks, "But *when* does it leave?" Cemal looks across to Murat: *Your ball.*

The final talk, given by a professor of philology from Parma, is about stereotypes of Turks. It's a PowerPoint parade of Italian insults, translated into Esperanto: to smoke like a Turk, think like a Turk, curse like a Turk; when all falls into chaos, the Italians cry, "*Mamma, i turchi!*" (Mama, it's the Turks!). I feel as I did at an Episcopalian wedding many years ago, when the bride's golf-pro uncle told an anti-Semitic joke, to raucous laughter: "What is the Jewish housewife's favorite wine?—'*Taaaake me to Miaaami!*'" It stung like soap in my eye, exactly as these insults do now, as if—what? As if Esperanto had made me, in Hamlet's words, "turn Turk"? As if, after years of touring what the Ottomans had rigged up or bitten away in their forays to Vienna, Budapest, Rhodes, and Jerusalem, the world had been remapped with Istanbul's tulip-ringed palaces and azure mosques at its center and, radiating outward, Murat's patience, Cemal's sad kindness, and the gentle wisecracks of the student chemists.

We're all silent, as if these Italian curses have cast a spell on us. Renato breaks the silence to ask whether anyone has heard of "Turk's head" contests, but no one has.

A week later, back in Princeton, I found an article from the May 9, 1854, *New-York Daily Times*. A gossipy dispatch from Paris by one "Dick Tinto," it described a peculiar diversion:

> In all the public dancing gardens at Paris, is a contrivance to test strength of arm. It consists of a wooden head of a man, covered with thick cloth and mounted upon a spring; upon being struck by the fist, it descends to a point proportionate to the force employed, and a finger moving along a graduated scale, marks the degree attained. This head has represented of late years, and perhaps from time immemorial, the head of a Turk, and the number of blows the Mussulmans have received in his person is quite incredible.

*   *   *

President Obama, fresh from the G20 summit, has followed me to Turkey. He's overshot the mark by three hundred kilometers, standing erect before the Turkish Parliament in Ankara. On the ferry back to Istanbul, on a big-screen TV, Obama mouths words while a female voice utters them in Turkish and Cemal loosely renders them in Esperanto. "He's talking," Cemal begins, "about lots of Turkish issues—normalizing relations between Turkey and Armenia, reopening the Eastern Orthodox Halki Seminary, the Kurdistan Workers' Party, lifting the ban on Kurdish broadcasting. . . ."

No, not just about Turkey; Obama's talking about everything,

everything we haven't been discussing the past three days: Iran's nuclear potential, America's role in Iraq, Al Qaeda, the reunification of Cyprus, a two-state solution for Israel and Palestine. *This is my president*, I think, as people all over the boat glance up from their tiny glasses of tea to watch and listen. "The work is never over," Obama concludes, and the Esperantists exchange a knowing glance: *We could have told you that.* Tadeusz observes wryly, "He was getting more applause at the beginning." When we disembark, saying *ĝis la revido* (till next time), Cemal warns me that by ten the next morning, when Obama is to land in Istanbul, all roads to the airport will be closed.

At 6:30 a.m., standing with my bags at the elevator of the Seven Hills Hotel, I step aside for the snipers in blotted camouflage who file up a spiral staircase to the rooftop garden. They're dragging rifles, ammo, and iron stanchions to give Obama cover for his visit to the Blue Mosque. All day they'll aim between the minarets, where just last night, gulls looped through rays of floodlight, patches of moonlight, and the darkness in between.

BIAŁYSTOK

4. Bridge of Words

Four months later, after sprinting through the Warsaw airport with my luggage, I barely make the bus to Białystok. I'm taking the Podlasie-Express to Zamenhof's native city, which is celebrating the 150th anniversary of his birth by throwing him a congress. Poland has often been the site of jubilees—the Warsaw Congress of 1987 drew nearly six thousand—but the Cold War is over, and during the grim post-1989 years, membership rolls declined all over Eastern Europe. Here in Białystok, fewer than two thousand have registered. Still, the assembly is large enough to fill a huge makeshift hall erected on the grounds of the Białystok Polytechnic, and avid enough to populate the endless round of ceremonies, meetings, gatherings, concerts, and lectures for six days. The congress has a cumbersome title—"'To Build a Bridge of Peace Among Peoples': Zamenhof Today."

Even in Zamenhof's era, Białystok was a city of yesterdays, scarred by

the paths of emperors and kings, tribes and armies. Today Białystok, minus its Jews, Russians, and Germans, watches the children of Zamenhof
fill its hotels and several dormitories of the Polytechnic. The green conference logo with Zamenhof's profile is emblazoned on buses and bus
shelters. Shopkeepers have been given Esperanto glossaries; restaurants
offer menus in Esperanto. An Esperanto-language city map tracks a walking tour of Zamenhof sites: his birthplace, the gymnasium where he
studied, the monument to the Great Synagogue (a grim reconstruction
of its mangled cupola), and the Zamenhof Center, which has a small exhibition about Białystok in Zamenhof's day. The Rynek—the large square
at the city center, once the marketplace—has been entirely given over
to an international arts festival. The city's arts venues all seem to have
thrown open their doors; an Israeli friend, thumbing through the program, counted thirty performances, about twice as many as usual. In
this city of three hundred thousand, unaccustomed to large groups of
tourists, I can't walk a block without seeing two or three Esperantists
sporting conference badges, in animated conversation.

At the fair traditionally held the night before the official opening,
representatives from dozens of Esperantist organizations set up card
tables and distribute pamphlets. Some of the groups have had a presence
for nearly a century. The UEA website recognizes, rather quaintly, associations of "doctors, writers, railway workers, scientists, musicians," "Scouts
and Guides, the blind, chess, and Go players," "Buddhists, Shintoists,
Catholics, Quakers, Protestants, Mormons and Bahá'ís." There is no Jewish group per se, nor has there been for many decades; in 1914 Zamenhof
worried that a proposed *Hebrea Esperanto-Asocio* would represent Jews as
a nation, which he was convinced they were not.

Among the "activist groups" are LSG, the Ligo de Samseksamoj
Geesperantistoj (League of Gay Esperantists); VERDVERD, the green Esperantists; TEVA, the Worldwide Esperantist Vegetarians Association; and
the pacifist Homaranisma Komunlingva Movado Kontraŭ Novliberal-
ismo, or HKMKN (pronounced "HoKoMoKoNo"): the Humanitarian,
Common-Language Movement Against the New Liberalism, who've
spent much of the past decade protesting the war in Iraq. The railway
workers are not in evidence, but most of the other groups are represented,
along with the famous Rondo Kato (cat lovers' circle). Also on hand are a
clutch of Esperanto publishers; the fine-arts journal *Beletra Almanako*;
TEJO, the youth wing of the UEA; and SAT (Sennacieca Asocio Tutmonda,

or World Anational Association), headquartered in France, an umbrella group for socialists, anarchists, and "anationalists" who since 1921 have used Esperanto as tool for promoting any number of left-wing agendas. Behind another table, a friendly young Cuban dispenses leaflets with the logo of a lighthouse advertising next year's Universal Congress, to be held in Havana. It's hard to imagine getting myself to Havana, though I pocket the leaflet.

At a table across the corridor, behind a sign reading "Bona Espero," sits an elegantly coiffed blond woman in her seventies with a creamy silk outfit, chatting with a couple of Koreans. Bona Espero, Esperanto for "good hope," is an orphanage in rural Brazil founded in the 1950s, run since the 1970s by German-born *Ursula Grattapaglia and her Italian husband, *Giuseppe Grattapaglia. It has always seemed more a legend than an institution, and I'm taken aback to be face to face with Ursula herself.

"Are you Ursula Grattapaglia?" I ask.

"Of course!" she says heartily. Her light blue eyes are flecked with coffee grinds.

"All the way from Brazil?"

"Of course! We come to the congress every summer, then we visit family for a couple of weeks. We'll go back at the end of the month." I tell her I'm an American professor writing a book about the Esperanto movement, and ask for a leaflet.

"A *leaflet*?" she says in disgust. "*Kara, kara,* you must come and visit," she says, as if Brazil were just north of Hoboken. "Here's my card, find a time that convenes and come and stay with us." We chat for a few minutes and then she says, "I will be hearing from you" with sublime certainty.

At the opening ceremony the next morning, some people are in ribboned, gaitered national costumes; others, sombreros or alpine hats. A substantial contingent sport Kelly green T-shirts bearing Esperanto slogans: *Vivu! Revu! Amu!* (Live! Dream! Love!), or *Ĉu vi parolas ĝin?* (Do you speak it?). One T-shirt features a grid containing the entire table of correlatives. As the temperature rises in the fiberglass hall, so does the noise level; the air grows pungent with summer sweat. People, mostly over fifty, shuffle about, embrace and chat, and move on. The ceremony is an irony-free affair of speeches, greetings, performances, anthems, all transacted with a sort of shabby pomp. Delegates from each national association approach the podium, offer a brief greeting from their country, and move offstage. Next, a few words from the organizing committee, several more from the mayor of Białystok, and a lengthy address by the UEA's president, *Probal Dasgupta, an Indian linguist. The guest of honor is "La Nepo"—the grandson of Zamenhof, small, wizened and puckish. *Louis-Christophe Zaleski-Zamenhof, né Ludwik Zamenhof, is affectionately referred to as "LoZoZo"—which is how you pronounce his initials, LZZ, in Esperanto. LZZ, who emigrated to France in the 1960s, is something between a household god and a mascot, and his story, thanks to Roman Dobrzyński's 2003 biography, *Zamenhof Street*, is well known.

After his father, Adam Zamenhof, was arrested and shot by the Nazis in 1940, young Ludwik and his mother Wanda escaped the Warsaw Ghetto and lived under assumed identities. To honor the Polish pseudonym that had kept him alive—Krzysztof Zaleski—he had embedded it in his legal name. His grandfather, LZZ now tells us, described Esperanto as a "peace bridge" over a river of incomprehension and intolerance, and now he, "La Nepo," is a builder of real bridges made of steel and concrete. Bridges are for crossing, and what better place than Białystok to ponder his grandfather's intuition that a language of peace might enable us to cross the bridge of understanding? Besides, he adds, 2009 is the UN's International Year of Reconciliation, and when has Esperanto ever been as timely? (Sotto voce, the goateed man on my right points out that 2009 is also the UN year of natural fibers.)

In sessions devoted to the conference theme, there's a lot of talk of bridges, some of it achingly sincere, much of it rather ironic. *István Ertl, a Hungarian translator for the EU Court of Auditors in Luxembourg, improvises on the theme: "Bridges? Bridges are crossed by refugees and armies. And what do we do? We celebrate, celebrate, celebrate; we're old people running to and fro with green flags." He speaks rapidly; hip, blunt, dry. Suddenly an elderly man in the audience stands up, and in a flat, American accent, blurts out his name and conference number. His hand trembling visibly, he points to István: "*That* man! *That* man is . . . incomprehensible! Esperanto is meant to be understood. I ask you: how many people here in Białystok could understand him?"

István deadpans, "Twenty-seven percent," and goes on with his oration.

Everyone agrees that bridges would connect Esperanto to those who lack language rights or suffer from linguistic inequality—bridges such as that built between the UEA and UNESCO in 1954, when the latter accorded the UEA the status of "organization in consultative relations." Esperanto's man at the UN, these days, is *Neil Blonstein, a retired New York City schoolteacher who runs the UEA's tiny New York office—or third of an office. Since NGO budgets are tight, the UEA shares a cramped basement space with the U.S. Federation for Middle East Peace and the Earth Child Institute. Neil has boiled the rationale for Esperanto down to an elevator pitch, and he undoubtedly spends more time in elevators than most people. Periodically he scouts the UN lobby, trying to snag a precious few minutes with ambassadors and their staffs. He makes his pitch, gets his picture taken, and attaches it to a mass email: "Subject: Four minutes today with Ban Ki-moon."

"The problem with bridges," remarks a gruff Slovenian, "is that people don't see themselves on the other side of anything. We have a solution, but people don't feel there is a problem."

Tonkin, the former UEA head, has heard it before. "We need to inform people, through outreach, clearly. But we also need to strategize how to be effective within institutions; we're one of the only NGOs devoted to language rights. And we have to do all this while we manage the paradox of inclusiveness and exclusiveness. So we start by spreading the problem. The problem isn't English. The problem is that *language is an institution of power.*"

* * *

Tonkin knows a thing or two about power. He is ex-president of a great many things: the University of Hartford, the UEA, and its youth wing, TEJO, before that. Though gray and eminent, he's anything but an éminence grise; witness the way he dashes from podium to podium, introducing, lecturing, even auctioneering in rapid-fire Esperanto. He brings to mind Alice Roosevelt's famous comment about her father, Theodore: "He wanted to be the bride at every wedding, the corpse at every funeral, and the baby at every christening." Now in his early seventies, Tonkin has been an Esperantist for more than half a century.

Like many Esperantists of his generation, he fell in love with the language in his teens, a time when identity is malleable and life itself is a grand experiment—at least one's own life is. In 1958 Tonkin attended his first TEJO conference, in Germany, a gathering that was "astounding to a relatively sheltered eighteen-year-old full of hormones . . . a sort of

Grand Awakening. And it filled a need for me to break out of a highly judgmental world." The following year, he traveled to Warsaw for Zamenhof's centennial, bringing with him a suitcase filled to the brim with English sweaters; selling these on the street financed three weeks in iron-curtain Poland. "Poland was waking up; there was energy all over. My friends in England had prejudiced assumptions about life in Eastern Europe, but I was discovering that these people in Poland were living complete lives; they had value systems that were coherent and integrated. Yes, they might be under pressure, they might not like their government, but they were *not* brain-washed."

During the mid-sixties, Tonkin became the first TEJO president to sit on the UEA board. He was being groomed for leadership by the UEA president, a charismatic Croatian jurist named *Ivo Lapenna. Lapenna's passion for discipline and his quest for world recognition would both leave a deep imprint on the UEA. Famously controlling and autocratic, he was not above humiliating his opponents; as Tonkin puts it, "He chewed up colleagues who were not as smart as he was." After a beat, he chuckles; "Well, I was sort of an arrogant son of a bitch myself." In 1974, Tonkin succeeded Lapenna as UEA president, trying to steer an even course amid bitter infighting. "I was willing to take insults and defeats without responding. I was accused of being a communist faggot in France. Nasty personal stuff. Since I was neither one nor the other, I brushed it off easily."

"Were you disillusioned by all this animosity among Esperantists?" I ask.

"No, Esperantists quarrel like crazy. People quarrel when they fail, or when they've screwed up in some way. But that said, here's the thing: *Esperanto works.* Its success is as a language community; it's a collection of shared values: the value of cooperation; openness to other ways of thinking; peace. Talking rather than fighting." It was on Tonkin's watch that the Esperanto world officially gave up its losing battle against global English. "Zamenhof was invested in the idea that diversity of languages was a curse, but since 1974, there's been a seismic shift in the way we think about language: Babel is good. Multilingualism is good. With respect to English, they need to convince people that using English is not value-free; we need to stop the aggression of English with more multilingualism. The real issue is not now; it's what happens a hundred years from now." If only Tonkin could stick around till then.

I ask him if there are any general characteristics that Esperantists share. "There's a bifurcation in the way they operate, moving between a career and Esperanto." He's talking about himself now, about making his career in an elite world of university intellectuals as skeptical of utopian solutions as they are of the "grand narratives" of history and knowledge. And he's talking about me, as I navigate between exuberant Esperanto gatherings and dispiriting English Department meetings where my colleagues grouse about a steep decline in the number of English majors (to which someone invariably responds that the decline is a national trend; small consolation). I'm sure Tonkin's heard the question I get at literature conferences when I tell colleagues what I'm working on. "Esperanto?" they ask in puzzlement. "Isn't it dead?"

If I'd wanted to work on a dead language, I'd have chosen Latin—so much more useful.

"Esperantists are more adventurous than ordinary mortals," Tonkin continues. While we've talked, his responses have become a bit looser, more improvisatory. "They're people who [have been] looking for something—and for themselves—and failing to find it. Often, people who don't fit in. Or people who understand something other people don't. I think there are some people who are Esperantists who never find their way to Esperanto at all; I call them virtual Esperantists." Clearly that doesn't mean me, on two counts: I've found my way to Esperanto and according to the Declaration of Boulogne, simply using the language qualifies me as an Esperantist. On the other hand, I'm always something of an outsider here. For one thing, Esperantists know that a Princeton professor can bring much-needed prestige to their cause, all the more so if she can enthuse about Esperantic fraternity—the *granda rondo familia*—while remaining unseduced by utopian dreams of a universal language. Ironically, I'm one of the few people in the Esperanto world to have a professional interest in it. Amid all the ravishing, free-flowing, multicultural conversation, my chats with Esperantists always involve a tacit exchange: they give me access so I'll give them status.

And for another thing, I'm a practicing, public Jew—not simply *judadivena* (of Jewish descent)—and when I hear condescension about particularism, I reach for my pistol. I wouldn't still be wandering in *Esperantujo* if I believed that Zamenhof regarded Judaism with condescension or contempt; in my mind's eye, while he "crosses the Rubicon" to universalism, he's carrying Judaism on his back. A decade ago, my children's school celebrated "United Nations Day" by asking parents to send in "the bread you eat in your culture." Instead of giving me joy in my bread-eating brothers and sisters, the hypercarb communion set my teeth on edge. It mattered to me that focaccia is focaccia and naan, naan; it still does.

Which is all to say that here in Białystok, among these meta-Jews—this "great family circle" of Esperantists—I suddenly realize what I am: a meta-Esperantist Jew.

5. Big-endians and Little-endians

The Akademio de Esperanto is about to hold its annual public meeting. "The academy," Tonkin once told me, "is a sort of fire brigade to watch out for misuses. Since most people write Esperanto before speaking it, there's less of a gap between the spoken and the written word than in many languages; it's used fairly conservatively. But there are some great fights. Take the famous 'ata-ita' debate, the Esperanto version of Swift's Big-endians versus Little-endians." I've heard of this famous controversy about whether Esperanto verbs express tenses (present, past, future) or aspects (whether an act is completed or ongoing). All discussions about the debate, which include several entire books, cite a famously contradictory statement of Zamenhof, who couldn't seem to decide himself. The "ata-ita" debate may be the only grammatical controversy with its own *Wikipedia* entry—in the Esperanto *Vikipedio*.

Seventeen of the forty-four academicians, four women and thirteen men, take their places on the stage, specialists in astrophysics, banking, education, literature, linguistics, mathematics. Among them are Tonkin, Löwenstein, and *Otto Prytz, a blind professor emeritus of Spanish from Oslo. Nearly half of the seventeen are native speakers of either English or French; no wonder the academy carefully monitors linguistic diversity among its membership. The term is nine years, renewable; every three years, one-third of the members are up for election. As Tonkin puts it, "Some of the members have been asleep for years; staying awake is . . . not an absolute requirement of membership."

The format is simple: the academy publicly tackles a series of written questions submitted by the general membership. *John C. Wells, a British phonetician and author of the leading English-Esperanto dictionary, presides. He reads the first question aloud, then passes the hand-held microphone to whichever academician reaches for it first.

"What is Esperanto for 'cluster bomb?'" The questioner uses the English term. A matronly Italian takes the mike. "*Grapola bombo*," she suggests, Esperantizing the Italian expression *bomba a grappola*. "No!" says another member, grabbing for the mike, "*Bombetaro*"—approval by acclaim for the latter. It is more . . . Esperantist.

"Which is the 'first floor,' the ground floor or the one above?" "We're not here to legislate among cultures," comes the reply. "Use the term you'd use in your own country."

"Should we say '*Birmo*' or '*Mianmaro*'?" Tonkin says, "These are political decisions, not academic ones; to stick with Burma is a critique of the regime." A question on the proper name for Mozambique snags a curt reply from Wells: "There's a published list."

"Which is the correct adverbial form: '*Sponte*'? '*Spontane*'? '*Spontanee*'?" Alas, Esperanto never did solve the problem of irreversibility that drove the Idists away. Wells takes a straw poll: *spontane*, hands down. When someone suggests that the Academy consult the frequency of uses on the Web, the Israeli physicist Amri Wandel protests, "That's not reliable. I've written about this . . . about *nanplaneto* vs. *nanoplaneto*." Heads bob knowingly; those who haven't already read it take down the reference.

Wells flips to the next question. "Why is the sexist '*shminkistino*' the preferred term? Not all makeup artists are women, right?" It's a rhetorical question; point taken.

"Which is better: '*Bluaj okuloj*'? '*Bluokuleco*'?" Blue eyes, or blue-eyedness? It's a question only an Esperantist could understand—or need answered.

"How do we properly refer to the parts of a person's name: '*Familiana nomo*'? '*Persona nomo*'?" "In some cultures," says Tonkin, "the word 'name' only refers to a family name; and there are other terms and usages." He does not say "Christian name," as the English usually do. "We're not here to make the world easier; we make easier the complication of the world." Wavelets of laughter. "Do as you like."

Most questions are lexical, but late in the session comes a grammatical question: "What about this trend of creating new verbs from participles?" The academicians sigh audibly, as over a teenager who has once again forgotten to take out the garbage. In fact, it once *was* a youth issue: a trend that began among Esperanto-speaking teens in the 1980s has finally filtered into the Esperanto mainstream. While Americans are now scandalously verbing every noun in sight, Esperantists have, since 1887, been licensed to verb almost any root. Instead of *Mi ludas gitaron* (I play the guitar), I can simply add a verb ending to the root "*gitar-*" and say, *Mi gitaras*. But now, something more extreme is happening: people are taking participles, adjectives already spawned by verbs, and using them as secondary verbs. "For example," says one academician, "they've been saying *bezonatas*, from the participle *bezonata* (needed), as in *Ĉio bezonatas samtempe*—'everything is being needed at the same time.'" More examples are thrown into the fray as the volume of the chatter onstage rises, until Wells wrests away the mike and says, a little impatiently, "You have a choice. You always have a choice." *Do as you like. You have a choice.* They may be the Academy, but they're not the boss of us.

When the session draws to a close, people file out in knots of two and three, seeking out a bit of shade to continue debating about participles. In my mind's eye, I see the delegates of 1905 doing much the same, before recessing to the cafés of Boulogne.

6. Adrian

"*Strangulo*"—"weirdo"—says Adrian, the retired public health professor I'd met in Iznik. Adrian's right; the young Japanese man who unicycles past our table in the beer garden, arms outstretched for balance, is a weirdo. I'd seen him the night before, playing the accordion on the esplanade in front of the polytechnic. Earlier today, clad in a green T-shirt and a white hachimaki headband, he pedaled his unicycle past the entrance to the *libroservo* (bookstore) as I entered. I was there to drop some złotys on books: anthologies of Hungarian poetry, back copies of *Beletra Almanako*, a history of Esperanto in Africa, Raymond Schwartz's novel *Kiel akvo de l'rivero* (Like River Water), the satirical magazine *La Kancer-Kliniko* (The Cancer Clinic), and the best-selling *Kulturo de Amo*, a sex guide in Hungarian and Esperanto, illustrated with exquisite stippled pencil drawings. It's been in print continuously since the seventies, the passionate couple still locked in their forty-year-old embrace, wearing mullet hairdos. While I stand paging through it, a plump French woman in Birkenstocks says over my shoulder, "Buy it now! You'll see, it always sells out." This was not the only erotica in the *libroservo*. There are erotic poems by one "Peter Peneter" (the pseudonym of Kálmán

Kalocsay), and the popular *ABC de Amo* (ABC of Love), a Danish best-seller of 1958.

Some weeks ago, Adrian emailed that he had applied too late for lodging in Białystok; now, he wrote, there were no rooms left in the bargain hotels and he wasn't in the market for luxury. "I'll find something; I've never yet spent a night under a bridge." By the time I catch up with him at the opening ceremony, he's rented a room for twelve euros a night in the priory of an onion-domed Orthodox church on the outskirts of town. Apart from the Doberman in the courtyard, he says, it's perfect: quiet, clean, and comfortable. He's left his B&B in Maastricht in the care of "*la lesbaninoj*"—a Bulgarian lesbian couple who get free lodging in exchange for housework—but takes all calls for the business on his smartphone. After he answers "*Hallooo*," it's hard to predict what language he'll speak next: Dutch; his fluent, colloquial English; his excellent French; or his functional German, Danish, Norwegian, Swedish, or Italian. He also knows enough of ten other languages to speak to cabbies. "Come to Maastricht and I'll give you the five-country tour," he offers broadly; "We start in Holland, lunch in Belgium, drive through France, a stop for a beer in Luxembourg, dinner in Aachen and then home." Only he has no car . . . but no worries, he'll borrow one. Adrian has been an Esperantist since his university days in Amsterdam, but raising four children (the younger two adopted from Korea) as a single parent has kept him away from congresses for many years. Now, pensioned and supplemented by his B&B income, he's back in Esperantic action.

Not that Adrian has stayed close to home all those years; quite the contrary. After retiring as a public-health professor, he had a second career as the international affairs director of an aviation university. He'd flown from Dar es Salaam to Jakarta, Sydney, Morocco, Cyprus—just about everywhere, setting up consortia, meeting with aviation officials, researching crashes. It takes half an hour to discover three places he has not visited: the Galapagos, Vietnam, and Princeton. Invariably, he finds an Esperantist to show him around town, put him up for a few days, perhaps drive him down to the beach. "I don't go places to see a valley or a tower," he says with disdain; he's a sojourner, not a tourist. His habit, on visiting a new city, is to find the best café or taverna and revisit it daily, shmoozing with regulars and flirting with waitresses. And here in Białystok, he's fast becoming a regular at the Esperanto Café on the Rynek, where he addresses the waitress in Polish: "I remember you from yesterday! Enneke?—no, Emilie!" After the congress, he'll head to Warsaw to see friends, "but perhaps I'll hit Belarus for a day from here, it's only just over the border." He'll look into a visa tomorrow. "You can plan and plan," he says, leaning back from his glass of Chianti contentedly, "but the best plan is no plan."

Adrian makes an excellent guide to the congress, by day and by night. He knows everyone, the *denaskuloj* (native speakers), the *gravuloj* (VIPs) and the *stranguloj,* who, besides our unicycling friend, include a bearded French teen sprouting three pontyails and several gray-braided elders dressed more or less like John the Baptist but for the Guatemalan bags draped over their shoulders. Rarely do the categories of *gravuloj* and *stranguloj* coincide, but when they do, Adrian supplies the deep background. We meet the five Kazakh teens who've come to Białystok by train, over three days and nights. We take in a concert by Guinness World Record winner *Jean-Marc Leclerq (known as JoMo), who sings in twenty-two languages. We watch the tender one-man show about Zamenhof written and performed by *Georgo (Jerzy) Handzlik, a Polish singer, actor, and broadcaster.

Adrian points out the long-married couples, the exes and their exes and theirs, and the *kongresedzoj*—elective "spouses," invariably from different countries where their husbands and wives are working or minding kids or parents. They meet once a year at the Universal Congress, their affair an open secret, fodder for gossip, but worthy of respect. They're fickle in their constancy, and constant in fickleness; some of them have been at it for decades. After the day's councils and talks, they'll meet for a glass of wine and dine in cheap eateries with plank floors. After dinner, they'll stroll into town, chatting in Esperanto until the light dwindles and they return to the hotel, the guesthouse, the B&B. And after that, Esperanto dissolves into the common language of flesh.

7. Flickering Shadows

During the run-up to Zamenhof's centenary in 1959, his Judaism became an explicit theme for discussion. That year, an Israeli Esperantist named Naftali Zvi Maimon published an exquisitely researched article about Zamenhof's Zionist activities. This was soon joined by Maimon's articles on Zamenhof's early years, student period, Esperantist activity, and

Hillelism; on the Zamenhof family, especially Markus; and on how little attention the Esperanto world had thus far paid to Zamenhof's Jewishness and Jewish milieu. Not until 1978 did Maimon collect the articles into his landmark book, provocatively titled *La Kaŝita Vivo de Zamenhof* (The Hidden Life of Zamenhof). But hidden no more: here in Białystok, Zamenhof's Jewish life has taken center stage. In the weeks before the congress, the "Zamenhofology" listserv was primarily concerned with various strands of Zamenhof's Jewishness: Yiddish, Zionism, Hillelism.

This morning, Tonkin launches a session called "Zamenhof Today" by asking us to put ourselves in his "shoes, beard, and spectacles" as a man of a specific place, time, and ethnic background. Only then can we get beyond our icon of the kind visionary grandfather and gauge the immensity of his decision to invent a new way, a new option. At the end of a series of questions to launch the session, Tonkin asks, "Did Zamenhof want to Judaize everyone?" I flash back to Zamenhof's strange statement to the *Jewish Chronicle*: "Instead of being absorbed by the Christian world, we [Jews] shall absorb them; for that is our mission." If "to Judaize" means, as Zamenhof put it, "to spread among humanity the truth of monotheism and the principles of justice and fraternity," then the answer is yes, that was precisely what Zamenhof had in mind. But if "to Judaize" means "to turn them into Jews," then the answer was, decidedly, no.

Our next speaker has been Judaized in the latter manner, but not by Zamenhof. *Tsvi Sadan, an Israeli professor of linguistics, looks far younger than his forty-six years. With his yarmulke, wire-rim glasses, scraggly beard, white shirt, and black slacks, he might resemble a yeshiva boy; he might, did he not resemble more closely a Japanese scholar in an Edo-period scroll. In his native Japan, Sadan had been Tsuguya Sasaki, but after emigrating to Israel, he changed his name, converted to Judaism, became an Israeli citizen, and earned a doctorate in Hebrew linguistics. (I'm told that he's the sole Israeli Esperantist who wears a yarmulke and sticks to kosher food.) His website lists his languages as follows:

Native: Japanese
Active: Hebrew, English
Quite active: Yiddish, Esperanto

Passive: German, French, Russian
Very passive: Arabic, Aramaic, Italian, Spanish, Polish

Sadan is lecturing today as part of the International Congress University, a series of carefully vetted, high-level lectures delivered mostly by academics. His lecture, "A Sociolinguistic Comparison of Two Diasporic Languages, Yiddish and Esperanto, on the Internet," has mustered a healthy audience who are rewarded for their attention with the news that Esperanto has a far larger presence on the Internet than Yiddish. Toward the end of the rather technical talk, the topic changes to Sadan's passion: traditional Ashkenazic dances. Suddenly he walks in front of the podium, strikes a dancer's pose, and begins to gambol across the stage, dropping low for a *kazatzka,* and all to the beat of a klezmer band that only he can hear. It's distinctly a man's dance, the kind flamboyantly performed at Orthodox Jewish weddings, and it brings on a familiar sour taste. I've done my time watching from the sidelines as schnapps-fueled men dance for the *hatan* and *kalah* ("groom and bride" is the phrase, not "bride and groom"). I always love their abandon; I always hate their complicity in a regime of separation, boundaries, limits. Today, the response is mixed. Some are charmed, but others seem put out by— what? The lack of decorum? The in-your-face display of Sadan's unlikely Jewishness?

A warmer reception is given to the next lecturer, Tomasz Chmielik. Trained in German and Polish philology and a novelist himself, Chmielik is one of the premier translators of literature into Esperanto; thanks to Chmielik, Samuel Beckett, Günter Grass, Friedrich Dürrenmatt, Georges Perec, and I. B. Singer have found places in the Esperanto library. Today Chmielik is screening two short films made by Saul and Moshe Goskind, owners of the Warsaw film studio Sektor. In 1939 the Goskinds, knowing that the days of Jewish life in Poland were numbered, set out to document Jewish life in six cities, Kraków, Vilna (Vilnius), Lvov, Warsaw, Białystok, and Łódź; all the films survive except the one documenting Łódź. Weeks before the invasion of Poland, the films were dispatched to New York, but went astray until 1942, when they were auctioned off by the dead letter office of the U.S. Postal Service. Only in the late 1960s did various portions of the surviving films make their way to Israel, where Saul Goskind, who had emigrated there, reedited them. Where the original soundtracks had been lost, new ones were recorded in Hebrew and English.

"So, are these the same films?" Chmielik asks. As my students say, he is "getting meta" on us: not only the Jews of prewar Poland, but also the films about them are among the lost. What we're watching, then, are flickering shadows of flickering shades. The narration's in Yiddish, the subtitles in English; no one translates into Esperanto. Białystok's 55,000 Jews—rich and poor, capitalists and bundists—bustle about their multilingual, sophisticated society. Places of worship and palaces of culture lie cheek by jowl. Here's the 1913 Great Synagogue (in which close to two thousand Jews were locked and set on fire in 1941, two years after the film was made) and there, the 1834 Khorshul (Choir Synagogue, destroyed by the Nazis in 1943) over which Zamenhof's father, Markus, had presided at the groundbreaking. Here's the Białystoker Yeshiva, and there the Musar Yeshiva, and in yet another neighborhood, on Lipowa Street, the progressive-Zionist Tarbut (Hebrew for "culture") School. This building, unlike the others, is extant, a repurposed craft school, devoid of Jews. When we see a glimpse of Zamenhof's birthplace (in Białystok) and later, his tomb (in Warsaw), it's like spotting a family member in a photograph of Times Square on V-E Day.

The final shots are of Jewish children lounging on a summer day in a large, leafy park, dappled sunlight playing on their faces. I recognize the Branicki Palace gardens, where just last night we had listened to JoMo under lanterns. Seventy summers earlier, in these gardens, Jewish children in crisp white uniforms had played circle games; Jewish teens, mugging at the camera, had comically flexed their muscles; plump Jewish babies had been prammed up the allées like stately galleons. Here and there a baby gazes, fascinated, into the lens, heedless of its nurse, pushing, pushing on. At the end, a subtitle tells us that "these children are precious; they are the future." The footage lasts three or four minutes; the children would last two or three more years, at most.

When the lights come up, people are sniffling. Quietly, Chmielik says, "I close my eyes and imagine how the story of all these people ended. We know the ending. They did not."

Suddenly, from the audience, an Israeli named *Josi (Yosi) Shemer rises to his feet. I know Josi from his weekly email of Jewish jokes translated—and laboriously annotated—in Esperanto. But Josi looks transfigured; as if seized by the gift of tongues, he exclaims: "This is holy work! From a non-Jew! To translate from Yiddish to Esperanto! To bring us this film! . . ." and trails off, in a paroxysm of acclamation. Chmielik is too embarrassed to respond. Announcing where we can order the DVD online (though no one had asked), he adjourns the session.

8. A Nation Without Pyres

Like Jewless Kraków, which hosts a huge annual klezmer festival, the city of Białystok has turned its Jewish quarter into a Jewish reservation. Shops sell tribal souvenirs: CDs, books, and postcards of Jewish life between the wars. In certain tourist restaurants, one can order "Jewish-style" food—borscht, herring, brisket with prunes. Tonight, on the Rynek's massive stage, an Israeli dance troupe performs to an accordion, a wailing clarinet, and a snare drum. But if these are meant to show us real, live, dancing Jews, they're unconvincing. There's something odd about their costumes, not Jewish but Jew-y: dresses made of tallit fabric, faux kapotas, phony black fedoras held on with rubber bands. Music blares, lights glare, and the dancers wheel about smiling red lipsticked smiles. It's a Ballet Folklórico, only hold the Mexicans.

Friday morning I board a bus full of Japanese Esperantists to the seventeenth-century synagogue at Tykocin. I recognize some of the Japanese from my hotel, where they move in flocks herded by their own professional guide. Apart from deferential bowing and a friendly "*Saluton!*" in the elevator, they fraternize mainly with one another. An Italian friend explained that the Japanese Esperantists, as enthusiastic as they are affluent, generally make a strong showing at world congresses, but most aren't comfortable in conversation. "You'll hear them crocodile," she said, and so I did; they spoke Japanese in the corridors, at breakfast, and now on the bus.

Twenty-five miles west of Białystok, Tykocin was the birthplace of Zamenhof's father. The Jewish community dates back to 1522 and, despite fierce competition from Christian guilds and an episode of blood libel in 1657, they had prospered. By the time Markus Zamenhof was born in 1834, there were nearly three thousand Jews in the town, about 65 percent of the population. Fortunately, I've read about the fate of Tykocin's Jews during World War II, since our slim, ponytailed Polish guide barely mentions it. A detachment of Nazi police entered the town on August 16, 1941, and secretly ordered the digging of three large pits in the nearby Łopu-chowo forest. On August 25, at six in the morning, Tykocin's Jews were rounded up in the market square, told they were being taken to the Białystok ghetto, and marched to a nearby school. Then by the truckload, men first and then women, they were taken to the forest and shot in the freshly dug pits. The next day, a sweep of the town yielded another seven hundred Jews, the old and the sick, who met the same fate. The synagogue became a storehouse for plundered Jewish goods. Most of the 150 Jews who escaped to the forest were murdered. By the end of the war, Tykocin's two thousand Jews numbered seventeen.

No sign of this catastrophe greets us when we descend a brief flight of stairs into the whitewashed masonry synagogue. Our Esperanto-speaking guide informs us that the synagogue floor had to be lower than the floor of the church of the Holy Trinity at the opposite end of the town. The descent makes the nine-meter height of the white interior seem more lofty, and the nine-bay floor plan more enveloping. The interior and the women's sections had been destroyed by the Nazis, but all was immaculately restored during the 1970s and 1980s as part of the regional Podlaskie Museum: the furnishings of the ark, the mahogany rails, the cut-glass chandeliers, and the Hebrew and Aramaic words painted in huge, carefully aligned black letters on the walls. Our guide points out that these enabled Jews to pray when it was too dark to read the prayer book. From cupolas high above come gashes of light on the letters, carving even holier words among the black Hebrew characters.

Most of the Japanese sit in silence on the benches, as our guide dilates on rituals and ritual objects—the women's section, the Hanukkah meno-rah, the Ark of the Torah, the bima. There's a perfunctory mention of the Nazi plunderers (not murderers), but anti-Semitism doesn't come up. No talk of Jews and Poles, or of the pogroms of 1936 and 1938, before the Nazis had ever set foot in Poland. "Poland," says our guide, "has always been a tolerant place."

A Japanese man in a golf hat raises his hand. "Diversity!" he says, cheerfully, "that is the key thing, diversity." He's the same man who an hour earlier had asked me where I was from. "*Usono*," I'd answered, and he'd beamed: "I'm from Obama, Japan! That is my hometown, Obama! So I love Barack Obama!"

On the matter of diversity, our guide agrees. "I think so, yes," she says haltingly. Then with more conviction: "Diversity is why Poland has always been a tolerant place."

I want to ask, and don't want to ask, and then I ask, "What about the Poles who looted Jews during the pogroms of 1936 and 1938? What about the complicity of the Polish police in the roundup and murder of Tykocin's Jews?" Does anyone else notice that I'm becoming my mother? Once, when I murmured my affection for Degas, she'd snapped, "That anti-Semite? Show me his ballerinas and I'll show you *Dreyfus*."

The guide swigs from her water bottle. "Poland is a country without scaffolds," she says evenly; it's part proverb, part trademark. She takes another swig, and shifts her purse to the other shoulder. "Poland is a nation without pyres."

* * *

That night in Białystok, after the crowds had thinned and the floodlights blinked out, a young hooded man threw a bottle of pink paint onto the monumental bronze bust of Zamenhof at the intersection at Białowny and Malmeda. The next morning, Zamenhof's lips, beard, and bust were bright pink, as though *la majstro* had just bitten the top off a bottle of Pepto-Bismol. Saturday morning's local paper, the *Kurier Poranny*, reported it as a "racist attack," which apparently followed a handful of other incidents throughout the week. The massive "Zamenhof tent" was set on fire the night before the inaugural. A group of skinheads entered the congress hall, some in black shirts with a star of David crossed by a red bar. An ad for the congress was defaced; bus tires were slashed in the parking lot. And late Wednesday night someone threw a bottle with burning liquid against the new Zamenhof Center, which, being stone, was left unscathed. While sound checks were under way for the final ceremony, a Brazilian *samideano* was wounded by a large stone hurled through the window of a dormitory.

All this I would learn later, from the independent webzine *Libera Folio* (Free Page). But the UEA's daily conference newsletter had been vandal- and violence-free. During the congress, according to *Libera Folio*, *Brunetto Casini, the editor, had been planning to publish a photo of the paint-spattered bust of Zamenhof and a brief article by *François Lo Jacomo. Anxious about repercussions, Casini had checked in with the local Congress Committee, who gave him a green light. Still anxious, Casini had followed up with a call to *Osmo Buller, the laconic Finnish director of the UEA. According to Lo Jacomo, "Osmo looked at the photo, [and] the three lines which I had written, and without any emotion whatsoever said simply, that he [Casini] must not publish it." Instead, the front page bore a photo of smiling Esperantists gathered around an eighty-millimeter telescope.

In the weeks and months following the congress, comments flew back and forth on the *Libera Folio* website. Some attacked the UEA for censorship, insisting that the crimes were racist and anti-Semitic; others minimized the events as adolescent hooliganism. The leaders of the Israeli Esperantist League wrote in fulsome praise of the Polish hosts and the city of Białystok. But it was Renato Corsetti, elder statesman, who posted the classic Esperanto rejoinder: "Violent nationalism and hatred of foreigners is found everywhere, not only in Białystok. The existence of these feelings in some part of humanity vindicates our work to eradicate them in Białystok and in the whole world." The paint, the fire, the skinheads: all the more reason to carry on talking, writing, believing—and planning for the next *granda rondo familia* in Havana.

PART THREE

THE HERETIC, THE PRIESTESS, AND THE INVISIBLE EMPIRE

1. The Heretic

In the fall of 1927, the Associated Press reported that Mrs. Mabel Wagnalls Jones, heir to the Funk & Wagnalls publishing fortune, had recently built a memorial to her parents. It was a rambling Tudor-Gothic edifice in Lithopolis, Ohio, with classrooms, meeting rooms, a library, and an auditorium that could seat three hundred people, the entire population of the town. Mabel was not only thinking big; she was also thinking in Esperanto, planning to turn Lithopolis into the Esperanto center of the United States. Within two years, she had acquired the entire library of the former president of the American Esperanto Association, and Esperanto classes for Bloom Township schoolchildren and their teachers, as well as night classes for adults, were in full swing. "This isolated village," rhapsodized a reporter, "miles from a railroad and not even touched by motor busses, may become the Capital of an invisible Empire, founded upon Esperanto, the Universal Auxiliary language."[1]

This is not something most Esperantists of the 1920s, American or otherwise, would have said. By almost every standard, Esperanto failed the test of an empire: it had no imperial center dependent on far-flung resources; no colonies to govern, and no infrastructure by which to govern them; and no army or navy. It lacked the essential requirement of an empire: *imperium,* that is to say, power. Even so, by the end of World War I, Esperanto had acquired a geographical reach that would have been the envy of any empire. It had spread beyond Eastern and Western Europe to the United States; to Asia, including China, Japan, and Korea;

to South Africa, Egypt, and North Africa; to Australia and New Zealand; and to Brazil.

But in the years between the world wars, far from Lithopolis, Ohio, the fate of the "invisible Empire" of Esperanto lay largely in the hands of the three most visible empires on the globe: Stalin's USSR, Japan, and Hitler's Third Reich. Speakers of "the dangerous language," as it was called by Stalin, were perceived as a menace onto which virtually any enemy could be projected: communists, Jews, Trotskyites, "bourgeois elements," and democratic socialists, among others. Ulrich Lins, in his landmark study, *La Danĝera Lingvo,* documents the brutality of totalitarian regimes in the USSR, Japan, occupied China and Korea, and Germany toward Esperantists and their organizations. Free to realize their own versions of the *interna ideo,* Esperantists coped with such regimes in vastly different ways. Some made common cause with imperial powers for ideological aims; some made compromises simply to survive; and many stolidly chose opposition, sometimes at the cost of their lives.

The vague *interna ideo* also allowed for competing visions of the movement itself. There were suprantionalists, like Hector Hodler, whose vision of the UEA was a decentralized network of consuls serving local constituencies. There were internationalists, represented by the Paris-based Central Office, who reconceived Zamenhof's vision of interethnic harmony as an affair of nation-states; the UEA would be dominated by the largest national organizations, which provided the movement with its largest financial base. There were anationalists, who split off from the UEA to bring Esperanto into the service of world socialism. There were anarchists, chiefly Chinese and Japanese reformers trying to usher a Confucian, pan-Asian vision of world harmony into a new century. And it was left to Zamenhof's own daughter, Lidia, to keep alive the universalist, transcendental strain of Zamenhof's vision.

Zamenhof himself had placed his hopes in yet another world power: the United States. In his early days, he'd envisioned the United States as a homeland for the Jews, and later predicted (wrongly) that the country would become a world center for Esperanto. He also believed that instead of flexing its imperial power, the United States would become increasingly woven into a pan-American union of states. Despite a flurry of interest around the 1910 Universal Congress in Washington, resistance to Esperanto in the States came from many corners: from xenophobic nativists, from those still in thrall to what Emerson called "the courtly muses of Europe," and from capitalists who associated Esperanto with socialism. Even so, its passionate advocates made it a Rorschach for diverse concepts of their country's identity as a multicultural and multiracial society, a nation-state, and a burgeoning world power.

This chapter is framed by two European Esperantists, a man and a woman, who refused to compromise with empires and, in vastly different ways, were undone by them. He called himself "the heretic"; people called her "the Priestess." He was a poor Catholic from a village in Normandy; she was a middle-class Jew born in Warsaw. He, a carpenter, educated himself at the feet of anarchists; she earned a law degree at Warsaw University but never practiced. He talked and wrote about *sennacieco* (anationalism); she, a Bahá'í, lectured ceaselessly about "the way." In 1936, he renounced his nation and left it forever; two years later, weeks after Kristallnacht, she sailed back to her homeland, where she was imprisoned, immured in the Warsaw Ghetto, and finally murdered at Treblinka. No two Esperantists had ever been more certain of Esperanto's *interna ideo,* and no two "internal ideas" could have been more different. In every way but one—their common tongue, Esperanto—they were poles apart. His name was Adam; hers, Zamenhof.

* * *

In 1879, six months after L. L. Zamenhof launched an early version of Esperanto at a birthday party, Eugène Aristide Alfred Adam was born in Saint-Jacques-de-Néhou, Normandy. In *Fredo,* his fragmentary autobiographical novel, the infant hero is baptized once with water, and a second time with cider, by his roguish, alcoholic uncle. Adam's childhood, like his protagonist's, was a battle between piety and skepticism, with the latter always getting the upper hand. It was also an education in the power of money; like Fredo, Adam saw his beloved sister, Nata, married off at twenty to a rich man whom she despised. It was as if she'd been stolen away, and when she died, a year later, he blamed the thief. A talented woodworker, Adam became skilled at making faux-antique furniture but when he learned how exorbitantly a merchant had marked up his work, he saw exploitation, not opportunity.

Gradually, he made his way to Paris, where the skeptical child grew into an iconoclast bent on smashing idols of all kinds: religion, money, and patriotism. By day he taught technical drawing; by night, he attended anarchist meetings. As an ambulance driver during the war, he insisted on treating German as well as French soldiers, and by the end of the war, he had renounced nationalism. Romantic love was the next idol to be smashed, when a brief marriage ended in separation. He would know better the next time, seeking a woman for rational partnership rather than love or marriage. The woman he found, a brilliant, well-to-do British Esperantist named Hélène (Nellie) Kate Limouzin, had an adoring nephew named Eric Blair, who sojourned with them and their Esperantic circle in Paris. Though Blair never became an Esperantist, under the name George Orwell he would later write the shrewdest statement in English about the role of language in politics.

Adam learned Esperanto in Paris, in his mid-thirties, among socialists and anarchists. Active in a group of left-wing Esperantists in Paris, "comrade" Adam took on the task of editing the journal of the Esperanto workers' group *Esperantista Laboristo*. And in its pages, in 1920, he began to publish the manifesto that would split the Esperanto world in two. *For la Neutralismon* (Away with Neutrality) called for a new movement that would use Esperanto as a tool for "overturn[ing] the capitalist order";[2] he called it the Sennacieca Asocio Tutmonda, or SAT (Worldwide Anational Association). National organizations would play no role in the new entity except to propagandize to ministries of education and local governments. As Adam demonstrated in a technical diagram resembling an elaborate system of pulleys, SAT would be decentralized. No particular political party would be endorsed, so that social democrats, communists, and anarchists could work together, promoting Esperanto among the working classes of all nations. Through Esperanto, the worldwide proletariat would arrive at a new social order.

Neutrality, Adam wrote, was false consciousness, and he exhorted his readers to disavow the "bourgeois miasma" of the "neutralist" UEA, with its "dandyism" and its "desire for prestige and other bourgeois affairs."[3] *Homaranismo* and even Zamenhof himself were cut down to size:

> The author of Esperanto lacked a clear concept about the ongoing, ceaseless, more or less bitter, battle among the social classes. . . . Tolerance about religion, race or nation, and the possibility of mutual understanding is not enough to do away with enmity and to bring about justice. And where there is no justice, war is latent.[4]

*Eugène Adam, or Lanti, the heretic
[Österreichische Nationalbibliothek]*

Adam also refused to align the group with bourgeois pacifists, including the pacifist UEA, though he had already distanced himself from a cell of anarchist terrorists in Paris. SAT members would not be *pac-batalantoj* (peace fighters); instead, they would wage class warfare, propelled by a revolution in language.

With the founding of SAT, Adam felt it was time to rename the workers' journal—and himself. The first issue of the new *Sennacieca Revuo* (Anational Review) came out over the name of "Lanty." It was a coy transcription of the French "L'anti," a nickname he had acquired by being tirelessly oppositional, and a fine nom de guerre for an iconoclast. There was another reason for a pseudonym, as E. Borsboom, Adam's biographer, points out. Having joined the French Communist Party at its inception in 1920, he was in danger of losing his teaching job; besides, the chauvinist Poincaré government fiercely opposed the teaching of Esperanto.

But this particular alias, the name by which Adam was henceforth known in the Esperanto world, was more than a pseudonym. It was, in Borsboom's words, "a metamorphosis"[5] by which he passed from one life to another. In 1921, he issued a press release noting the suicide of his "predecessor" Eugène Adam, and duly printed a death notice in the next issue of the *Sennacieca Revuo*. Teo Jung, the editor of *Esperanto Triumfonta*, realized the hoax, but Edmond Privat, editor of the UEA's monthly *Revuo Esperanto*, composed a somber obituary:

E. Adam, editor of *Sennacieca Revuo*, killed himself in October 1921. He wrote thus in his will: "Be silent about my death. If I have friends, they should be not be funereal, but on the contrary, joyful." . . . In spite of the desire of the deceased, we can't be silent about his disappearance and we must remember that he was an experienced, large-thinking, and progressive Esperantist with real ideas. He energetically led the interesting *Sennacieca Revuo*, now edited by E. Lant[i].[6]

A new name for Adam, a new name for the journal, and a new name for the *lingvo internacia*: *lingvo sennacieca*—the nationless language.

* * *

In 1922 Lanti—as the name was commonly spelled—traveled to the Soviet Union to see the workers' revolution firsthand. He went in search of a laboratory for putting Esperanto to work for worldwide, classless anationalism. What he found on the streets, as he reported in "*Tri Semajnoj en Rusio*" (Three Weeks in Russia), were potholes, beggars, prostitutes, and peddlers; in the halls of government, a warren of corrupt, heavily guarded bureaucrats, hopelessly disorganized and overworked. He assailed Lenin's New Economic Policy of 1921, which permitted a modicum of capitalist enterprise, as an egregious compromise of socialist principles: "Politically, the Proletariat won; but economically, the victory still seems far away."[7] Most *samideanoj* received him warmly, especially the intellectuals who edited *La Nova Epoko* (The New Era), none of whom was a party member.

Language was a crucial reason for the visit. Lanti knew that the Comintern was debating the role language might play in unifying the Soviet Union's diverse ethnicities and educating its largely agrarian society. A year earlier, at the Tenth Congress, Lenin had rejected a proposed Russification program, an act that appeared to open the door, even a crack, to an auxiliary language. But as Lanti learned in Moscow, the commission set up in 1919 to study the matter had already been liquidated. In future, language matters would be under direct control of the Comintern. In Lanti's view, this failure put Esperanto into eclipse, a condition exacerbated by the cowardice of Esperantists who were party members. After a visit to the Moscow Esperanto Club, Lanti wrote:

I have the impression that the Esperantist communists are almost embarrassed by their Esperantism. Since the leaders of

Sennacieca Revuo, "Three Weeks in Russia," 1922

the Comintern are not interested in the thing, it seems that our *samideanoj* are afraid of compromising themselves by propagandizing in communist circles. Severe communist discipline, for many, suffocates the enthusiasm and fervor for Esperanto.[8]

And in Lanti's eyes, the one Esperantist with the fervor and influence to convince the Comintern to endorse Esperanto was too preoccupied with his own prestige to be counted on.

Ernest Drezen was a young Latvian-born engineer from a family of means. After serving in the Red Army, he attained a post in the Comintern as the right-hand man of Mikhail Kalinin, the president of the All-Russian Central Executive Committee, and officially the head of state. Recently, Drezen had become president of the newly formed Soviet Esperanto Union (SEU). In a striking photograph Lanti included in his articles, Drezen appears in his Red Army uniform, his aristocratic features and broad forehead topped by thinning hair. His face is swiveled toward the camera, half in shadow; his gaze is intense; his lips are pursed, as though he is choosing his words carefully.

Lanti and Drezen were Esperanto's Hitler and Stalin; its Rabin and Arafat. Our sole source for their meeting was Lanti, who lambasted the

*Ernest Drezen, President of the Soviet
Esperanto Union (SEU)*

phalanxes of guards and paper-pushers barring access to Drezen's lair in
the Kremlin. Finally reached after hours of effort, Drezen told his French
visitor to come back later. At five p.m., after scant minutes of conversation, Drezen phoned for a car to whisk them off to his house, where his
wife (a non-Esperantist) had prepared a lavish dinner. Once home, Drezen
showed off his Esperanto library, trying to impress Lanti with his love of
"nia afero" (our affair), but Lanti's "affair" was the recently inaugurated
SAT, and he and Drezen most definitely did not share the same view.
"[Drezen] doesn't want to collaborate with anarchists and social democrats," wrote Lanti. "But, strangely, he is president of the Soviet Esperanto
Union, in which are not only anarchists but bourgeois of a certain type.
This contradiction, thus far, I haven't been able to clarify."[9]

After three weeks of visits to party bureaucrats, cultural commis-
sars, electrical stations, cooperative farms, and Esperantist intellectuals,
as well as after-hours wandering in the streets of Moscow and Leningrad, Lanti lamented "the ruin of my beliefs." In his bitter "Post-voyage
Reflections," he reviled the Soviets for compromising their communist
principles by endorsing capitalist stimuli for industry and agriculture.
He was still, he asserted, a communist, and he confirmed his support
of the Third International. But, he asked, "must a communist close his
eyes when he sees something bad or ugly? Is communism a new religion [in which] . . . no one can discuss anything, unwilling to risk being
considered as a heretic?"[10] He would never shed the name "Lanti," but

in 1924 began to write under yet another pseudonym: "Sennaciulo"—the anationalist.

* * *

Lanti underestimated the rigor, tenacity, and stealth with which Drezen would strive, for nearly twenty years, to convince the Comintern that Esperanto was indispensable to the success of the Soviet empire.

Drezen was as much of a contrarian as Lanti himself. For years, he fought the intellectuals who, in line with Marxist thinker Antonio Gramsci, dismissed Esperanto—or any other planned language—as "rigidified and mechanized."[11] Not until the late 1920s did the Comintern endorse the materialist, class-based linguistic theory of V. Y. Marr who, though not an Esperantist himself, claimed that Esperanto might indeed play a role in a world-language revolution. Drezen published a monograph theorizing the role of Esperanto in the victory of world socialism with an introduction by Marr, whose views were endorsed by Stalin in 1930 at the Sixteenth Congress of the Communist Party.[12]

Meanwhile, to settle scores with Lanti and prove his mettle to the Comintern, Drezen pummeled SAT, claiming that its "anarchists [and] social democrats are more dangerous enemies for the revolutionary movement than the openly bourgeois."[13] After *La Nova Epoko* printed a satirical piece about him, Drezen had the journal suspended. Rumors, probably with some degree of truth, began to rumble: Drezen had had a hand in the disappearance of a *Nova Epoko* editor; Drezen had betrayed a fellow Esperantist who had protested Soviet persecution in the Ukraine. Within months, eighty anarchists, among them several leading Soviet Esperantists, had been killed in purges in Moscow and Leningrad.

Even as he was failing to Sovietize SAT, Drezen advocated the use of Esperanto to Sovietize European workers. In 1924 he saw his moment, when the Comintern set up a system of worker-correspondents to propagandize to socialists and syndicalists in Western Europe. Drezen enlisted Soviet Esperantists to participate, hoping not only to propound Stalinism, but also to expand the use of Esperanto among Soviet workers.[14] The SEU organized Esperanto correspondence campaigns in several cities and translated Esperanto letters from other countries into Russian. According to Lins, in the early days of the campaign, about two thousand Esperanto letters per month were sent from the cities of Minsk and Smolensk alone.[15] Meanwhile, an Esperanto group in Belarus sent more than four thousand letters to workers on five continents and received even more. In 1926, the official Soviet newspaper *Izvestia* declared the Esperantists' correspondence program a model for the whole Soviet Union, and the Komsomol (the Communist Party's youth wing) published a brochure entreating youthful comrades to learn Esperanto. Textbook sales soared, and Esperanto classes were held in factories and offices. The more successful the Esperanto correspondence project became, the more Drezen was emboldened to pressure Lanti's SAT to fall into line with the SEU.

But the very success of the project alarmed Drezen's Comintern superiors, who worried that propaganda composed by so many hands— Esperantists, no less, whose loyalty was always suspect—was not reliable. They demanded that Drezen take tighter control of the campaign. In 1927, he instructed correspondents to confine themselves to talking points for Sovietizing—read: Stalinizing—Western European organizations. But by this time, Lanti in Paris had published an anonymous Soviet letter describing unemployment, homelessness, housing crises in cities, and ignorance in the countryside.[16] Drezen's drastic response was to monitor *all* Esperanto correspondence, screening all incoming and outgoing letters and translating them into Russian to allay the Comintern's suspicion.

After 1927, when Stalin officially turned his back on international communism, advancing nationalistic "socialism in one country," Lanti would never again pay dues to the Communist Party. To Soviets, he was a "heretic"; to Soviet-backed communists within the SAT, a "neutralist"— an ironic slur for the author of *For la Neutralismon*. Once Drezen accused Lanti of "sins and crimes . . . against the revolutionary tradition,"[17] schism within SAT was inevitable, though the endgame took three years of internecine plotting, extortion, and threats to play out. Finally, in 1931, when the SEU denounced SAT as "counterrevolutionary," the rupture was official. But the boycott of SAT did not keep European Stalinists from the 1931 SAT Congress in Amsterdam. They went to heckle Lanti, whose concluding remarks were disrupted by cries of "charlatan," "fascist," "liar," "bourgeois," "Spinozist," "schismatic," and "cheater."[18] For a man who had stood up to the will of Stalin, it was all in a day's work.

* * *

In 1934, Lanti took a page from Zamenhof's book, resigning the presidency of SAT to become, as he put it, one of the ordinary "*SATanoj.*" Having done so, Lanti had more pressing business than lamenting "the ruin of [his] hopes." With seventeen years of journalism behind him, he began to publish books and collections of essays. He was no philosopher; he abhorred theory as a tool of absolutists. His articles about language and anationalism rumble like city buses in plain, fluid prose, stopping short, from time to time, to admit a metaphor. In a controversy over the introduction of neologisms by Esperanto poets, Lanti argued that neologisms were essential to the growth of the language. And somehow he found time to translate Voltaire's *Candide*; Lanti's remains the standard Esperanto version. In 1930 he published the first comprehensive dictionary entirely in Esperanto, in an unlikely partnership with the UEA; it has been in print (in revised editions) ever since.

The same year he resigned the presidency of SAT, Lanti was married for the second time, this time to the woman who had already shared his life in Paris for eight years. Nellie Limouzin, nine years Lanti's senior, taught school in her native Burma before moving to England shortly after 1900.[19] While she and her sister Ida were both suffragettes and Fabians, Limouzin found her way to Esperanto and began to write for Lanti's *Sennaciulo* magazine over the signature "EKL." She met Lanti in 1923, and in 1925 invited herself to join him in Paris for, in Borsboom's words, "a shared life of two friends with equal rights, with full liberty to break relations when it convened, or when the feeling of friendship evaporated."[20] Their bond remained unbroken—that is, until they married.

Our clearest picture of the Lanti-Limouzin ménage comes from Nellie's nephew, George Orwell. During the period memorialized in *Down and Out in Paris and London*, Orwell was a frequent visitor to their apartment; another Esperantist family had hosted him while he searched for digs.[21] According to his biographer Gordon Bowker, Orwell was close to Lanti while the latter was wrestling with the SEU for control of SAT, and the young writer clearly would have been aware of Zamenhof's trials as well. As Orwell wrote in 1946, "For sheer dirtiness of fighting the feuds between the inventors of various of the international languages would take some beating."[22] Lanti's defiance of Stalinism led, in Bowker's view, to "spirited debate . . . that probably helped define more clearly the kind of socialist [Orwell] would become."[23] Shortly before he died, Orwell wrote, "I have never fundamentally altered my attitude towards the Soviet regime since I first began to pay attention to it some time in the nineteen-twenties," a statement Bowker reads as an homage to Lanti.[24] And Lanti may well have been the first pseudonymous writer Orwell ever met.

During the mid-thirties, Lanti retired his pseudonym "Sennaciulo" and took on a new one: "Herezulo" (The Heretic). It was what Drezen had called him, and he took on the sobriquet partly as a provocation. But it was also the name Lanti had used for his hero, Rabelais, whose clerical and political satire, he wrote in 1929, made him "more current than many of this century."[25] This time, Lanti didn't announce the death of his earlier incarnation; he didn't need to. For those committed to anationalism, something was dying all over Europe, as Hitler glided to power on wheels greased by anti-Semites, xenophobes, thugs, and arsonists.

The ordeals of the past decade had aged Lanti; at fifty-five, he looked about seventy-five. For years, disillusionment had been his daily bread. His face was pinched and lined, his dark eyes hooded, and his boar-bristle beard, now white, seemed thinner. He looked more like an impressionist painter than a crusader for an impossible cause. In what turned out to be a farewell speech, he told the Netherlands Esperanto Workers Union that they should make no mistake: Stalin was as much a dictator as Hitler and Mussolini. The USSR was invested in patriotism, not world revolution; and the Comintern elite were busy vacationing at French spas, ignoring the vast discrepancies in workers' salaries.[26] To his Stalinist challengers, he was relentless:

> You still think that in the USSR the workers and the peasants rule. This rule is symbolized by the ubiquitous hammer and sickle. For believers, this symbol is indubitable proof of the existence of the reign of the workers and peasants. . . .
>
> It is truly marvelous and worthy of tears, the realization that generally people are easily deceived and mystified by words, symbols and slogans.[27]

Lanti had given his best years to using language to transform the world, worker by worker, mind by mind, but now he had come to the same conclusion his nephew would reach, one war and millions of deaths later:

> Statements like *Marshal Pétain was a true patriot* [wrote Orwell], *The Soviet press is the freest in the world, The Catholic Church is opposed to persecution*, are almost always made with intent to deceive. Other words used in variable meanings, in most cases

more or less dishonestly, are: *class, totalitarian, science, progressive, reactionary, bourgeois, equality*. . . . Political language—and with variations this is true of all political parties, from Conservatives to Anarchists—is designed to make lies sound truthful and murder respectable, and to give an appearance of solidity to pure wind.[28]

By 1935, there was little to hold Lanti in place: not SAT, whose congresses he no longer attended; not the new journal that he had named with his pseudonym, "Herezulo"; not even the long-suffering Limouzin, of whom he unkindly remarked, "She could drown in a glass of water."[29] Offered an early retirement from his post teaching technical drawing, he grabbed it, on the assurance that he could receive his pension abroad. Before leaving he saw to it that, in the event of his death, Limouzin would inherit his meager estate.

"Even in revolutionary circles," he had told the Dutch workers' group, "one finds very few people who could sincerely declare: to lose my nationality doesn't bother me; on the contrary, I yearn to lose it and consciously strive to acquire the mind of a world-citizen."[30] He was describing himself, and on June 11, two days after the wedding of Eric Blair and Eileen O'Shaughnessy (which he skipped, along with his own going-away party), he left France forever. After a brief stay in Spain and Portugal, he set sail for a new destination: Japan.

2. "Language of Ne'er-do-wells and Communists"

From the Ido schism emerged the myth of an Esperanto movement "purified" of soulless language fanatics. Similarly, the SAT schism spawned its own mythology: that Lanti had gone beyond the pale, replacing the *interna ideo* with class warfare. On this telling, what Lanti called anationalism was simply a version of international socialism, and Lanti was far less independent of the Soviets than he led people to believe. The truth, of course, was more complicated. In fact, SAT revitalized Esperanto for the postwar era. When the Bolsheviks overthrew the reign of the czars in 1917, the international left was galvanized, and as we see from SAT's swelling membership rolls in the 1920s, many leftists found Esperanto consonant with their international aspirations.

The schism, in part, was a reaction against the increasing prominence of national units in the governance of the Esperanto world. By the end of World War I, Hodler had seen his supranationalist vision for the UEA fall on the battlefields, along with several of the movement's future leaders. Because of SAT's prestige and the UEA's weakness, the schism had a powerful impact on the perception of Esperanto in the wider world. Perhaps the chief legacy of the SAT schism was to identify Esperanto, for the world at large, with socialism; sometimes, with the cause of world revolution. The immediate result was to blight Esperanto's prospects in the nascent League of Nations.

When Hodler learned of the plan for a League of Nations, he warned Esperantists to keep their expectations in check. Hodler knew that the motivation to form a league was not to develop a coordinated, international government, but rather to protect national interests and the right of self-determination. And the emergence of the league was all carefully orchestrated by three world powers—the British, Americans, and French—to reduce the stature of both Germany and the USSR on the world stage. The proposed league, Hodler predicted, would be a "heavy organism," dominated by anglophones and francophones. Even if language policy became a matter for deliberation, Esperanto would have to prove its practical use to a commission that would be politically biased.[31] Hodler, who died of tuberculosis in 1920 at the age of thirty-two, did not live to see his apprehensions realized, but his skepticism was well founded.

In the eyes of Inazo Nitobe, the Japanese undersecretary of the League of Nations, Esperanto was a promising prospect "for meeting the demands of science and commerce and the still higher needs of an instrument for international understanding." But when he visited the 1921 Universal Congress in Prague, his attention was absorbed by the emergence of SAT: "The poor and humble make of Esperanto a lingua franca for their exchange of views," he wrote, declaring Esperanto a language for "the masses."[32] That Esperanto appeared to be a language for "the masses" doomed its claim to be a fourth working language (besides English, French, and Spanish) for the elite delegates of the League of Nations.

From the start, the League confined its interest in Esperanto to a debate about Esperanto instruction in the schools of member nations. A proposal to study the matter was signed by thirteen countries, including

China, Japan, and India.[33] According to the historian Carolyn Biltoft, the secretariat convened an "International Conference on the Teaching of Esperanto in Schools," following it up with a survey about current Esperanto activities. Respondents reported Esperantist activity in Albania, Bulgaria, Japan, China, and Germany; in Brazil and Russia, commissions were studying the matter. Even in British-dominated India, a nascent Esperanto movement propounded internationalism as India's path to modernity. And from Persia came a blank survey with a ministerial pronouncement at the bottom: "As soon as all the member states of the League admit the teaching of Esperanto in their countries, the Persian government will follow also their example."[34]

But in the ensuing 1922 debate, Raul de Rio Branco of Brazil denounced Esperanto to the League of Nations as a language of "ne'er-do-wells and communists."[35] He then published a paranoid anti-Esperanto pamphlet, warning that "in the hands of that subversive party and its subaltern clients, a universal language would eventually be the language of an anti-national army."[36] In France, the same year, Léon Bérard, the minister of public education, issued a circular expressly prohibiting Esperanto instruction because it would destroy "the Latin spirit and French genius in particular"; the minister even forbade the use of school facilities for any Esperantist activity.[37] Neither brokered compromises nor amendments could compel the League's Third Assembly to endorse Esperanto instruction; instead, the assembly transferred the question of Esperanto to the International Committee on Intellectual Cooperation (ICIC),[38] the earliest incarnation of UNESCO. There, President Henri Bergson was under strict instructions from Bérard to "drown" Esperanto,[39] which he did, filing a report so ridden with misapprehensions that it verged on libel. (Bergson, a French Jewish philosopher who had declined to support Dreyfus publicly, may well have been among those seeking to distance themselves from the Judaic aura of Esperanto.) In August 1923, in the penumbra of Bergson's report, the ICIC announced to the assembly that it was "incompetent" to decide on the matter of an international artificial language.

For a time, two proponents of Esperanto well placed within the League struggled on. One was the delegate from the dominion of South Africa, Lord Robert Cecil, author of the failed 1922 resolution on education; the other, the wily, irresistible Edmond Privat, Hodler's friend and collaborator, who at eighteen had wangled an audience with President

Theodore Roosevelt and later became an intimate of Gandhi's.[40] To promote Esperanto, Privat had exchanged his translator's post for an unpaid position within the Persian delegation.[41] Perhaps this is why the last significant act of the League regarding Esperanto was a Persian initiative: Esperanto, a tongue that tens of thousands of people spoke fluently, was upgraded from "code" to "clear language" in telegraphy. Those who yearned to hear the nations address one another in Esperanto would have to be content with saving a few coins on the tariffs on telegrams.

* * *

After three calamities—the SAT schism, Esperanto's failure to gain a purchase in the League of Nations, and the death of founder Hector Hodler—the UEA was in a precarious position. The Paris-based Central Office, which was in thrall to powerful national organizations, pressed the Geneva-based UEA to accept an integrated, international structure. At the Universal Congress of 1922, to avoid a second schism, the UEA accepted the Helsinki Compromise, an uneasy balance of power between national organizations and the loose alliance of individuals in the UEA. On the one hand, the compromise was too weak to stave off nationalist interests permanently; on the other, it brought a modicum of stability for the next decade, which fostered Esperantic activity in the fields of commerce, science, education, and culture.

The 1920s saw the emergence of several conferences designed to promote Esperanto among the elites of various professions. In 1925, a conference to promote Esperanto in science and technology took place in Paris; participants, mostly non-Esperantists, came from thirty-three countries, with ten governments sending official emissaries.[42] Coinciding with this conference was another to promote the use of Esperanto in commerce. The conveners set out to adapt for commerce mini-dictionaries invented in 1905 by a German chemist named Herbert F. Höveler. Within a year of their appearance, Höveler's "keys," as he called them, became wildly popular: a British major general named George Cox reported in 1906 that they had already been published in eight European languages, with "Chinese and Japanese editions . . . in preparation." Soon they would be available in eighteen languages. Cox described the key as "a tiny book, costing 1/2d . . . weighing 1/5 of an ounce . . . containing a vocabulary of over 2500 roots, with explanations of the suffixes, formation of words, etc etc. gives you the language in a nutshell"[43]—quite a contrast to Cox's own 416-page grammar of Esperanto.[44]

Esperanto in schools, even after the defeat of the League of Nations resolution, remained a focus of UEA activism. A 1927 multilingual conference called "Peace Through the School" convened nearly five hundred, of whom three in four had some competence speaking Esperanto.[45] Meanwhile, the UEA also capitalized on the presence of scholars among its rank and file, sponsoring an "Esperanto Summer University" at each Universal Congress. In addition to erudite lectures on "Esperantology," one could hear university faculty lecture on psychoanalysis, "long distance cables, magnetism, standardization of monetary systems, and Spanish folklore."[46] The tradition persists to this day, though the Summer University became the International Congress University in July 1987, when it took place during a Brazilian winter.

With every expansion of Esperanto's reach into these and other fields, the "language of ne'er-do-wells and communists" leaped forward with the accretion of new, specialized glossaries. Whereas the period before World War I saw a variety of idealist and religious groups embrace Esperanto, the 1920s saw the emergence of affinity groups based on a common profession or hobby. An article from 1928 lists "aviators, bankers, blind people, boy scouts, Catholics, doctors, engineers, Freemasons, free-thinkers, lawyers, pacifists, philatelists, policemen, postal servants, railwaymen, stenographers, scientists, teachers, vegetarians, etc. . . ."[47] For each constituency, the pattern was to hold an inaugural meeting at a congress, then launch a journal such as the *Internacia Pedagogia Revuo* (International Pedagogical Review), which brought the number of Esperanto magazines to "nearly 100."[48]

The language was also enhanced by poets, who coined new words to replace cumbersome compound words that were unsuited to metered verse. Zamenhof had made a distinction between new words that were coined to expand the range of Esperanto, and neologisms which went head-to-head with sanctioned words already in use. Zamenhof's attitude toward neologisms (and he contributed some himself) was rather lenient: the community would eventually decide the matter by using or not using them, and time would tell. But after Zamenhof's death in 1917, neologisms became a polarizing issue. Lanti endorsed them, but their opponents maintained that they threatened the integrity of the language; why retire words that had only recently been minted for circulation? And all for the sake of making Esperanto poetry sound more like French and Italian verse? Indeed, most neologisms were drawn from romance languages. Because the negating prefix *mal-* was a particular bane of poets, about seventy-five *mal-* words (by the count of Esperantologist David K. Jordan), have at various times been supplanted by sleeker romance alternatives. *Mallonga* (brief), for example, was sometimes replaced by *breva*; *malĝoja* (sad), by *trista*. But as Zamenhof had predicted, time *did* tell. Most *mal-* words remained in use alongside their neological rivals; as Jordan notes, many neologisms, if they survived at all, would in time take on a more narrow semantic reference than the words they challenged.[49]

One of the great champions of neologisms was the Hungarian poet Kálmán Kalocsay. While a few notable poets emerged in Esperanto's early years, Kalocsay presided, in Budapest, over the first literary "school" of original Esperanto writers; others would emerge in Spain, Italy, Scotland, and elsewhere. Chief of medicine at the Budapest Hospital for Infectious Diseases, Kalocsay published in 1921 his accomplished debut volume of poems, *Mondo kaj Koro* (World and Heart). Into exquisite poems written in traditional forms, Kalocsay wove seductive, off-kilter metaphors and coined neologisms that would permanently enrich the language. Just as Zamenhof's publications had found a patron in the wealthy Wilhelm Trompeter, Kalocsay was bankrolled by Esperantist Teodor Schwartz, also known as Tivadar Soros. (His son, a young Esperantist named George Soros, would use the occasion of the 1947 Universal Congress in Bern to defect to the UK.[50]) Kalocsay's journal, *Literatura Mondo*, printed on huge, creamy pages with lavish art nouveau woodcuts in seafoam and crimson, also became the venue for his translations of Hungarian poets, as well as "Baudelaire, Dante, Goethe, Heine, Pushkin, Shakespeare and Keats, among others."[51]

Kalocsay's coeditor on *Literatura Mondo* was the versatile Julio (Gyula) Baghy, actor, dramatist, poet, and feuilletonist. The same year *Literatura Mondo* was founded, Baghy debuted with *Preter la Vivo* (Beyond Life), a wrenching volume of poems about his ordeal as a prisoner of war in Siberia. Baghy's 1927 *Dancu, Marionetoj* (Dance, Marionettes) was one of several popular collections of stories, sketches, and satires. Kalocsay was a poet's poet, but Baghy was, in Auld's phrase, "the people's poet"; it was Baghy who always sold more books. Kalocsay and Baghy collaborated not only on *Literatura Mondo*, but also on the *Hungara Antologio*, one of the many national anthologies of poetry translated into Esperanto. Taken together, these books are Exhibit A to defend Esperanto when it's charged with dissolving national cultures.

During the 1920s, with the institutional future of Esperanto in limbo, Esperanto became a go-to metaphor for cultural boundary crossings of many kinds: among them, radio broadcasting, cinema, and museums for working-class audiences. In 1924, Esperanto was propelled into the world of broadcasting—the "empire of the air"—delivering cultural capital to eyes and ears around the world. That year, a Geneva conference attended by delegates from nearly forty radio companies and societies unanimously passed a resolution supporting "*an* Esperanto"—but not Esperanto per se.[52] Soon radio would be known as the "Esperanto of the Ear," and cinema the "Esperanto of the Eye." What we now call "the media" were still called miracles in the 1920s; in the words of the American novelist Edward S. Van Zile:

> The disappearance of the last frontier, the solving of Earth's ancient mysteries, the coming of the wireless and of the Esperanto of the Tongue and of the Eye, seem to presage some new revelation to the soul of man that shall remove forever from the entrance to the garden of eden, that angel with the flaming sword.[53]

In the case of cinema, for a few pennies virtually anyone—in Van Zile's words, "illiterates and even morons"[54]—could have access to content that was unconstrained and unmanaged. In the United States, fear that federal authorities would censor the "Esperanto of the Eye" provoked the film industry to begin to self-police, issuing guidelines that came to be known as the Hays Code.

"A new Esperanto" is what the Viennese social theorist Otto Neurath called his Isotypes, a visual language he developed for his "Museum of Society and Economy," which was open at night for the education of workers. "The problem of an international language," Neurath recalled in a memoir, "attracted me fairly early. Volapük had come and gone; Esperanto reigned uneasily in its place."[55] Collaborating with the artist Gerd Arnzt and the designer Marie Reidemeister (whom he later married), Neurath created an immutable, self-evident symbol—a faceless, monochrome pants-wearing human—that would be accessible across classes and cultures. Isotypes, Neurath wrote, were "as neutral as maps"—a dubious proposition, since as Phil Patton has shown, Isotypes were not

free of stereotypes: in one chart, racial types were indicated by tur-
bans, derbies, and "coolie" hats, as well as by various "skin" colors.[56]
Nonetheless, two-dimensional and cheaply reproduced, Isotypes had legs.
Today, they're the abstract silhouettes that tell us whether we're pushing
open the door of a men's room, a ladies' room or, with a new symbol
combining male and female silhouettes, an "all-gender" bathroom. But
in 1933, when Neurath presented his Isotypes to the Russell Sage Foundation in New York, they were still a novelty. According to a bemused
New York Times reporter, Neurath's "Picture Esperanto" was "understand-
able to all peoples"; but "two interpreters and a prompter" were required
"to translate from Dr. Neurath's German into English."[57]

3. *Amerika Esperantisto*

Had Neurath addressed the New Yorkers in Esperanto, it would hardly
have helped.

The history of American indifference to Esperanto is rooted in an
American paradox, articulated best by the historian Jill Lepore: "American nationalism has universalist origins." A supreme deity had blessed
the new republic, and rights were conveyed by nature, rather than ceded
by governments. Thus, to be American, in the early days of the Republic,
was to be a universalist—in theory, at least, leaving nativism, racism, and
intolerance aside. However, as Lepore has argued, the universalist impulse to cross cultures was eclipsed by the more pressing need to distinguish the young republic from Great Britain. Even though one in every
four Americans spoke English as a second language, the burning question
of the day was how to distinguish American from British English.[58] Cross-
cultural universalism became the domain of evangelicals, of phoneticists
such as Alexander Melville Bell, and by the 1860s, of the creators of the
telegraph and telephone (invented by Bell's son, Alexander Graham Bell).

By the early twentieth century, after waves of emigration from Ire-
land, Italy, Germany, and the Pale of Settlement, the United States was
home to three million non-English-speaking immigrants[59] who had to
fend for themselves when it came to learning English, mostly in night
schools. Thus, while Esperanto was exploited in the Soviet Union for its
centrifugal, international reach, in the United States, a few intrepid indi-

viduals seized upon its centripetal potential to unify a multiethnic, multilingual populace. Race, too, played a role in the history of Esperanto in the United States where it was used to offer Afro-Americans a new identity as world citizens. And while Esperanto was used to promote social ideals about ethnicity and race, as well as to reject isolationism, American Esperanto groups tended toward pragmatism, strategically presenting the language as a practical boon to travel and commerce.

The history of Esperanto in the United States starts with an eccentric, immigrant adventurer with a gift for languages. Richard Geoghegan was a young Irish linguist studying Chinese at Oxford when he struck up a correspondence with Zamenhof, who asked him to translate the *Unua Libro* into English. Geoghegan's *Dr. Esperanto's International Language, Introduction & Complete Grammar* (1889) immediately became the standard English version. Two years later Geoghegan, his widowed mother, and several siblings emigrated to the state of Washington, where he supported himself as a stenographer, learned Japanese, and wrote papers on linguistics in his spare time. In 1903,[60] Geoghegan took up a post as a court stenographer in Fairbanks, Alaska, where he secretly married a Martiniquais woman and eventually wrote a classic dictionary and grammar of the Aleutian language.[61] To recognize his dedication and linguistic accomplishments, Geoghegan was elected, in absentia, to the precursor of the Academy of Esperanto in 1905. That year, the first American Esperanto club met in Boston, and within three years, there were sixty-six Esperanto clubs in the United States.[62] In 1908, the *Esperanto-Asocio de Norda Ameriko* (EANA, or North American Esperanto Association) was founded and the first American Esperanto congress took place at Chautauqua, New York, a mecca for progressives in the fields of culture, religion, and philosophy.

Early debates about Esperanto in the United States address the practicality, feasibility, and ideology of the language in a distinctly American framework:

> "So the horse is a [organic] growth; yet man makes the iron horse, and this marvelous creature of strength, speed, and endurance goes from New York City to Chicago in twenty hours." It is preposterous for an age that can talk through a thousand miles of wire to say that it cannot speak any language that has never been used for centuries by savages and barbarians.[63]

Esperantists testified that the *lingvo internacia* was an irresistible and inevitable form of progress, well suited to promote U.S. commerce:

> [I]n this age of commercialism . . . there is certainly not the "natural charm" to coin that there is to wheat or corn, meat or vegetables, wool or silk, products of the earth beautiful in their growth, but the members of the family of nations need one basis of exchange. . . . This place Esperanto will fill in the meeting of the nations in business, science, literature. . . .[64]

On the con side were two distinct voices. One was an elite, Europhilic voice that lampooned Esperanto's naiveté about international relations. Its tireless spokesman was William L. Alden, the London correspondent to the *New York Times*, who in 1903 declared Esperanto to be "a sort of Italian gone wrong in company with some Slavonic tongue."[65] When the Touring Club of France endorsed Esperanto, Alden acidly remarked that "it is an extremely patriotic club, as it proved when it expelled Zola because he asked for justice for Dreyfus."[66] A year later, he conceded that "Esperanto is rapidly becoming a fashion. . . . [I]t is spoken by hundreds of thousands, and there is actually growing up what the Esperantists call an Esperanto literature." But lest Esperanto make a claim to high culture, he added:

> The advocates of Esperanto seem especially anxious that it should be spoken by all persons who ride bicycles or rush about the country in motor cars. Their idea probably is that when the cyclist or the motor car driver runs down somebody and is charged with the offense he can pretend to speak nothing but Esperanto, and by that trick may tire out the constable who questions him. [67]

Only Alden's death in 1908 stemmed the tide of ridicule. That year, a similar position was voiced by Arkád Mogyoróssy, a Hungarian immigrant who wrote under the Latinized name "Arcadius Avellanus." Esperanto was as useless, he wrote, as "the respective idioms now spoken in Italy, France, Spain, and other countries; . . . those idioms," he lamented, "are nothing else than as many 'esperantos.'"[68] No wonder Mogyoróssy was exercised; he had already translated *Treasure Island* into "Living Latin," his own candidate for a universal language.

The other opposing voice regarded Esperanto as inimical to American capitalism. In August 1907, a *New York Times* article observed the coincidence of the closing ceremonies of the International Socialist Congress in Stuttgart and of the UEA Congress in Cambridge, England. Trading on the myth that Esperanto sought "to obliterate the literature of the world and the beauties of national speech," the writer propounded a linguistic Darwinism: "The political institutions which experience will prove the most worthy . . . will survive. . . . It is the same with languages. In neither category is there room for an artificial social system or a language that lacks a history."[69]

Esperanto seemed poised for such a Darwinian selection in 1906, when it came before the Delegation for the Adoption of an International Auxiliary Language in Paris. That December, George Brinton McClellan Harvey, the editor of the widely read *North American Review*, launched a serialized teach-yourself Esperanto textbook. Harvey, an Esperanto enthusiast, solicited a contribution from Zamenhof himself, who assured American readers that "Esperanto is, and always will remain, the language of freedom, neutrality and international justice."[70] In the throes of yet another revision of *Homaranismo*, Zamenhof vowed that:

> the actual golden light of Justice and Brotherhood among the nations will come not out of chauvinistic Europe, where almost every spot of land bears the name of some tribe; where, naturally, each of those sections are guarded as the exclusive property of its particular tribe, and those not of that tribe born within that territory are regarded as strangers. No, that light must come out of great, free, democratic America.[71]

Zamenhof's Esperanto name for the United States was *Usono*, a word derived from Usona or Usonia, two contemporary coinages designed to distinguish U.S. citizens from those of other North and South American countries.[72] But writing in the penumbra of pan-Americanism, Zamenhof used the word "America" to mean "the countries of America."[73]

> Absolute equality—which has become a kind of Americanized goddess—and voluntary federation of all countries on the American continent—the hope of many of the best men in the

Western Hemisphere—will be completely attainable only when a neutral language will come into use for general communication.[74]

* * *

While the Paris delegation was thrashing out the relative merits of Esperanto and Ido, the *Times* reported "trouble in the rank of the local Esperantians."[75] The defection of the New York Esperanto Society's leadership to "Elo," as it was erroneously called (a month later, the paper would call it "Ilo"), garnered a four-tier headline in the *Times*:

> **Give Up Esperanto, Will Now Speak Elo [sic]**
> **Members of New York Society Decide**
> **That Esperanto Is an Impossible Language**
> **Say It Is Full of Defects**
> **They Vote to Take Up Elo in Its Place—**
> **Col. Harvey Defends the One They Abandon**

Ido partisan Andrew Kangas wrote a lengthy letter to the *New York Times* charging that Esperanto lay in the clutches of a "pontifical orthodoxy"; Ido, he argued, deserved the embrace of freedom-loving Americans. Even the president of the New York Esperanto Society, Max Talmey, resigned to embrace Ido, which he called "a more melodious and a modulated Esperanto." Like so many Idists, Talmey soon became disenchanted, and by 1924 had developed Arulo (Auxiliary Rational Universal Language) which, renamed Gloro (*Gloto Racionoza*, rational language), he presented in 1937 to the "Jewish Club" in New York City. In his bid for publicity, Talmey had one distinct advantage: as a medical student in Munich, he had befriended ten-year-old Albert Einstein, lending him recondite texts in mathematics and physics. Reunited with Einstein in the United States in 1921 after a nineteen-year hiatus,[76] Talmey popularized Einstein's theory of relativity and gave interviews about his now famous mentee. No surprise, then, that at the unveiling of Gloro, in the words of a reporter from *Time*, "one of the most interested auditors was Friend Einstein."[77]

The Ido melodrama in New York turned on charges of a very American malfeasance: false advertising. To Arthur Brooks Baker, the founder and editor of *Amerika Esperantisto*, Ido was snake oil; Kangas, "with one exception the most rapid talker the writer of this article has ever heard."[78]

Before the Idists surrendered the Esperanto brand, wrote Baker, "they used it for one last spasm of advertising, us[ing] the crude method of the dishonest grocer, and offer[ing] the public something 'just like Esperanto,' 'as good as Esperanto,' 'simplified Esperanto,' 'dessicated Esperanto,' 'boneless Esperanto,' etc."[79]

Marketing Esperanto was Baker's expertise. He lectured at civic centers, schools, and public halls, flogging Esperanto at the New York Electrical Show in Madison Square Garden: "Electricity is the quickest and most modern force of its kind. Esperanto is the quickest and most modern language."[80] No profession was beyond an appeal; the researcher Ralph Dumain attributes to Baker an article called "Esperanto for Clay-workers," published in *Brick* magazine in 1908:

> Have you received in your office letters written in German, French or Spanish, which you, as a layman, could not decipher? . . . If so Esperanto might be a friend in disguise! . . . Might not some worker in clay on the Continent, in Africa, in Japan, be encountering the same difficulties that you are trying to overcome?[81]

In such pitches Baker, who also advocated lower tariffs in his *Insurgency* magazine, was tacitly pitting Esperanto against American isolationism.

Quite another type of sales pitch was used by eighteen-year-old Edmond Privat during his 1907–1908 American tour: sex appeal. After he lectured to the women at Normal (later Hunter) College, "fifty names were given of girls who will take lessons in a class which [he] will start this week. . . . The Normal College girls say they are going to talk nothing but Esperanto among themselves."[82] The girls from Washington Irving High School, eager for lessons, had to get in line. As a concept, rather than a language, Esperanto had already percolated into popular culture, and once waltzes, tony brownstones, and schooners had been named for it, Esperanto was ripe for seedier settings. Bennet C. Silver, a Jewish extortionist who targeted Jewish victims, signed himself "Esperanto, Chief of the Black Hand." And in Kansas City, "a romance which sprang from the warm and mutual interest in Esperanto, the international language," ended in the murder of Frank W. Anderson, the manager of a department store, by Peggy Marie L. Beal, a Dayton nurse. The weapon—a revolver; the motive—"the eternal triangle." As if life imitated art, a sensation novel was found nearby, its cover depicting "a woman dancer, dagger in hand, standing over the prostrate form of a man." Tawdry, familiar tabloid fare, except that the lovers' "letters contained frequent passages in Esperanto."[83]

4. Vaŝingtono

In 1910 Ludovik and Klara Zamenhof, along with eighty-one other European Esperantists,[84] boarded the SS *George Washington* for New York. It was the Zamenhofs' first trip to the United States, and the first time the Universal Congress was held in the Western Hemisphere; most of the 357 conferees were Americans who had never before been to a congress. A group of "one hundred and twenty lady Esperantists" from Torquay, England, delegated a fellow Briton to convey their greeting of one hundred and twenty kisses,[85] and thirteen governments, as well as the U.S. Department of War, sent official representatives.

Mobbed at Washington, D.C.'s Union Station by a throng of Esperantists, Zamenhof spoke to the press through an interpreter: "New York completely dazzle[d] him. . . . He says that it is so colossal, so splendid in what might be termed a semi-barbaric manner, so vibrant with energy that it literally stunned him. He wishes me to repeat that he is amazed, startled, astonished and everything else that expresses the superlative degree of wonderment."[86] American "semi-barbarity" notwithstanding, Zamenhof stressed that his mission was to cultivate the seeds of Esperanto in American soil. At the inaugural session, he delivered a rapturous salute to the "land of liberty":

The Tenth Universal Congress, Washington, D.C., 1910

> Thou land of which have dreamed and still dream multitudes of
> the suffering and oppressed . . . [l]and of a people which belongs
> not to this or that tribe or church, but to . . . all her honest sons,
> I am happy that fate has permitted me to see you and to breathe
> at least for a little while your free and unmonopolized air.[87]

Newspapers in Washington, New York, Baltimore, Boston, and else-where were less interested in Zamenhof's rhetoric than in the lively ancillary events. They sprinkled their coverage with Esperanto phrases: "'Kiel Vi Sanas?'/This is How Esperantists, Gathering in Washington, Greet Each Other";[88] "'Bonan Vesperon' the Greeting on All Sides in Washington."[89] At a Washington-Cleveland baseball game, "umpires' decisions were given in Esperanto, and books of baseball rules, printed in the international language, were distributed."[90] The linguist and grammarian Ivy Kellerman Reed furnished the congress with her new translation of *As You Like It,* staged to high acclaim. The fluency of the participants, as well as the ease with which Esperanto could be learned, was cause for wonder: "Nothing but Esperanto is used by the delegates in conversation, and four Washington policemen . . . were taught the language in a few weeks."[91]

While the Washington gathering did not achieve the full harvest Zamenhof had hoped, Esperanto did attain a new degree of respectabil-ity. By 1912, a course was offered at Stanford, and an Esperanto Club boast-ing twenty members had formed at Cornell.[92] Already in the lists of the debate about Esperanto were two Princeton professors. Theodore W. Hunt, the first chair of the department of English, closed the 1908 Modern Language Association meeting with a statement dismissing Esperanto and other constructed languages: "Whatever purely commercial or util-itarian purpose they may subserve, they can never rise to the plane of language as the expression of thought for the highest ends. . . ."[93] Hunt's opposite number was Esperantist George Macloskie, a retired Princeton biologist, who chatted amiably to the *North American Review* about his *samideanoj*: "army and navy officers . . . London business people . . . French priests." Esperanto's phonics, he pointed out, were no harder to understand than his own Scottish brogue. Besides, as the translator of the Gospel of Matthew into Esperanto, Macloskie could well claim that Es-peranto was a far more flexible language than English: "English has not two words [as does Esperanto] to denote the difference between the two kinds of baskets used for the crumbs left after two different occasions of feeding the multitude."[94]

On June 21, 1911, Esperanto entered the halls of the Capitol in Washington. Veteran Esperantist Richard Bartholdt of Missouri, a German-born congressman and former editor-in-chief of the *St. Louis Tribune*, introduced HR 220, a proposal to study whether Esperanto might facilitate "the social and commercial intercourse of the people of the United States and those of other countries." After the House passed the resolution, the Esperanto Association of North America swung into high gear, distributing a million free copies of "A Glimpse of Esperanto," which doubled as propaganda leaflet and brief grammar.[95] But in February 1914, having failed for two years to "get action," Bartholdt put forward a radically pared-down proposal "that Esperanto be taught as a part of the course of study in the schools of Washington, this being the only jurisdiction we have in the matter of education."[96]

The hearing on HR 415 took place on Tuesday, March 17, 1914. A Professor A. Christen, of Columbia, testified about the importance of Esperanto for Americans. First, "in at least 87 cases out of 100, you will find [that Esperanto] words connect with one or many English words."[97] Second, Esperanto could aid in assimilating the nation's immigrants, upwards of 14 percent of the population.[98] Third, Americans had already registered their enthusiasm in Chautauqua, Buffalo, New York, Philadelphia, Pittsburgh, and Washington; moreover, elite universities, including Columbia and the University of Pennsylvania, "have shown their open-mindedness to the extent of engaging a paid lecture . . . [and] so has the Department of Education of the city of New York."

Brandishing tourist leaflets in Esperanto from Milan, Poitiers, Innsbruck, and Davos, Christen thrust before the committee a heap of forty commercial catalogues in Esperanto:

> For instance, here is a very elaborate, costly, and handsome catalogue from the biggest firm of photographic instrument makers in Germany, and, I believe, in the world. . . . Here is a bookseller in Paris issuing a catalogue entirely in Esperanto. Here is a leaflet about the Panama Exposition published in Esperanto. Here is a catalogue issued by the Oliver Typewriter Co. printed in Esperanto. Cook's famous touring agency has used Esperanto for the last seven years. Here is a Scotch tea firm publishing a circular in

Esperanto. Here is a bicycle saddle maker in Germany using Esperanto for publicity. . . . Here is a very big Anglo-American firm of medical supplies, Burroughs, Wellcome & Co., and they use Esperanto in many of their circulars. . . .

With some mendacity, Christen described the UEA as "purely a commercial league for the coordained [sic] use of the language," assuring his audience that "Esperanto is only an 'auxiliary' language. Nobody dreams of its being a universal language."[99]

HR 415 never made it through committee, and the Sixty-Third Congress adjourned without debating whether to provide the children of Washington, D.C., nearly one-third of them African American, with lessons in Esperanto.[100] But as Dumain has shown, a young black man from the deep South was already advocating Esperanto to help African Americans cross racial barriers, access foreign cultures, and become citizens of the world.[101]

Born in South Carolina in 1881, William Pickens earned a BA in two years at Talladega College, then matriculated at Yale, where he earned a second B.A. in classics.[102] When Pickens, in his mid-twenties, seized on Esperanto as a novel means of racial uplift, a humorist in the *Boston Herald* was mocking it as "a new inter-racial language": "[With Esperanto] one might travel at will . . . among the Kalmuck Tartars or people of Borneo, and ask for koumiss or headmoney and get it every time."[103] But for Pickens, Esperanto fit snugly into the ethos of self-improvement espoused by *Voice of the Negro*:

> The writer saw his first book on Esperanto less than a week ago. [Some books] arrived and were perused one evening between the hours of six and ten; and the next morning he wrote letters in Esperanto to some European Esperantists. . . . Any man of any language of Europe or America, who is of sound mind and well trained in his mother tongue, can master the syntax of Esperanto in a week.

With a modest investment of time and effort, African Americans would never need to fear being "socially embarrassed when we go abroad"[104]— probably not an issue for Pickens, who spoke six languages.[105]

In Pickens, Esperanto had attracted an eloquent, impassioned evangelist; his harsh riposte to the "natural language" skeptics is worth quoting at length:

> Nature is an extravagant and erratic idiot who pampers variety rather than utility. She lays within the stream a myriad eggs to raise a dozen fishes; she sows a hundred acorns to sprout two or three sickly oaks. Everywhere she wantonly mixes and mingles the useful and the useless. Just so in these natural tongues she will write a half dozen words meaning the same thing. . . . She will obey no single rule without a half dozen exceptions. All in all, she has so mixed and muddled and anticked in the every-day speech of men . . . [that] the masses of mankind, so far as Nature's languages are concerned, will never be intelligent beings save in that tongue to which they were born.
>
> By the scheme of Esperanto, Dr. Zamenhof, the Russian, has removed the whole difficulty. . . . Science can be frugal if Nature is prodigal.[106]

Embracing an artificial language, Pickens offered his readers a glimpse of a world in which nature—savage, wasteful, unjust, and amoral—no longer determined human opportunity. Although Pickens's advocacy for Esperanto, which earned him a certificate from the British Esperanto Association, was apparently short-lived, he devoted his multifarious career as an academic, NAACP field director, and seller of War Bonds to African Americans to this pitched battle between nature and culture. When he died in 1954 during a cruise to Jamaica, he was buried neither on Southern nor on Northern soil but, at his wife's request, at sea.

5. A Map in One Color

Whereas Soviet *samideanoj* endorsed the imperial reach of the USSR and Americans proposed Esperanto's value to a multicultural yet isolationist superpower, Esperanto in the Far East emerged within an anarchist, anti-imperialist milieu. In the early decades of the twentieth century, Esperanto empowered East Asian reformers to cross boundaries as they strove toward a pan-Asian alternative to the Western norm of a sovereign, territorially bounded state.[107] It may seem unlikely that a language comprising the "dismembered" tongues of Europe could help to define modernity in Japan and China, but Esperanto did.

In the wake of the Russo-Japanese War of 1904–1905, Tokyo became a breeding ground for the new "non-war" movement,[108] a group of young anarchists devoted to an anationalist, peaceful vision of the future. From within this subversive nest, the Japanese Esperanto movement was hatched in 1906 by the anarchist Osugi Sakae. His most influential student was the Chinese scholar Liu Shipei, who predicted, as Lanti would some years later, that Esperanto would become the crucial bonding agent of a world socialist movement. Though Esperanto would never replace the cultural heritage of the Chinese language, Liu Shipei wrote from Tokyo, it was the only foreign language the Chinese would need in the twentieth century. And once the Chinese dictionary was translated into Esperanto, he prophesied, Chinese could be made accessible abroad.

Liu Shipei's view of the Chinese language as a sacred trust was opposed by a radical circle of Chinese anarchists based in Paris. They deemed Chinese a "barbaric" obstacle to modernization and democratization,[109] advocating its replacement by a phonetic language; Esperanto would fit the bill. But even those Chinese who were favorably inclined toward Esperanto quailed at this extreme position, putting forward a gradualist program instead. The charge of "barbarism" provoked journalist Zhang Binglin to call Esperanto an "unnatural" language of "the whites" that would reify China's inferiority and hasten its deracination. Ultimately, his journal espoused a more moderate position on Esperanto, as part of a three-point agenda: standardizing the pronunciation of Chinese; requiring knowledge of one Western language to qualify for high school (and two to qualify for university); and teaching Esperanto in schools as soon as it became feasible.[110]

The third point was not as far-fetched as it sounds. In 1912, Minister of Education Cai Yuanpei decreed that Esperanto be offered as an optional course in teacher-training schools.[111] Meanwhile, the progressive New Culture Movement turned its attention in 1915 to the reform of Chinese characters, and Esperanto gained new advocates as a transitional resource for modernization. When he became rector of Peking University in 1917, Cai Yuanpei established both an Esperanto major within the Chinese-language department[112] and a research school, the Peking University Esperanto Institution. After a Zamenhof Day congress at Peking University drew two thousand people, Cai Yuanpei was emboldened to

set up the Peking Esperanto College in 1922, hiring the eminent writer
Lu Xun, as well as Russian and U.S. Esperantists, to teach literature.[113]
Though he did not write in Esperanto, Lu Xun became a distinguished
advocate for the *lingvo internacia*:

> In my opinion, humanity will certainly have a common lan-
> guage, and for this reason, I approve of Esperanto. Nonetheless,
> I can't be certain whether Esperanto will be the future universal
> language. . . . But now only Esperanto exists, so one can only
> begin by learning it. . . . To speak metaphorically, [if you need]
> a powerboat [and refuse to even] build a canoe or get around in
> one . . . the result [will be] that you never invent a powerboat
> either, and never cross a river.[114]

Substitute "bridge" for "powerboat," and voilà—Zamenhof's own favorite
metaphor for Esperanto.

* * *

Until the end of World War II, the fate of the "invisible empire" of Esperanto in Asia was inextricably linked to the imperial ambitions of Japan.
While in China, anarchists dominated Esperantic circles, the situation in
the Japan Esperanto Association (JEA) was more fractious. Like the Esperantist theosophists in Europe, many Japanese pacifists and anarchists
sought spiritual meaning in Esperanto. For some, this meant embracing
Zamenhof's Homaranism; for others, a young offshoot of Shintoism called
Oomoto (Great Source), which was founded and led by a sequence of child-
less women. By the early 1920s, the Oomoto sect had adopted Esperanto as
their world language, according Zamenhof the status of a minor divinity.

But when the repressive government stepped up surveillance of anarchists and Bolshevists, self-proclaimed Japanese "neutralists" of the JEA
split off to form the centrist Japanese Esperanto Institute (JEI). The neutralists avoided ruffling the feathers of the government, but as Lins has
shown, even a Homaranist faction in the JEI tacitly acquiesced in Japan's
occupation of Taiwan and annexation of Korea.[115] Although Japanese
police surveilled, harassed, and occasionally arrested Esperantists, several
defiant *samideanoj* openly criticized the government, propagandizing
against the regime both within Japan and outside it. Among those who
protested Japanese aggression, at great personal risk, were three Espe-

rantists who led extraordinarily itinerant and multicultural lives: Vasili Eroshenko, Ooyama Tokio, and Hasegawa Teru.

Born in what is now Ukraine in 1890, Eroshenko was blinded at age four by a case of measles. In the romantic annals of *Esperantujo*, Eroshenko's blindness was the source of his radical egalitarianism; as a Japanese journalist put it, "His eyes see people's skin in a single color and also the map of the world in one color."[116] By the time he graduated from a school for the blind in Moscow, Eroshenko was an accomplished violinist and competent in both Japanese and Esperanto. In April 1915, he was dispatched to Tokyo by the Russian Esperanto Federation,[117] where he propagandized for Esperanto, studied massage, and in short order became a celebrity. But for his traditional peasant shirt, Eroshenko might have stepped out of a portrait of a young quattrocentro nobleman. His broad, clear brow was framed by long blond ringlets, and he garnered huge crowds when he sang folk songs accompanied by his balalaika.[118]

Restless and venturesome, he left Japan two years later, sojourning in Thailand, Burma, and India; keeping a low profile was out of the question, and in 1919, probably on suspicion of Bolshevist activities, the British deported him from Calcutta. Via Afghanistan[119] and Russia, he soon returned to Japan, where he lived above a sweet shop frequented by Japanese transnationalists known as "worldists." According to Gotelind Müller, police archives reveal that Eroshenko was kept under close watch, not because he was under suspicion for Bolshevism but because of his "worldist"[120] entanglements. In 1921, after taking part in both a May Day demonstration and the congress of the Japanese Socialist Union, Eroshenko was again deported, this time from Japan to Russia, where his frank criticisms of the Bolshevists provoked a charge of espionage.

How Eroshenko managed to escape from a Russian prison ship to China is not known, but six months after his expulsion from Japan he appeared in Shanghai. By February 1922, he was living in Peking in the home shared by writer Lu Xun, his brother, and his brother's Japanese wife. By day Eroshenko worked as a masseur in a Japanese-owned spa; by night, appointed by Cai Yuanpei to a post at Peking Esperanto College, he taught Esperanto to more than five hundred students, supplementing his income with various lecturing jobs. That summer he traveled to Helsinki for the Universal Congress, returning to Peking. But the following summer, he left China to attend the Universal Congress in Nuremberg, never to return.

Vasili Eroshenko in China
[Österreichische Nationalbibliothek]

For the remainder of his life, Eroshenko tried to use his celebrity to ride not under the radar, but well above it. Like Zamenhof, who could tailor his self-presentation to his audience, Eroshenko was a chameleon. Back in the Soviet Union, he preserved himself by teaching at the Comintern's Far East University, a training school for East and South Asian communist operatives. (It had more colorful names, too: "Communist University of the Toilers of the East" and "Stalin School.") But even after translating Marx, Engels, and Lenin into Japanese, Eroshenko's true colors could not be concealed, and he was dismissed for being "ideologically unreliable."[121] He next became an ethnographer, documenting the condition of the blind among the indigenous Chukchi people in Siberia. Though he rarely if ever taught Esperanto, he published his Chukchi writings in an Esperanto Braille journal. He also knew when *not* to depend on his celebrity for safety; by fleeing to Turkmenistan in the 1930s, he managed to escape the Great Purges during which several hundred Esperantists were assassinated or sent to labor camps. The remaining twenty-three years of his life are not well documented, in part because the KGB burned his files.[122] After teaching stints in Tashkent and Moscow, Eroshenko returned to Ukraine, where in 1952, the man who had crisscrossed the map of the world as if it were indeed "all one color" died in the town of his birth.

Another multinational Esperantist who worked to undermine the Japanese regime was Ooyama Tokio. Born in Japan in 1898 and raised in Korea, Ooyama was the son of a Japanese bureaucrat in the occupation government. Against his parents' wishes, he married a Korean woman and together, after studying at Doshisha University in Kyoto, they made their home in Korea. Under his Esperanto pseudonym, "E. T. Montego," he wrote fervent appeals to Koreans, in Esperanto, to defy the Japanese colonization of Korean culture and hold fast to their right to use the Korean language. To promote Japanese-Korean relations, Ooyama founded a "Society for the Just Way," publishing a monthly magazine for the Japanese living in Korea.[123] The Japanese-language pages fiercely attacked Japanese stereotypes of Koreans, translated Korean writing for a Japanese audience, and unsparingly documented the Japanese colonization of Korea; the Esperanto pages featured translations of Korean writing as well. As a Japanese researcher recently revealed at a joint congress of Korean and Japanese Esperantists, Ooyama's transnational activism extended to a non-Esperanto journal as well. How risky a venture this was became clear when the journal was examined in 1997: entire articles were effaced by the censor, and on most pages, the censor left behind a trail of thick black tire-treads.[124]

The activism of Hasegawa Teru, another Japanese Esperantist who chose a transnational life of protest against her own government, took place mainly in China. Following the Chinese Revolution of 1925–1927, when the Guomindang banned anarchist unions, the majority of Esperantists made common cause with the Communist Party. In September 1931, following the Japanese invasion of Manchuria, twenty-one Chinese Esperanto groups jointly published a manifesto that skewered Japan's claim to be striving toward "All-Asian" harmony and against aggression by Western powers: "Although . . . the Japanese people is our brother . . . we unhesitatingly prepare to fight against those who damage world peace and dishonor the history of humanity, and principally against all those barbarities performed by fanatical patriots and imperialists."[125] An important voice of protest was the Shanghai-based "Ĉinio Hurlas" (China Howls), whose Manchuria reportage included sensational accounts of enslavement, the injection of Chinese youth with opium, and the suppression of the Chinese language.[126]

Hasegawa Teru, a Tokyo Rose in reverse

In the pages of this journal, Hasegawa Teru became a Tokyo Rose in reverse, exhorting Japanese Esperantists to protest their government. Born Hasegawa Teruko (she dropped the feminine diminutive "ko"), she was known in Esperanto circles by her pseudonym, "Verda Majo" (Green May). In 1932, at the age of twenty, she was arrested and expelled from college for her involvement in a proletarian literary movement. Her first Esperanto publication, commissioned by the Shanghai-based *La Mondo*, was an exposé on the condition of women in Japan, with a focus on the exploitation of women workers. Four years later, she secretly married Liu Ren, a Chinese student and Esperantist living in Tokyo, and scandalized her parents by following him to China. There she joined the Chinese resistance, calling on Esperantists of the world to boycott Japan.[127]

During the battle of Shanghai in August 1937, Hasegawa went into hiding for a time, then escaped with her husband to Canton (now Guangzhou), where she wrote blistering exposés of golf-playing Japanese generals sporting dapper European uniforms.[128] After an official order mandating the separation of Chinese-Japanese couples, Liu Ren tried to present her as an overseas Chinese, but the Guomintang were not fooled. The couple were deported to Hong Kong,[129] but with intervention from influential writers, they managed to relocate to Hankou, where she began propagandizing against the regime—this time, on the radio, and in Japanese, not Esperanto. It was a matter of time before the Japanese press denounced her as a "coquettish traitor,"[130] publishing her family's address and demanding a statement from her father, who, according to one memoir, received anonymous letters urging hara-kiri.[131] Hasegawa remained defiant: "Whoever calls me a traitor to my country, go ahead! I'm not afraid of this. I'm even ashamed of being a compatriot of those who not only invade another's territory, but also unrestrainedly make life hell for those who suffer innocently and helplessly."[132] She went on to write articles about Japanese war crimes such as sex slavery and medical experimentation, framing the Chinese resistance to Japan as part of a worldwide struggle against fascism.[133]

The optimism Hasegawa expressed when the war ended was crushed by the civil war between the Guomintang and the Communist Party. She, Liu Ren, and their two small children wandered through Manchuria for months in search of a livelihood and a stable home; she then became pregnant for a third time. Hungry, desperate, reluctant to bear a child for whom, in Müller's words, "she [saw] no future," Hasegawa had an abortion, contracted an infection, and died on January 10, 1947. She was thirty-five. Liu Ren, weakened, ill, and impoverished, died four months later of kidney failure, and their children were sent to an orphanage.

Since then, many have sought to redeem the tragic denouement of their lives. In 1980, they were Romeo-and-Julieted by a Chinese-Japanese television production; in the new millennium, however, the story has assumed a more optimistic ending. On August 18, 2000, a group of Chinese Esperantists brought about the first encounter between Hasegawa Teru and Liu Ren's two adult children and Ozawa Juki, their mother's sister. That Esperantists continue to honor Hasegawa's courageous activism (and, to a lesser extent, read her writings), belies the despairing title of her 1941 collection, *Whisper in a Hurricane*.[134]

Just as Hasegawa Teru's story can be told as an abysmal tragedy or as an affirmation of transnational, Esperantist values, there are also two ways of telling the subsequent story of Esperanto in China. For most Western historians, the glory days of the movement were the early, anarchist period. On this telling, once China's anarchist Esperantists made the liberation of China their primary agenda, they relinquished their freedom to be critics of nationalism. Such an account ignores the fact that, in that time and place, to sup at all was to sup with devils, whether the

Moscow-controlled Communist Party, the craven Guomintang, or the Japanese invaders. On the other hand, for those who write from within the eighty-year history of Esperanto's embrace of Communism, the telos of Esperanto in China was ever and always the founding of the People's Republic on two sturdy pillars: the evolution of Chinese society through popular revolution and the promotion of world peace. Figures are not available, but it is probable that the People's Republic of China has channeled more funds toward Esperanto, in absolute terms, than any other nation. For decades, the most handsomely produced magazine in the Esperanto world was *El Popola Ĉinio* (From the People's China), a dead ringer for *Life* magazine and as glossy as it was anti-Western.

It is difficult, if not impossible, to imagine a third story: what the future might have held for China's Esperantists, invaded, bombed, banned, and persecuted by the Japanese, had they not lived in the shadow of Japanese imperialism. As the *Concise History of the Chinese Esperanto Movement* (2004) bluntly puts it, "The guns and cannons of Japanese militarism took neutrality, pacifism, and Homaranism away from the Chinese Esperantists, and they were on the way to national liberation."[135]

6. "A Bastard Language"

Perhaps the unholiest alliance between Esperantists and a militarized, nationalist state occurred in Nazi Germany, under the dubious slogan "Through Esperanto for Germany." In 1933, soon after Hitler declared himself chancellor, the Universal Congress took place in Cologne with neither apology nor accommodation for Esperantist Jews, pacifists, and communists, to whom Nazism was anathema. Certainly no apology was forthcoming from Gunter Riesen, the Nazi mayor of Cologne, who according to Lins, saluted the nine-hundred-odd congress-goers (about half the usual number) in his brown shirt.[136]

In Cologne, the fragile Helsinki Contract fell apart, and the UEA surrendered to pressure to become a federation of national organizations. The revamped UEA was led by a French general named Louis Bastien; its vice president, a German banker named Anton Vogt, was a member of the Nazi Party. Schism finally came in 1936 when the federalists relocated their headquarters to London, forming a new entity called the Internacia Esperanto-Ligo (IEL). Within a year, membership in the Geneva-based

UEA had dwindled to 1,300, whereas the London-based IEL claimed 13,500.[137] And for ten years, despite repeated efforts to reunite the two groups at annual Universal Congresses, the UEA and the IEL were separate organizations, each with its own ideology, headquarters, executive, finances, yearbook, and journal.

In Germany, between the years 1933 and 1936, hundreds, perhaps thousands, of Esperantists did a perilous two-step with the Nazis. The National Socialist case against Esperanto, painstakingly compiled by Lins, took the high road of an argument about the mystical purity of German culture. Esperanto was "artificial, international, [and] pacifist"; a "bastard" language; "a purely mechanical, soulless creation." Like a worm in an apple, it sought to "latinize" German from within.[138] Esperanto, which Goebbels would call the "language of Jews and communists" (and which the Gestapo would call "the secret language of communists"), was for Hitler a way to conjure two imperial phantoms: Jewish hegemony and communist world revolution. In *Mein Kampf* (1925), he denounced a troika of Esperantists, communists, and Freemasons:

> On this first and greatest lie, that the Jews are not a race but a religion, more and more lies are based in necessary consequence. Among them is the lie with regard to the language of the Jew. For him it is not a means for expressing his thoughts, but a means for concealing them. When he speaks French, he thinks Jewish, and while he turns out German verses, in his life he only expresses the nature of his nationality. As long as the Jew has not become the master of the other peoples, he must speak their languages whether he likes it or not, but as soon as they became his slaves, they would all have to learn a universal language (Esperanto, for instance), so that by this additional means the Jews could more easily dominate them![139]

The Nazi language police, the Allgemeiner Deutscher Sprachverein, expressed contempt for Zamenhof's "bridge" language—a bridge over which foreign words would march to despoil German.[140] Hitler, as so often, spoke more plainly: "in one hundred years, [German] will be the language of Europe"—a glimpse of the future that prompted him, in 1940, to substitute gothic for roman lettering on official documents.[141]

Most vulnerable were the two-thirds of German Esperantists who belonged to the leftist German Labor Esperanto Association. The Nazis, having come to power in 1933, wasted no time in outlawing the GLEA. It was the first legal persecution of Esperantists in Germany, though slurs in the media, along with scattered acts of harassment and vandalism, went back to the twenties. Once Hitler arrested left-wing activists, banning both the GLEA and SAT, the "neutral" German Esperanto Association offered to propagandize for the Nazi regime. In articles proclaiming the motto "Through Esperanto for Germany," the GEA submitted to the Nazi protocol of *Gleichshaltung*, the compulsory, ideological "making same" of formerly independent bodies. Thus, at the Universal Congress in Cologne, the GEA passed a resolution to revoke the membership of persons with a "counter-state attitude," although a proposed clause barring membership for "non-aryans, marxists or communists" failed to carry. Despite the defeat of the "non-aryan" clause, Arnold Behrendt, the president of the GEA, asked all those running for president of a local group to submit papers attesting that they were neither Jewish nor Marxist.[142]

By then, a new Esperanto group created expressly to endorse the Nazi Party had emerged. Founded in 1931, it had a distinctly German name—Neue Deutsche Esperanto Bewegung (New German Esperanto Movement)— and a distinctly Nazi agenda: to obliterate dissent. In an Esperantist *Anschluss*, the NDEB deposed the GEA's president, put in a puppet, and annexed the group, who weakly protested that they had been fellow-travelers all along. By the time the alliance collapsed, the GEA's mission had become entirely Nazified: to spread "through Esperanto our national-socialist world-concept in all states of the world."[143] When in 1935, the GEA expelled Jews from its membership rolls, the NDEB was not to be outdone: they expelled Zamenhof himself, excising his name from all propaganda.

If the GEA thought to save Esperanto in Germany by embracing the Nazi Party, it was too late; it had always been too late. A cache of documents recovered from East German archives reveals that throughout the thirties and into the forties, Esperanto preoccupied the most powerful operatives of the Nazi state including Hitler, Himmler, Hess, Heydrich, Bormann, and Goebbels.[144] Contempt for Esperanto was axiomatic, since the Esperanto mind was as different as—say, the Jewish mind. In Heydrich's exquisite phrase, "Our conscience is German ... the 'human consciousness' is a Jewish creation and doesn't interest us."[145] In 1935, Heydrich attempted to ban Esperanto absolutely, but Goebbels preferred to have local police harass Esperantists and shut down their clubs. Esperanto was banned from schools; Nazi Party members were forbidden to join Esperanto organizations. By June 20, 1940, when Himmler announced a complete ban on Esperantist activity, it had already ground to a halt.

Even the Geneva-based UEA, which had resisted the encroachment of nationalism, took neutrality as its byword. Hans Jakob, the Swiss socialist who edited *Esperanto Revuo*, declined to print protests against the Nazification of Esperanto in Germany lest he violate "the chief principle of our association," political neutrality.[146] Nonetheless, *Esperanto Revuo* did publish "The German Viewpoint About the Race Problem" by "E. W.," who expressly adapted the Nazi Party's racist platform for Esperantists. In a farrago of quotations from Hitler and other leading Nazis, the author contended that strict laws against racial mixing were no more than a sign of respect for other cultures. Moreover, the Nazi state was on the side of human rights, insofar as it strove to guarantee each race's "right" to racial purity. After all, what was more universal than laws against racial mixing?

In the same issue appeared a contrary voice, an impassioned diatribe against militarism, chauvinism, and racism. In "Our Mission," the author reminded readers that Esperanto was not a language, but a sacred cause. It is a stern sermon full of grotesque, imposing metaphors—tsunamis, hydras, bone-gnawing dogs—that render graphically the grim stakes of the moment: "The world today is like a drowning person." Esperantists must not betray the *interna ideo,* "the desire to understand and empathize among ethnicities." The author was in no doubt that Esperanto could guide an armed and armored world toward peace, and she signed her full name: Lidia Zamenhof.[147] The "mission" she described in 1934, as she was turning thirty, had for a decade been the mission of her life. She inherited it from her father, but she had made it her own.

7. The Priestess

Born in Warsaw in 1904, Lidia Zamenhof was the youngest of three children. Because her sister, Zofia, was fifteen years older, and her brother, Adam, sixteen years older, she was raised as a coddled only child. At five, in a full-length studio portrait taken for an Esperanto magazine, she gazes soberly at the camera, accustomed to being taken seriously. She is dressed entirely, theatrically, in white: white-laced boots and socks, white parasol, white flouncy dress tied with a white bow, her rag curls framed by an enveloping white headdress. Fingers curled tightly around a parasol propped between her feet, she looks like an ingenue setting out for a stroll.

Her childhood was comfortable but not lavish, except in the attention her parents paid to her. She painted, played the piano, and culled stamps from the envelopes sent by her father's far-flung correspondents. At the age of nine, Lilka, as she was known, was bribed to learn Esperanto with the offer of a trip to the Universal Congress in Bern. She soon became a fixture at congresses, the Esperanto world's blond darling. Her mother, Klara, offered an ear when her gentle, affectionate father was preoccupied, as he so often was, meeting with visitors from abroad, typing in his study late into the night. Even before she entered her teens, Lidia asked hard questions, having already been the victim of anti-Semitic mockery at school. Despite the gemütlichkeit of the Zamenhofs' drawing room and the banal routines of the clinic downstairs, she saw her father as an embattled, prophetic figure on a religious quest. And he had come to believe that the future of Esperanto would someday depend on her.

Ludovik Zamenhof's death in the last months of the war left Lidia, at fourteen, the caretaker of both her mother and her father's legacy. In 1921, Lidia, Klara, and other close associates of the family founded an Esperanto circle in Warsaw, Konkordo, expressly devoted to keeping her late father's *interna ideo* in full view.[148] After the Vienna Congress of 1924, she became secretary of the International Student Esperanto Association, calling on "students of all countries" to unite.[149] By the end of that year, her mother died of liver cancer. Though she received her law degree from Warsaw University the following year, she never practiced. Her biographer, Wendy Heller, points out that "the Polish bar association was strict about admitting Jews—very few were accepted."[150] More likely, she was diverted from practicing law by a fateful encounter with proponents of the Bahá'í faith.

At the 1925 Universal Congress in Geneva, the International Bahá'í Bureau held a session to show that their universalist faith dovetailed with Esperanto's *interna ideo*. American Esperantist Martha Root, who had given up a career as a society journalist for Bahá'í, read aloud Zamenhof's 1913 comment that "the Bahá'ís will understand the *interna ideo* of Esperanto better than most people."[151] Under Root's influence, Lidia Zamenhof became "convinced . . . [that] Esperanto was created directly under the

Lidia Zamenhof, 1909
[Österreichische Nationalbibliothek]

influence of [Husayn-'Alí] Bahá'u'lláh, although the author of the language"—her father—"did not know it."[152] At the start of Bahá'u'lláh's ministry, the Tehran-born, Farsi-speaking leader had enjoined his followers to adopt a universal language. Returning to the theme in 1891, four years after the publication of Esperanto, he mentioned that "a new language and a new script" had already appeared. It fell to his son, 'Abbás Effendi (known as 'Abdu'l-Bahá), to identify that language as Esperanto and advocate for it: "'I hope that the language of all the future international conferences and congresses will become Esperanto, so that all people may acquire only two languages—one their own tongue and the other the international auxiliary language.'"[153] He exhorted Esperantists to dispatch teachers to the Bahá'í community in Persia, and encouraged Persians to study Esperanto in Europe. Within months, he had begun to speak of his injunction to learn Esperanto as a "command," but the level of compliance among his followers is hard to determine.[154]

Although both Bahá'í and Esperanto saw a crucial role for language in promoting interethnic harmony, the two movements parted ways on at least one crucial point: the Bahá'í faith was led by a dynasty of self-proclaimed prophets, by their own account the heirs to Moses and Jesus. The creator of Esperanto, by contrast, had entirely relinquished his

leadership of the Esperantists. His willingness to forfeit his own prophetic stature to the sovereignty of the Esperanto community was his
signal characteristic as a leader; perhaps even as a man. But if there was
one Esperantist poorly placed to see this crucial difference between the
Bahá'í faith and Esperanto, it was Lidia Zamenhof. In her eyes, Ludovik
Lazarus Zamenhof had always been a prophet, and now that he was
gone, she was looking for another.

* * *

By the time Lidia Zamenhof embraced the Bahá'í teachings, Shoghi Effendi Rabbani,' the grandson of 'Abdu'l-Bahá, had become spiritual leader.
Known as the Guardian, he was educated in Beirut and Cambridge and
was fluent in English; only seven years Lidia's senior, he became her
spiritual advisor. Lidia Zamenhof spent her twenties yearning to make a
pilgrimage to the Holy Land, but not for the sake of Zionism; instead, she
desired to visit Haifa, then the seat of the Bahá'í faith. She sought permission from the Guardian but was told that the time had not yet come. In
Warsaw, she taught Esperanto. While the UEA struggled to rein in the
increasing power of its largest national units, she reminded *samideanoj* to
remain faithful to the *interna ideo;* they were to be, like her, high-minded,
pacifist, and anti-nationalistic. In one allegorical essay, she figures Esperanto as a golem in danger of losing its "inner spark"; another describes a
journey through a xenophobic, violent land called Chauvinia.

Soon she began to use Esperanto to spread Bahá'í teachings. Like
Lanti when he founded SAT, she was now working *"peresperante, ne
poresperante"*; through Esperanto, not for it. As she told Root in confidence in 1926, "Esperanto is only a school in which future Bahá'ís educate themselves. The Bahá'í Movement is a step forward. It is larger." But
Root quoted her in a Bahá'í magazine, and to Lidia's embarrasment the
quotation was soon picked up in the Esperanto press, which responded
harshly. Instead of answering her critics, Lidia stayed focused on pilgrimage, learning Farsi that she might answer 'Abdu'l-Bahá's call to live
among the Persians and teach Esperanto. In fact, it was already being
taught there in Bahá'í schools, and most of the early Persian delegates to
the UEA were Bahá'ís.[155] A 1925 photograph taken at Hamedan, Persia,
shows thirty grave, fezzed men and one grave fezzed little boy, almost
entirely hidden behind a large white Esperanto standard.

When Lidia did finally journey to Haifa in 1930, she was depressed and anxious, unable to feel the rapturous presence of holiness: "'Every morning I would go to the Holy Shrines . . . and, forgetting my Occidental stiffness, I would beat my head against the Holy Thresholds. But . . . the heavens seemed to be closed to my supplications.'"[156] She was not the first Eastern European Jew of her era to seek a more rapt, raw piety in the Middle East than European Judaism offered, nor the first to strike her head on the ground simply to feel it. The historian Susannah Heschel quotes an account by the Jewish orientalist Ignác Goldziher of a visit to a Cairo mosque: "In the midst of the thousands of the pious, I rubbed my forehead against the floor of the mosque. Never in my life was I more devout, more truly devout, than on that exalted Friday."[157] Lidia's hours of prayer in Haifa, however, were far less exalting than Goldziher's in Cairo. The only episode of religious rapture she recorded from that trip was an encounter with a spider, saved from "the abyss" by a slender thread of his own devising. Heller claims that Lidia had an audience with Shoghi Effendi, but if she did, an account of that meeting is conspicuously absent. Before returning to Warsaw, Lidia made another pilgrimage, this time to Jerusalem, where she presented the manuscript of her father's grammar of Yiddish to the newly founded Hebrew University. (A Jewish Bahá'í presenting the Yiddish manuscript of a once-Zionist Esperantist to Hebrew University in Israel: all the contradictions of modern Judaism in one brief encounter.)

Lidia Zamenhof spent the better part of the 1930s teaching Esperanto in Lyon, hosted by Marie Borel, the co-founder of the Union of Esperanto Women. She used progressive, immersive teaching methods; biographer Zofia Banet-Fornalowa estimates that between 1932 and 1937 she taught Esperanto to more than three thousand students in more than fifty courses.[158] From France, Lidia followed closely the developments in Germany. To awaken Esperantists to the coming cataclysm, she wrote frantic allegories about voracious beasts tearing one another's flesh, tigers who couldn't be contained, bloodthirsty monsters on the loose. In *Esperanto, La Praktiko, Pola Esperantisto,* and other journals, she denounced Nazi militarism and fascism, chauvinism, anti-Semitism, even Nazi eugenics.[159] And she made public her contempt for the UEA's cowardly concession to federalism at Cologne. When schism came in 1936–37, it split the Zamenhof family; her sister Zofia joined the IEL, but Lidia sided with the Geneva-based UEA.

Lidia's life in the Bahá'í faith was woven into a fabric of intense friendships with women: first, in Poland, with Root; in France, with Borel; and still later, with Roan Orloff (Stone), an American Bahá'í said to have been

Lidia Zamenhof, 1925
[Österreichische Nationalbibliothek]

cast out by her Orthodox Jewish mother. Lidia spoke on Bahá'í themes to the Union of Esperantist Women, and in 1936, venturing beyond both Esperanto and Bahá'í, she addressed the International Council of Women in Vienna. With the Rhineland re-militarized and Austria about to cede its independence to Germany, she decided to speak about war. All wars, she declared, had special import for women: men waged wars, and women paid for them with sons and suffering, with hunger, fear, bitterness, and dislocation. She enjoined women to keep "lead soldiers and wooden swords" from their children:

> Show your children . . . that glories exist more noble than the
> bloody crowns of Caesars and Napoleons. Tell them that concord
> builds up, discord destroys. Teach them that "love" is not merely
> a banal harangue, that "brotherhood" is not just a utopian dream.

And she urged them to bring into their children's lives children of other ethnicities, nationalities, and races. This, they could—indeed, *should*—do through Esperanto, which was far more than an affair of "postage stamps and picture post cards." Esperanto would empower children to "recognize the true face of their neighbor and see that that face is the face of a brother."[160] Above all, she said, unity among women was the key to bringing the world back from the brink of disaster.

* * *

Lidia Zamenhof's Bahá'í friends were now imploring her to get out of Poland—out of Europe altogether. Though Shoghi Effendi had been counseling Lidia to work on her Farsi and sojourn in what had recently become Iran, he now wrote to urge her to visit the Bahá'ís of the United States since they "are so eager to meet you and accord you a hearty welcome."[161] When the official invitation from the American Assembly of the Bahá'í Faith finally came (the Guardian had written to them himself), it stipulated that the Bahá'ís would pay for her round-trip passage from Poland, but the Esperanto Association of North American (EANA) would have to take responsibility for setting up the Esperanto classes by which she hoped to pay her way.

When she arrived in New York on the ship *Batory* in late September 1937, she felt much as her father had on his arrival in 1910. She, too, was thrilled by the skyscrapers, traffic, and bustle of New York; she, too, felt small, overwhelmed, and agitated, though her letters home would wax ecstatic about ice cream, which was happily ubiquitous. Like her father, she was mobbed by journalists, whom she addressed through an interpreter. But unlike her father, she was asked how tall she was (barely five feet) and how much she weighed. Diana Klotts, a reporter for the *Jewish Sentinel,* questioned "the Modern Minerva" about what Esperanto might mean to American Jews. In reply, Lidia Zamenhof quoted her father's Esperanto translation of the following lines from Zephaniah 3:9: "For then will I turn to the peoples/ A pure language/ That they may all call upon the name of the Lord/ To serve Him with one consent." It was Klotts, remarking on Lidia's "strange inner light," who dubbed her "the High Priestess of Esperanto."[162]

From the outset, the American journey was mired in complications. Among the Bahá'í, there was official respect for Esperanto, but beneath it neither warmth nor urgency. The American Esperantists, on the other hand, saw in Lidia a lit match that could ignite interest in Esperanto. Tensions mounted within the joint Bahá'í-Esperanto sponsoring committee. The Esperantist Samuel Eby, declaring his reservations about Lidia Zamenhof's skills as a lecturer, eventually resigned from the committee, but not before lodging a formal complaint with EANA about his two Bahá'í colleagues, Della Quinlan and Josephine Kruka.

As she trudged from city to city, Lidia Zamenhof could not count on enough interest even to enroll a course in Esperanto. She abhorred the dingy Bronx house with terrible food in which Eby had installed her. Apparently, Shoghi Effendi heard of her struggle and wrote reminding her to "persevere and be confident." The encouragement was well-timed; by winter, suffering from jaundice and exhaustion, she had become the butt of a series of bizarre, anonymous allegations: she was a liar, she stole money, she was a communist. Her Bahá'í handlers suspected a disaffected Esperantist but Lidia may have had another idea, for she asked Shoghi Effendi whether he advised her to remain a Jew. For her, she wrote, Jewishness was a legal status and an expression of solidarity with the Jewish community of Warsaw; renouncing Judaism wasn't necessary, was it? After several months, she received a reply. A formal renunciation was not necessary, his secretary wrote, but, "he hopes later on conditions will develop to a point that would make it advisable for you to take further action in this matter."[163] Around this time Lidia learned that Shoghi Effendi was telling his followers that Esperanto was less important as a language than as an idea; she also discovered that he had never actually learned Esperanto.

In February 1938, she traveled westward to Detroit, where she lectured to all comers: vegetarians, masons, women lawyers.[164] It was among her most successful visits, with dozens of articles about her appearing in seven languages. Still, she lamented that "not one Negro" had attended her classes. Even before coming to the United States, she had noted twice her desire to teach a class in Harlem,[165] but it never happened. When she tried to schedule a class at the black YMCA in Detroit, she was told that doing so was "impractical." When she expressed an interest in lecturing to the NAACP, she was told that their programs were "too full."[166] (A meeting between Lidia Zamenhof and William Pickens is tempting to imagine, but such did not occur.) Discrimination was on her mind, not only against blacks and Jews, but also against Asians. In Detroit, she wrote an essay declaring that Esperanto belonged to Asians as much as to Europeans and predicting that they too would leave their mark on the language.

When news of the *Anschluss* reached her in Detroit, she responded tersely: "the great drama is already beginning."[167] Her American friends entreated her to seek U.S. citizenship, and she wrote to Shoghi Effendi for advice. He replied that the matter was up to her: "Persevere in your historic task," he wrote, "and never feel discouraged."[168] Meanwhile, she applied for an extension of her visa by eight months, confident enough in the outcome to plan classes in Cleveland and Minneapolis for the coming fall. But the day her visa expired, she learned that her extension had been denied on the ground that she had violated employment regulations. If there had been any doubt, it was now clear: she had been ill-advised and ill-served by her handlers, who had failed to apply for an available waiver of employment laws. Though her friend Ernest Dodge did his utmost for months to plead her case, he was only able to secure an extension until early December.

Advice from friends streamed in: she should go to Cuba, Canada, France, California—anywhere but Poland—and reapply for a visa. Panic was not in her nature, but anxious and fearful, she once again turned to the Guardian for advice. Heller quotes her cable in full:

> EXTENSION SOJOURN AMERICA REFUSED. FRIENDS TRYING
> TO CHANGE GOVERNMENT'S DECISION. OTHERWISE
> RETURNING POLAND.
> PLEASE CABLE IF SHOULD ACT OTHERWISE.

His response was decisive:

> APPROVE RETURN POLAND. DEEP LOVING APPRECIATION.
> SHOGHI.[169]

Still she waited, hoping that her fate would turn for the better. For a time, an invitation seemed to be forthcoming from Canada, but "the Canadians aren't courageous enough. . . . they 'see difficulties.'" This time, when she requested Shoghi Effendi's permission to meet him in Haifa, she was seeking refuge, not transcendence. He cabled his reply:

> REGRET DANGEROUS SITUATION IN PALESTINE NECESSITATES
> POSTPONEMENT OF PILGRIMAGE.

She wrote, with the humility of a medieval pilgrim, that she knew it was because "such a privilege is not often received and that certainly one must deserve it, and second—because of the war in Palestine." Indeed, Haifa was dangerous. Strategically important because of an oil pipeline, Haifa had been the target of attacks by displaced *fellahin*, by the Irgun, and by the Royal Navy trying to stem the tide of gunrunners and terrorists. Surely Shoghi Effendi knew that to ensure Lidia Zamenhof's safety, he would have to shelter her in his compound, and this he was not prepared to do.

She told her anguished friends that she intended to return to Poland: after all, Shoghi Effendi had advised it, and it was God's will that she rejoin her family in a time of trouble. She sent messages of appreciation and farewell; she prayed; she packed. At the port of Hoboken, the Staten Island couple who drove her there made a final, desperate plea for her to come home with them, but she refused. On November 29, 1938, she sailed for Poland on the *Pilsudski*. It was the day after Thanksgiving and twenty days after Kristallnacht.

8. Vanishings

Ernest Drezen, Lanti, Hasegawa Teru, and Lidia Zamenhof all met tragic ends.

Drezen, highly placed in both the Comintern and the Soviet Esperanto Union, was closely watched. When the SEU was censured by the Komsomol, Drezen regrouped, striving to immunize the movement against the suspicion of "bourgeois elements" by increasing the percentage of workers in the ranks. His efforts were effective: the percentage of workers grew from thirty to forty-five and, with an influx of interest among Ukrainian youth, membership rates nearly doubled over three years.[170] The onset of the Great Purge in 1936 found the SEU keeping a low profile, publishing theories of language pedagogy and advertising its usefulness to foreign-language instructors. But once the purge began in earnest, Esperantists were persecuted as individuals with suspicious ties to those in other countries. One by one, the luminaries of the Soviet Esperanto movement disappeared from view. Rank-and-file members were also arrested, interned in labor camps, and killed. Precise figures are hard to come by; one Soviet Esperantist estimated that upwards of thirty thousand *samideanoj* were arrested and several thousand died. The father of the Ukrainian poet Aleksandr Logvin, who spent two years in exile in Arkhangelsk, stashed his son's Esperanto writings in a beehive. Both Logvin and his poems survived the purges.[171]

The date of Drezen's arrest in 1937 is not certain. Lins elaborates the many possible grounds for his arrest: "As a non-Russian, erstwhile czar's officer and then one of the earliest on active duty with the Russian Army, a university professor, head of the Soviet Society for Cultural Relations with Foreigners . . . [and] as a person who often traveled to foreign countries, he offered up a bouquet of reasons to be suspected as a 'spy.'"[172] Reports on the manner of his death also conflict; some say he was shot in October 1937; others, that he died later in prison. The only date on which the sources agree is May 11, 1957, when, some twenty years after his arrest and execution, he was posthumously rehabilitated and cleared of all criminal charges.

* * *

Lanti never learned of Drezen's death. The year 1937 found him in Yamashiro, a hot springs town by the Sea of Japan, lodging with a Japanese *samideano* named Takeuchi Tookichi, a devout Buddhist. For a time, Lanti immersed himself in Japanese culture, visiting shrines, temples, and sacred mountains; he read Buddhist tracts with keen attention, though it was hard for him to muster any reverence. (He once confessed to eating the little cakes pilgrims had left out for the Buddha at a shrine.) Looking out over rice fields, he wrote letters comparing the Ginza to Paris; he ate sushi and hobbled about in getas. But the charm of Japanese culture was no match for his distaste for Japanese nationalism, especially once he realized that his Japanese host was a police informant.

Before leaving Japan for Australia, Lanti developed an abscess on his left hand.[173] The symptoms were alarming: swelling of the hand, fingers, and forearm, and intense pain all the way to the elbow. The carbuncle subsided for a time, but in early 1938, a few months after he arrived in Sydney, it returned with redoubled menace. He was hospitalized for six weeks and improved, but in August, suffered another outbreak of carbuncles on his ear, back, and leg. At the best of times, Lanti could wear out a welcome fast; now, anxious and miserable, he ranted about how expensive, uncultured, and materialistic Australia was, not to mention the inhabitants' abysmal competence in Esperanto. In November 1938, he arrived in New Zealand, which, although cheaper and less class-stratified than Australia, did nothing to relieve his perpetual restlessness.

His letters to Limouzin were cordial but infrequent; if he missed her, he didn't let on. Soon after Lanti's departure for Japan, she returned to England, where she moved into a damp, remote farmhouse in Hertfordshire with the newlyweds, Eric Blair and Eileen O'Shaughnessy. She stayed two months, and the tense ménage a trois did little to gladden the young bride in her marriage. As O'Shaughnessy wrote to her friend Norah Myles: "I lost my habit of punctual correspondence during the first few weeks of marriage because we quarreled so continuously & really bitterly that I thought I'd save time & just write one letter to everyone when the murder or separation had been accomplished."[174] By the time the Blitz began, Limouzin was in London cowering for safety. She survived the war and died in 1950, without ever seeing Lanti again.

From New Zealand, Lanti made his way to South America; on May 6, 1939, he reached Montevideo.[175] His wanderings continued, to Argentina, Brazil, Chile, and finally Mexico. At the war's end, the French consul in Mexico offered him free passage back to France but, suspicious of the French government and tainted by his history as a communist, he doubted he would be readmitted. When a group of leftist *samideanoj* in Los Angeles invited him to join them, he started trying to secure an American visa. Intermittently, he was suffering painful attacks of carbuncles as well as generalized inflammation and dermatitis; his fingernails fell off, and he could barely move his fingers. At sixty-five, to better keep his skin clean, he shaved off the beard he had worn since his anarchist days in Paris.

Late in 1946, he developed an abscess on his scalp. A friend, the Spanish socialist exile Francisco Azorín Izquierdo, took him to the French hospital, where a doctor recommended drilling a hole in his skull to excise the infected tissue. When Azorín agreed to cover expenses, an appointment was made for the following day. But the narcotics Lanti brought home from the clinic were not enough to dull the pain, and already unmoored from his Mexican life, he found nothing to anchor him. That evening, overwhelmed with despair, he hanged himself from a shower head. He left a note in Esperanto directing his survivors to notify the French consul, send Nellie Limouzin 750 pesos "as my legal wife," and edit and republish his writings. The doyen of the best-selling Esperanto dictionary of all time niggled over diction to the end:

> I'd like to say much more, but this would only prolong my martyrdom (martyrhood? now I don't know).
> This is my testament. Eugène Adam-Lanti.

His suicide was his last protest: his life had become a torment and he was against it.

* * *

Protest was not an option for Lidia Zamenhof when she returned to Warsaw in the winter of 1938. She was reconciled to her fate, and when her faith needed shoring up, she wrote long letters to her Bahá'í friends: "If I left America," she wrote, "perhaps it was because God preferred that I work in another land." She was writing bleak allegories: Christmas trees with candles that burn for a moment and go dark; a country called "Nightland," "where the sun had not risen for so long that it had nearly been forgotten."[176] After she wrote to Shoghi Effendi that she planned to stay in Poland a few weeks, then go to France, his secretary replied:

> Although your efforts to obtain a permit [in the United States] . . . did not prove successful, you should nevertheless be thankful for the opportunity you have had of undertaking such a long and fruitful journey. He hopes the experiences you have gathered during all these months . . . will now help you to work more effectively for the spread of the Cause in the various European countries you visit, and particularly in your native country Poland, where the Faith is still practically unknown.[177]

In a postscript, the Guardian himself wrote that he looked forward to meeting her "face to face in the Holy Land" at a time "not far distant." In the meantime, she was to bring Bahá'í to the Poles, lecturing, paying calls, and translating sacred Bahá'í texts into Polish. After eighteen months of effort, she could count all the Bahá'ís in Poland on one hand.

In 1939, she did not go to France, nor did she travel to Haifa; she would never leave Poland again. Three weeks after the Nazi invasion, the Zamenhof home in Warsaw was bombed to rubble. Within days Zofia Zamenhof, Adam Zamenhof, and his wife, Wanda, were arrested in the hospital where they worked; Lidia was arrested at the home of a relative. Adam was incarcerated in the Daniłowiczowska Street prison; the women, in the notorious Pawiak prison. On January 29, 1940, to avenge an assault on a Nazi officer by the resistance, fifty prisoners were taken to the forest near the village of Palmiry, north of Warsaw, and shot, among them Adam Zamenhof.[178]

After five months in the Pawiak prison, Lidia, Zofia, and Wanda Zamenhof were sent back to Warsaw to eke out survival among the

400,000 Jews from all parts of occupied Poland sequestered within the three-and-a-half-square-mile Ghetto, an area that normally housed less than half as many people. Exactly one year after the Polish Jews were first required to wear a white badge with a star of David, the Warsaw Ghetto was sealed off, and Jewish life in Poland was itself imprisoned.

An internal report of Heydrich's Reich Main Security Office glimpses Esperanto's creator through what Lins calls "Nazi spectacles."[179] The "Jew Zamenhof," the office reported, had engineered three methods to achieve his goal of worldwide Jewish domination: the Esperanto language; "unbridled" pacifism; and *Homaranismo*, which was doubly offensive to Nazi sensibilities—it not only aimed to blend all ethnicities and races into one people, but it did so for the express purpose of preparing the world for Jewish domination.[180] Examined through Nazi lenses, the invisible empire of Ludovik Lazarus Zamenhof was starkly, menacingly visible.

In July 1942, "translocations" began in Warsaw, ostensibly to a labor camp "in the east." Between five and ten thousand Jews were rounded up daily, many lured to the Umschlagplatz with a promise of three kilos of bread and a kilo of beet marmalade. Years later, an Esperantist railway worker named Arszenik claimed to have offered to smuggle Lidia Zamenhof out of the Ghetto and hide her, but she refused to endanger him. Interviewed in France in the 1990s, her nephew Louis-Christophe Zaleski-Zamenhof could not recall her ever mentioning Arszenik, but he believed her response would have been in character: "There was something holy in that little person."[181]

Toward the end of September 1942, at the age of thirty-eight, she was among the 300,000 Jews from the Warsaw Ghetto who were packed into cattle cars and sent to Treblinka. (Zofia had gone voluntarily, perhaps thinking she could be of service as a medic.) Eva Toren, then a fourteen-year-old girl who had met and befriended Lidia that spring at a Ghetto seder, would survive to remember Lidia's final hours in Warsaw. In 1993 Toren recalled the Nazis whipping, shouting, and pushing Jews into the Umschlagplatz, where they stood without water from early morning until evening. In the afternoon, the Germans and their Polish minions arranged the Jews in lines five deep for the selection. Lidia was several rows behind Eva, and they exchanged a pregnant glance. When she was selected for deportation, Lidia "walked regally, upright, with pride, unlike most of the other victims, who were understandably panicked."[182]

On the fifth of September, Lidia Zamenhof boarded the train to Treblinka, where, upon arriving, she was killed in the gas chamber.

A few months after the war ended, the Bahá'í National Spiritual Assembly of the United States and Canada began to plan a memorial service for Lidia Zamenhof. They consulted Shoghi Effendi: shouldn't she be designated among the martyrs for the Bahá'í faith? On January 28, 1946, the eve of what would have been Lidia's forty-second birthday, Shoghi Effendi cabled his American followers:

> HEARTILY APPROVE NATIONWIDE OBSERVANCE FOR
> DAUNTLESS LYDIA ZAMENHOF. HER NOTABLE SERVICES,
> TENACITY, MODESTY, UNWAVERING DEVOTION FULLY MERIT
> HIGH TRIBUTE BY AMERICAN BELIEVERS. DO NOT ADVISE,
> HOWEVER, THAT YOU DESIGNATE HER A MARTYR.[183]

She had intended to give her life for the Bahá'í faith, but died as an Esperantist, a Zamenhof, and a Jew.

Samideanoj III
Hanoi to Havana, or *Usonozo*

===

HANOI

1. *Usonozo*

I'm late to register for the Sixty-Third International Youth Conference because the Hanoi University School for Foreign Languages is hard to find. Like most Esperanto venues, it's not in the city center; it's barely on the city outskirts, nestled among curving, branching arteries of concrete clogged with motorbikes. It's a sweltering day in August, and after forty-eight hours of travel, punctuated by twenty minutes in a shower booth at Narita airport, I feel off-kilter, atilt, strange to myself. I've just looked up the Esperanto word for jet lag, *horzonozo: hor/zon/-*, a compound root meaning "time-zone," plus the *-ozo* ending, meaning "a sickness." Timezonesickness.

I've come in search of a cure for *Usonozo*, the malady of being American. *Usonozo* is a chronic, if not fatal, condition; it attacks with every suburban barbecue and peaceful election, every rectangle drawn around violence, whether by television, laptop, or iPhone. Glaciers melt, empires fall, journalists garbed in saffron jumpsuits are beheaded, but the rectangles remain, only smaller and smaller. From time to time, *Usonozo* abates, as when I send my son off to West Africa for a semester, or my daughter to a kibbutz in the Golan Heights. And as soon as that happens, I feel anxious. I sleep fitfully; I'm distracted, unable to pay attention. Then, when I throw my arms around my son or daughter at the airport, the symptoms of *Usonozo* kick in again: Complacency, comfort, a consummate faith in the order of things.

So I'm here to break out of the rectangle; to see Vietnam not on the black-and-white TV of my American childhood but among Esperantists.

The taxi threads between two ranks of ochre stucco buildings as we look for Building 14A, but find only Building A. When we pull up close, we see a shadowy one and four, ghosts of the missing numbers. V. D. Lien Hall, where the opening ceremony is to take place, stands at the far end of a cinderblock complex. Along the pathways lie several pools dotted with pale pink lotus flowers. The scene is so serene, it might be a painting, but for a faint urinous reek. I follow a concrete arcade toward the lecture hall, stepping over a syringe tossed carelessly on the walkway. The hall is already crowded, and though the stage is bare, people are snapping pictures, some standing on skimpy folding chairs. The air is hot and close and I take a seat near the door.

Sitting beside me is a sandy-haired fortyish woman in shorts, sipping a liter of water. Her nametag reads "Sylvie 282," and she calls to mind a Birkenstocked French teacher I'd had in high school. This is ostensibly a youth congress, but because Esperanto congresses are open to all, there's a smattering of middle-aged people and a handful of the elderly.

"*De kie vi estas?*" I ask her; where are you from?

She's from Marseilles, a lawyer, but she mainly wants to talk about teaching Occitan, the ancient Provençal language still spoken in pockets of southern France and Catalonia. "*Kaj vi?*"—and you?

"*Usono.*" Zamenhof's name for my country cuts it down to size; the "n" is for *north* America. "*Mi loĝis en Francio kvar monatojn—antaŭ dudek jaroj.*"

Hearing that I'd spent four months in France, albeit twenty years ago, she immediately switches from Esperanto to a fast, emphatic French: "Have you been to the city center and isn't the traffic *frightful*? Just yesterday I was on a bus and it hit a *dog,* and no one helped until finally the police came and lifted him up *covered* in blood, but he was already *dead!*"

As a tall ponytailed guy in his twenties, the president of TEJO, takes the podium to offer a brief welcome, Sylvie leans toward me: "*Les Croatiens ont les meilleurs accents, non?*" Time to draw a line in the sand; I've never crocodiled and I haven't come here to do so.

"*Jes,*" I say firmly in Esperanto. "*Kroatanoj havas la plej bonajn akcentojn.*"

Next, a slim, tall Vietnamese woman, like a candle with arms, takes the lectern. She is *Lai Ty Hai Ly, the president of the Vietnam Organization of Young Esperantists, clad in a traditional *ao dai,* a long, clinging tunic in pea-green silk over gold silk trousers. By day, she works for the refrigeration company whose logo appears on the orange plastic fans that were distributed at registration. By night, she devotes herself to nurturing Esperanto among the youth of her country. She's the person who recruited and trained the squadron of beaming *helpantoj*—the twenty student volunteers in Kelly green T-shirts. Four months ago, she advertised a free Esperanto course and enrolled some eighty students. After six weeks, she gave an exam and weeded out half of them. Of the forty who were allowed to continue, half were weeded out a few weeks later by a second exam. The remaining twenty, the crème de la crème of Hanoi's young Esperantists, are avid, sharp, ambitious. What drove them to learn Esperanto was the same impulse that had sent them to intensive English classes, to the CNN website, and to train for jobs that have the words "international" and "global" in them.

At Hai Ly's signal, we all rise to our feet. The Vietnamese flag—a yellow star on a red field—is raised, followed by what must be the national anthem; then the karaoke system begins to blare a peppier tune: "La Espero"—"The Hope," Zamenhof's anthem for his para-nation. Set by a French composer, Félicien de Ménil, it sounds like the Marseillaise arranged as a polka.

The president of the Vietnamese Esperanto Association, a dark-haired pudgy man of about sixty, takes the lectern. He gives a little background about Esperanto in Vietnam, which dates back to 1897, when one J. Ferra became the first European on record to speak Esperanto in Indochina. He mentions that Ho Chi Minh learned Esperanto during his sojourn in London (1914–17); light applause. Apparently, the national movement was catalyzed in 1932 by Lucien Péraire, a French Esperantist who visited Indochina during a four-year bicycle trip across Europe and Asia. Soon government-licensed groups sprang up in the central region known as Cochin China, spawning congresses, journals, radio transmissions, and publishing ventures. After the Geneva Accords of 1954, when the country was divided into northern and southern zones, Esperantist activity persisted in the northern sector only; not until the 1980s did Esperanto return to the south. And only in 1995, when Vietnam was opening up to the West during a period of rapid economic reforms, did the Vietnamese Esperanto Association became an official member of the UEA.

The president closes his speech by applauding the audience, then steps to one side where, assuming a braced, athletic stance, he becomes the

Vietnamese interpreter for the benefit of local reporters. I know I'm jet-lagged when I catch myself struggling to comprehend his Vietnamese instead of the speaker's Esperanto.

Like every other PowerPoint lecture ever given at an Esperanto congress, "Vietnam En Route to Renovation" begins with four or five people huddled around a dysfunctional projector. To relieve the tedium, a young girl gets on a chair and with a long pole rescues a blue balloon from a whirling fan. As applause for the rescuer abates, the association president praises the *Esperantistoj kaj Usonanoj*—Esperantists and Americans—who protested the "American War," offering "solidarity, friendship, and cooperation" to the Vietnamese people. (Unmentioned is the martyrdom of *samideano* Alice Herz, an elderly Holocaust survivor, who immolated herself in Detroit in 1965 to protest the war.) Suddenly two bullet points appear on the white screen:

- 1 million handicapped
- 4 million poisoned by dioxin from Agent Orange

Next, photos of craters, defoliated jungles, bombed paddies, and mangled bodies flash on the screen.

For the young Esperantists fanning themselves all around me, this war is ancient history. But after two days in this country, I've realized that for Vietnamese and Americans of a certain age, echoes of the "American War" still reverberate. My husband, Leo, and I saw them this morning, the Agent Orange victims, huddled by a footbridge at a nearby park, showing us their stunted limbs and begging.

2. The American War

The congress agenda for the next day—a demonstration by a blind masseur; an exhibition of Vietnamese crafts; a "getting-acquainted" social—couldn't compete with my desire to see the Cu Chi tunnels, a two-hundred-kilometer subterranean network that brought the Saigon regime to its knees. I decided to take the day off and head for Cu Chi; Leo stashed his laptop in a fragile-looking room safe and came along.

The cab wove among motorbikes bearing lawn mowers, eggs, painted shrines of red and gold. On either side of a divided boulevard, skeins of utility wires stretched limply between poles, then every so often snarled into nests for absent wire birds. The spindly apartment buildings were one-room-wide structures of three or four stories, trimmed in lilac, aqua, orange. We passed the ironwork district, the granite district, the furniture district, the water-tank district. Billboards with smiling faces hawked invisible products called "Top Life" and "E-Town." One featured two young women with identical hairstyles locked in an earnest gaze; staunch red capital letters at the bottom told us what was on their minds— "HIV." Here was the English abbreviation, not the French (VIH); while French is still lodged in the Vietnamese language in words like *ga* (from *gare*, station) and *kem* (from *crème*, ice cream), most recent borrowings are from English: *tivi, hambogo, guita.*

After driving through miles of rubber plantations, dodging bony, dusty cows, we parked in the Cu Chi tunnels lot and were led to a reception area to await the English-language tour. A huge portrait of Ho Chi Minh hung up front, and one hundred empty folding chairs stood at attention in neat rows. Even in the shade, the heat was leaden; a dozen flushed, enervated Germans filtered in and took seats, sipping water bottles and fanning themselves with brochures.

Suddenly from nowhere, music blared, as if a stereo left for dead by a power outage was shuddering back to life. A TV screen lit up with grainy black-and-white images of fire and explosions; a voice intoned in Vietnamese, and over it, high and wrought, another chanted rhythmically in English: "Like a crazy flock of devils, the bombs and bullets of Washington, D.C., fell on women. Children. Trees. Leaves. Buddhas. And into pots and pans." In the next frame, a pigtailed young girl was waving merrily, swathed in the black-and-white plaid Vietcong sash. "This schoolgirl," the shrill voice said, "cute and gentle, lost her father. Her hatred lifted her higher. Single-handedly she killed one hundred eighteen Americans. For her courage she was decorated as 'Brave Exterminator of American Soldiers.'" Amid images of peasants at play, dancing, singing, picnicking, the pinched voice continued: "The peasants fought in the morning and plowed in the evening. Bombs could not silence their songs and music. Their sweet country songs pushed them forward to national victory." At the end of the video, to throbbing strings, a date appeared: 1983.

This is the rectangle the Vietnamese have been watching, ever since the fall of Saigon.

Our English-speaking guide was a uniformed Vietnamese soldier. Exotic yet bland, like the token Asian actor in a forties movie, he led us tourists out of the pavilion, up a dirt path, pointing out a huge crater with a tiny placard: B52 BOM. Further on, we reached a covered pavilion in which a small group of epicene mannequins with painted Asian eyes squatted on mats, frozen at their work: sawing open unexploded B52 bombs, filling ersatz grenades, slicing rubber tires up into sandals. In the longest, narrowest pavilion, a painted mural showed six large pink figures in American uniforms, each the victim of a different booby-trap, spurting blood from the neck, the belly, the stump of an arm.

Begun in the 1950s, during the First Indochina War, and elaborated in the mid-1960s, the Cu Chi tunnels were designed to be too narrow for large American GIs to enter. Although General William Westmoreland had an exquisitely detailed map of the tunnel system, its dormitories, mess halls, magazines, factories, and hospital, even its secret underwater entrance, the U.S. forces had never been able to penetrate it. When they had sent in dogs, the Vietcong rubbed their own faces with American soap to confuse the animals. And once the dogs began to bleed to death in booby traps, their American handlers quailed. Twenty-five thousand Vietnamese, soldiers and civilians, had died in this underworld, said our guide. "It's a little cramped," he added, like a young man leading us into his first studio apartment, "don't try to stand up." I followed Leo down earthen steps into damp, cool utter darkness. At the bottom, I put my hand on his sweaty back and kept it there, afraid to lose contact. The air smelled foul, the way the earth must smell to the dead. Playing Eurydice to Leo's Orpheus, I followed close through the darkness until light fell and we began to climb the stairs.

I thought of Rose Harrington, my childhood neighbor, whose eldest son, Jimmy, was killed in action somewhere between Saigon and the Mekong Delta. From the Department of Defense came a gold star, a folded flag, and Jimmy's remains. Rose, whose name belied her ashen pallor, was the only Gold Star mother in my town, and at the Memorial Day parade, while we Girl Scouts broke ranks to flog the Good Humor truck for free pops, she got a big round of applause. An ovation, since everyone was already standing.

3. *La Finavenkisto*

For fifteen years, there was one air-conditioned room in Hanoi, and it belonged to the corpse of Ho Chi Minh. Contrary to the express wishes of "Uncle Ho," as he is still known, who had requested cremation, the Politburo decided that if embalming was appropriate for Lenin, Ho deserved no less. In the early 1970s, they quarried the innards of Marble Mountain near Da Nang and commissioned an architect to build a mausoleum in the form of a lotus. A less floral building is hard to imagine: a stubby gray marble cube mounted wedding-cake style on granite plinths, it looks like a grim communist parody of the Lincoln Memorial. Across the top is the legend "Chu Tich [President] Ho-Chi-Minh."

We're lucky the mausoleum is open. Each summer "Uncle Ho" is sent off to Moscow to a spa for the corpses of embalmed dictators, from which he returns, refreshed with bright cosmetics, a few weeks later. Sunday's the busiest day of the week. Coiled around the base of the monument three times, the line moves slowly under hot sun, like a snake after a large meal. Up and down the line, on the other side of an iron grille, women are hawking bottles of water, postcards, lentil pancakes. To pass the time, I'm chatting with one of the congress *helpantoj*, a serious, fresh-faced girl named Tring Ha. She asks where I'm from.

"*Usono.*"

"*Usono!*" she says loudly. "There are no *senatoroj* from Washington, D.C., and why is that?" I don't have a good answer. She's something of a Usonophile, reciting the names of all the states she knows—sixteen, including New Jersey. Suddenly, from a dark opening at the top of the marble staircase tumbles a whoosh of cool air. With each step we take, it gets cooler and cooler until, at the top, uniformed guards bark in English, "Hats off, hats off!" and we're in.

We've entered a huge, draped, darkened chamber, and our eyes come to focus on the sole source of light, as in a painting of the Nativity: the spotlit, pasty face of Ho, who lies serenely, hands folded, a long, gray, wispy beard spread out on his torso, extending to his wide black belt. In my mind's eye, I see Harpo Marx in *A Night at the Opera,* scissoring the beards of the three snoring Russian aviators. By contrast to Ho's stillness, the line is moving fast: in a macabre peristalsis, we're suddenly expelled from the chamber and the building. Blinking in the sunlight, Tring Ha asks Roddy, a roly-poly pastry chef from Melbourne, "*Ĉu vi ŝatis ĝin?*"

"Yes," says Roddy diplomatically, "indeed, I did like it." He pauses, thinking of what else he could possibly say. "It's a most important thing."

A young man in a "Floating Village, Thailand" T-shirt says to me quietly, in English, "That's a lot of fuss for one dead man." It's Eran Regev, a twenty-six-year-old computer geek from Tel Aviv, former president of the Israeli Esperanto League's youth wing. Like every other ex-intelligence officer with a degree in mathematics from the Hebrew University, Eran launched an IT start-up, which, now a 24–7 commitment, is sapping his time and cramping his style. I'd been introduced to him by Renato Corsetti, the president of the Universal Esperanto Association, who told me afterwards, in an impressed *sotto voce*, "He has a Jordanian girlfriend!" After a tour of Ho's official study, Ho's country-pavilion study, and the famous one-column pagoda, I sit next to Eran on the bus and ask whether we can continue speaking English. I have a feeling he's worth a little crocodiling.

"Of course," he says, with a plummy British accent. I ask where his Jordanian girlfriend lives, and his face sours.

"I don't have a girlfriend," he snorts, like a teenager who wants his closed door to stay closed. "Did Renato tell you that?" There is one Jordanian member of the Esperanto youth group in Jerusalem, he tells me, but she lives in Jordan and doesn't come to meetings. "She's a friend," he says, loosening a bit, "not my *girlfriend*."

At ten, Eran decided to invent a language. When he showed his father his early attempts, he was told, "You don't need to do this; someone already has." His father hired an Esperanto tutor and took him to the Esperanto "museum," a single dusty room at Hebrew University that was open a few hours a week. From time to time, a couple of old men would show up, gossip, read newspapers, and leave; the space has long since been reallocated. After a few months, Eran lost interest; it was another fifteen years before he saw an ad for an Esperanto group convening in Tel Aviv. In 2004, with a shaky command of the language, he found himself at the International Youth Congress in Sarajevo. For the first two days he said nothing to anyone; on the third he started speaking and didn't look back. "It's even stronger in Zagreb," he said. "Downtown, kids volunteer to wear signs telling what languages they speak to help foreign visitors: 'Esperanto spoken here.'"

Eran knows I'm interested in Zamenhof's Judaism, and he recommends a few of Zamenhof's speeches and articles about Jews, Judaism, and Zionism. From the perfunctory way he fills me in, I can tell it's not really an interest of his, but you can't be an Israeli Jewish Esperantist and not know all this. It would be like not knowing what a seder is.

So what is Esperanto's attraction for Eran? "First I'll tell you what many other people would say," he starts, like a debater prepping the "cons" of gun control. "They'd say it's great for getting hospitality in other countries. They'd say if you travel using Pasporta Servo"—the free international hosting service—"you'll see places no tourists go and do things no tourists do. They'd say that you show up at an Esperantist's door and in an hour they've given you the keys to their car. And they'd say you can only do this in Esperanto.

"But they're wrong. I've done it in English plenty of times.

"People also say, 'Use Esperanto to fight English.' But that's not right either. First of all, most people in the world who talk English are really speaking 'Globish,' not English. Second, English is encroaching on Esperanto every day. For example, people say '*futbol*' but the proper Esperanto word is '*pied pilko*': Foot. Ball. People say '*interneto*' but they should be saying '*interreto*,' since *reto* is Esperanto for 'web.' Or '*komputero*' instead of '*komputilo*.'" He's authoritative, peremptory, a one-man academy. "Besides," he says abruptly, "English won't last. Look, French didn't." I've heard this before from Esperantists: Yesterday, French. Today English. In fifteen minutes, Chinese.

"So why do *I* do it? Partly because I love the language. It's compact, it's ingenious. It's rigorous but flexible. It's vital. One can invent new words, easily, and one does. Do you know any Esperanto slang?" he asks. I think of the last page of the "Esperanto Phrases" website, the page with all the asterisks: P*u*s*s*y—*piĉo*; C*o*c*k—*kaĉo*.

"No," I say.

"Well there's *kancerfumi*—to cancer yourself smoking. And *mojosa*, slang for 'cool.' It's an acronym, MJS, for *moderna-juna-stilo*, which means 'modern youth style.' There's another word that means 'getting good at Esperanto and losing interest'—named after the writer Kazimierz Bein, who did just that." It's a verb created from Bein's initials—KB, pronounced "ka-be"—hence, *kabeismo*.

"I keep hearing," I say, "that Esperanto's easy to learn because there aren't any idioms. But Zamenhof assumed that the language would grow as natural languages do. So how could there not be idioms?"

"There are some," Eran says; "You already know what it means to croc-odile; then there's *gufejo*—literally, an owlery—a hang-out for night-owls."

"I have a word for you," I countered. "*Elmuri.*" He's mystified; I've just stumped a star.

"To take something out of a wall?" he asks.

"To get cash from an ATM." His dour face cracks a goofy grin; "*el-muuuur-i,*" he says, as the homunculus in his brain writes it down.

"Also," he says, "I've translated several Beatles songs into Esperanto, but there's a lot of original Esperanto music out there too—*Viro kai Virino; Esperanto Desperado.*" I've heard them on YouTube; the former sounds like Ian and Sylvia, the latter, like leftover Eagles.

"Do you know the song 'Fina Venko'?" he asks.

"No. What does *fina venko* mean?"

He scans me sharply, as though trying to decide if I'm worthy of the answer. "Well, I don't think it's Zamenhof's phrase, but it means 'final victory,' the moment when everyone everywhere has realized that Espe-ranto is the way to go. There's an irony of course, because *venko* means both victory and defeat. So something will be lost, and something gained. We'll lose the benefits of being small, the intimacy, the bonds, but I really think this is the way the world is headed." He lowers his voice; here comes the confession. "I'm optimistic about the *fina venko*. That's not why most people do it. But it's why *I* do it. "

Till now, he's sounded like a Starbucks-swilling Israeli hipster hang-ing out in Nepal. Now he sounds like his own bundist great-grandfather—or mine—patiently awaiting the final, inevitable triumph of socialism. He's a *finavenkisto*, at once much older and much younger than I am.

"Did you grow up in Tel Aviv?" Yes, he says; when he was six, his par-ents went through a messy divorce, and moved to opposite ends of the city. He and his sister were shuttled back and forth from mother to father.

"Week by week?" I ask.

"No," he said, "every other day."

A child shuttled daily between parents who don't speak? No wonder he's waiting for the *fina venko*. "Are your parents still living?"

"If you call it living . . ." he retorted. Would I have said this about my parents at his age? About my father, taking my cancer-ridden mother from one continent to another in pursuit of colonics, albumen deriva-tives, cocktails reeking of garlic? About my mother, always packing and unpacking, going along with it all with queenly detachment and writing, on the backs of old syllabi, acid poems about marriage and chemo? I might have thought it; I would not have said it.

Eran's father has remarried and moved to Glasgow; Eran rarely sees him. His mother, a year ago, moved to Mumbai, where she does yoga and volunteers at a day care center. "Midlife crisis," he says, rolling his eyes, and my breath catches.

What does he think I am doing here at this youth congress, turning myself back into a child? I ask him how old his mother is. "Forty-nine," he says.

"I'm older than she is," I blurt out. If Eran is surprised, he doesn't let on.

4. The English Teacher

We're on the bus to Ha Long Bay, and four hours of incessant beeping—at cars, scooters, minivans, and the skinny gray steers who shuffle along the shoulder—have left everyone shell-shocked. Glad to disembark at a roadside restaurant, we sit down at a round table bearing a huge platter of watermelon. Eran starts a contest: who can say *watermelon* in the most languages? Predictably, he wins by saying it in Esperanto, Hebrew, English, Yiddish, French, Spanish, Polish, German, Italian, Dutch, Danish, and Vietnamese. Turns out I know one he doesn't: the Greek *karpouzi*. "That's new to me," he says, "but of course, *karpo* in Turkish is a gourd."

Back on the bus, a slender, boyish *helpanto* sits down next to me. Introducing himself as Phong, he tells me he *loves* to speak English—so could we? *Please?*

Phong, who is twenty-four but looks eighteen, loves English because it earns him a living. Mornings, he teaches English grammar at an elementary school; afternoons, he tutors English to high school kids. He earns four to five hundred thousand dong a month (eighteen U.S. dollars), depending on how many hours he tutors. Every morning he wakes up at five a.m. to do housework for his mother, then rides his scooter forty-five minutes to work; evenings are for Esperanto classes. He gets home around midnight.

It's just Phong and his mother; no mention of siblings. His father, he tells me, died a couple of years ago.

"Oh, I'm sorry," I say automatically.

"No problem!" he assures me. Phong's father fought both the French and the Americans, and Phong himself spent two years in the army. Before I can ask what he did there, he changes the subject abruptly: "Do people buy power with money in the United States?"

"Well," I venture, "running for national office is an expensive proposition; it costs lots of money to advertise, and there are spending limits, but there's a way around it if you are willing to forgo federal funding."

"No," he interrupts, "I mean lobbyists. Do they buy influence from the people in the Senate? In the House of Representatives?" When I concede that there are favors, considerations, ethics inquiries, he seems unsurprised. Then he asks about gun control, divorce rates, drug abuse, HIV, and education reform. He even asks about "No Child Left Behind."

The barrage of questions leaves me nonplussed; how exactly does he keep up with all these issues? "I watch CNN," he says, unable to conceal his pleasure at having impressed me. I'd been told by a retired American diplomat never to ask the Vietnamese directly about the one-party system. But if not now, when? "Do you belong to the Party?"

He pauses and says slowly, "I don't think so." Is he being evasive or has he not understood my question? Hard to tell; his English is fairly grammatical but far from colloquial. (The next day, at the university bookstore, I purchase the textbook he'd used to study English. Published in Vietnam, it is riddled with grammatical and factual errors. Even the pagination is wrong: 64 followed 27, 28 followed 72, and eighteen pages are missing.)

"Well," Phong says, "it's not what you think. If you don't like who's running, you vote someone else in. In time it will change. We have elections every four years but it's very different from America. There aren't many speeches, no one's on TV, and there are few posters. *Very* different."

And why, when he's so devoted to learning and teaching English, did he take up Esperanto?

"Esperanto is a peace language," he says simply. End of story.

We're not even halfway to Ha Long Bay, but he suddenly asks for my email address, as if we could possibly lose contact during this four-day congress. I give him my card, and in my notebook he prints in clear, small letters, "Phongsado2@yahoo.com."

"Phong *sad*?"

"I started email when I was in the army. I was far from my family and
my friends, I missed my mother. I was so lonely, I thought I would always
be sad, so Phongsad is how I called myself." I tell him I promise to write
and hope to hear, before long, that he's changed "Phongsad" to "Phong-
happy."

*   *   *

A month after Leo and I returned home, and days after our middle son
left for college, our Siberian Husky died, and not of her own accord.
When cancer left her too weak to walk, we drove her to the vet, held her
on the floor and "released" her, as the vet put it. We'd talked it through; it
was the humane thing to do. But her death felt like a judgment on us, as
though we had let the census in the still, quiet house drop to an uncon-
scionable level. I found an old photo of her, a sort of glamour shot that
showed off her blue eyes, and emailed it to all the graduate students
who had ever cared for her. And I sent it to Phong.

After a month, he replied.

> Dear Ms Esther,
>
> Thank you so much for your letter. I'm so sorry that I can
> write to you now. Because I have to work so much, not enough
> time to check mail and answer your letter.
>
> I also want to talk to you much more about me not my familly
> because it's not happy. As you know I was born in unhappy
> familly, my father died when I was ten, and my only younger
> brother died of accident three years ago. It's the worst thing in
> my life. All remaining time, I will have to live in torment of con-
> science as I didn't save his life. When my father died, maybe I was
> still too little to feel losses but when my younger brother died, I
> felt all the pangs of parting. I really slumped down and I thought
> I can't continue my life. However, I have to live, live to continue
> his way that he chose, studying and become a good person.
>
> Now, my familly has three members: my mother, me and an-
> other younger brother but I have not accepted him as my brother,
> I considered he also died. He caused so much suffering for me. And
> it's too enough!
>
> At the moment, I wish you were here. I will take you visit Ha-

noi streets in autumn, it is so beautiful, as your soul, and you will
feel fresh of life, weather . . . also feel typical perfume of a typical
flower in Hanoi autumn, milk flower, I like autum as it's sad and
nice. . . .

I was so regretable for your dog. He was piteous.

> Warm wishes to you,
> write soon,
> Nguyen Trang Phong

Too enough, I thought, and yet too little. How had his brother died? How
was the youngest implicated, and why the estrangement? Why the dis-
avowal? And why did Phong blame himself? I knew I couldn't ask; perhaps next autumn, in a sad moment among the milk flowers, he would
disclose more. Instead, I thanked him for telling me about painful losses
and ongoing struggles.

Phong's next message arrived on New Year's Day:

> Dear Mrs Esther H Schor
>
> On occasion of New Year and Christmas, I wish you and your
> family would have a peace avatar heal, happiness new annual
> plant and satisfaction swamp.
>
> > With all best wishes!
> > Nguyen Trang Phong

In response, I sent him a photo of my family at Bryce Canyon. "I have a
question," I wrote. "Did you use a computer-translation program in writing your message? I am trying to learn more about them," I added, a little
lie to let him save a little face.

He replied swiftly.

> Dear Mrs ESTHER!
>
> I am so sorry. I sure that you were disappointed to me when
> reading my letter. Maybe I not good at writing, and wrong
> grammar so you asked me: "<u>I have a question: did you use any
> computer-translation program in writing your message? I am try-
> ing to learn.</u>"
>
> Maybe I have to study more about that, because I not good at
> English.

I promise I will study harder to improve this.

For that letter I used computer-translation program, it's a website to translate.

Best wishes.

Nguyen Trang Phong

Attached was the photo he'd promised on the bus ride: two soldiers, barely past boyhood, wearing green Soviet-style peaked caps with red bands, fringed epaulets, and wide, latched belts. They stand at ease, one boot slightly in front of the other. The boy on the left, draping a brotherly arm over Phong's shoulder, is a full head taller. Next to Phong, who is downcast and impassive, the boy looks almost jovial. Rail-thin, sad Phong leans against a whitewashed colonial balustrade, solemn as a figure on a banknote.

5. VIPs

Hanoi's State Guest House is a white marble colonial manor; its grand staircase, worthy of a ballroom in *Dr. Zhivago*, affords a sweeping view of Hoan Kiem Lake. Here the Hanoi municipal government has lodged the first couple of *Esperantujo*, UEA president Renato Corsetti and his wife, the Esperanto novelist Anna Löwenstein. Not every world capital would regard them as VIPs, but this one clearly does; Renato and Anna have been given an Esperanto-Vietnamese translator and assigned a driver for the week.

Between them, Renato and Anna have been speaking Esperanto for some eighty years: forty years with Italian gestures and twirled consonants, the other forty in clipped British sentences and damp London sighs. Their two sons, now adults, were raised trilingually: Renato spoke Esperanto with them, Anna raised them in English, and they acquired Italian from babysitters, schools, and television. Renato estimates that 50 percent of *denaskuloj*—Esperantists from birth—stay in the movement and the rest have nothing to do with it (at least, that's what his domestic laboratory suggests).

Renato's fascination with his children's multilingualism—that and a major heart attack—led him from banking into linguistics. He's a plump man in his early sixties, with benign, wide-set eyes above flushed cheeks. Decked out in a white straw hat and khakis, he looks more like a picnicker on the Appian Way than the president of a worldwide NGO. He taught himself Esperanto at twenty while studying economics, leafing through Esperanto journals in a communist bookshop. It was the sixties; it was Rome; the streets were aswirl with Maoists, *manifestazione*, and the occasional Red Brigade bombing. Within a couple of years, Renato became president of TEJO, the Esperanto youth wing, exchanging demonstrations for interminable meetings, lectures, and discussions.

Anna interrupts: "Remember when you created a sensation by tearing down the flags?" He's amused by the question, but passes on the opportunity to expand. Renato and Anna both reminisce with alacrity, at a rapid tempo, but in slightly different keys. Renato's speech has two or three sharps, Anna's a couple of flats.

Anna had always known that her great-uncle, a Nuremberg Jew killed by the Nazis, had been an Esperantist. Perhaps that was why at thirteen, weary of memorizing French irregular verbs, she purchased a book called *Teach Yourself Esperanto*. At fifteen, she went to a youth meeting but was too shy to open her mouth. Then, like so many Esperantists, she dropped the language for years, going on to study medieval English literature and comparative philology at the University of Leeds. After a spell in Edinburgh, she joined her parents in Israel in the mid-seventies. Anna's father, a West End actor known as Heinz Bernard, a refugee from Nazi Germany, had put himself through school by waiting tables and skinning rabbits. When he learned that he was adopted, he emigrated to Israel to seek out his birth family. There he married, acquired fame and stability, and appeared four times a week on television in a children's show written by his wife, Nettie. The days of skinning rabbits were over.

"Do you know the Hebrew verb *l'hizdangef*?" Anna asks. I do; it's slang for aimlessly strolling down Tel Aviv's Dizengoff Street, full of cafés and shade trees. "My Esperantist friends and I used to say *'Dizengofumi.'*"

Renato and Anna have lived their lives in Esperanto since the 1960s, when the language became a magnet for activists. "First, peace activists, protesting the war," Renato says, "then in the eighties it was all about sending food to Africa and raising money for an AIDS vaccine and HIV awareness." For Anna, however, the seventies stand out: "In those days, I was very involved in women's liberation and the La Leche League." She's the author of the first Esperanto guide to breastfeeding, or *mamnutrado*. "Those were the days of *Sekso kaj Egaleco* [Sex and Equality], the first feminist magazine in Esperanto. I was working in Rotterdam at the world headquarters of UEA and I wrote it, produced it, and mailed it out. The Eastern Europeans couldn't send money, so we sent it free to Eastern Europe and Brazil. It was very much of its time—lots of articles fearing nuclear war—it was even translated into Japanese." The links between feminism and Esperantism, she tells me, "are still alive today in the women's movements of Korea, Pakistan, Bhutan," but *Sekso kaj Egaleco* had long since gone the way of all cheap, mimeoed feminist newsletters.

"Older Esperantists, those our age"—Renato points to Anna—"are still ideologues, but not the young." After this slightly melancholic pronouncement, he takes the tempo up a bit. "Today Esperanto is growing in Asia, Africa, Latin America. When I'm in Asia, I feel the tremendous enthusiasm; when I'm in Brazil I'm always hearing that Brazilian Esperantists are going to save the world. And in Cuba—their slogan used to be 'I am a soldier of Esperanto'—it's been supported by the regime for decades. There are still about ten thousand Esperantists in Cuba." In fact, they've had an outsized impact on the movement, hosting the Universal Congress twice: in 1990, when Castro himself received the Esperantists at one of his residences, and again in 2010.

"You see, the idea of neutrality is still central, and it has always been," says Renato.

"So, is that the *interna ideo*, neutrality?"

"The *interna ideo* is equality among people," he says serenely. "In the movement, every culture is worthy"—in his Roman-accented English, it rhymes with "swarthy"—"every culture is to be preserved. International linguistic relations should be fair, but with English comes American culture. And less than 10 percent of people speak English worldwide." I should be disturbed by this, but I feel oddly complacent. Perhaps it's congenital, my *Usonozo*—a missing gene for universalism? Or do I harbor a few lurking cells of chauvinism? Maybe my suburban American childhood left a hairline fracture of the soul.

"So the *interna ideo* isn't the *fina venko*?" I ask.

Anna chuckles: "The *fina venko*? Nowadays, anyone will tell you—the *fina venko*'s a joke." Anyone, but not everyone.

We've been talking in the bar of a boat headed for the limestone karsts and spiky islands of Ha Long Bay. From the upper deck comes a blast, and the boat joins three or four tiers of wooden picnic boats already ringing a tiny dock. A boy of fifteen in mirrored shades takes Anna by the hand and indicates that she's to mount the chair, cross to the next boat, wait for him to collapse the folding chair and jump over, then repeat the exercise on the next two boats after that. I'm betting Renato will take a pass, but when I look again, Renato has already crossed to the next boats after that, and when I see them next, Anna's walking slowly and carefully down the gangplank toward the beach, with Renato close behind.

Whoever told us we'd be back by eight this evening was wrong. Without traffic or any discernible delays, we reach Hanoi around midnight. The kitchen in the *studentoklubo* has remained open and serves up spaghetti Bolognese for the weary, sunburned arrivals. But after, at the dorms, there's no hot water.

In fact, there's no water at all.

6. Number One

At lunch the next day, I sit across from Malik, a mustachioed Pakistani whom I recognize from the morning session. We'd just seen images of a Korean demonstration against the *"Usona Bazo"*—the American base at Pyongtaek. Frame after frame, smiling students bearing Esperanto placards: *"Mi Amas Pacon"* (I Love Peace); *"Pacon al Irako"* (Peace to Iraq); *"Faligu Pafilojn"* (Down with Guns). In one image, a student waves an Alfred E. Neuman–style caricature of George W. Bush, reading "BUSH: REIRU AL VIA STELO!" (Go Back to Your Star!); boisterous laughter from the audience. I might have laughed along at this laughingstock of a president, but somehow I felt uneasy and isolated. To my left, Malik rose to speak and, since it's the custom to recite one's congress number, held up his badge, declaring "I'm Number One!" Evidently he was the first to register online for the congress. Whether he meant to comment on Bush or not was hard to say; waves of laughter drowned him out.

In the cafeteria, wearing a pale blue Izod shirt, Malik has the bluff, well-met manner of a businessman at the club, a man who knows his own importance. He's a Canadian citizen from Montreal, Pakistani by birth, who speaks eleven languages. The rest of the story takes two hours, and yes, he'll get to Bush, eventually.

In the early 1970s, during the Indo-Pakistani War, Malik moved to Tehran. One day, while reading a magazine in a butcher shop, he saw an ad for Esperanto, bought a teach-yourself book, and then enrolled in a course. Esperanto in Iran, having been dormant for forty years, was enjoying a revival. At its height, before the cultural revolution of 1980 shut it down again, Esperanto was taught at Tehran University and in clubs, schools, and mosques; the city boasted seven hundred trained instructors. Among them was the man who taught Malik's class of five hundred students, droning into a microphone for an hour. Malik soon started attending Tehran Esperanto Club picnics. "They knew what they were doing," he said; "they got you to speak Esperanto by fining you for every word of Farsi spoken."

In 1979, when Ayatollah Ruhollah Khomeini left his house near Paris to board a plane for Tehran, Malik realized his days there were numbered. The day the Tehran Esperanto Club members were bused to an audience with Khomeini, he'd missed the bus. It was an accident, he said, "but if you had to miss a bus, this was the bus to miss." That particular meeting was uneventful, but Esperanto would soon be throttled by the grip of Islamic law; by the end of three months, Malik had made his way back to Pakistan. Back in Islamabad, wondering if he were the only Esperantist in the country, he resolved to teach Esperanto, putting into practice what he'd learned in Tehran: enroll eager students, go for picnics, and fine the crocodiles.

No dog is as shaggy as the story of how Malik tracked down the famed Mr. Muztar Abassi, the founder of Esperanto in Pakistan. (Abassi had also published an Esperanto-Urdu dictionary and would later translate the Koran.) Suffice it to say that Malik met with an imam who had known Abassi only to find, after a day doing the imam's errands, finding a proper gift, and sitting patiently for hours, that Abassi had been waiting for *him* in the mosque the entire day.

The lunchroom has been emptying steadily for a half hour, and we're the only ones still sitting with trays. Suddenly Malik picks up a greenish banana from his tray, frowns at it and excuses himself. He strides to the kitchen and brandishes the banana high in the air until a cook runs over to replace it with a bright yellow one. From across the room, Malik waves his new banana at me, like a crescent of moon he'd personally plucked from the night sky, then returns and takes his seat.

"*Usonanoj*," he says—had this been our topic all along, Americans?— "they're all brainwashed."

They? Me? All of us?

"It's Bush this, Bush that," he says with disgust, "Bush, Bush. For Americans it's work, the game, sleep, and more brainwashing. They need to be liberated."

Suddenly he says in English, "Why do I learn Esperanto when I can just speak English? Esperanto has changed my life. I have friends around the world; I am open-minded; in *Esperantujo* I have, believe me, a different personality. Esperanto means love your language and country while loving all others." He gestures around the near-empty lunchroom, then lowers his voice a shade. "All the Pakistanis I know in Montreal have no idea how to love other people without prejudice. They're sending their kids to English-speaking schools. Why? Because *maybe*"—mockingly—"*someday*"—pause—"*maybe someday* they'll be going back and then where would the kids be if they didn't know English? But not me," he says, shaking his head vigorously. "My child will learn French; I'm not afraid of that.

"Look," he says, leaning in; he's about to say something personal—about me. "*You're* Jewish"—I hadn't told him—"*I'm* Muslim, but in Esperanto we're both speaking one language. Where did I get my first Koran in Esperanto?" A beat. "From an Israeli at an Esperanto congress."

It's past two p.m. and we're both a little talked out, so he asks a ponytailed volunteer, mid-flirt with an Australian at the next table, to take our picture. We pose as she zooms in and out, in and out. Malik breaks the pose, takes the camera from her and refocuses it on me. Then he surrenders it and resumes the pose. She has turned the camera vertically this time, and he doesn't like it. "*Ne ne ne*," he says, going over to her, taking the camera and refocusing it. "*Tiel!*"—like this! Biting her lip, she holds the camera tightly and snaps before Malik can resume his grin. "*Denove!*" he says—again!—and she snaps it again, and then again. I know he wants me in his album of open-minded Esperantists who love our languages and countries while loving all others. But I'm finding it hard to hold the pose.

* * *

It's Friday afternoon, and the closing ceremony is getting under way. The humidity, as always, is suffocating, and many of the younger Esperantists, out late "owling" the night before, look sleepy and sullen. Some of the *helpantoj* nod off during the "bird-of-paradise dancers," three svelte, balletic young Hanoians with bare midriffs. They even sleep through the next act, a fellow playing an earsplitting piccolo directly into the microphone, and the next, a deep serenade on what looks for all the world like a Vietnamese didgeridoo.

Hai Ly, seraphic in an immaculate white *an doh*, thanks five groups

of people with five different speeches, each culminating in a reading of a
dozen names. The day before, I'd asked her whether she saw any conflict
between the staunch nationalism one encounters everywhere in Vietnam and the internationalism of Esperanto. She'd hesitated, as if summoning the effort to correct my most basic assumptions about both
Vietnam and Esperanto. After a moment, she said simply, "No." What it
meant was, *We are already living in two worlds: Asian and Western, communist and capitalist. One world scarred and maimed by war; another
nurturing and cherishing peace. One, a world we inherited; the other
which you Americans have thrust upon us and which we are frantically
making our own.*

Each person thanked, without being asked, ascends the stage. When
Hai Ly's salute ends, a trumpet fanfare blares on the PA, then a loud,
thumping disco. The ranks of the thanked wave rhythmically to the beat.
From either side of the stage comes a *helpanto* bearing an armload of long-
stemmed red roses, one for each person onstage. When it comes time to
thank the *helpantoj,* Hai Ly's voice cracks with emotion; tears roll down
her face. She has nurtured them, encouraged them, motivated them to
learn the language of peace. Most *helpantoj* weep openly. "In Esperanto,"
Hai Ly says, over the din, "we don't say goodbye. We say *ĝis la revido*"—
"till we meet again."

I can't make out what Hai Ly says next, but the entire audience gets
up and shuffles onto the stage. The official photographers are shouting in
Vietnamese and trying to wave the crowd toward the center, as if by remote control. But the mass congeals slowly, as the *samideanoj* hug and
weep and move on to hug and weep again. I follow them up to the stage,
and we huddle together, sweaty and damp, amid the rank, close odor of
our bodies. It strikes me that they're expert at something Zamenhof was
adept at, too: this life in two worlds. What Zamenhof did in Białystok,
Vietnamese teens are doing today in Bien Hoa.

And somewhere in heaven, where the lingua franca is surely Esperanto, Zamenhof must be watching his youngest children, posing
like the Boulogne and Dresden and Warsaw delegates before them, for
the official congress portrait. Perhaps he is shivering—as I am, despite
the tropical heat—to hear the youth of Hanoi, Hue, and Ho Chi Minh
City belting out "*La Espero,*" karaoke-style, to the timeless whirring of
fans.

7. You Got *That* Right

After giving away dozens of Princeton decals and amassing a heap of paper flowers and fans, I left the congress, picked up Leo, and we headed for the airport. We'd planned a brief trip to what the tourism industry calls "the imperial capital of Hue"; in fact, we wanted to see the site of the brutal, protracted battle in which the Americans and South Vietnamese wrested Hue from the Vietcong, who had occupied it during the Tet Offensive of 1968. Since arriving in Vietnam, we'd been treating our *Usonozo* with pilgrimages of various kinds—to the Cu Chi tunnels; to the Hoa Loa prison, aka the Hanoi Hilton; to the Vietnamese Women's Museum, with its strange relics of the war, all made by Vietcong women: a three-inch metal comb in the shape of a shot-down American plane, ersatz lamps made from U.S. grenades, and a flower vase made from a fifty-seven-inch shell on which the names of thirty-two girls were inscribed. And now, Hue; the name itself conjured U.S. Marines in bandoliers running through city streets, sprayed by gunfire.

Our guide was Tran Dinh, a stocky, olive-skinned fellow in his late thirties with thick brows and a black baseball cap. When he met us at the airport, he haltingly read out our names from his clipboard, greeting us in slow, deliberate English—an act, as it turned out. Snapping shut the folder, he grinned and said, "Let's get this Boeing going!" When I praised his pronunciation, he said, "You see, I clooooose my syllllllables with connnnnsonants. I make my tongue work! I exercise my muscle! Most Vietnamese never learn this. They *wah* instead of walk. They *ta* instead of talk."

Tran Dinh showed us the tower where the Vietcong had raised the flag in Hue. Inside the citadel, the geomancers had done their work, laying out in fortuitous arrangements courts within courts, each defined by who was permitted to enter it. Less than a third of the citadel had survived the battle for Hue, and we spotted a bullet-pocked octagonal concrete emplacement set in the rear gate by the Americans. Outside in a park were several mangled American cars and copters on display.

After answering a barrage of questions from Leo and me, Tran Dinh took a deep breath and laughed. "Hey, guys, you remind me of one of my American clients who asks a lot of questions. She's a child psychologist and a writer. A Jewish person."

There was a brief, uncomfortable pause. Leo said, "We're Jewish too."

Tran Dinh lit up. "Yeah? Jews?" he said delightedly. "I love Jews! Jews are so smart, they want to know everything. I have many Jewish clients from America. Do you know the Morowitzes?"

"Well," I managed, "there are a lot of Jews in America, about six million. We couldn't possibly all know each other."

"But tell me," he continued, "don't you Jews know each other when you see each other? You can tell, can't you?" There seemed to be no point in weighing the consequences of one particular answer over another, so I said, "Sometimes. It's not a simple thing; there are so many Jews who have intermarried. I teach courses on Jewish subjects, and you never really know for sure which students are Jewish."

For sure? Did I really say that—*for sure?*

"Well," he said confidentially, "I'll tell you something. I'm the only guide I know who volunteers to lead Israelis. Most of the guides I know just refuse—they say they ask too many questions, they demand and demand, they interrupt constantly, you can't tell them anything. But me, I can take them! I can take them any day! I love Jews!"

My mother used to say that the line between philo-Semitism and anti-Semitism is very faint; Leo changed the subject. "So you're collecting American expressions?"

"Yoooooooou *betcha*," said Tran Dinh, showing us a Chinese knockoff of a PalmPilot.

"Do you know 'What-*ever*'?" asked Leo, imitating a disaffected teen.

Tran Dinh shrugged it off. "What-*ever*? Old hat."

"Well," said Leo, "here's how you do 'what-*ever*' in sign language." He made two *v*'s with his thumb and forefinger, merged them into a *W* and pushed it forward. Tran Dinh looked bored. "Thanks," he said flatly.

"Okay," I said, "try this: 'Stuff happens.' It's another way of saying 'What-*ever*.'"

Tran Dinh pondered. "Is it vulgar?" he asked.

"Well, no," I said, "in fact it really means 'Shit happens,' which *is* vulgar. In fact, 'Stuff happens' is sort of polite. You want to be colloquial without being vulgar, right?"

"You *said* it."

"Tran Dinh," Leo cut in, "try this: 'You got *that* right.'"

Tran Dinh said it softly to himself once or twice then tried it out loud. "*You* got that *right*."

"No," said Leo, setting the bar high for a performer like Tran Dinh. "It's 'you got *that* right.'"

"*You*-got-*that*-right," said Tran Dinh with relish and took out the PalmPilot. "I'm adding that to my list, and 'Stuff happens.' And also 'Shit happens.' That makes eight hundred forty-four phrases. When I get to one thousand I am going to publish them and sell them to all the tour guides." While the Esperantists in Hanoi had been dreaming of a better world, here was Tran Dinh's dream of betterment, selling his English in exchange for—what? A reprieve from taking graying American vets through Khe Sanh, weekend after weekend? For a brief vacation in the Tonkin Alps?

"And with this list," he said, waving the device, "I will make a *killing*."

* * *

An hour later, on a high bluff overlooking the Perfume River, we mount the steps to the seven-level Thien Mu Pagoda. In a flat pine grove on the summit lies a monastery. Outside, a few young boys of ten or eleven, shorn but for a single hank of black hair, mill about in baggy beige tunics doing chores: some sweep; others, wearing yellow rubber gloves, scrub steps. Tran Dinh jokes with the chore-doers, who agree to pose for a picture with him, then return to their tasks. When we reach a temple containing the Buddhas of past, present, and future, I ask whether he and his family are practicing Buddhists. "Long story," he sighs, like a student asked why he'd switched majors from pre-med to English. "I believe in God, I am a spiritual person, but I don't practice. But my father . . ." He sucks on his water bottle.

"My father is now a mendicant monk—but he wasn't always. During the war, it was a terrible time; you didn't know within a family who was what, some were fighting for the SVA [South Vietnamese Army] in the day-time and reporting to the NVA [North Vietnamese Army] in the night-time. My father was in the SVA and felt very, very bitter when the Americans left in '73. When the war was over, the government tried to make him speak, tried to make him bend"—he holds his forearm up rigidly—"but he wouldn't bend. Would. Not. Bend." He fake-pushes the rigid arm with the other arm but it doesn't budge.

"Then they took him away for four years of 'reeducation.' Up a creek. No paddle."

He's skipping decades, now, but the present presses. "So not long ago, he asked my mother to grant him his freedom to become a monk—he had to ask her, that's the rule—and she did. So he left to become a monk. He lives very simply with other monks, he eats little, only vegetables; he spends little. I don't see him much, and when I see him, he won't joke with me anymore." There's sorrow in his eyes, and I can see what he's lost: the joy of making his father laugh, his apprenticeship for a career of clowning with tourists.

We've reached what appears to be an open three-car garage. In the first bay is a rusty vintage sedan in robin's-egg blue; behind it, on a wall, hangs a large black-and-white photograph. It's weirdly familiar: a slight man sits in the street, straight-backed in a lotus position, a white plastic canister of gasoline tossed onto the roadway beside him. There's a brightness in the center that the photo can't entirely capture; he's on fire, this meditating man, wild tongues of flame licking his shaved head and bare feet. He seems to lean back slightly on his throne of fire, his contour clear, black, and motionless, tiny bright flames at his collar and sleeves. To his left, a small knot of monks in flowing white robes stand like Graces in front of a crowd and opposite them, a large grey sedan with its hood agape, as if in surprise.

Only it wasn't gray, it was robin's-egg blue, and this is the car.

From this monastery, in the summer of 1963, a seventy-one-year-old monk had driven to a major intersection in Saigon to protest the oppression of Buddhist monks by the American-backed Diem regime. He parallel-parked, and while nuns wept and monks chanted, he went into the road and sat cross-legged until someone emptied a canister of gasoline over his head and shoulders. In one hand, he clutched beads; with the other, he struck a match, and in what Diem's sister-in-law blithely called a "barbecue party," sat motionless within the flames, lips moving in silent sutras, counting out the days until the coming war.

My six-year-old self, cross-legged on the lineoleum, watched on TV.

HAVANA

8. The True Believer

As I'd told family and friends all spring, *"I'm going to Havana legally, from Miami; there are permits for writers; did you know there are ten direct flights a day?"* I soon learned that for me, no permits were on offer. Instead, I was to look up the categories of travel excluded from the U.S. embargo, which was still in place at the time, choose the most applicable, and book a charter. Upon my return, I was to show documents validating my claim for an exemption to whichever Immigrations and Customs Enforcement agent happened to be on duty. In my case, he was Cuban-American and decidedly unimpressed by my credentials. After barking that I'd just flouted the embargo and incurred a $250,000 fine, he waved over another agent, who ushered me into a detention room, where I sat for forty-five minutes before being sent into the next room, which turned out to be an agriculture check, and in two more minutes I was outside, waiting for a cab.

But I am getting ahead of myself. Let me go back, which is what one does here in Cuba, where the cars seem to be driven by relatives who've been dead half a century.

When I arrive at the opening ceremonies in the vast Convention Center, which the government has let the Esperantists use gratis to suck some hard currency into the economy, a Hungarian history teacher accosts me: "José Antonio is looking for you," she says. I had never met *José Antonio Vergara, a Chilean physician and public health official, but he is known by all: "You couldn't hope to find a more optimistic Esperantist," an elderly *samideano* once told me; "he's a true believer." I find Vergara, in an ironed shirt white as a lab coat, and he asks if I've come to Havana legally.

"Yes," I say hesitantly, without expanding on the complications.

"Wonderful!" he says, "because we need you! We need you to give the official greeting from the Esperantists of the United States to the people of Cuba! Please say a few words and use this phrase of José Martí: in Spanish it's *'Patria es humanidad'*—you understand? Only *say it in English.*"

My throat constricts; I'm a Cold War baby boomer raised on *Get Smart* and civil defense drills. What can I possibly say to the people of

Cuba? I'm feeling a little faint, but before I can bow out, Vergara ushers me to a seat on the stage.

I have five minutes to craft a salute to the Cuban people in Esperanto and deliver it to an audience of two thousand.

There are preliminaries, of course: greetings from the minister of culture, a boisterous rendition of "La Espero," and a performance by an improbably sexy twelve-year-old accordionist in braids. Then the traditional salutations begin, alphabetically: *Argentinio, Aŭstralio, Belgio* ... Someone reads a salutation in Quechua; a Khazakh woman in a red scarf sings hers. By the time they call *"Usono,"* cameras are flashing, tripods trained on the lectern. I grab the podium to steady myself. It's hot under the lights.

(Breathe. Breathe. Breathe.)

> *Kiel vi scias, la vojaĝado al Kubo estas malpermisata al civitanoj de Usono. Tamen, kelkaj verdegaj, kuraĝaj usonanoj suksesis alveni al Havano por partopreni tiun gravan kongreson ĉar, en la vortoj de José Martí, "Our homeland is humanity."*

As you know, travel to Cuba is forbidden to American citizens. Nevertheless, some very green [i.e., Esperantist], brave Americans succeeded in coming to Havana to participate in this important congress, because, in the words of Jose Martí, "Our homeland is humanity."

Applause gathers, grows, rumbles, amid football hoots and vuvuzelas droning from the mezzanine. Later, listening online, I'll count the seconds of applause: thirty-four.

Afterward, when I reach the coffee bar, people surround me, pumping my hand, patting me on the back, thanking me for the risks I've taken in solidarity with the Cuban people. Besides, says a young man from Brazil, it is so brave of me to go on national television, given that I am there illegally.

"But I'm here legally," I say. "I'm *not* one of the brave Americans"— but the young Brazilian isn't listening. "Don't worry, Esther, I've already erased my video of you," he says. "I don't want to get you into any trouble."

I hope all the videos will have been erased by the time I reach Miami.

* * *

José Antonio Vergara loves to speak English and says he *prefers* to speak it with me. His English is everything my Esperanto is not: fluent, exacting, nuanced; perhaps the prospect of a long interview in my uneven Esperanto seems a chore. While he speaks, his right hand is always moving; for emphasis, he points to something in the air, slightly above his head.

"When I was a child in Valdivia, Chile was a very poor country," he says. "Not as poor as it became during the dictatorship, but poor. I was hungry for ideas, looking outward to the world, and at seventeen I spent two months in England as an exchange student. Esperanto always caught my attention, and in the early eighties, when I entered medical school, I took a correspondence course and soon began to teach it. Esperanto was peripheral to my life, then; I was teaching it to protest the dictatorship. I joined the Youth Communist League at university and in medical school." He grows quiet; his hand stills. "I myself was never tortured, but I had friends who were killed." His demeanor is grim, but periodically his eyes dart to someone waving at him in the distance; he brightens for a second, then locks my gaze again. "But in eighty-nine, when the communist regimes fell in Eastern Europe, I felt betrayed. I had put my intelligence and prestige on the line to support these regimes, and when I learned what they had really done, I became personally depressed. . . ." He trails off, uneasy about recounting the fall of Communism as an identity crisis. But that is the story he needs to tell.

"In 1992, I finally left the party. For a time I was like a refugee. I had been a militant atheist, always resisting the concept of spirituality. But when I read a book about Buddhism, I thought, This is what I stand for: Protection of life. Compassion. Lovingkindness. I was amazed. It's an ethical tradition, not a transcendental faith. Besides, I was always a solitary man, even as a doctor. I specialized in epidemiology, and after six years in primary care, became a regional public health officer." He's now in charge of a region of 800,000 people.

"Esperanto became a part of my life because it meshed with my hopes for peace and equality. It was always pure," he says, a man who knows what it is to suffer diseases of both body and soul. "It enables me to stand for what I believe in—in a practical way. The idea itself is genius; I don't care about power and I know [the numbers] are modest. What's important is that people choose it. In 2003, at the congress in Fortaleza, I decided to improve my involvement in Esperanto. I'm an activist for Esperanto. And for linguistic diversity. And for biodiversity. And for scientific literacy."

Suddenly he grins, his finger tracing 360 degrees in the air. "You know, Havana, *here*, was my first congress in 1990, and now. . . ." It's as if he has been sitting here in the convention center for twenty years, waiting for it to fill up again with Esperantists. And it has. "Esperanto is not *the* answer," he says, then points to himself. "*I'm* happier because of Esperanto, here, meeting my friends from abroad. It is not enough to think about happiness of the group—we have to think about happiness as an individual attainment." He shrugs; the statement doesn't quite fit with his announced credos, but he stands by it. "I'm a true believer," adds José Antonio Vergara, as if he needed to.

9. "Tiel la Mondo Iras"

The highlight of Vergara's first congress—the Havana Congress of 1990—was Fidel Castro's lavish garden party for the Esperantists. A video, posted on YouTube by Michael Cwik, shows a barrel-chested Fidel in full military regalia. He stands before a banquet table, flanked by a bespectacled translator whose head doesn't quite reach Fidel's epaulets. The mode is vaudeville: Fidel bellows his greeting, clasps his hands and waits for the translation, but the translator sounds like a field mouse. "*Alto! Alto!*" (Loud! Loud!) roars Fidel, to explosive laughter, and the Esperantists chime in, "*Laute! Laute!*" "If you are dismayed," says Fidel, "remember that Christianity started with a smaller group" (laughter). "Sure, they were persecuted and crucified" (guffaws, as he grotesquely mimes a crucifix); "sure, some were thrown to the lions" (chuckles). "But in the end it spread to many parts. I hope you won't be crucified" (high hilarity) "and thrown to the lions" (shrieks of laughter), "but nevertheless, you will win because the idea is very just." Thunderous applause; they've all succumbed to it—Fidel fever.

Before closing, Fidel thanks the Esperantists for choosing Havana: "I'm sure that this congress will improve interest in Esperanto for our people." It could hardly do otherwise. Since the first Cuban Esperanto organization was founded in 1909, Esperanto has endured through corruption, revolution, famine; an article here, a lecture there, a class somewhere else, with few congresses and very little of the usual hosting and guesting of international visitors. Twenty years after the revolution, in 1979, the Cuba Esperanto Association (KEA) was founded; within ten years the UEA opted to hold the 1990 congress in Cuba. Fidel's prophecy was correct; membership rose in the aftermath of the 1990 congress, and in the decade between 1997 and 2007, it rose by 20 percent.

The Cubans running the present congress are fluent, sophisticated, worldly; among them are a publisher, a radio producer, a lawyer, a translator, a professor of philosophy. They're all decades-long veterans of the movement and well known, since every summer a couple of them are sent by the government to attend the Universal Congress. Fidel hasn't shown up this year, but our Cuban hosts are following his lead by throwing us a party—daily. Every afternoon, while sessions plod on in the partly air-conditioned convention center, three or four live bands, all lavishly costumed, play while teenage *helpantoj* fan out onto the dance floor like bar mitzvah motivators. Monday, merengue; Tuesday, salsa; Wednesday, cha-cha; Thursday, rhumba; Friday, samba. Each muggy afternoon, to the beat of bongos and claves, Esperantists from Europe, Asia, Australia, and North America dance with the Cuban rank and file. Those Cubans who are bused in from remote areas are hard for me to understand; they swallow Esperanto syllables in the best Cuban style and, anyway, it's tough to hear anything above the music.

The *habanero* volunteers can afford to come only because the UEA pays their daily bus fare. They attend the congress gratis in exchange for volunteer duties, as do the *samideanoj* from Camaguey and Santiago de Cuba. Toward the end of the congress, each Cuban will receive a voucher for 33 CUC (Cuban convertible pesos, keyed to the U.S. dollar) to spend at the on-site Esperanto bookstore. In a country where the average monthly wage is the equivalent of 15 CUCs, this is fairly miraculous. It's clear they won't be buying Esperanto books to resell them; to whom? What is usually a high point of a Universal Congress—the comical auction, run by auctioneer Tonkin—is embarrassing; our Cuban hosts sit together quietly on the sidelines, as affluent Europeans outbid one another for trinkets.

Adrian, the Dutch public health professor whom I first met in Turkey, is here in Cuba; it's his fourth visit, and he has promised to introduce me to some friends in Old Havana. While I wait for him in the lobby, I overhear Geraldo, a slim thirty-something Cuban in black skinny jeans, lecture two young Germans on the history of U.S.-Cuban relations—in detail, at length, and vehemently. (In fact, Geraldo has been living in Switzerland for the past ten years, as I learned when I met him yesterday during a tour of Hemingway's house, where the guards themselves panhandle for tips.) It's all news to them, and it's not the version I was taught in my sixth-grade social studies class. "For the U.S.," he concludes, "it's the politics of ripe fruit, as if it all just fell into their hands. So that's what the revolution was fought for: to return their rightful property to the Cuban people."

On the plane, when we'd started our descent fifteen minutes after leaving Miami, I could already glimpse the island that was once my country's toy, playground, whore. Along the wide avenues tread the ghosts of gamblers, rumrunners, and babes, but their automotive legacy's distinctly less ghostly. Among the Ladas and Volgas run plump '50s Chevrolets and Packards, painted in only three colors: Caribbean blue, pine green, and salmon. "Coco Island," the amusement park near the convention center, was once "Coney Island"; a grand clubhouse along the beach now provides recreation for the machinists' union. And inexplicably, the famed Tropicana still sells eighty-CUC tickets for the nightly open-air burlesque show, which even the revolution couldn't disrupt. The showgirls may be adolescent, but the tassels on their nipples just turned seventy.

* * *

Except for a few square blocks refurbished with UNESCO funds, Old Havana is in ruins. The buildings' elegant scrolled facades are weed-ridden and crumbling; bits and pieces of stucco the size of cinderblocks fall onto puddled, cratered streets. Walls inside the doorways are festooned with electrical wires, strung to ersatz apartments built on platforms in what were once cavernous mansions. "Here you're a walking purse," says Adrian as we reach the Malecón, a bayside esplanade overlooking rusted iron piers, from which small boys are jumping into the water. "Be careful," he says, gesturing toward a woman approaching with an infant. She points to my water bottle, then to her baby. I hand her the bottle, thinking she wants to give him a sip, which she does, then she pockets the bottle and moves on. In the park, a man asks to borrow my pen and I give it to him; he pockets it and strolls off. Just yesterday, on a tour bus, I took out a bag of nuts and raisins and held it open to a Cuban *samideano* across the aisle. "*Dankon*," he said earnestly, taking the bag; he ate a handful and put the rest in his backpack.

I've seen people this poor and poorer in Mexico City, in Dakar, in the Bronx, but they did not look this healthy. Men, women, and children are well nourished and able-bodied, their limbs whole, their skin—whether the color of espresso or of café au lait—clear. There are many teeth and few pregnant bellies: the government supplies both dental care and contraceptives. I see plenty of older people around (though it's difficult to say how old), ambulatory and self-sufficient. In fact, Cuba comes out ahead of the United States in a few major health indices including life expectancy (78.3 compared to 78.2) and infant mortality (6.95 deaths per thousand live births, compared to 7.07). Cuba's fertility rate is distinctly lower than that of the United States (1.48 compared to 2.05 in the United States and nearly 5 in Senegal).

The next day, along with seven volunteers carrying fifteen bags of toys, I board a van for the National Institute of Oncology and Radiology. Beside me is *Julián Hernández Angulo, the charismatic president of the KEA. He's a sturdy, dark man in his mid-fifties with wise, luminous eyes; he's an educator. There's an air of nobility about him, as though he were posing for a heroic bust. (So that Julián could learn Esperanto in the late 1970s, a friend laboriously transcribed, in its entirety, *Teach Yourself Esperanto*.) When I ask him to fill me in on his life in Esperanto, Julián cuts to the chase: "I work *every day* for Esperanto." I know what this means for a middle-aged Cuban man: working a full-time job; supporting a family; queuing for bread, medical care, and rations; yet somehow setting aside time for Esperanto. As the bus stops at a red light in front of the Necropolis Cristóbal Colón, Julián points out the final resting place of La Milagrosa. Dying in childbirth, she was buried with her stillborn child at her feet, but years later, when her casket was opened, the baby lay cradled in her arms. Her tomb is a holy site for pregnant women and mothers of sick children.

As in the tomb, so in the pediatric cancer ward: mothers stay close to their children. They're admitted along with their kids, sleep beside them, and remain there for the duration of treatment. These children are the most serious cases in the country, sent here from twelve other oncology centers in Cuba. One by one, they're accompanied to the community room by their mothers, to select the offered toys: a toddler on an IV, a boy with an eyepatch, a bald teenage girl who rolls her eyes at the toys with a look that says "I haven't been six for a decade." A few minutes later a wild-haired young pediatric oncologist hurries in to greet us. The statistics

are very promising, she says cheerfully; 70 percent of these patients survive for at least five years. Silently, I do the math: if we come back in five
years, four of these fourteen children won't be alive.

When the kids are settled in with their toys, Julián grabs his guitar
and stands up. He explains that we're Esperantists from countries all over
the world; being Spanish-speakers, the mothers seem to catch the word
for hope. "We are *so* happy to be here with you," says Julián, "that we want
you all to join us in a song." Julián begins to strum and in a sweet tenor
voice, sings an upward swing of melody.

> *Tiel la MONDo iras,*
> *Tiel la MONDo iras,*
> *Tiel la MONDo iras,*
> *Tiel la MOND—*

"This is how the world goes"—it's a song about hard times and heart-
ache, violence and loss. At the end of each sad verse, Julian knocks twice
on the guitar, as if waking us up to yet another day in such a world. And
like the world itself, the chorus goes and goes, around and around, and
we Esperantists all join in; some of the mothers are singing, too. Not the
children, busy with their toys—all but three or four who, nestled in their
mothers' arms, have surrendered to sleep.

10. Devil's Advocates

The following afternoon, the Esperantology session provides some unexpected comic relief. Amri Wandel, the wiry, ingratiating astrophysicist
who heads the Israel Esperanto League, chairs a session called "Esperanto
in the Shadow of English."

"The old arguments for Esperanto," Wandel begins, "that it's neutral,
easy to learn, and equal to any occasion, are no longer enough. It is time
to radically change our arguments for Esperanto." To make the point, he
has posed six provocative questions that stack the dice against Esperanto,
the last of which is "In fifty years, will the UEA have 100,000 members or
100?" What follows is a public debate between proponents of "universal"
Esperanto and "global" English. Taking the pro-English side are two of
the most diehard and devoted Esperantists in existence—UEA President

Probal Dasgupta and José Antonio Vergara, joined by a Finnish professor of media studies.

The three pro-English debaters warm to their roles instantly. They
argue vehemently, confidently, contemptuously, rapidly ticking off the
points against Esperanto: that English is clearly dominant in every branch
of international activity and communication; that it matters how many
people speak the language; that while Esperanto is a nice idea, it will never
be more than a coterie pursuit. The audience finds the incongruity of it
all comical, and clearly the debaters are amusing one another as well.
Maybe there's something cathartic for these three in assuming the voice
of doubt, as they've encountered it in all the cocksure colleagues and
friends who treat their abiding passion for Esperanto as nothing more
than an idiosyncrasy; at best, a quaint quirk. What Wandel had hoped for
was to point out a middle way forward, a secure place for Esperanto in
a world dominated by English, only it hasn't quite worked out that way.
"Well," he jokes when the applause dies down, "I suppose there really isn't
a need for Esperanto *after all.*" Given his Esperantist credentials—former
TEJO president, Israeli Esperanto League President, academician, and
father of three *denaskuloj*—I marvel at his aplomb. But it dawns on me
that this game of devil's advocate has been played before on the Esperantist stage—more a ritual, perhaps, than a game.

* * *

This year, the talk of the congress is a lecture by Spomenka Stimec, an
eminence in the Esperanto world of letters. A Croatian novelist and dramatist writing exclusively in Esperanto, Spomenka's in her late fifties, her
coppery hair bobbed in a Dutch boy cut. She has just pulled off something
remarkable: winning a competition for EU funds to support the translation of children's books from Bengali into Italian, Croatian, and Slovenian, and the reverse. The proposal, undertaken jointly by the Croatian
Esperanto League and publishers in Slovenia, Italy, and India, acknowledged that there are no literary translators from Bengali to these three
languages. Instead, the translation would be transacted through an "as-yet-
undecided" bridge language.

"We did not parade the word *Esperanto* before the EU," Spomenka
says drily, which may be why they won the grant of thirty-three thousand
Euros, half of the project's total cost. After the books were translated
twice—first into Esperanto, then into either Bengali, Slovenian, Italian, or

Croatian—and published, Spomenka persuaded embassies and consular offices to sponsor highly publicized book launches. Visitors from India were invited to the three European countries to give children hands-on involvement with Bengali clothing, food, and songs, challenging them to write essays for a contest. Spomenka's lecture concludes with a slide show of the six children's book covers—the three European books, printed in Bengali; and the three European translations of the Bengali original.

When the lights come up, there is a hushed homage to Spomenka's genius. A moment later, Vergara's hand shoots up. "It's ironic," he says slowly, "that you've had to hide the role of Esperanto just when it's playing a crucial role at the highest levels." Ironic? He might have said painful, exasperating, excruciating.

"Then where would we have found the money?" Spomenka shoots back. "We'd have sold our own blood to make this happen."

11. The Director

Adrian first met Arnoldo Garcia at the 1990 Havana Congress. The two have visited a few times over the twenty intervening years, mostly in Havana, sometimes with Arnoldo's wife and son, and sometimes not, when the couple are separated. Some of the credit for cementing this friendship goes to Arnoldo's frequent appeals for money—his annual Christmas appeal is a photo of snow-covered Niagara Falls with the caption "Feliz Navidad de Havana"; the rest of the credit goes to Adrian's periodic dispensations of cash. "Arnoldo's a character," says Adrian in English, leading me over to a slight, gray-haired man sporting a slim cane and a black Florida Marlins cap. With considerable effort, Arnoldo rises on his cane and greets me with a one-armed hug; "*Saluton, Profesorino!*" He has agreed to tell me the story of his life as an Esperantist—and for Arnoldo, all stories begin in 1959.

"When the Revolution came, I was thirteen, a student in a private Catholic school run by Americans. English was all-important at my school; English and business. In my spare time I read *Reader's Digest* and listened to Voice of America; I still remember Miss Anderson, my English teacher. I was the best writer in the class." We're speaking Esperanto, but he's proud of his English, which pokes through here and there. "My family didn't have much money but there was a rich boy at the school who used to visit whorehouses in the afternoons." He draws closer, conspiratorially. "One day he saw one of the priests dressed as a tourist on his way to the whorehouse!

"When the school was nationalized in the Revolution, everything changed: suddenly we were all wearing khaki. No more emphasis on English; no more three-years-of-business-training. The school emptied out and my friends vanished. Now most of my friends from school are dead or in Miami." He pauses and I chuckle, to be polite. "Around that time I played a chess tournament with a kid who turned out to be Fidel's son. I didn't know until I saw it in the newspapers." As an afterthought, he adds, "It ended in a draw.

"The first Esperantists I met in the 1970s—they're also in Miami now—showed me a map of the world: There was Spain! There was France! We became activists, ran courses, ads, expositions, but we never registered with the government. It was all illegal, so Esperanto was passed off as a cultural affair." This is a theme I've encountered before: keeping Esperanto out of politics by proclaiming it to be a cultural pursuit—in Nazi Germany, in 1930s Shanghai, 1980s Tehran. Only in my own country did Esperanto ever try to pass itself off as a purely commercial affair. "You had to be careful. In every group, whether religious, philosophical, or cultural, there was one policeman. I once visited a [Brazilian] spiritismo group: even there, a policeman!

"It wasn't until 1988 that I left the country to spend three weeks at a Cseh course [Esperanto teacher-training] in Poland. There were thirty women in the class and very few men. A Bulgarian woman with big glasses asked me to dance. She watched my feet the whole time but afterward I was able to get her alone for a few minutes. As soon as we were alone, she started crying, 'I miss my children!'"—he fake-wipes his eyes— "and that was that."

When I excuse myself to keep an appointment, Arnoldo offers to continue the conversation over dinner in Old Havana, where he lives. "Come pick me up," he says, "and we'll go to the Hanoi. There's no bell, but Adrian knows the drill: a black flag hanging from the third-floor window means I'm out.

"But I'll be in. Yell up and I'll throw you the key."

* * *

En route to pick up Arnoldo, we stop in to visit Fortunato and Bertalina, a couple in their eighties who run a *casa particular*—a tiny mote of free enterprise in a sea of nationalized commerce. Fortunato, now in semi-retirement, worked for years as a bellhop in a big hotel. "They were all owned by the mafia," he says in Spanish; then shaking his hand from the wrist, *"Muchas drogas."* Now, while Bertalina wet-vacs the bedrooms (*"Ay! Ay!* There's been *so* much rain"), Fortunato lounges in a floral-upholstered recliner watching TV. Framed photos everywhere, children and grandchildren; weddings, graduations, *quinceañeras.* Fortunato channel-surfs, stopping when a woman appears on the TV dressed up as a Hasidic boy, singing in a pulsating vibrato. *"Yentl!"* he says, beatifically. *"Me GUSTA Bar-bar-a!"*

Bertalina makes tea and sets out a plate of fruit for each of us—guavas, pineapples, melons. She hums as she sets out the food, then settles down to chat about their family, the weather, the couple with a baby due in to-night. Ten or fifteen minutes go by and suddenly Fortunato launches from his chair, changes the station, and turns up the volume. "Fidel!" he tells us, gesturing toward the screen.

Indeed, it's Fidel speaking about the upcoming Día de la Rebeldía Nacional on July 26, which commemorates the 1953 assault on the Mon-cada Barracks. Red, white, and blue Cuban flags are already strung from windows over the street; bands are rehearsing everywhere. At seventy-four, Fidel seems much smaller than he did in the 1990 Universal Con-gress. He stands erect, but he's flanked closely by aides alert to any signs of infirmity. He's wearing a track suit; his beard is grizzled, his face lined; his voice is reedy and his delivery halting. As he reads, he holds up the text of his address in two gnarled, shaking hands.

"See?" says Fortunato proudly. "Fidel! Steady as a *rock*!" Fortunato and I seem to be watching the same screen, on the same television, but clearly we're not. Adrian and I exchange a glance, and Bertalina quietly goes on pouring tea, humming a chorus of "Waltzing Matilda."

* * *

Arnoldo drops the key from the third floor into the darkness; a second later it plops right into Adrian's hand. We climb a flight of stairs strung with wires, and Arnoldo's waiting at the top. He's Adrian's age, but framed by the doorway he looks hunched and bent, perhaps fifteen years older. *"Saluton! Bonvenon!"* he says with pride, welcoming us into a small, dimly lit room piled high with dusty, yellowing books, videocassettes, and magazines, largely in Esperanto. There is very little room to move, since a table occupies most of the space; the table top is taken up by a squat PC that resembles a Pleistocene artifact. The air is musty and stale, as if the windowless room hasn't been cleaned in fifty years. A faded curtain printed with palm trees and coconuts hangs over a small recess; through a two-inch opening I can make out a stove, but it's too dark to gauge how greasy it is. Just as well.

"So now we will meet Dolores," says Arnoldo. "She's turning one hundred next week. Good thing I put her down for free diapers from the Convent de Belén." We enter a smaller, darker room that fronts on the street, and he flips on the light.

A forty-watt bulb, high overhead, illumines a bed set against a pale green wall. In it, a tiny, birdlike woman with wispy white hair lies on her side, asleep. The sheets are thrown off, exposing her pale blue gown and chalky legs. Arnoldo reaches over and pinches her calf, hard; she doesn't move. "She's not skinny," he says, "she could last a long time. Mostly she lies in bed, but she wakes up for a couple of hours every evening. We shout at each other for a while and then she goes back to sleep. And then, sometimes, I go out."

Her face is in shadow, her open mouth sunk around her gums. Whether she'll die with Arnoldo at her side, or all alone, and when, is anyone's guess. But clearly she'll die here.

"Where is your room?" I ask.

"*This* is my room," he says quickly. Two pillows lie on the bed, one under Dolores's head, and the other beside her small bare feet. I don't need a diagram: Arnoldo and his hundred-year-old mother share a bed, sleeping head to foot.

He flips the light off, and we go back to the other room, which by comparison looks bright. I'm suddenly eager to get to dinner. "Shall we?" I say, pointing to the door. No one moves.

"Show her," says Adrian.

"The *Profesorino*?" Arnoldo's clearly taken aback. "No! No!"

"Don't worry about her," says Adrian, mischievously. "In fact, I'm sure she'd like it."

"You're *sure*?" he asks Adrian, who nods with conviction. Arnoldo turns to me, half excited, half resigned. "Okay, *Profesorino,* come and look at my movies."

He sits at the PC, which at his touch whirrs like a sewing machine. Up comes a photo of two busty, leggy women in red bikini tops, hot pants, and thigh-high boots eyeing one another nastily. Their red fingernails are long and tensed, as if ready to scratch the other's eyes out.

"I am the director," says Arnoldo matter-of-factly, "and this one's called *Cat Fight*."

Adrian leans into the screen, squinting. "Is that Judy?" he says, pointing to the woman on the left.

"Yes, but she's been missing the last few days," says Arnoldo. "I'm afraid they've picked her up again for streetwalking—which she is *definitely* not doing anymore."

It's not quite a movie, rather a series of stills with Spanish subtitles. "I will claw you, my little kitty," says Judy to her nameless adversary. "I will pull your hair, bitch," answers the other. In the next several stills they're play-fighting in various poses; in each, twenty red fingernails claw into mounds of curvy flesh. "It's no more than you see on the beach," Arnoldo points out, and he's right; tops, shorts, and boots stay on. After some more clawing and wrestling, the women end up in a faintly erotic embrace, smiling. The final image has no caption, but Arnoldo supplies one: "Friends forever!" he says happily.

On the screen, behind the embracing women hangs a faded curtain printed with palm trees and coconuts; through a two-inch opening I can make out a stove.

"You shot this *here*?"

His shrug says, "I'm supposed to rent a studio?"

We're late for our reservation; Arnoldo grabs a plastic bag on the way out the door, anticipating leftovers. "For a Cuban," he says waving the bag, "*this* is a body part."

* * *

We're treating Arnoldo to dinner at the Hanoi restaurant; were he to treat us on his meager pension, he'd be forfeiting ten months of rations. It's a rare occasion, a dinner out, so Arnoldo's eating slowly. When we're all finished and I suggest that it's time to go, he calls over the waiter and orders an almond ice cream for dessert. As soon as the waiter leaves, Arnoldo shows us the silent code with which people criticize Fidel in public places. "They never name him, but they do this," he says, pulling on an imaginary beard.

After two or three Bucaneros, the wonder of eating food worth piles of pesos has paled and Arnoldo becomes pensive. "Be glad you were born in Holland and America," he says. "Psychiatrists have studied the Cuban people. They just follow, follow, follow what they're told. They suffer from *ŝafeco.*" It's one of those Esperantisms that doesn't carry well to English. They follow like sheep, he's trying to say, they suffer from . . . not sheepishness. Sheephood? Sheepiness? Sheepity?

"What are you doing on July 26?" I ask him.

He clutches his chest, clowning. "Probably having a heart attack," he says.

On the way back from dinner, I notice for the first time that Arnoldo's not using his cane, nor is he limping. "Arnoldo, your leg's better!"

"Muuuuuuch better," he says. "You see, I signed up to volunteer at the congress, but for the first few days, the UEA refused to pay bus fare. So suddenly, I was lame!"

I'm the director.

The street is dark, except for bobbing, floodlit flags. Arnoldo saunters toward home, where Dolores, in the pale green room, rests up for her final call.

PART FOUR

ESPERANTO IN A GLOBAL BABEL

1. Reinventing Hope

By the end of World War II, Zamenhof's hope of transforming all humanity into one great family circle was a thing of the past. His dream of a Hillelist people had failed; Homaranism lived on only in rarefied Bahá'í and Oomoto circles. Stalin had silenced and murdered Esperantists who had claimed a voice in the new Soviet empire, and under Hitler Esperantists had fared no better, even those who expressed allegiance to the Third Reich. The Second World War would force the Esperantists, once again, to reinvent their movement and, after the Holocaust, to reinvent hope itself. They needed a new kind of hope, open-eyed and scathed by war, one that took account of evil and vowed to oppose it.

The man who reinvented hope for Esperanto was a Yugoslavian jurist named *Ivo Lapenna. Like Lanti, he was inveterately oppositional, redefining the *interna ideo* as "unambiguous and uncompromising antifascism." The positive version of this ethos was human rights, but an agenda this vague could not protect Esperanto against the corrosive impact of Cold War–era politics. On Lapenna's watch, the movement's vaunted neutrality yielded to bitter infighting among Eastern Europeans in the Soviet orbit, leftists in the West, and those who feared the movement's infiltration by communist operatives—chief among them, Lapenna himself.

His leadership was paradoxical. Vindictive and often paranoid, Lapenna celebrated the collective while favoring an elite of "cultured and well-intentioned people";[1] trusted the collective will while reviling "the

enemy within"; affirmed the strength of the movement while declaring it
to be imperiled; and, above all, espoused "principles of full democracy [to
promote] culture and tolerance [and bring] illumination, learning, progress and success," while disciplining individuals of diverse or wayward
opinions. Beneath it all was a grim certainty about human nature: that
individuals, left to their own devices, could not be trusted to treat one
another as equals. Zamenhof's benign trust in human nature had found
its opposite number in Lapenna's paranoia.

Born in Split in 1909, Lapenna was the son of a professor of engineer-
ing and a pianist.[2] At twenty, he and *Emilija Heiligstein (whom he soon
married) founded the student-run Akademia Esperantista Klubo; a fellow member recalled his magnetism: "All of us, men and women, were in
love with him."[3] At twenty-four, Gino, as he was called, received his doctorate in law from the University of Zagreb. He had long been moving in
anti-fascist circles and eventually fought for the resistance; Lins, interviewing his youthful associates, found a web of associations with prominent Communists. That Lapenna became a government official after the
war, in Lins's view, points to Party membership, though there is no concrete evidence to prove it.[4]

*Ivo Lapenna, beneath a portrait
of Zamenhof
[Österreichische Nationalbibliothek]*

In 1937, poised to become president of the Jugoslavia Esperanto-Ligo, Lapenna published a series of anti-fascist articles in the league's monthly, *La Suda Stelo* (The Southern Star). He began at fever pitch: "Non-neutral 'neutrality,'" he declared, "is the cancerous wound of the Esperantist movement. . . . There never existed, nor could exist, completely neutral human beings." Even the Olympians, he joked, were biased. Only *as a collective* could the Esperantists achieve an ideal of neutrality. "Thus," he wrote, "[we are] not a society of neutral esperantists, but a neutral society of esperantists."[5] The following year, after his first, fiery speech against fascism before the breakaway International Esperanto League (IEL) in London, he was asked to join the leadership.

When the IEL and the UEA joined forces to become a single Universal Esperanto Association after the war, Lapenna saw his moment to shape the future of the movement. At the 1947 Universal Congress in Bern, he put forward a motion condemning Nazi war crimes, exhorting:

> all Esperantists, Esperanto-organizations and the Esperanto press, ceaselessly and most energetically, to battle against the remainders and new hotbeds of fascism . . . ; to unmask those who are preparing and provoking a new war; to actively support all democratic and peaceful tendencies.[6]

Asked to limit the resolution to the condemnation of Nazism, Lapenna adamantly refused; the resolution failed with 20 in favor, 126 opposed, and 34 abstentions. Whatever goodwill he had incurred with his extraordinary rhetorical gifts, Lapenna quickly frittered away, denouncing his opponents as having "fascist leanings"; others, he ridiculed as "frivolous"[7] oddballs who brought mockery on the Esperanto movement.

During 1948, when the Communist Party of Yugoslavia began cracking down on the Stalinist-leaning Esperanto league, Lapenna fled to Paris. Though he was granted asylum in France, he subsequently moved to the United Kingdom and within a few years secured a professorial post at the London School of Economics. In due course, he became a British subject, to all appearances, a tweedy academic tending the roses at his Wembley home. But into the executive of the UEA, he channeled his ferocious sense of purpose, focusing on two agendas: first, to centralize and bureaucratize the organization; and second, to propagandize aggressively against fascism to both institutions and individuals.

For the membership rolls of the UEA, it was an era of expansion. With a new rule granting membership gratis to all who belonged to national Esperanto associations, membership rose from 17,707 in 1948 to 20,000 in 1955 to nearly 34,000 in 1963.[8] Attendance at the annual Universal Congress also climbed. The prewar high had been just over 2,000 (Stockholm, 1934), but by the early 1950s, registration over 2,000 became the norm. Esperantists in Warsaw-Pact countries had travel restrictions, both legal and financial, but when congresses were held in iron-curtain countries, participation rose dramatically. The Warsaw Congress (1959), celebrating Zamenhof's centennial, garnered 3,256; Sofia (1963), 3,472; and Budapest (1983), 4,834. The 1987 Centennial Congress in Warsaw registered nearly 6,000 people, a record that still stands.

While the UEA expanded, Lapenna compiled an impressive list of achievements. As before the war, there were two offices, but instead of competing for influence, they neatly complemented one another: London handled administration and propaganda; Geneva, delegates and publications.[9] The Language Committee and its Academy had already been restructured as a single fifty-member Akademio de Esperanto, an oratory competition was set up for youth, and, at the initiative of the poet Reto Rossetti, a fine arts competition was launched. The keystone of the propaganda effort was the new Center for Research and Documentation of World Language Problems (CED), founded in 1952. Lapenna housed it in his home, with his (second) wife, *Ljuba Knjažinska-Lapenna, in the role of secretary. The CED's mission was to document the efficacy of Esperanto based on rigorous academic research so that the UEA's propaganda would be taken seriously, at last, by discerning, influential readers.

Lapenna not only reconceived the *interna ideo*, built up the movement's infrastructure, and expanded its membership; he also took Esperanto oratory to a new level. So inspiring were his plenary addresses that recordings of them have been sold by the UEA ever since. Typically, a Lapenna speech opens with fulsome praise of the host city, trumpets the unity of the UEA, and sounds an alarm about threats to unity. Toward the end his timbre rises, and his delivery becomes emphatic and rhythmic; the speech is followed by thunderous applause. Some listeners reported more than a "weak ecstasy": to twenty-year-old *Birthe Zacho, a handsome blond Dane with excellent Esperantist credentials, Lapenna's 1956 address "sounded like classical music; for me the most sublime art. I had the impression that the entire speech [was] only for me, and that we [were] in reciprocal contact."[10]

Fantasy became reality when they met at a ball a few days later. Thereafter, though Lapenna never did divorce his second wife, he and Zacho became publicly linked. Ljuba remained Mrs. Lapenna, as did Emilija Lapenna, who had refused her ex-husband's request to drop his name. When Birthe had a son in 1965, Zacho, not Lapenna, was his surname, but his given name was Ivo. For the rest of Lapenna's life, he and Birthe were together openly, if intermittently, and only after Ljuba died in 1985 did they become engaged. Months before his death in 1987, Birthe Zacho became the third Mrs. Lapenna.

* * *

Lapenna set his sights higher than a rationalized, flourishing organization. In 1950, at his instigation, the UEA delivered to the UN a petition for official recognition bearing 900,000 signatures and the support of five hundred organizations with a combined membership of over fifteen million members. In a familiar pattern—proposal, study, delay—the UN turned the matter over to UNESCO, which resolved to survey member states and address the matter at the next General Conference, two years hence, in Montevideo.

If Lapenna hadn't already been an Esperantist for twenty-five years, the work of lobbying UNESCO delegates in Montevideo might have converted him. With most, he spoke French; with the Italians, Italian and with the Russians, Russian; with others, his weaker German, Spanish, or English.[11] Lapenna persuaded the Mexican delegation to put forward a resolution endorsing Esperanto, but it failed after a Danish linguist observed that Esperanto was culturally useless, invented by an amateur, and "suitable only for Uruguayan menus."[12] No insult had ever helped the cause of Esperanto more: it was one thing to offend Esperantists, quite another to offend the host country. After a clamorous protest, the vote was retaken and the resolution passed giving the UEA, thirty-two years after the debacle at the League of Nations, the status of "consultative relations" with UNESCO.

UNESCO's legitimation brought few significant changes to Esperanto's standing in the world, Humphrey Tonkin has argued, because Lapenna restricted the UEA's involvement to language issues.[13] Instead, the effects were more deeply felt within the movement itself. Lapenna used the UNESCO relationship as a stick with which to shame the Esperantists into an unprecedented—and unwelcome—degree of "self-discipline," as he called it. Public relations, he believed, was the burden of *every* Esperantist, and to the end of "destroying prejudices" in the world at large, a set of directives was issued cautioning Esperantists to avoid any activity that would give the appearance of being a sect.[14] But in Tonkin's eyes, the real benefit of Montevideo was self-esteem and unity among the Esperantists themselves. "It gave the movement a sense of direction," wrote Tonkin, "which channeled the energy of activists and created a certain level of consensus about the way forward."[15] But that consensus was to prove shortlived.

2. Aggressor

While Ivo Lapenna was rebranding the *interna ideo* as antifascism, his doppelgänger was living on West Sixteenth Street in New York City doing much the same thing—but with a dark, anti-Soviet twist. The Cold War strained relations among Esperantists in Eastern and Western Europe, but in the McCarthy-era United States, it wreaked havoc.

In 1947, *George A. Connor, born in Nebraska in 1895, was president of the Esperanto Association of North America (EANA). Like Lanti, Connor had eked out a living teaching industrial drawing; he had also traveled to the Soviet Union between the wars, where he detected an acrid whiff of corruption. Unlike Lanti, he never wrote about his sojourn there, but in later years, his niece gave out that "he saw a number of his friends killed or all of their rations cut off."[16] Whatever Connor witnessed or endured in the USSR, his hatred of the Soviets and their influence was bitter, personal, and limitless.

Living on veteran benefits and (for obscure reasons) a disability pension, Connor crisscrossed the country for Esperanto. He gave lectures while his engaging wife, Doris, taught her signature "Connor Course" in public libraries and YMCAs. She also cleverly marketed her course as a record-cum-textbook and gave interviews for local television stations. Back in New York, with the assistance of a Ukrainian immigrant named *Myron Mychajliw, they ran EANA out of their apartment. Always pressed for cash, they attended congresses abroad thanks to the largesse of other Esperantists. "The long crossing is just to our liking," George

Connor wrote, "because we hope to give our usual *Esperanto-Kurso* aboard ship both ways."[17]

But if Connor's anti-Soviet sentiments germinated on Russian soil, his descent into paranoia eerily mimics that of his native country. In 1947, just as the House Un-American Activities Committee (HUAC) held its first set of hearings, Connor demanded "undivided support and loyalty to EANA," complaining that "individualistic institutions," "foundations," and "book services" were "promoting disharmony."[18] During the weeks following Senator Joseph McCarthy's famous 1950 "Wheeling" speech denouncing "enemies from within," Connor published a similar diatribe denouncing corruption in the ranks:

> If a band of robbers, opium contrabanders, or other criminals would use Esperanto, the neutral Esperanto-movement would be by no means obligated to express joy about this and propose its help. Similarly, when Esperanto is used to spread obvious lies or to subvert the democratic constitution and the liberty of our country, our "neutrality" hardly obligates us to tolerate this without protest.[19]

This attack was composed by then-president of EANA *William Solzbacher who, like McCarthy at the second round of HUAC hearings in 1951, was ready to name names. He started by naming the Soviet Union, which he portrayed as the sworn enemy of Esperanto. Conversely, wrote Solzbacher, Esperanto was inimical to the Soviet Union, since it had the power to *"punch holes in the Iron Curtain"*: "As a two-way street enabling people in Communist countries to learn how the common man in the 'capitalist' world lives and how he thinks [Esperanto] imperils totalitarian isolation." There was a prophetic grain of truth in Solzbacher's assessment. In the decades to come, Esperanto would become, for a new postwar generation in "iron-curtain" countries, a symbolic resistance to totalitarianism; for many it was the sole way of making contact with the West. But when it came to American Esperantists, Solzbacher's rhetoric was inflammatory and extreme. What was at stake, he wrote, was a clear choice between "liberty and slavery."[20]

During the 1950s, Connor led a schizoid existence. On the one hand, he was becoming increasingly vindictive to those Esperantists whom he flatly accused of being communist informants. On the other, Connor was the chief propagandist for Esperanto in the United States, and as such was highly successful. Under Connor's leadership, Esperanto was making its way into the American mainstream. Each issue of *Amerika Esperantisto* rejoiced in record-breaking numbers of new members and announced new courses. In October 1955, in New Jersey alone, seven new courses in the language "approved by UNESCO" were advertised, both in the working-class cities of Newark and Elizabeth and in elite suburbs such as Millburn.

Sightings of Esperanto in the press and on television were zealously announced. Nineteen fifty-three was a bumper year for Esperanto on network television: Groucho Marx interviewed Joseph Scherer, the Los Angeles *samideano* who had written Esperanto lyrics for the hula-dancing "natives" in *The Road to Singapore* (1940), and Art Linkletter's *House Party* featured Edward Kalmar, a Polish Jew who, in words of the *Los Angeles Times,* had "literally talked himself to life"—that is, saved his own life—by identifying himself to a guard as a fellow Esperantist.[21] The same year, Helen Keller wrote to thank *Esperanto Ligilo*—a Braille journal—for translating her recent speech at the Sorbonne into Esperanto. "How free and flexible Esperanto has grown!" she wrote, requesting a subscription.[22] Six months later, as a publicity stunt, *Life* magazine began to send notices in Esperanto to delinquent subscribers.[23]

But Esperanto's most imposing presence in mid-century America was not in the realm of culture at all. In 1947, when the U.S. Army developed a dummy enemy called "Aggressor" for training maneuvers, the language they assigned it was Esperanto. In the tortuous words of Field Manual FM 30-101-1, Esperanto "is not an artificial or dead language. It is a living and current media [sic] of international oral and written communication [which] . . . can assimilate new words that are constantly being developed in existing world languages."[24] Like the "Aggressor" faction, which was bent on "assimilating" U.S. citizens, the Esperanto language depended on the "assimilation" of words from other languages. As innocuous as this description sounds, onto Zamenhof's language of peace, equality, and world harmony the army projected its terror of—and disgust for—communist aggression.

The association of Esperanto with communism is writ large in a U.S. Army public relations film.[25] As an army officer begins to discuss training, black-clad Aggressor stormtroopers burst into the office, speaking a very stilted Esperanto, and frog-march him out the door. The commander of these marauders then perches on the desk, explaining that he represents the military arm of the "Circle Trigon Party"—its logo a green triangle aping the Esperanto green star. (Never mind that the UEA had dropped the logo because it resembled the Red Star of the Communist Party.) The dark uniforms and insignia of the Aggressor forces mimic Soviet regalia, though when called to attention, the Aggressor soldier gives an unmistakably fascist salute.

The program was so successful that in 1959, the Department of Defense published a standalone textbook called *Esperanto: The Aggressor Language* (FMN 30-101-1a). In addition to an introduction, a grammar, and a vocabulary, it featured a lengthy dialogue naming—in Esperanto—all the weapons in Aggressor's arsenal: "pistol, rifle, machine gun, mortar, recoilless rifle, gun, howitzer, rocket, rocket launcher, missile, tank, and armored carrier."[26] The Aggressor force's armor included vinyl cannons, tanks, and trucks, to be pumped up for maneuvers. In its paranoid Cold War fantasy of Esperanto, the U.S. Army was courting an inflatable enemy.

As for the role of U.S. Esperantists in the Aggressor program, no names have ever been named;[27] the conventional wisdom, these days, is that no dedicated *samideano* would have produced Esperanto so stilted and error-ridden. Connor improbably asserted that support flowed not from Esperantists to the military, but the other way: "The special tactical force in our U.S. Army . . . has brought us a number of members from the armed forces."[28] Whether Connor played a hand in creating the war game that would last the better part of two decades, we'll probably never know. Not until 1967 was the Esperanto field manual officially rescinded; as a Pentagon officer told American Esperantist William Harmon, "We don't need a make-believe enemy anymore. . . . We're getting all our training in Vietnam."[29]

* * *

Nineteen fifty-two was a turning point for Connor and EANA. For the first time, EANA refused membership to Connor's "carping critics," those who resisted his co-optation of Esperanto for anti-commmunist propaganda. At the EANA Congress in Sacramento, two of the *refusés*, *Dittlof and *Elvira Zetterlund, convened a disaffected "reorganization committee," which became the new Esperanto League of North America (ELNA). "It was more than a dictatorship," said co-founder Roan Orloff Stone of Connor's EANA; "it was tyranny; [Connor] was the Saddam Hussein of the Esperanto world in the United States."[30] At the Bologna Universal Congress of 1955, barely six months after the U.S. Congress condemned

Joseph McCarthy, the UEA censured Connor for "intransigence," officially recognizing ELNA alongside EANA.

Furious about the UEA's endorsement of ELNA, Connor blamed Lapenna, denouncing him as a "communist partisan." To Connor, Lapenna
was not simply soft on communism; he was a Soviet apologist and fellow
traveler, as evidenced by his deceitful claim that "the famous [iron] curtain is
beginning to rise."[31] Moreover, Connor alleged an official cover-up of Lapenna's intrigues, accusing the respected journal *Heroldo de Esperanto* of collu-
sion. Connor's *Amerika Esperantisto* carried satires of Lapenna as a moral
dwarf, and cartoons of the Soviet bear hooking the UEA like a flounder.[32]

Lapenna's stature might have permitted him to ignore the American
gadfly, but his pride did not. (The United States may be a superpower,
but the American Esperanto community is a rather minor constituency
in the UEA.) Bitter and outraged, Lapenna blamed Connor's defamation
for the fact that he, Lapenna, was twice denied British citizenship.[33]
Compelled by Lapenna's wrath, the governing committee of the UEA voted
to expel George Alan Connor from the UEA in an unprecedented, never-
repeated act. The Connors moved to Oregon, leaving Mychajliw to run
the central office out of his Brooklyn apartment and take over the book
franchise. As Mychajliw's daughter, *Tatiana Hart, recently commented,
"He subscribed to Dr. Zamenhof's theory that if everyone in the world
spoke Esperanto ... there would be less misunderstanding among nations. Unfortunately, as the Connors' employee he was not in a position
to disagree with them openly."[34]

After Connor died, his widow, Doris, donated his Esperanto library to
the University of Oregon, where it remains the largest Esperanto collection in the United States. An archive overview of 122 pages mentions
Connor's "opportunity to apply his trade in the Soviet Union in 1930–32,"
but gives away no secrets. The only man ever expelled by the Universal
Esperanto Association died in 1973. Had he lived one more year, Connor
would have seen Ivo Lapenna barely escape a similar fate.

3. Lapenna Agonistes

Elected president of the UEA in 1964, Lapenna struggled to hold the Cold
War Esperanto movement together. A refugee from a Communist regime
living in the West, a scholar of the Soviet legal system, and the leader of

an organization on both sides of the "iron curtain," Lapenna was in a delicate position. When he was suspected of being a communist sympathizer, he denied it vehemently; when he suspected *samideanoj* of working for the Komintern, he lashed out. To complicate matters, the pendulum in the Esperanto movement was swinging from Western to Eastern Europe.

Ever since the Soviet Union quashed the Hungarian uprising of 1956, Esperanto provided those living in the Eastern bloc with an internationalism that would never censor speech, never arrest a writer, and never be compromised by a repressive show of force. Some Eastern-bloc Esperantists joined the socialist organization Esperanto Movement for World Peace (MEM), but many more joined the UEA, which in the decade after Montevideo grew by 52 percent. Most of the increase comprised Poles, Bulgarians, and Hungarians, though the financial benefits to the UEA were diminished by currency restrictions on outgoing funds.[35]

As the era of Hitler, Stalin, and Mussolini receded, Lapenna's anti-fascist slogan of "active neutrality" (or "positive neutrality," as he rebranded it) seemed increasingly abstract; during the Cold War, neutrality itself came to seem chimerical. To exhibit his own neutrality as UEA President, Lapenna tacked back and forth between East and West. In 1967, he traveled to Moscow and Leningrad to visit the emerging Soviet Youth Esperanto Movement, but he also distanced the UEA from the Eastern-bloc MEM, and in Vienna he interrupted a pro-Soviet speech by the East German ambassador.[36] As Lins recalls, Lapenna approved publication of an account of the Soviet persecution of Esperantists, but when the World Esperantist Youth Organization (TEJO) passed a resolution against U.S. military aggression, Lapenna refused to back them.

In the time-honored way of those who govern riven states, Lapenna directed Esperantists' attention away from the rift. Trying to capitalize on his victory in Montevideo, in 1966 he applied to the Secretariat of the UN for official recognition of Esperanto and for concrete support. But times had changed; Lapenna's Eurocentrism had not kept pace with a body whose membership had been radically altered by two decades of decolonization. Thus the 1966 petition to the UN, though it bore a million signatures and the support of organizations totaling seventy-two million members, failed even to prompt a study commission.[37]

What Lapenna later called "the beginning of the end"[38] was brought

Lapenna and Humphrey Tonkin, 1965
[Österreichische Nationalbibliothek]

about neither by Eastern-bloc opponents nor by "enemies within," but by TEJO, led by Lapenna's former protégé, Humphrey Tonkin. After the student demonstrations of 1968, a moment of "radical change in the role of youth in society," TEJO rebelled against all the hallmarks of Lapenna's presidency: the immersion of the individual in the collective, centralization, and autocratic governance. In the Declaration of Tyresö [Sweden], TEJO declared Esperanto to be a liberatory movement on behalf of individual freedom. The gravest threats to individuality, TEJO declared, were social conformism and technology-driven alienation, which destroyed the environment and "undermined the human psyche." Decrying "linguistic imperialism," TEJO committed itself to "working for the elimination of every misuse of language for economic, cultural or political suppression." But "enlarg[ing] the dimension of the individual," as the declaration put it, was quite simply an unheard-of agenda in the history of Esperantism.

In fact, the Declaration made no mention whatever of Esperanto as a language, a movement, or an ideal. As *Giorgio Silfer, then a member of TEJO, later observed, reframing the *interna ideo* around the individual, rather than the *granda homa familio*, left it radically open: "Maoists saw in it an *avant-garde* toehold in the bourgeois Esperanto movement; socialists considered it a forward step toward the democratization of the Esperantists; Western progressives enthused that its spirit conformed to their ideas; pragmatists accepted it as a realist adaption to the present."[39]

TEJO, being politically multifarious, rebelled not against Lapenna's politics but against his leadership. Lins, like Tonkin a Lapenna protégé, was among many "wearied by his revolutionary pathos, his martial conduct and his inflexibility." Quick to make enemies and vilify those who trusted him, Lapenna couldn't (in Tonkin's words) "use the good features of people [while he] ignored, or neutralized, the bad [ones.]" Under Lapenna's leadership the movement was being torn apart, East from West, and along generational lines; even among the stalwart Esperantists who had given years to the movement, morale was abysmal. Warned by the UEA executive that his allegations of "attacks" and "misrepresentations"[40] were endangering the movement, Lapenna escalated the conflict: a "putsch" was in the works, he charged, funded and fomented by Moscow, with election tampering sure to follow.[41] By so doing, he alienated his supporters in the USSR and Eastern Europe.

In the weeks before the Hamburg Universal Congress of 1974, Lapenna used his bully pulpit to issue a "Warning to the Membership" in *Esperanto Revuo*. He reminded his readers that he had fought against "Hitlerism" when most Esperantists had been silent or fallen in line with Nazi strictures. He went on to name his "perfidious" enemies, among them the senders of forty anonymous telegrams from what he called the "Paris Esperantist Tribunal."[42] "There can be no 'peace' between truth and lie, between aggression and defense, between good and evil," he admonished; "even Christ . . . whipped the merchants out of the temple."[43] The man who was, in Tonkin's words, "more papal than the pope"[44] had begun to anticipate a Christlike martyrdom. Echoing his 1937 article about "the cancerous wound" of false neutrality, he gave his readers a choice: "Either one desires to 'have Lapenna' without abscesses on the organism of the UEA, or one will have the abscesses without me."[45]

At the 1974 Universal Congress in Hamburg, a single round of voting revealed that Lapenna had lost his base of support. It was Tonkin, now the ex-president of TEJO, who opposed him. As vice provost of the

University of Pennsylvania during an era of sit-ins, marches, and take-overs, Tonkin had withdrawn from leadership positions in the UEA; he had not intended to run for the presidency. But a consensus emerged that Tonkin was the best hope of depriving Lapenna of yet another term. "I thought, 'He'll take this defeat like a gentleman," Tonkin recalled, "but nothing doing. Lapenna had fought with Tito's partisans."

Preempting the next round of voting, Lapenna announced that he would be stepping down, not because he had failed to garner enough votes but because the UEA constitution regarding neutrality had been flagrantly violated in a rigged election. Invoking Zamenhof's vow "to sit among you" when he resigned the presidency in 1912, Lapenna vowed *never to sit among them again.* He left the room, left the congress, and left Hamburg, never again to return to a UEA gathering.

Within months, Lapenna was composing the angriest screed in the history of Esperanto. *Hamburgo en Retrospektivo* (Hamburg in Retrospect), which deserves a prominent place in the annals of wounded narcissism, launched a campaign to clear Lapenna's name and attack his suspected opponents. In 1977 he founded the Neutral Esperanto Movement (NEM) and published its journal, *Horizonto,* meting out defamatory diatribes in national languages, and placing them in the U.S., British, French, and Danish press. His rage had become his life, and he would die embattled. Lapenna was a totalitarian among universalists, a warrior among pacifists, and a bureaucrat among those for whom Esperanto was a balm for the blisters of alienation, system, and convention. In *Postwar,* Tony Judt remarks of the Communist state that "it was in a permanent condition of undeclared war against its own citizens";[46] the same was true for Lapenna and the Esperantists. Without ever surrendering, he died on December 15, 1987—Esperanto's centennial year, and Zamenhof's birthday.

4. *Many Voices, One World*

Tonkin's agenda was to extend the reach of the UEA beyond its power base in Western Europe. He devoted resources toward national associations in Iran, India, Turkey, and Japan, and coaxed delegates from non-European countries onto the executive committee. The Rotterdam office was expanded; new satellite offices were opened in Budapest, Antwerp, and New York. It was Tonkin's innovation to hold the Universal Congress

outside of Europe every other year. The Chinese, emerging from the pre-
dations of the Cultural Revolution, hosted the 1986 Universal Congress in
Beijing, where Tonkin learned that "the higher the level of the banquet,
the deeper in the ocean they went to catch the seafood."[47] Since the congress in Beijing (which hosted again in 2004), the Universal Congress has
been hosted by Cuba (twice), Korea, Australia, Israel, Brazil, Japan, Vietnam, and Argentina. The generation that reframed Esperanto as a liberatory movement was making new voices heard on a global scale.

Like Lapenna, Tonkin visited the Soviet Union, meeting with Esperantists in Leningrad in 1975. Meanwhile the Esperanto youth wing in
the USSR was engaged in a battle of wits with the Communist Party
and its apparatchiks. *Mikaelo Bronŝtejn, *Anatolo Goncharov, and *Boris Kolker were three of the young Esperantists who, armed with nothing
but moxie and a sense of the absurd, maneuvered among KGB agents,
petty party officials, and local bureaucrats. The strategy was to convince
the authorities that Esperantists were loyal to the party while running
weeklong under-the-radar encampments. In the Soviet Esperanto Youth
Movement, "youth" was broadly defined; a typical gathering included
two to three hundred people ranging in age from about twenty to sixty.
Goncharov recalls one such event outside Tikhvin in 1976, when a stray
camper inadvertently tipped off local authorities. Several Volgas pulled
up, disgorging officials who ordered them to disperse. Goncharov organized the three-hundred-odd campers to resist by conversing peacefully
with the officials, who eventually drove off. The next day, they returned,
threatening to bring police and soldiers if the Esperantists did not
disperse. Again, the Esperantists stood their ground; again the Volgas
drove off. When the officials returned a third time, they said, "If you can't
leave, then at least observe the sanitary regulations." A promise to dig
latrines farther off seemed to satisfy the officials, who drove off and did not
return.[48]

Russian-born *Dina Newman, now a reporter for the BBC, traveled
to these encampments to converse with Lithuanians, Siberians, Ukraini-
ans, and Uzbeks. "The encampments were an oasis . . . with very little official control. People were frank; I was never aware before that people
were critical of the Soviets," recalls Newman:

> There was lots of effort to translate folk songs from the Ukraine
> and Moldova into Esperanto, but [Yiddish] songs too, such as

"Dona Dona" and "Tumbalalaika." This was amazing, since the
Jewish context was never mentioned. Why . . . were they interested in Jewish songs?—these people didn't look Jewish. Well . . .
I thought, they do Georgian songs and all other ethnicities, why
not Yiddish? They were very inclusive.[49]

Goncharov, when asked in later years about the impact of Soviet anti-
Semitism on young Esperantists, asserted that "there was absolutely no
odor of anti-Semitism."[50] Kolker, however, had caused a scandal in 1984
by reviewing an Israeli book in *Esperanto Revuo*, the same issue in
which Lins reviewed a memoir about one Esperantist's years in a Soviet
prison camp. When Kolker was censured for "this audacity," he resigned
as president of the Association of Soviet Esperantists. Not until 1989
would he resume the post; shortly afterward, the association collapsed
anyway, in the rubble of falling walls.

Tonkin saw an opportunity in 1977, when UNESCO set up a "Commission on International Communication." It was led by the prestigious
Irish politician Seán MacBride, winner of the Nobel Peace Prize and the
Lenin Peace Prize and co-founder of Amnesty International. The commission's mandate was to frame a universal "right to communicate" and
develop a "New World Information and Communication Order" among
developing and Non-Aligned nations. Commissioners were to ponder
unequal information flows, access to literacy, advertising, distortions of
reportage of Third World and Non-Aligned nations, and the cultural
domination of mass media by the West, which commanded nearly
90 percent of the radio spectrum. In Tonkin's view, to democratize global
communication without addressing linguistic justice would be like
setting out to build a world-class hotel without two-by-fours. Enter
Esperanto.

To develop relations with the commission and to strengthen Esperanto in Non-Aligned nations, Tonkin invited the UNESCO director-
general, Amadou-Mahtar M'Bow of Senegal, to the Universal Congress
in Iceland. M'Bow and Tonkin discussed the work of the commission and
the symbiosis between UNESCO and the UEA. It was all very promising
until the MacBride Commission issued its report. *Many Voices, One
World* was many things: a witness to injustice; a brave, if misguided
attempt to prophesy the future of communication technology; and an in-

Humphrey Tonkin, Rotterdam 2012 [UEA]

transigent refusal to address, head-on, linguistic imperialism. "A certain imbalance in the use of international languages" was observed, prompting the weak suggestion that "studies might be undertaken with a view to improving the situation."[51] To compound the UEA's disappointment, M'Bow was a highly divisive figure, autocratic and nepotistic; *U.S. News & World Report* charged that he had used UNESCO funds to build a rent-free penthouse in Paris for his family.[52] In 1987, when twenty-six governments threatened to quit UNESCO if he ran again, M'Bow stepped down.

Originally the MacBride report was approved for publication in English, French, Russian, Chinese, Spanish, and Arabic. Had it been more attentive to language rights, it might be available today in more than three languages—English, French, and Spanish, the first languages of less than 15 percent of the world's population.

5. *Sekso Kaj Egaleco*

In 1975, the UN International Women's Year, "the UEA for the first time became actively interested in its women members," recalled Anna Löwenstein. To be sure, the women's liberation movement, in tandem with the

Declaration of Tyresö's emphasis on individualism, empowered Esperanto's women members. But in fact the UEA had first embraced the cause of women's rights nearly seventy years earlier.

In 1911, the UEA proclaimed the creation of the Universal Women's Association (UVA) as a freestanding section of the organization. That year, a *Women's Bulletin* appeared as a free supplement to the UEA magazine; its lead article, written by C. L. Ferrer, a suffragist from Monaco, was a call "To our Women Readers":

> We must not only propagandize Esperantism, but through Esperantism, strive for our own women's interests and . . . use this new strength to improve our material and intellectual condition, to facilitate relations among our sisters in all countries, to draw closer to them, and to weave among them strong bonds of solidarity and of reciprocal esteem.[53]

In the struggle for suffrage, Ferrer saw an important role for Esperanto. A year earlier, she had proposed Esperanto to the congress of the Women's International Suffrage Alliance as a language of international cooperation. Ferrer herself was a member of the network of volunteer "consuls" who provided services to *samideanoj*. The special needs of women travelers were already being addressed: a woman traveling alone could write ahead to the local consul, who would meet her at the train station, orient her to her new surroundings, and accompany her to her lodging. Ferrer, however, conceived of a network of women consuls, calling on them to advise their sister *samideaninoj* on employment issues and civil rights. In addition to alerting women to their mission to provide "international aid and protection,"[54] these consuls were also to research women's lives, compile statistics, and submit the data for publication.

The *Bulletin* also dwelled on the trials of women in the workforce, informing its readers about an international petition for equal pay for women workers;[55] an article (signed "A. R.") reported on an effort to regulate the number of nighttime hours women could be required to work. "Is a required break between nine in the evening and five in the morning too much?" she asked. "How are we to understand people who already are cursing the 'socialism' (?) of this new law!"[56] Other articles compared the salaries of women stenographers, typists, bookkeepers, governesses, and others, and listed respectable, secure residences for women workers. In the third issue, Emma Herzog of Davos lauded the state of Colorado for hiring a young Chippewa secretary named Mary Finn: "Only the bronze-colored face of this gracious woman, whose eyes intelligently looked out over gold-rimmed glasses, revealed her Indian heritage."[57]

The poet Marie Henkel, a German widow who first learned Esperanto at age sixty-one, exhorted women readers to change the culture if they wanted to change their lives. In an article entitled "Choice of a Profession for Our Daughters," Henkel wrote:

> Just as [they do] for a son, parents must choose a profession for their daughter. . . . Not every young girl marries, and not all husbands live forever. . . . Women who learn nothing practical are without doubt a heavy charge on human society.
>
> To you I direct my words, to you, parents. . . . Accustom the little girls to the idea: "I'm going to be this or that." Complete equality: . . . they must plan *only* on this.[58]

Henkel also asked readers to deflate three antifeminist stereotypes: the "old maid," the intrusive mother-in-law, and the wicked stepmother. The *Bulletin* also ran features on "cooking in a paper bag" and child care— "microbes multiply in the nose and the mouth before they go anywhere else." In each issue, the journalist and Tolstoy translator Jeanne Flourens wrote a "Fashion Chronicle" under the whimsical moniker "Roksano, Vice-Chief Vagabondess":

> Must I say something on skirt-pants? . . . If we are to put on pants, wouldn't it be necessary, to differentiate the sexes, that men put on skirts? And for those charmers who mockingly ask, "Won't moustaches do it?"—in our country, perhaps, but in those where men are clean shaven . . . ? It's indeed wiser to keep our own clothes. If our skirts are too narrow and obtrude on our movement, tailors must make them larger, instead of thinking up something totally unsuitable.[59]

In this and other articles, the *Women's Bulletin* aimed squarely at its middle-class, middle-brow audience of UEA members.

A riposte from the left came during the 1920s, when the women of

SAT attacked their bourgeoise sisters for class blindness and complacency. As Reine Rippe scolded in the SAT journal *Sennacieca*:

> Revolutionary feminists don't use their energy to conquer empty
> rights, for example, the right to vote, which makes it necessary
> that they delegate Peter or John to the bourgeois parliament to
> "forge" laws strengthening capitalism; [SAT's] feminists fight
> with their male comrades and participate in the important
> emancipation movement which every day becomes more lively,
> more widespread and more high-minded.[60]

A 1927 survey, according to Garvía, shows that women comprised over
one-third of the Esperanto community, but the data are not reliable: the
survey was never sent to working-class Esperanto clubs; besides, anglophones were disproportionately represented. Still, as Garvía has
shown, women had a far more vigorous presence in *Esperantujo* than
among the Volapükists and the Idists; moreover, the prevalence of
women is signaled by Esperanto's detractors, who called the movement
"effeminate," "emotional [rather] than rational, and lacking virile values such as patriotism and militarism."[61]

Marcelle Tiard, Esperanto feminist
[Österreichische Nationalbibliothek]

In the annals of Esperanto, feminism comes into focus and out again, but Marcelle Tiard, born in Paris in 1861, was a leading presence for decades. She had accompanied Zamenhof on his 1910 trip to Washington, D.C., and thereafter presided over the Provence Federation of Esperantists. In 1929, at the age of sixty-eight, she became the founding president of the Union of Esperantist Women (UDEV):

> They elected as president of the newly established association Mrs. Marcelle Tiard (Paris) and as secretary, Mrs. Nora Kozma of Budapest. (The aforementioned secretary asks all women Esperantists please to report . . . specifically on suffrage, women's work, admission to universities, the obtaining of official state and city posts, etc.)[62]

By March 1933, shortly after Tiard's death, the focus had changed. Within days of the Reichstag fire, by which Hitler burned his way to power, *Esperanto* ran the following notice from UDEV:

> [Women] are the mothers, the teachers; in every country, they can sow in children's hearts feelings of solidarity, tolerance, brotherhood, love, which above all make war impossible. To many men, this self-defense against war seems a bit cowardly, [an attitude] responsible for a thousand years of prejudices, according to which they're obliged through arms to protect the *patria*, the home territory!—Many prejudices have disappeared, but unfortunately not yet this cruel, massive misery, [spreading] death and suffering. . . . [O]nly complete nonviolence guarantees the true evolution of humanity.

A few months later, at the twenty-fifth Universal Congress in Köln, 106 members of the German Esperanto Association, representing only 5 percent of the membership, unanimously approved the Nazi policy of *Gleichschaltung*, bringing their statutes into line with party protocol.[63] In this milieu, only twenty members of UDEV convened to discuss pacifism: "For reasons which we don't especially need to mention here," reported *Esperanto*, "public propaganda for this meeting was not possible."[64] Lidia Zamenhof was not in attendance at Köln, but she addressed UDEV members at the 1934 Universal Congress in Stockholm, the 1935 congress in Rome, and the 1937 congress in Warsaw. She spoke to the women of *Esperantujo,* then as always, against Nazism, against fascism, and for peace, a still small voice amid the clamor.

* * *

Second-wave feminism hit the Esperanto world in the mid-1970s. In 1974, in preparation for the UN International Women's Year, the UEA founded the Commission on Women's Action (KVA); soon after, at the Universal Congress in Copenhagen, the first conference on women's leadership was held. "We taught women basic things," recalled Ursula Grattapaglia. "How to organize, how to run things, how to speak within the sphere of men. We said, this is how, *now go do it!*" *Julie Tonkin (Winberg) taught workshops on public speaking and organized lectures by women about their professional lives. Still, women were underrepresented in both the leadership and in the rank and file because, as Grattapaglia remarked, "the way of women is roundabout—we have children, we nurse them, we raise them—and the way of men is much more straight. So this was a necessity, that women's lives shouldn't keep them from being leaders."

*Eliza Kehlet, a Danish (*denaska*) Esperantist and retired interpreter for the European Parliament, noted that the Commission was set up to stimulate women to be more active Esperantists. The 1966 figure of 24 percent women UEA members had risen only to 25.58 percent by 1980, though the figures probably understate the proportion of women, since many couples bought only one membership, in the husband's name.[65] Though women are today well-represented on the UEA Board and Academy and have served twice as UEA general director, no woman has ever been president; only one has presided over TEJO.

In the late 1970s Löwenstein (then Brennan, as she was known and will be referred to here) wrote a seven-part series called "Women and Men" for the youth magazine *Kontakto.* Timely and well-received, the series prompted her to launch a feminist newsletter with contributions from both women and men. In October 1979, seven years after the founding of *Ms.* (United States) and *Spare Rib* (United Kingdom), she published the first issue of *Sekso kaj Egaleco* (Sex and Equality). Her watchword was that of the women's liberation movement in general: nurture, not nature, was accountable for the plethora of differences between the sexes.[66] Soliciting contributions from readers, whatever their proficiency in Esperanto, Brennan published lively forums on such topics as workplace discrimination, how to combine motherhood and professional life, and the unequal distribution of child care and housework. No issue was too mundane for a forum, and no forum failed to offer vivid snapshots of women struggling to realize themselves in a world of dirty diapers, impatient bosses, and overworked husbands. As Brennan wrote in later years, "the women . . . didn't write long theoretical articles about women in another part of the world, but warmly felt accounts of their situation in their own homes, schools or workplaces."[67]

The inaugural issue of *SkE* was a low-budget, samizdat affair; Brennan typed it and *Dermot Quirke in the UK mimeographed it gratis. Like other Esperanto publications during the Cold War, it was distributed free of charge to the "nonpaying" Eastern bloc countries, where Brennan actively sought contributors. And just as Tonkin was doing in the UEA, she strove to give a voice—and visibility—to women in Non-Aligned nations who disclosed their stories, convictions, and hopes, always within a cultural matrix. A lengthy article by the Indian sociologist *Manashi Dasgupta (which appeared in Esperanto translation) discussed how the Indian reverence for motherhood paradoxically kept even elite women in a second-class status. In the same issue, an Estonian *samideanino* wrote that in her country, heavy reliance on examinations mitigated discrimination against women. Writers from Eastern bloc countries pointed out that their regimes offered women more equality of opportunity than did the West. "Generally, I can't imagine, that after the school years young women would desire not to learn a profession," wrote *Lembe Laanest of Estonia, "although of course stipends in departments, institutes and universities are usually not equal in salary."[68]

So ecumenical was the journal that two Japanese Esperantists, *Yamakawa Setsuko and *Hukunaga Makiko, published a widely distributed Japanese-language edition. Conversely, *SkE* also published excerpts from the mainstream press about feminist milestones—the first woman police commissioner in Italy, Conservative rabbi in the United States, cosmonaut in the USSR—and Brennan also spotlighted institutions such as the Berlin Philharmonic, which had (and still has) an abysmal record for employing women. In *SkE,* one size of emancipated liberalism did not fit all. "Discrimination against women can be an inextricable aspect of specific cultures," Brennan wrote. "How do we face this fact? Do all cultures have an equal right to life; or are the lives of the individual women within it more important?"[69]

Language reform, in the best Esperantic tradition, became a flash-point for controversy. Polemics ranged from the need for a neutral rather than masculine pronoun (*ri* for *li*); the abandonment of *fraulino* in favor of *sinjorino* (now to mean "Ms."); fierce objection to the use of the suffix *-ino* to denote women professionals (*verkistino* instead of *verkisto*); and the use of the prefix *ge-* to signify a person of either sex. (The plural *gepatroj* meant "parents," so why not use the singular *gepatro* to denote either parent?) The eminent translator and psychotherapist *Claude Piron, while arguing that strict rationalism was not the surest way to language reform, nonetheless offered a detailed four-part recommendation on how to reform use of the feminine *-ino* suffix.

Opposed to such reforms was the poet and Zamenhof biographer Marjorie Boulton. What business did Esperantists have debating pronouns, she asked, in a world full of workplace discrimination, religious bigotry, unwanted children, unequal rights in marriage and divorce, female circumcision, and the rape of political prisoners?[70] When Brennan published her own exposé of sexist fairy tales, she drew an outraged response from the journalist *Bernard Golden: "Today . . . children's tales, tomorrow she'll tell us a new version of classical mythology, and the day after it will be Shakespeare's turn, and inevitably, a rewritten 'Holy Bible' according to the 'Brennanist' heresy."[71] Printing Golden's response, Brennan wore his insult as a badge of honor.

Brennan not only edited *SkE*; she also helped to write the first mission statement for the Commission on Women's Action, which included the following:

1. To make Esperantists aware of the social problems of women.
2. To educate Esperantist women to overcome these problems.
3. To make contact with international women's organizations.
4. To raise the proportion of women in the Esperanto movement.[72]

The Commission was beholden to the UEA's goal of propagandizing Esperanto to the world; hence three of its four goals focused on Esperantism. But *SkE*, by contrast, was independent. It approached international women's issues *peresperante*, not *poresperante*—through Esperanto, rather than for it. The *SkE* sourcebook on discrimination for the 1980 Universal Congress, for instance, made little mention of Esperantism. From Sweden came a graphic description of female circumcision and infibulation, with grisly testimony by a circumcised Malian woman. From West Germany came a personal essay from a blind German woman urging more "independence and integration in the world of the sighted."[73] And from Iranian *Ĵila Sadigi (one of the five commissioners) came a revolutionary manifesto vindicating the wearing of a black veil:

> I can't—even in Esperanto!—define the courage and even the brashness of women when they cover themselves with this veil. Without these veils, they are more beautiful, but at the same time, cowardly, passive, shamed, silent and emotional.[74]

At the 1980 congress on discrimination, women outnumbered men in the sessions on anti-feminist discrimination, but according to the British Esperantist *Diccon Masterman, men's voices dominated. "One had the impression," wrote Masterman, "that men were more eager to defend the rights of women than women themselves." (Though a Gambian man addressed the group on female circumcision, no African women attended the congress, and the scarcity of non-Western women was duly noted.) In search of a way to "activate the passive women who never dare to open their mouth[s]," *Pepita de Caspry of Norway proposed that a seminar on public speaking techniques be offered to women Esperantists.[75]

After the congress, in a column entitled "Practical Steps," Brennan announced a new priority: to train women in public speaking and coach them in practicing their skills.[76] "We need to educate ourselves if we are to reach others," she wrote. She set up an archive of speeches to provide models and resources, and offered a packet of materials for anyone willing to run a public-speaking workshop. The most successful workshop, led by Brennan and three others, was a one-week intensive held in July 1983 in Pisanica, Bulgaria. The eighteen participants practiced skills in enunciation, breathing, reading aloud, and reducing anxiety. Toward the end of the week, they each wrote and presented a speech on a choice of themes and offered one another feedback.

In the same issue in which *SkE* proudly reported the workshop's success, Brennan published an open letter by the Iranian *Turan Sagafi: "Reading in *SkE* articles about . . . lectures to help women who have problems with speaking in public . . . I ask: 'Are all the other grave problems of life already solved?' Not in Iran."[77] Sagafi told of remote villages, impoverished schools, and women compelled to make fifteen trips a day to draw well water; wives who were beaten, locked up, and excluded from all public deliberations; daughters who skipped school rather than leave their mothers alone with flocks, fields, wells, childcare, and household tasks. While leftist feminists in the 1920s accused the UEA of class blindness, six decades later, Sagafi's letter pointed up the enduring ethnocentrism of the mainstream movement.

Reading *Sekso kaj Egaleco* from the vantage of the twenty-first century is like walking into a multicultural meeting of 1970s feminists, sometimes embracing in solidarity, sometimes fiercely debating; you can almost smell the patchouli oil. *SkE* also yields an intimate glimpse of one woman's struggle to live out the ideals of both feminism and Esperantism amid the turbulent 1980s. In the editor's note with which Brennan began each issue, she described the trial of producing it, accomplished with carbon paper, postage stamps, and liberal applications of Tipp-Ex, amid the demands of her growing family. Between Issues 10 (July 1982) and 11 (January 1985) there was a gap of almost three years: "A NIGHTMARE COME TRUE," she groaned, after two issues were lost in transit before printing. Multitasking on work and child care, Brennan wrote: "One has to avoid the tendency to sit for hours in front of the magic screen, while

Anna (Brennan) Löwenstein and Renato Corsetti, 2012
[Fabio Corsetti]

the children draw on the walls and spill milk onto the rug, fighting to solve a simple problem such as . . . how to center the title." In one issue, Brennan quoted a "striking" comment by the British Esperantist *Sybil Sly: "Of the three occupations—work, family and Esperanto—it's possible to combine two, but probably not all three."[78] She was trying to do the impossible, and somehow managing.

In the wake of the 1986 nuclear accident at Chernobyl, Brennan found feminist magazines covering "pacifism, the nuclear menace, racism, poverty, health, homosexuality, lifestyle, etc."[79] It was a sign that the women's movement had matured, as had young activists like herself, many of whom were now preoccupied with balancing work and family. Kehlet recalls that by the end of the UN Decade on Women in 1985, the energy had dissipated: "It was the same fifteen women at every meeting—just not interesting anymore."[80] *SkE* sought a new editor, but to no avail. Since the women's movement had entered the mainstream— "although . . . in a diluted form," Brennan wrote, the phase of passion and discovery had passed. But another, for gay (mostly male) Esperantists, was in full swing.

6. *Samseksemuloj*

Seven years after the 1969 Stonewall riots in New York City, a British Esperantist, *Peter Danning, founded the Ligo de Samseksamaj Geesperantistoj (LSG). Born in Berlin in 1928, Danning fled with his Jewish family to England at the age of nine. A renovator of flats and owner of a gay-friendly guesthouse in Twickenham, Danning was also active in the founding of Britain's Gay and Lesbian Humanist Association. In 1977, by changing the Esperanto word *samseksema*, meaning "inclined toward the same sex," to *samseksama*, "same-sex loving," Danning brought homosexuality itself out of the closet. Guiding the group with probity and discretion, he ensured that its membership rolls were held in confidence.

American Martin Factor, retired linguist and former actor, recalls that before the collapse of communism in 1989, "LSG was often the only gay organization to which closeted men in Eastern Europe belonged. It was their connection to another world"—a world they trusted to keep their identities concealed. Until 1988, all LSG gatherings during the Universal

Congress were held in gay-friendly venues elsewhere in the city, allowing LSG members to maintain their privacy, as well as mingle with locals. Founded a year before the International Lesbian and Gay Association (as it was then called), the LSG calls itself the oldest international LGBT organization.

Membership was especially strong in Germany, Russia, Poland, and Hungary; the UK, where Danning founded the LSG, was another stronghold. It was a Briton who brought homosexuality into full view in the pages of *SkE*. In August 1987, Dermod Quirke, the production manager, wrote a piece called "A Male Feminist?"

> I'm a feminist because I believe that humanity is NOT split neatly into two groups according to sex. . . . I possess the biological capability of becoming a father, but I don't use this capability; that is to say, I'm a homosexual. . . . My lover is a man; and our relations are just as loving, just as intimate, as the relations between a happy heterosexual couple.[81]

The topics Quirke treated were very much at home in *SkE*: division of labor, prejudices about sex roles, nonsexist marriage and partnership. But the explicit emphasis on gender identity and sexual orientation was a portent of changes to come—but not in *SkE,* which folded after the next issue.

In the months before the 1980 Stockholm Congress on the theme of discrimination, *Franklin van Zoest of the Netherlands wrote to *SkE*: "In various publications there have already appeared articles about racial-ethnic, anti-feminist, economic and language discrimination, but nowhere does one see an article about discrimination against gays (homosexuals). Could this perhaps be intentional?"[82] Gay issues, though not part of the pre-congress publicity, were indeed on the agenda; in his keynote speech, British phoneticist John Wells mentioned "discrimination against homosexuals—against gays, as we now prefer to say—that is, discrimination on the basis of sexual orientation."[83] Like the Jewishness of Zamenhof, homosexuality was a ticklish subject for an organization that lived on both sides of the iron curtain, but in the revolutionary year of 1989, Wells became the first openly gay president of the UEA.

A decade later, at the Berlin Congress, Danning pressed the UEA for official recognition of LSG as a "collaborating organization." The governing committee's vote was fourteen in favor, five opposed, and eighteen abstentions. General Director Osmo Buller later mused that the number of abstentions was high because at that time votes were still taken by a show of hands.[84] When Danning, suffering from Parkinson's disease, died of a heart attack in 2002, the obituaries from gay Esperantists tenderly referred to him as "our dear founder"—the same terms used of Zamenhof at his obsequies.

According to a thirty-year veteran of LSG, the organization continues to have "considerable trouble attracting women." The LSG journal *Forumo* features pictures of semi-clad young men. Aside from women in crowd shots of marches and demonstrations, very few are pictured, and articles specifically about lesbians are rare; about transgender people, even rarer. To find a lively discussion about lesbians, one turns to the comments on the website *Libera Folio*, where in the best Esperantist tradition, men debate how best to refer to lesbians: as *lesboj* (without the -*ino* suffix)? as *lesbaninoj*? as *gejinoj*—gay women?

The 2010 Universal Congress in Havana was to celebrate the twenty-year anniversary of the UEA's collaboration with LSG. But for LSG, meeting in a country with a history of persecuting homosexuals—a country with no gay advocacy organization or publications—was out of the question. Besides, the LSG was loath to present gay Cubans with the choice of shunning the gathering or risking ostracism or even personal injury. In a *Libera Folio* interview, Buller agreed that the organization should not hold its congress in a country where the LSG would be banned—but, he pointed out, that was not the case in Cuba.[85]

In Buller's view, the hostility and anxiety shown toward gays among Esperantists had certainly lessened, but he discreetly alluded to the *gejofobio* (homophobia) that had fueled a crisis within the Central Office in 2000–2001, when a gay staffer was accused of sexual misconduct with a young male volunteer. To this day, the events are mired in controversy. Since the staff was too divided to mediate and resolve the issue, the UEA, headed by Kep Enderby, a former minister of justice for Queensland, Australia, took the matter on. When the board found neither for the complainant nor for the staffer, three longtime, respected staff members expecting exoneration of the staffer resigned in anger. One of those was Buller, who returned three years later as general director.

Asked by *Libera Folio* whether he was a member of LSG, Buller replied, "I take my neutrality seriously to the point where I don't join any allied associations. . . . And to prove the rule," he added, "I made an exception and joined the Association of Nonsmokers."

7. Rauma's Children

In *Esperantujo*, where many things happen late, the 1960s did not end until 1980. In the small Finnish town of Rauma, a group of youthful Esperantists pulled down the curtain, Wizard-of-Oz style, around the *fina venko*. "We believe that official adoption of Esperanto is neither likely nor essential during the 80s," wrote Giorgio Silfer, Amri Wandel, and *Jouko Lindstedt:

> The undersigned observe a contradiction in the Esperantists'
> attitude, resembling a conflict between the ideal superego and the
> ego: our superego causes us to preach to other people about some
> myths—a second language for all; the English language is our
> enemy; the UN must adopt Esperanto, etc.—and . . . at the same
> time, among us, we enjoy and use Esperanto in accordance with
> what it in fact is, independent of its founding principles.[86]

Just as Zamenhof had seen a crisis of inauthenticity among the emancipated Jews of the Russian Empire, the Manifesto of Rauma addressed an identity crisis in *Esperantujo*: "The search for our own identity causes us to conceive of the Esperantists *as if belonging to a self-elected diasporic language minority*" (my italics). For the Raŭmists, Zamenhof's ideology of the "family circle" was a liability rather than an asset, because it "repel[led] those outsiders who are interested." Nor did the Raŭmists endorse the para-peoplehood that Zamenhof had envisioned. Rejecting metaphors of archaic unity based on blood, they preferred the centrifugal metaphor of a diaspora unified by culture and affinity. Esperanto culture was more than a cradle for an infant language, and more than a platform for utopian ideals; in the course of a century, it had flowered into a distinct tradition and a source of a shared supranational identity. And with the centennial of Esperanto approaching, this culture deserved to be celebrated. "Outsiders" who found something to admire in *Esperantujo*, whether ideological or aesthetic, would be welcomed, but the utopian goal of an Esperanto-speaking world was declared moot.

As much as the Raŭmists abjured bonds of family and blood, the practical matter of sharing a cultural heritage was hard to distinguish from the "as-if" of Esperantic peoplehood. Ironically, to authorize their claims in Zamenhof's writings, the Raŭmists quoted his letter envisioning the Hillelists, "a group of people who accept [Esperanto] as their family language."[87] And perhaps it was no coincidence that the Raŭmists found their way back to Hillelism; the previous decade had seen a renewed interest in Zamenhof's Jewish context, and with it, the birth of "Zamenhofology." In 1973, Ito Kanzi, a Japanese editor of medical texts, published the first volume of forty-three in the *Complete Works of Zamenhof.* For his legendary efforts—and for his seven-volume Japanese-language novel about Zamenhof—Ito garnered every prize to be had in the Esperanto world. Proud of his achievement, he grafted Zamenhof's first name onto his own and nicknamed himself "Ludovikito."

Another landmark of Zamenhofology was N. Z. Maimon's *The Hidden Life of Zamenhof,* the first study devoted to the founder's Jewish milieu. Its impact was considerable; when Tonkin wrote an essay for the centenary celebration of 1987, he likened Zamenhof to a "Jewish prophet," an astonishing turnabout from the days when Zamenhof was ridiculed for being exactly that:

> The beautiful visions of the early Jewish prophets [wrote Tonkin] accompanied ... the Egyptian captivity and its emblematic successor, the pogroms. Also in the heart of Zamenhof, perhaps, the optimistic thread of Jewish thought was constantly accompanied by the cruel reality, which was interwoven with it. . . . Persecution opened his vision; the vision accompanies the persecution. . . . Doktoro Esperanto took upon himself that heaviest, almost Mosaic responsibility, to guide his people (all humanity) out of captivity to the promised land.[88]

For most Esperantists, Raŭmism was not a revolution but an *esprit de jeunesse* in tune with the spirit of the liberatory 1960s and 1970s; to many, it vindicated Zamenhof's dream of a para-people united by culture and affinity, even if it forfeited idealism in the process. But Raŭmism had its critics as well. One of the charges was that the manifesto transformed the *interna ideo* into a pleasure principle; Esperanto had lost its idealism, as well as its pertinence to other progressive ideals. It was as though the youth of *Esperantujo* had collectively gone upstairs and slammed the door—to party. But there was a darker objection: that because Raŭmists did not seek to extend Esperantic culture to the world at large, their vision insidiously resembled that of a nation, unlike Zamenhof's vision of an ever-expanding Hillelist community. For some, their worst fears were realized in 1998 when Giorgio Silfer, one of the three authors of the Manifesto of Rauma, claimed legal *sovereignty* for the Esperanto community among the world's nation-states.

Born Valerio Ari in Milan in 1949, Silfer earned degrees in modern languages and belles lettres. In his twenties he co-founded a cutting-edge literary magazine called *Literatura Foiro* (Literature Fair), which is still in print after half a century. In 1980, he started the first multimedia Esperanto venture, the *Literatura Foiro* Cooperative; along with the Esperanto Cultural Center, it is now based in the home of Silfer and his wife, *Perla Martinelli, in La Chaux-de-Fonds, Switzerland. (Martinelli is also the founding editor of *Femina,* currently the only feminist magazine in *Esperantujo.*) In 1998, Silfer and Martinelli inaugurated the first Esperanto PEN center, which soon joined forces with the Esperanto Radical Association to proclaim the "Pakto por la Esperanta Civito."

The pact declared that "the Esperanto community is a stateless diasporic language-collective to which people belong by free choice, or by a free confirmation, in the case of *denaskaj* [from birth] Esperantists." For the first time, the Esperanto world was conceptualized neither as a community, a people, nor a movement, but as a city-state, or *civito*. Although the Civito did not break away from the UEA, relations between the two organizations became more acrid than in any schism in the history of the movement. While the UEA struggled through internal crises and declining membership, the Civito boasted of its vitality and autonomy by comparison to the UEA, without making public its membership statistics. Instead of comprising citizens, the Civito initially comprised a federation of organizations; four years later, individuals were permitted to apply for *civitaneco* (citizenship) provided they belonged to one of the signatory organizations. All applications had to be approved by an undefined "registry," on unspecified criteria. Citizenship was free, and for life, though the pact contained detailed procedures for either side to sever relations between an organization and the pact.

Silfer rightly claims that the Civito is the only Esperanto entity to officially endorse the 1948 Universal Declaration of Human Rights; according to its website, this declaration and the pact itself are the Civito's two guiding principles. But for those outside the Civito, the medium is the message. Since its founding, the Civito has been widely perceived as a mysterious entity that thrives on the mystification of its own procedures. Its website features Piero della Francesca's painting *The Ideal City*, a cluster of noble structures drawn in single-point perspective, devoid of human life. Indeed, there is something austere and inhuman about the fiercely elaborated institutions that emerged from the Civito in its early years, including a constitution, a judiciary, senators, and a parliament. Red, white, and green political parties (the colors of the Italian flag) also emerged. Presiding over the Civito was a strong executive comprising a "consul" and up to seven "vice consuls," some appointed, some elected. Together they were known as the "Capital." In 1998 *Walter Zelazny, a Polish sociologist, became the founding consul, succeeded in 2006 by Silfer. At this writing, the Civito has a woman consul—*Marie-France Conde Rey—with Silfer, Martinelli, and three others serving as vice consuls.

The legal jargon of the charter, with its frequent recourse to Latin, carries through to the official dispatches of the Civito, posted on the Web with no space for reader comments. The Civito's arcane regulations make the bylaws of the UEA seem like those of a tree-house club. For example:

> The Forum approves rules in the form of directives and the Senate approves norms in the form of laws. Both branches of Parliament approve regulations which apply the directive or law. Usually the directives pertain to relations among the pact's entities, and laws regulate relations within the citizenry. Directives are named by the family name of the delegate who proposes it—for example "Hiltbrand Directive. . . ." and one indicates laws by a Latin epithet—for instance, *"Lex suffragatoria*—on the election for the Senate."[89]

To the stalwart Esperantists of the UEA, the arcane legalism of the Civito was baffling and alien. Silfer was viewed as a provocateur, and not without reason. He had an irrepressible habit of disparaging the UEA and its members; as he announced on the tenth anniversary of the pact, "We're more than *samideanoj*: we're *civitanoj*." (In Silfer's emails, *"Civitane,"* not *"Samideane,"* is the customary closing.) In person, Silfer is cordial and hospitable, a witty, erudite raconteur who is deeply versed in Esperanto history and literature. Tall and graceful, he has an august air about him, as if he were the head of the opposition (with him, one quickly stops speaking of "*the* movement," "*the* Esperantists"), except that the "governing" party doesn't acknowledge him until he commits a grave transgression.

In 2006, conflict between the Civito and the UEA flared up over an Esperantology conference Silfer organized in Togo. The UEA, having given more than 30,000 Euros to its Africa Office, was scandalized when that office issued a press release praising Silfer and the conference, followed by an email blast from Togo Esperantist *Gbeglo Koffi joyfully anticipating more such conferences. Provoked by Silfer's audacity and Koffi's disloyalty, the UEA abruptly severed its ties with the Africa Office.

To many, it seemed that Silfer had founded a quasi-state, a suspicion he confirmed by claiming that the Civito is "subject to international law."[90] Maria Rafaela Urueña, a professor of international law at the University of Valladolid, considers the idea ludicrous, since the Civito is neither a state (which draws its sovereignty from territory, people, or internal organization) nor a sovereign entity acknowledged by other subjects of international law.[91] But Silfer, with no time for naysayers, simply maintains that *civitanoj* are dual citizens of the Civito and their own country.

In 2000, on the twentieth anniversary of the gathering at Rauma, a retrospective was held at Helsinki. The Civito, thought to crystallize the nationalistic tendency of Raŭmism, had spurred the defenders of Raŭmism to disavow Silfer and rehabilitate it. On three points a consensus emerged. First, the distinction between Raŭmist goals and the "ancient" goals of the movement was false. Esperantists had, for more than a century, managed to be both a diasporic community *and* an activist, idealistic movement. *Finavenkismo*—the ideal of the final victory of Esperanto—was a corner into which sophisticated Esperantists had somehow managed not to paint themselves, generation after generation. At the heart of lived Esperantism was the capacity to be many things at once: part of a community and a universalist; a citizen and a transnationalist; a dreamer and a pragmatist.

The second general consensus was that the Civito, with its ever ramifying, Orwellian government, not only betrayed the Manifesto of Rauma; it also betrayed the Esperanto language by forfeiting clarity and accessibility. *Detlev Blanke, an Esperantist who came of age in the former

GDR, complained, "The text [of the compact] swarms with such notions as 'constitutional charter, pact, sovereign collective, code, laws, transnational culture, collective identity . . . , sovereign functions, lawgiving power, executive power, arbitration power, senate, consul . . . court, prefect.'"[92] Blanke also regretted that it "entrench[ed] the already sufficiently widespread opinion, that the Esperantists (without distinguishing between Esperanto-speakers, Esperanto activists, Green DonQuixotes, etc.) are an . . . unserious sect and dreamers, whom it doesn't make sense to engage."

The third point was that the Civito betrayed Zamenhof's abhorrence of nationalism; in the words of the Esperanto poet *Jorge Camacho, it espoused an "E-nationalism" led by an autocratic elite. No one has invested more effort in satirizing Silfer and the Civito than Camacho, who wrote two satires eviscerating what he dubbed "*Foirismo*" (after Silfer's journal) and its "liturgy." In 2007 Camacho, along with other (mainly) Spanish and Portuguese Esperantists, founded the parodic Esperanto Respubliko.[93] The Republic conferred the status of minister on all its founding members: there was a Minister of Hangovers and Aspirin; a Minister of Missed Turns, Non-urgent Affairs and Spanish Cursing; and Camacho himself served as Minister for [the] Sexes, Eclipses, and External Relations with the Esperanta Civito. A Finnish woman became president and Minister of Military Affairs, and (in lieu of seven vice consuls) there was one "president-in-law." The republic vowed to conduct all its international affairs in Basque and one-upped the Civito's heraldic coat of arms by taking as its insignia the triangular road sign for a bull crossing. If it did nothing else, the Esperanto Respubliko made the point that had the Civito itself not been deadly serious, it would have been savagely funny.

8. Global Babel

Tonkin once quipped that the Berlin Wall was holding up Esperanto in Eastern Europe; indeed, when it came down in 1989, UEA membership began to plummet. Distracted by shortages and recession, anxious to navigate changing institutions, Eastern Europeans had neither the motivation nor the leisure to pursue Esperanto. In the twenty years following the collapse of the Soviet Union, UEA membership fell nearly 60 percent, from 39,829 to 15,815. But the decline of participation in Eastern Europe was only a partial cause for this precipitous downturn. Another cause was the expansion of the English-instruction industry, after the Cold War, to Eastern Europe and East Asia, where English and opportunity became synonymous.[94] Technology, too, has contributed to the decline in UEA membership. But while the advent of the Internet has undermined the centrality of the UEA, it has also expanded and altered the ways in which Esperanto is learned, used, and accessed—that is, for those who have access to the Web; Esperantists are quick to point out that about 40 percent of the world's population does not.[95]

Those who regret the marginalization of the UEA note an irony here: that the UEA has been a world wide web (unplugged) since its inception in 1908, when Hodler founded a supranational network of consuls. Given the expense of traveling to congresses and the scattered nature of the community, Esperantists have always relied heavily on written communication. No surprise, then, that Esperantists were quick to seize on the potential of email; correspondences that once relied on sluggish mail services (including a legendary thirty-year postal chess match) could be carried on instantaneously, cheaply, and frequently. Listservs, chat rooms, and instructional websites soon followed. Vikipedio, the brainchild of Chuck Smith, an American Esperantist living in Berlin, has a disproportionately large volume of articles on the Internet (however difficult it is to count Esperantists), and Esperantists created the Czech, Slovakian, Georgian, and Swahili versions of Wikipedia.[96]

Thus, depending on whom you ask, the Internet has either revolutionized *Esperantujo* or has simply made its customary activities more rapid and accessible. *Peter (Petro) Baláž thinks the former. Since 2007, Baláž has directed a youth collective called E@I (pronounced "eh-cheh-ee") that has irrevocably changed the way people learn Esperanto. Unlike the Civito and the UEA, it is ecumenical in conception; its mission statement does not even mention Esperanto. Instead, the collective fosters "intercultural education, communication and collaboration" in Esperanto, Slovak, and Czech, with other languages to come; its global education website is available in nine languages. Membership is free. As of 2012, the collective comprised almost 15,000 signatories, all (by statute) between the ages of fifteen and thirty-five.[97]

From the inaugural E@I working seminar in 2000, there emerged lernu!, which teaches Esperanto online in forty-two languages. According to 2015 figures, lernu! reports nearly 200,000 registered users, which puts it at a 40-to-1 ratio to the UEA's individual membership. The lernu! web-

ESTU
TRANKVILA
KAJ
LERNU
ESPERANTON

Global Esperanto

site attracts young Esperanto learners, most of whom have no interest in joining an Esperanto organization. The same can be said for users of the popular Duolingo website; within the first week of its online Esperanto course, launched in 2015, it logged in 20,000 users. Facebook, too, reflects the marginalization of the UEA. At this writing, the ratio of "likes" on the unaffiliated Esperanto page compared to the "likes" on the UEA page is six to one.

But the comparison between the UEA's individual membership and the myriad of online learners is a false one. Those who join the UEA have *chosen* Esperanto. They affiliate, they receive the monthly magazine and yearbook, and about a third of them attend the Universal Congress. They pay, though not much; to join with an e-version of the magazine costs about $35 USD annually. Whenever and wherever they engage with UEA members, officeholders, or publications, they do so in Esperanto.

Lernu! and Duolingo, on the other hand, are not a choice but a click. One reaches them by visiting or surfing, not by flying to Iceland, Turkey, or Buenos Aires. And one can learn Esperanto with pedagogical support in one's own language and never be asked to serve on a committee or a board, or to run for a spot as a delegate. Lernu! is not choosing, but *friending* Esperanto, but that is precisely the point: with lernu!, E@I has managed finally to put Esperanto into the media stream, along with Facebook, YouTube, Tumblr, Instagram, Amazon.com, and all the other sites you visit daily. Sooner or later, lernu! is up on your toolbar, and beside it, *Reta Vortaro* (an online dictionary); Google Translate, which recently added Esperanto as its sixty-fourth language; and the hip English-Esperanto Dictionary developed by Sonja Lang (herself the inventor of a language called Toki Pona, designed to inculcate Taoism). Sonja's dictionary is where one turns to find the Esperanto for "genetically modified organisms," "baba ganoush," and "labia majora." On the language-teaching sites, interactivity is paramount: one engages with Duolingo's owl tutor "Duo," just as one does with lernu!'s feline mascot, Zam, who greets you on your birthday; a click on lernu! can even connect you to a human tutor or interlocutor. As a twenty-something Esperantist recently asked, can Zamcoin be far off?

The Web not only provides novices with language instruction and easy access to the community; it has also diminished the impact of the UEA's prime channel for delivering information, *Esperanto Revuo*. While TEJO's *Kontakto* has a website, *Esperanto Revuo* does not, though PDFs of issues are available online for subscribers. Esperantists looking for movement news online turn to *Libera Folio* (Free Page), a webzine that offers an independent point of view on the UEA and the movement in general. The unpaid editor and primary contributor, *Kalle Kniivilä, by day a reporter for the prestigious Swedish *Sydsvenskan*,[98] was formerly a leading public relations manager for the UEA. He edited the journal *TEJO Tutmonde*, served as the UEA's commissioner for information from 1997–1998, and later sat on the executive board of the UEA. But Kniivilä's disenchantment in 2003, during a season of controversial resignations in the Central Office, spurred him and István Ertl to start an independent forum with the highest journalistic standards. He recalls:

> It was very frustrating to see the chaos in the chief organization of the Esperanto world, and at the same time, to see that the vast majority of members were barely aware of [it], since there was no forum for serious, critical journalism in *Esperantujo*. The [UEA's] *Esperanto* . . . painted a completely rosy picture of the events, which made no room for critical viewpoints.[99]

These days, on the *Libera Folio* site, Kniivilä whets his axe against the Esperanto world's "[sect-like] isolation from the surrounding world . . . with green bulletins preaching the all-saving power of the perfect language and the imminent *fina venko* to a shrinking cohort of *samideanoj*."[100] Though various UEA operatives openly express annoyance with *Libera Folio*, they frequently grant Kniivilä interviews, knowing his reportage is sharp, well-written, and sophisticated. Such willingness has not been shown by Silfer, who regards *Libera Folio* as a "scandal rag" and whom Kniivilä treats unsparingly. For *Libera Folio,* there are no sacred cows. Shortly before the 2008 Beijing Olympics, the Chinese government came in for a scolding from *Libera Folio* when it defamed the Dalai Lama on its Esperanto website, *El Popola Ĉinio*: "The Dalai [Lama]'s clique ceaselessly interferes with and undermines the soul-migration of the Buddha." *Libera Folio* published an angry response by American Steve Brewer: "In China perhaps one can forbid the liberal expression of the people, but . . . not everywhere in the world." Kniivilä, in a wry follow-up, ventured that "the editors of the official Chinese website will choose other responses for publication."[101]

9. Esperanto in 2087

In an essay called "The 21st Century—Is the Esperanto Movement Ready?" Baláž argues that the UEA must either adapt vigorously to changed circumstances or lose its claim to be Esperanto's preeminent institution. Esperantists, he claims, have a great deal to learn from the success of E@I. First, because it is necessary to professionalize, funding must be aggressively pursued. To date, E@I has secured more than a million Euros in EU grants. Second, Esperantists need to collaborate with other institutions devoted to multiculturalism. Third, if the UEA categorically keeps the world of commerce at bay, it forfeits a crucial way to make Esperanto known, used, and funded. Finally, collaborations of the future must be Web-based and thoroughly transnational. (E@I's headquarters is a tiny office in Partizánske, Slovakia, rented from the city for one Euro per year; it might as well be on the moon.) Whether or not the UEA is prepared to learn these lessons will depend on whether a new generation of leadership—for now, digital immigrants; before long, digital natives—can seize the opportunities realized by the wildly successful E@I.

Unlike Baláž, most seasoned Esperantists don't dwell on the future; at least where Esperanto is concerned, they don't much like to contemplate it. They know that the number of people who develop competence, join the UEA, and go to annual congresses is trending down, even if the websites are getting hits. They know that English is, for all practical purposes, the "universal language"—at least for now. And they fear they'll inevitably be asked whether Esperanto is going to disappear, a question to which there is no good answer. Saying "yes" raises the question, "Why go on doing it?"; saying "no" makes one sound like a *finavenkisto*. Nonetheless, when I invited *samideanoj* to envision Esperanto at its bicentennial in 2087, they complied with a blend of gravitas and absurdity, the way Esperantists have always responded to unfathomable questions.

Several respondents felt that Esperanto will always speak to those seeking reassurance in a world that is violent, unstable, and short on certainties. Writing from Spain, Camacho commented that as long as this is the case, "the Esperanto affair will go on attracting those individuals just as a planet captures driving asteroids and transforms them into voluntary, fervent satellites." From her home in rural Brazil, Ursula Grattapaglia mused that in the twentieth century, Esperanto provided succor to those who suffered the horrors of war:

> [A]fter the First and Second World Wars, Esperanto grew vigorously, chiefly among those people who had survived the horrors.
> (I was among them in Berlin.)
> Because of wars, people seek out some concrete way in which to act against the violence of war, and Esperanto, willy-nilly, was and probably remains the bearer of ideas of peace, respect, tolerance, and solidarity.

The unending question of how to attract new Esperantists evoked fantasies of Esperanto's "normalization," when a wide range of people, rather than a self-described community, will speak it. In 2087, wrote Bronŝtejn, former leader of the Esperanto underground in the USSR, "three world-wide television channels, broadcasting in Esperanto, completely refuse to accept advertisements, since they receive enough funding on account of educational and cultural programming." Farther afield, Bronŝtejn imagined the day when "colonists who had come to Mars in 2025–45, and their thousands of descendants, proclaim Esperanto the state language of Mars." (Bronŝtejn has already been proven wrong; the Mars One project recently declared that the lingua franca on Mars will be English.) More modestly, Vergara, of Chile, imagined Esperanto at a pinnacle of academic and political prestige, as did Blanke in Berlin, who offered an (admittedly utopian) scenario in which the "centers and institutions on interlinguistics and Esperantology will be a common occurrence in universities."

Israeli astrophysicist Wandel imagined how profoundly the internet will have altered the Esperanto world. Like novelist Gary Shteyngart's prophecy of corporate mega-mergers ("LandO'LakesGMFordCredit"), the Wandelian future merges the maverick *Libera Folio* and the staid UEA: "Millions will follow its website, '*Libera UEA-Folio*,'" where reader-contributors will "write, discuss and respond in real time." Meanwhile, le-rnu! will have absorbed many functions of the weakened UEA, an acronym that in 2087 will stand for "Universal Esperanto Administration." Online students, Wandel predicted, will be "invited . . . to participate in virtual conferences and in this way be immediately integrated into the virtual Esperanto community." Wandel also predicted that "the popular social network Space Book will feature hundreds of Esperanto groups," with young people messaging in an Esperanto-rich cyberslang.

At Esperanto's bicentennial, Wandel wrote, there will remain one outpost of the print-and-paper world: The Academy of Esperanto, whose "official votes continue to be taken by snail mail, since some of its eminent members, on principle, don't own a computer . . . or use email." Like Wandel, former UEA president Corsetti reimagined the UEA—but re-centered in Brazil: "The headquarters," he wrote, "will be in Brazil, and they will soon present a proposal for the . . . use of Esperanto in the UN." Another century, another hemisphere, yet another campaign for UN recognition.

From Luxembourg, Ertl offered a topsy-turvy prediction in which technology vindicates Esperanto's humanism. "To have an immediate translation," wrote Ertl, himself an EU translator, "one no longer needs a computer screen":

> By 2030, after a transitional period with projecting Google Glasses, it will be possible to project translations directly into the brain. . . . At least [this will obtain] among the well-off portion of humanity, two or three billion of the ten billion living on earth.

Possibly, paradoxically, [the others] will more often be multi-lingual than the 'rich,' of whom only a few seriously study languages.... [Precisely this] will be beneficial for Esperantists ... :
The most utilitarian arguments fall away, and there remain the most intimate: the plea for authentically personal contact.

While other humans and their devices whirr in tandem, Esperantists will still be able to turn away from the screen, take off the Google Glasses, and unplug the brain from its electronic language-nodes. At least while they speak Esperanto, they will still be able to recover an authentically human life, and authentic contact with others.

With a changing world and a changing constituency, several respondents observed, the Esperanto language would inevitably be altered. From Rome, Löwenstein wrote: "Esperanto will still be spoken after seventy years, but what Esperanto will this be?" Löwenstein foresaw the eclipse of English by Chinese as the dominant world language, wondering if Esperanto might be used to bridge East and West, as in the early twentieth century: "[Will] the Chinese government conclude, at some point, that Esperanto could be the solution to the international language problem? Or will some Chinese Zamenhof create an Asian Esperanto, based on Asian roots ... ?"

Corsetti has argued that the omnipresence of Chinese would inevitably impact the Esperanto lexicon, just as the proportion of French, English, and scientific roots to German and Slavic roots grew by almost 20 percent between 1893 and 1970.[102] (To make the point that non-Europeans find Esperanto estranging, Corsetti masterfully rewrote a stanza of "La Espero"—retitled "La Tojvo"—using roots drawn only from non-Western and Slavic languages.)[103] Corsetti wryly predicted that "the growing use of Chinese will cause holy alliances among the English speaking countries, which will try to halt its progress ... through Esperanto.... Meanwhile, linguists continue to declare that we must attend to the meaning of tones, since linguists indeed know who pays the stipends for their research projects."

Just as the community and language will have evolved, so will the *interna ideo*: the leading contender for the role was environmentalism. From Rotterdam, U.S.-born *Roy McCoy wrote, "The disagreement among climatologists seems to be whether humanity will die off in 2040, 2050, or 2060.... If Esperantists—and everyone—don't start to care for the environment at this point . . . questions about the future of Esperanto will make no sense whatever, since there won't be people around to speak it." With black humor, Corsetti sketched a future doomed by climate change:

> [By 2087] few regions on earth will still be habitable. The most vast of these will be Siberia. Thus, in 2087, the war to take over Siberia, begun in 2085, [continues] between the remaining Chinese and the remaining Americans. [As for the *declared* reasons for war,] the Americans decided that this is the moment to transfer democracy to the last living ethnic Germans in Siberia and the Chinese entered to defend the shamanism of the Yakuts. . . . In this vision, Esperanto will be completely forgotten and . . . in the few remaining years, one will speak English or Chinese.

Japanese Esperantist *Usui Hiroko was more pessimistic about the present than the future: "In the present moment in history, when the idea that humanity progresses is so exhausted, [people] mockingly speak not only of the *fina venko* but also of the *fina velko* [final fading]." Usui disclosed that the nuclear accident at Fukushima in 2011 spurred him to move to China. "I'm now convinced that at some point humanity will perish," he wrote, "not because of nuclear war, as I believed during my adolescent years during the eighties, but because of nuclear centers."

It was Usui who named the one resource above all needed for Esperanto to survive: patience. He quoted an excerpt from "On the Future of My Poems," by the Esperanto poet Edwin de Kock. In English, roughly:

> If the barbarians at some point
> put the torch to civilization,
> wouldn't there remain, somewhere, egg-patiently,
> through the death-dark winter of the centuries,
> my little poems, to hatch
> under some new, reborn sun
> and in a doting, dreamy heart,
> to make my past thoughts resound
> in archaic Esperanto?

If classical scientific knowledge was preserved in Arabic; if neo-Confucianism influenced the European Enlightenment; and, moreover, if the ideal of Chinese ideograms is enshrined inside early modern language projects; then, Usui argued, "egg-patience" is clearly warranted. Corsetti, in a confessional tone, agreed: "When I was young, I thought that good people always won and bad people always lost. Unfortunately, I was more influenced by films, in which it indeed falls out this way. In reality, good people usually lose, but nonetheless, in the long run, they win. Sometimes the wait can be very long."

And whence this "patience" for a "very long" wait—what Ludovik Lazarus Zamenhof simply called "hope"? As Ursula Grattapaglia wrote, "Esperanto is virtually a mantra . . . which immediately creates sympathy, which identifies itself in irrational desires [for such things] as solidarity, equality, peace, and mutual understanding without hegemony." At its bicentennial in 2087, then, Esperanto will still be what it has always been: a litany of rational arguments driven by an irrational desire to make a better world.

When it comes to irrational desires, Ursula knows whereof she speaks. Back in the summer of 1974, there was nothing rational about her and her husband Giuseppe's decision to leave behind their comfortable lives in Turin, sail to Brazil, and foster abused, abandoned children in the rural savanna. No one can say whether their farm-school, Bona Espero, will still be there in 2087. But forty years after arriving in Brazil, Ursula and Giuseppe are still at it, teaching Esperanto and saving lives. In July 2009, Ursula invited me to visit, and the following May—on a clear fall day, in the Southern Hemisphere—I went.

Samideanoj IV
Bona Espero, or Androids

=====

1. "A Little Piece of Heaven"

These days the 150 miles from Brasília to Bona Espero are paved, all but the last four. After several hours driving due west, just as the scrub gives way to rolling hills, Ursula Grattapaglia swerves right onto a red sun-baked road. Months since the flash floods of summer—January, February, March—the road is still riven with gullies. To the left, on the hill, stands a white post topped by the Esperanto symbol, two green *E*s locked in a mirrored kiss.

After several bumpy minutes, Ursula slows and noses us through a white wrought-iron gate. As a trio of yapping dogs give chase, she honks a little song—*honk-a-honk-a-honk*—and from all directions, kids come running to the car, coffee-colored arms and legs in bright T-shirts. They don't know me, but when I step out of the car, they wrap their arms around me one by one, little lapping waves, then drift away. The scene arranges itself: a few low-lying cottages flanked by banana groves, pink hibiscus, flitting hummingbirds, aluminum-foil clouds, and, on the horizon, a stately mountain lying like a beached whale. "My God, it's paradise," I say, and Ursula's heard it before. I get her stock reply: "If this were paradise," she says, waving toward the kids, "these would be angels."

In 1974, Ursula and Giuseppe Grattapaglia came from Italy to start a new Esperanto world in Brazil. With their two teenage sons in tow, they left behind two jobs, two homes equipped with washing machines and dishwashers, two cars, family, and friends to live on the savanna with no electricity, no phone, and a couple of dozen illiterate peasant children. Ten miles away was the nearest town, a clutch of clay cabins with straw roofs. Brasília, a planned city barely a decade old, could be reached only after a fifteen-hour drive on dirt roads via a handful of improvised bridges.

Children during World War II, Ursula and Giuseppe were not strangers to scarcity. Ursula was born in 1933 and raised in Berlin. According to Roman Dobrzyński's *Bona Espero*, nine-year-old Ursula and her brother, along with other children of high-ranking Nazi officials, were handpicked to sleep in Hitler's bunker for eight months, until her family were relocated to Poland for safety. Later in the war, she and her family returned by stealth to Berlin, living hand to mouth. At the war's end, Ursula stood on the steps of a Franciscan high school and begged the nuns for an education, graduated in the top four, and then worked her way up at a department store from secretary to administrator. Both Ursula and Giuseppe became Esperantists while still in their teens; they met for the first time after a six-year Esperanto correspondence. When he wrote soon after, asking her to marry him, she told him he was crazy and warned him that she "abominated" children. Despite the warnings, he persevered, and Ursula agreed to a "provisional" marriage. They took their vows in Esperanto, and have now been provisionally married for fifty-three years.

Moving to Turin with Giuseppe, Ursula made a career of her gift for languages. For Fiat executives, she interpreted German, French, Italian, and English. (It was Ursula who translated for the Italian press corps during the 1972 Munich massacre, when eleven Israeli Olympians were assassinated by Black September.) Giuseppe, like his father, was nursed in the bosom of Fiat, and from age fourteen was one of a small cadre of youths groomed for a technical post among Fiat's engineers. Apart from a stint in the military, he had always lived in Turin.

By the 1970s, the Grattapaglias were in their early forties and highly placed in the Italian Esperanto Federation, organizing its annual congress—most famously, on a cruise to Morocco. (Ursula, in a rare burst of English: "*It was absolutely the top!*") One day Giuseppe came upon a circular advertising a school in rural Brazil founded by Esperantists, dedicated to making a "better world and a happier human race."

Boasting of telephone lines and a hydroelectric plant that would soon be up and running, the director, *Arthur Vellozo, entreated Esperantists worldwide to come to Bona Espero and join in the new venture. Ursula wrote to Vellozo proposing to visit at Christmas, but there was no response.

In accordance with rural Brazilian protocols, her letter sat in someone's kitchen for six months until a sufficient volume of mail accumulated to be delivered. After one or two more protracted exchanges, it was agreed that the Grattapaglias would spend Christmas of 1973 at Bona Espero.

What they didn't know was that the circular *when they received it in Turin* was already two years out of date, its luminous vision emitted by a dying star. After multiple flights and the grueling off-road journey, Ursula and Giuseppe found a handful of adults in charge of twenty-eight children in a crude, candle-lit building known as Pioneer House. There was no hint of a hydroelectric plant, and the only phone service to speak of was a generator that transmitted signals from one building to another. Unexpectedly, in lieu of Vellozo, they found another Esperantist named *Renato Lemos. But where others would have seen failure and fraud, they saw both need and potential.

Each day for two weeks, they dove into the daily routines and then, toward evening, grabbed an eight-millimeter movie camera and filmed the rosy watercolor sunsets. Back home in Turin, they wistfully watched the sun set over Bona Espero again and again. Giuseppe wrote up the adventure for *Heroldo de Esperanto* in utopian cadences, summoning Esperantists to this "little piece of heaven" soon to be the cultural center of the region, where children were instructed in "the ethos of the life-ideals of Zamenhof." Only two Esperantists heeded the summons: themselves. ("Be careful about filming the sunsets," Ursula jokes, "it can be very dangerous.")

In July 1974, their Italian lives packed into thirty crates, the Grattapaglias and their sons boarded the *Christopher Columbus* at Genoa and sailed to Rio de Janeiro. They had tasted the frontier life and made their choice, eyes wide open. They knew what lay before them: working in an isolated, rural locale alongside Lemos, whom they barely knew; grueling days and nights of physical labor—building, repairing, washing, cooking, and cleaning; the arduous work of teaching these children and shepherding them into the fold of *Esperantujo*. And they would need to find a way to educate their sons. They knew the elements would not be kind; they'd weather floods, fires, wolves, and anacondas, not to mention the breakdown of every machine brought in (some improvised from abandoned parts) to move earth and build on it. What they didn't know was that these would be minor trials next to those they would suffer at the hands of other human beings.

Bona Espero, Esperanto seminar, 1983
[Österreichische Nationalbibliothek]

* * *

I'd been told not to expect Internet or cell service; the closest internet connection is in Alto Paraíso, a fifteen-minute drive away. But the day I arrive, someone points out that two miles down the dirt road, if you hold your phone high overhead, it's possible to text. After stashing my belongings in the guest house, I head out. At the creak of my front door, Samba scrambles to attention, like a canine butler. A black-and-sand cimarrón with a feral past, she's also an opportunist, lurking on the guesthouse terrace in hope of favors.

With Samba beside me, I start down the road. It's cooling off, and the air is clear and frank. Under puffy clouds, the road slopes down, crossing a shaded one-lane bridge, and rises to a ridge where it suddenly cleaves the landscape in two. On the right, against the backdrop of massive Whale Mountain, I look down on a deep valley of eucalyptus and jacaranda trees. It's primal, pristine, as though at any moment a triceratops might poke its head out among the leaves. On the left lie the scrubby grasses of the cerrado, dotted by agaves and buriti palms, daubed with yellow begonias. On either side of the road sit red termite mounds the size of lambs and flirty purple *quaresma* trees. The name tells when they flower—

during Lent—which is what Elizabeth Bishop calls them in one of her Brazilian poems, "Electrical Storm":

> The cat stayed in the warm sheets.
> The Lent trees had shed all their petals:
> wet, stuck, purple, among the dead-eye pearls.

The only sound is cicadas, though I have an ear out for the rattle of the *cascavel*—rattlesnake. Ursula's told me not to walk down the dirt road alone, but this is how I do things these days, I want to tell her, alone. Still, I'm glad to see Samba trotting gamely along.

This evening I'm introduced to the other couple on the premises: Tia (aunt) Carla, a diminutive, radiant former student who, twenty-two years and two degrees later, is head teacher and residential director; and Paulo, a fifty-year-old Italian with a round, shaved head. A few years ago, he came here from the state capital, Goiana, to meet with Giuseppe, a *paisan*. Soon after, he had a vision that he should farm the land. When he tried to purchase land from the Grattapaglias, they told him it was famously infertile, then offered him ten hectares for a trial run. Paulo surprised them twice over. First, he grew a garden so lush and fertile that it feeds twenty people three meals a day; second, he married Carla, helping her to raise her teenage son, Nestor, in an apartment in the children's house. When I introduce myself to Paulo in Esperanto, he blurts in English, "I don't speak Esperanto." There are few matters on which Ursula is resigned, and this is one of them. "Paulo," she says gravely, "is *neesperantista*."

Then there is Sebastian, a tall forty-four-year-old volunteer from Argentina, handsome enough to be a soap opera character, that dark, sexy cousin who's just moved back to town. In fact, he's a rock star in the Esperanto world, the linchpin of two bands: a punk band called La Porkoj (The Pigs) and a Latin-rock band called Civilizacio. This is his third stint at Bona Espero. During an earlier visit, he composed the official Bona Espero anthem, a lullaby of gentle arpeggios. The kids, however, find a backbeat in it, and rock it out:

> En *Bona* Es*pero* ni *lo*ĝas
> *pace* kaj *en* harmo*ni'*,

*ti*un trezoron ni *hav*as
kaj *em*as *do*naci al *vi.*

In Bona Espero we live,
peacefully, in harmony;
This treasure which we have,
we'd like to give you as a gift.

Sebastian works in the fields between six and eleven a.m., teaches Esperanto and music to the kids for a couple of hours, and all afternoon memorizes the Hindu mantras he downloads at the Internet café in Alto Paraíso de Goiás. After supper, he watches Brazilian telenovelas side by side with Ana, the maid, who lives in a cabin on the premises. She's a matronly woman with low-slung breasts and a shuffling gait, probably a decade younger than she looks. Her gentle, high-pitched sing-song doesn't hint at the fact that, while sweeping up after the kids of Bona Espero, she is serving out a twenty-three-year prison sentence, without bars.

We'll get back to her.

This evening, the kids sit at two long tables, as at every meal. The adult table is set for five adults and four languages. Ursula, Sebastian, Carla, and I speak Esperanto; Paulo and Giuseppe, Italian; Carla, Paulo, and Sebastian, Portuguese; and Paulo and I, English. Ursula and Giuseppe alternate among their three common languages. On the highway, when someone changes lanes without signaling, they yell out in Italian. They speak to the workers in Portuguese. And at lunch, they wander from Italian to Portuguese and back, until they finally hit Esperanto, the clear channel on the dial.

When Sebastian enters the dining hall, five girls fall on his arms—"*Se-bas-ti-an!*"—begging him to sit with them. When I enter, one small boy, Leandro, catches my eye—*Esther! Esther!,* he calls out, patting the place next to him. I sit, humbly, but within a few minutes they've all wolfed down everything on their plates and shuttled over to the sinks.

The daily routine emerges quickly. A wild, kid-clanged bell calls us to breakfast at eight: two slices of stiff flaxseed bread, one with salami and one with mango marmalade. Then, for the kids, chores, homework, lessons, and play; farmwork for Paulo, Sebastian, and the laborers; food prep for Carla, who readies a substantial vegetarian lunch for all, with the ubiquitous rice and beans. At about twelve thirty p.m. a school bus arrives to disgorge another fifteen children, town kids who will return to their families when school ends at six. Around three there's a break for *lunch* (Portuguese for "snack"), and after the town kids board the bus, a simple supper of soup or sweet rice with pumpkin. At seven thirty, with a modicum of prodding by Carla, the kids clean up, shower, and go to bed exhausted. Carla and Paulo watch DVDs in their apartment; Ursula and Giuseppe watch CNN in their house. For the rest of us, the plump night sky, with its brilliant constellations and shooting stars, provides the sole entertainment. It is ravishing, the stars so close you want to eat them.

But you can't, and the nights are long.

2. Androids

Most Esperantists never visit Bona Espero, but they all know about it. For the young and the venturesome it's a place of pilgrimage, since the Grattapaglias give volunteers room and board for up to six months, sight unseen, hoping they won't make nightly runs to the taverns or hang out at the nearby *ayahuasca* commune. (Not a few marriages have resulted from all this volunteering, and not a few breakups.) But for the vast majority of Esperantists, Bona Espero is a living, breathing embodiment of the myth that all Esperanto needs is a little infrastructure and a lot of commitment and it can save the world. Supported by Western European Esperantists (largely Germans) who have full pockets if not deep ones, Bona Espero is the one place on earth where Esperanto is an immovable feast, an entire society, a way of life.

Immersed in the mythology of the place, armed with an invitation from Ursula, whom I met in a noisy, crowded room in Białystok, I came to Bona Espero with two misconceptions. First, I thought that the children are raised bilingually, in Esperanto and Portuguese, but this was not true. Sure, what with daily classes in conversation and the ebb and flow of Esperanto-speaking volunteers, even the newer kids can follow simple commands and utter a couple of gentle insults (*"Li estas freneza!"*—"He's crazy!"). At birthdays, they sing in Portuguese, then Esperanto: *"Feliĉan Naskiĝtagon al VIIIIII . . ."* For those who've been here longest, Esperanto is the kitchen language in which they banter back and forth. But for most of Bona Espero's children, Esperanto is a language of tall, white transients, and a tool for drawing wide smiles of approval from Ursula. In most cases, when they leave Bona Espero, they leave Esperanto behind as well.

Second, I thought Bona Espero was an orphanage, but not one of the current group of children is literally parentless. Most of the "orphans" in fact come from fractured, improvised families. "The real orphans are easier to deal with," says Giuseppe. "Because when these kids come back from home after the school breaks, we just have to start all over with them. One July I offered a prize for anyone who would collect garbage around their house and bury it in a hole in the ground. When they came back, no one had done it. Sure, a few tried, and their families said, 'What is this craziness the foreigners have put you up to?'" The Grattapaglias' identity as "foreigners" has become a pretext for all manner of accusation and scapegoating; almost forty years since their arrival, it has still not fully abated.

What the Grattapaglias have done at Bona Espero, foreigners or not, is to take Esperanto to a destination undreamed of by its maker. I do not mean Brazil; Zamenhof fully expected his *lingvo internacia* to flourish in both South and North America. I mean that Zamenhof, the patriarch of a large Jewish family, built Esperanto on the foundation of family affections, which in the farms and towns of rural Brazil are in short supply. Zamenhof's vision for humanity was "one great family circle" because he deemed the family a fundamental source—even a guarantor—of fellow feeling among people of different religions, ethnicities, nationalities, and races.

But where Zamenhof had seen enough light to infuse his vision of world harmony, the Grattapaglias had found darkness, guilt, and shame. Here in Brazil, for the eight million to ten million children who fend for themselves in the streets, family affections are at best fragile, at worst, betrayed and travestied. Ursula and Giuseppe have found no end to the ways parents fail their children. Women often have five, six, seven children with several different men, who tend not to stick around to raise their kids. New boyfriends rarely embrace their partner's brood. Kids who get in the way of frustrated parents, or who cross paths with a drunk adult, are beaten. Sexual assault and abuse are rampant. Girls are raped by male relatives, sometimes with such force that they require surgery; boys are raped by boys a few inches taller, goading them to "play trains."

Because those who should protect them are absent—in mind, in body or both—boys of eleven and twelve accept protection from drug dealers, who force them to commit crimes for which the dealers would be jailed. These kids are proud of the risks they've taken—at least, the ones who elude the juvenile justice system are proud. And even when their parents are around, children are being deprived of schooling and health care. Often they're left on their own for days at a time, which usually means wandering from neighbor to cousin, aunt to neighbor. Grandmothers rarely take up the slack; how could they? Many are barely out of their thirties, with their own young children to care for.

Women are abused, as well. Sometimes they fail their children because they fear for their own lives. Such was the claim of Ana, the prisoner-maid, who'd stood by while her eight-year-old daughter was raped by the girl's father. When an older son reported the rape, Ana was arrested, taken from her riverside shack to the prison in Alto Paraíso, and barred from access to her children. There was no women's prison, so she slept on the floor of the prison kitchen. Since Bona Espero had educated some of Ana's children, a social worker phoned Ursula and proposed that Ana serve her sentence as a maid at Bona Espero. Ursula gave her customary reply: she would try it. It seems to be working, though Ursula has had to teach her how to clean a toilet and wash a window, since Ana had never lived with either. While Ursula is not permitted to pay Ana, she pays a monthly sum into a pension for her; together, they opened the first bank account Ana has ever had.

* * *

Any hour of the day, Ursula looks as if she's en route to a swanky French restaurant for lunch. This morning, sitting in her book-lined salon, she's in a two-piece, flowing cream-and-blue ensemble, her hair in a blond upsweep, not a strand out of place. She's ready to start the interview, smiling, her hands clasped as if she were a sign-language interpreter awaiting my first sentence.

I'm a little nervous. I haven't spoken Esperanto much lately, so I've prepared my opener. "Most people use Esperanto as a bridge between cultures, but here you're teaching Esperantist values to kids. What are they, and how do you teach them?"

Her hands become windshield wipers, sweeping aside my question.

"Esperanto," she says, "is for people who aren't hungry. For educated, literate, comfortable people. One percent of the world's people live this way. What we deal with here are *basic* problems: hunger and illiteracy.

Every person is entitled to dignity and civility, and Esperanto is a tool for us. What we do here, we do through Esperanto; it's not our goal."

This is a little pat, and she feels it herself, starting over. "After World War II, we were people who wanted peace," she says, "and we were pursuing peace through Esperanto. These were hard days in Berlin. But we were living in the American sector, in love with American culture, watching American movies, listening to American music; we were colonized by the American soldiers. When they offered free Esperanto classes at the American culture house, I took two courses at once and was fluent within three months. Esperanto was my passion," she says, warming to her subject. "My father wouldn't let me go out dancing, but I hitchhiked in 1956 all the way to Italy to the Esperanto encampment Giuseppe organized. All day I worked as a secretary at a department store; at night I was trying to finish high school. All my money went to feed my mother and siblings, and everything there was to eat I had to divide into seven parts. I had only my clothes," she says, tugging at the shoulders of her dress, "nothing else." Her engagement photo, she tells me, shows her in a dress donated by an alumna of her Franciscan high school, an older Jewish girl who had escaped to England on the Kindertransport. When Ursula learned the origin of the dress, she wrote to her benefactor to thank her. Twenty years later they met in New York, and they've been friends ever since.

Ursula doesn't forget much.

Yesterday, on the long drive from Brasília, she had rattled off the goals of Bona Espero: First, to live off the land, with pure air and clean water, "which you'll be drinking *krane*"—from the tap. ("Don't worry," she added, "we've tested it and it has never made anyone sick.") Second, they are there to help the local community. Third, they are there to be a bridge between rich and poor, via the world of Esperanto. It's a mission statement, ready for recitation at any time.

But this morning her tone is more confessional. "Esperanto is not really why we came here. We all have motives for what we do. I was forty years old with a family, two kids in good schools, a good job, pouring myself into Esperanto and it came to me, this uneasiness, this distaste for materialism, this desire to do more. *There must be something else, some other way.*" She's singing in the key of midlife crisis, a tune I recognize.

"People look outside themselves," she says, leaning close to me on her elbow, "and some turn to religion. Brazil is a supermarket of religions:

Catholicism, spiritualism, magical cults—and everyone is shopping. I'll take this religion, and that one, and that one. Religions all promise to connect you, they know that much." She looks me up and down as if to ensure that the next pearl will not be wasted. "But perturbation of spirit leads to spiritual evolution.

"Everyone is searching for something," she continues, searching my face. "Look around you, at Paulo, at Sebastian. Even you, coming here, all by yourself."

Is she fishing for information? Or can she read it in my eyes?

"I'm . . . in transition," I said, transition from weeping daily (sometimes most of the day) to weeping every other day. Here in Brazil, I'd left behind, in a rented apartment on a man-made lake, the few things I'd taken from my marriage of nearly thirty years—a crate of majolica dishes, a drawing of Bologna, photos of the kids. And, to save my life, left behind the man I thought I'd give my life for—kind Leo; funny, brilliant Leo— back in Princeton, bewildered, grieving.

"Your marriage," she says without hesitation, though we've never discussed it.

"Yes, my marriage . . . especially here, I sometimes forget I'm alone now, and it whacks me from behind."

"So your hands are empty," she says, stipulating a fact. "How are you doing?"

"*Tago post tago*"—it's day by day.

Tears are welling up; I've said all I'm going to say, for now.

She goes to the bookcase and returns with an English-language paperback called *The Subterranean Gods*. "Do you read science fiction? There's a novel by Cristovam Buarque—a Brazilian senator!—that accounts for it all. God creates human beings, but an era of disasters leads them to go underground. So they have to create substitutes for themselves: *androjdoj*. And these androids, they're coarse, imperfect, dim, dense. They bumble around the earth, they don't get what they're doing there, they don't get one another, they don't get anything.

"And they're us. Androids, that's all we are." So that's why I've been numb since November, stumbling through errands, not returning calls. I'm not really human at all.

She pauses, then resumes. "And given that we are androids, what is amazing is that my husband and I both felt it at the same time, the need for something more. Well, we're both egotists, Giuseppe and I," she says brusquely. "Altruists *have to* be egotists; they want to remake the world the way they think it should be."

She hands me the book; it's an assignment, not a recommendation. "Look," she says firmly. "No wonder men and women don't understand each other; they're androids, we're androids. Women want to make life, preserve life, they love twenty-four hours a day. I love everything: the children, the trees, the grass. I love everyone. Sometimes pride gets in the way of love; it's so hard to say, 'Come back to me, I want you back.'"

I'm nodding, mute.

"*Androids*," she affirms; QED. "But even for androids, love is the essence of life."

* * *

Androids don't flirt and tease the way these kids do, especially the pubescent boys and girls. "Do you give them sex education?" I ask; I meant safe sex, but before I can clarify, Ursula guffaws. "They know more about sex than we do. Most of them have been initiated at home; they live in tight quarters, they've seen sex at a young age. I tell them sex is part of love; sex is for when you are older and ready for it. I ask them, 'Would you eat a fruit that was green?'"

Eleven-year-old Clemente looks like green fruit. He and his brother were brought here when a local judge realized that his own cowherder's two boys were being kept out of school to help their father. This was fortunate for Clemente, who was more cut out to be a maître d' than a cowboy. Even in the hairnet he wears for kitchen chores, he is friendly and unself-conscious, with a wide, goofy smile and buck teeth. Lately Carla has noticed a nervous tic, and she tells Ursula. They agree to watch him; in fact, they are already watching him. A few months ago, when the class was assigned to compose a letter to someone outside Bona Espero, Clemente wrote a sexually graphic letter to Amelia, one of the girls bused in from Alto Paraíso.

She had caught my eye, one of two girls who'd crossed the invisible frontier past which girls start to hike up their skirts when it's freezing and wear bright scarves when it's sweltering. (The other, Edite, is eleven but still can't read and write, so she sits in the three-to-eight-year-olds' class. To save face, she plays teacher during recess.) Clemente's letter to Amelia ran through the sex acts he wanted to do with her, telling exactly which positions he wanted her to assume for each and narrating in detail his (several) orgasms. When he finished the letter, he signed it and handed it in. Carla was incredulous, as was Ursula. The punishment was obvious: he would have to read it aloud to them, and he did. It has not happened again.

A week ago, a boy named Flávio arrived. He's about twelve, tall and muscular, with light skin and an arsenal of gleaming teeth. Recently, he'd stopped going to school, had acted out at home, and was increasingly sullen and withdrawn. Deposited at Bona Espero by a social worker, Flávio seemed ready to make things work. But the following morning, Carla found two urine-soaked sheets stuffed into his dresser. She took him aside and explained, patiently, that it was okay if he wet his bed. She even showed him the washing machine that devoured all the previous night's sins every morning.

The next morning, while I was interviewing Ursula, Carla poked her head in, carrying a white laundry basket. Flávio had done it again. Ursula took him aside and explained that there were only two rules at Bona Espero: you don't hit and you don't lie. Wetting your bed would have no consequences, she said, but balling the sheets up and hiding them was not clean and not healthy. The next morning after breakfast, while the kids were picking the tiny stones out of the day's allotment of rice, Carla stormed into the dining hall, where Flávio was leafing through a comic book. She walked to within four inches of him—they're about the same height—and began to yell at him in Portuguese, jabbing the air in the direction of the dormitory. The other children left off their work in awed silence while Carla marched him out of the dining hall, to the abode of Ursula.

"I told him," Ursula tells me at lunch, "I know what you've been through, Flávio. I know what the older boys have done with you. You don't need to hide anything anymore; we already know. That will not happen anymore, and you can erase that from your life as long as you make the right choice here. So this is your choice: either you live the way we live here or we'll send you back to your mother. And soon you will be back on the street with the boys and we can't help you then. So sit here, Flávio, and think to yourself, 'I have a choice.'"

All through the day, Flávio sits on the slate ledge on Ursula's veranda, crying fat slow silent tears that neither he nor anyone else bothers to wipe away. Sometimes he simply stares off into the distance.

When Ursula and I pass by later that afternoon, Flávio asks, "May I study?"

"No," he is told, "you may not. Sit. Think."

The next morning, Flávio's bed will be dry. And the next. And the next.

But Sunday morning the soaking sheets will be once again stuffed into the bureau, and when it's time to get ready for a hike to the waterfall, Flávio will be sitting alone on the slate ledge, sniffling and thinking some more, if he had anything left to think.

3. Utopians

They were a strange group of utopians, the six Brazilian Esperantists who founded Bona Espero in 1957. According to Dobrzyński, it began with Arthur Vellozo's dream vision from the spirit world. Vellozo dreamed that he was to serve abandoned children; instruct them in ethics, solidarity, and brotherhood; live off the land. As a devotee of the spirit world, Vellozo, a bank officer, was not unusual. To invest time and belief in the world of spirits is an everyday affair in Brazil, even among the educated elite. The followers of the nineteenth-century French medium Allan Kardec (né Hippolyte Rivail) number among the millions here, where generals and transit workers alike wait on line late into the night for an audience with a medium.

Kardec's epitaph—"To be born, die, again be reborn, and so progress unceasingly, such is the law"—might serve as a motto for Brazil's vast, enduring culture of spiritual recycling. In the 1950s, a spirit known as Ramatis informed his Brazilian followers that there was an Esperanto Academy in the spirit world, and all should learn Esperanto. Since then, the links between Esperanto and spiritism in Brazil have always been strong; an estimated 80 percent of Brazilian Esperantists are spiritists.

That October, the six "pioneers" set out overland by Jeep and wandered the savanna for months, watching for signs. In February, when their Jeep was commandeered to transport a woman in labor to a clinic, one of the Esperantists suddenly exclaimed, "This is the place!" There was the small problem of acquiring the land. Vellozo put the matter before Abilio Czerwinski, the ethnic Pole who owned the land, mentioning the "Polish" creator of Esperanto, and soon Czerwinski agreed to sell them five hundred hectares for a nominal fee.

In 1963, after Vellozo's advertisements for a new Esperantic farming colony fell on deaf ears, he struck a deal with the Brazilian Justice Department. They designated Bona Espero a "custodial institution" for delinquents, and followed each child with financial support. By 1965, disputes over money drove Vellozo and Renato Lemos apart, but the contretemps did not prevent Lemos from marrying Vellozo's daughter. Together the couple had full charge of the community which, hand to mouth, and quite dystopically, endured. When Giuseppe and Ursula arrived in 1974, Giuseppe asked Lemos for financials. "Dear man," replied Lemos, "we're family here!" Lemos—who, as Dobrzyński tells it, sold off his prized entomological collection to fund the school—had no better aptitude for management than did the other five Esperantist pioneers, four of whom had since gone their separate ways.

However incompetent, Lemos remained until, a decade later, he awoke to learn that three teenage boys had left during the night, ridden horses to Alto Paraíso, and refused to return. One of the three, age fourteen, told Ursula and Giuseppe that he had been covertly having sexual relations with Lemos for upwards of a year. Lemos initially denied the charge, but when detailed accounts from several boys tallied, he confessed, claiming that he himself had been abused as a child. Lemos's considered suggestion was that he go off for a month, have some much-needed dentistry, and resume his post. He was summarily dismissed and the three boys were gradually sent away.

A second scandal involved a young Esperantist from Brasília, a hardworking civil servant whom the Grattapaglias had taken under their wing. "Rosa Maxima," as Dobrzyński calls her (at Ursula's request), traveled with them in 1980 to the Universal Congress in Stockholm, after which she took up a volunteer post in the Central Office in Rotterdam. Soon she wrote to Ursula that she and the British UEA director, Victor Sadler, were in love. Ursula fantasized that the two would become their successors at Bona Espero, but when they arrived in early 1983, they surprised Ursula by asking for separate quarters.

What followed next, Dobrzyński calls a "revolution"; Giuseppe, a putsch. In a bid for control, Rosa proposed to liquidate the school and transform Bona Espero, at long last, into a "true" Esperanto center. The Grattapaglias barely prevailed against Rosa's manipulations of Bona Espero's board of directors. Rosa avenged the defeat by composing a diatribe accusing the Grattapaglias of beating the children, exploiting their labor, and profiting from donations intended to feed and clothe them. By the time Ursula and Giuseppe read it, Rosa had already mailed the document (at the expense of the Brazilian government) to three thousand Esperantists. It was a curse in the form of a pamphlet, as quoted by Dobrzyński:

> We now urge that the Fire of Truth consume every brick of this lie that is Bona Espero, so that out of the cinders, the only authentic ESPERANTISTS, those who live or sincerely strive to live out the internal idea . . . reconstruct the new, true Bona Espero and to make of it a lighthouse for the world, a nucleus of this race and culture and ONE UNIQUE BROTHERLY ESPERANTIST PEOPLE.

In a postscript, anticipating challenges, Rosa offered to have her mental health certified. The Rosa Maxima scandal, like the Lemos scandal, had no neat conclusion. Rosa's rage eventually burned itself out; Ursula and Giuseppe returned to welcome back the children after their winter break and begin another school term. Periodically, they still feel reverberations, to which they are resigned, as if the echoes simply obtain in the physical laws of the universe. Reflecting on the ordeal, Ursula quotes proverbs that are agnostic about the balance of good and evil in the world—proverbs of endurance.

4. Paper Kids

In the dining hall, Leandro strums the opening bars of "Smoke on the Water" on a guitar—"da da *daaaa,* da-da da-*daaaaa*"—over and over again. When he arrived as an eight-year-old, he told Ursula: "My mother is a whore." This is not why he was taken from her. Leandro was brought here because instead of sending him to school, his mother had made him her receptionist. He opened the doors to her clients, seated them until she was ready, and made small talk. I could see why she'd asked him to do this: a delicate boy, eyes glinting like schist, Leandro wore an air of authority, minus the fringe of self-importance. In his three years here, there has been not one phone call asking after his well-being.

His Esperanto's strong, and it's good practice for me to banter with him. Last Saturday, during our three-mile hike to the waterfall, he took my hand and asked, "Would you be my mother?" It's like being asked to be a summer girlfriend; we both know it'll be nice and then it will end.

"Would you be my son?" I asked, and the deal was struck. Today, when we set off for the same hike, I look about for Leandro, but he's nowhere to be found. Paulo explains that Leandro's being punished. He'd found a weasel in the meadow and beaten it senseless with a two-by-four. When Carla had moved the mauled animal deeper into the cerrado to live or die, Leandro went back to finish the job.

Leandro, along with Clemente and Clemente's half-brother Edílson, are the companions of choice for eight-year-old Rafael. Rafael has a round head of curly hair and saucer-eyes that roll around to comic effect; with a floppy coat and a horn he'd be a Brazilian Harpo Marx. He clowns for the big boys and ingratiates himself by doing their bidding. Halfway through today's hike, Carla notices that Rafael is struggling with a heavy backpack. This is odd; usually Bona Espero's kids bring nothing but hats—no towels, water bottles, sunscreen, bug spray, Baggies of grapes, or smartphones. Carla asks Rafael what he's carrying and he shrugs: "I'm not sure, it's Clemente's and Edílson's stuff." Carla frowns and points to the dirt; he swiftly dumps the backpack and walks on, knowing Carla will

Left to right: *The author, Ursula and Giuseppe Grattapaglia, Bona Espero staff and children, 2008*
[Esther Schor]

send his taskmasters back to retrieve it. She does, and we don't wait up for them.

Rafael likes to play with Toys That do Significant Things: yesterday, a bow and arrow he fashioned from bamboo; today, a tiny plastic tow truck whose string he unwinds to retrieve pods and seeds. When I let him play with my laptop—a first for him—he swiftly masters the space bar, shift key, backspace, and delete, then types the numbers from 1 to 157, leaving off at the peal of the lunch bell. The next time I let the kids take turns with my laptop, he shows up with plastic headphones—who knows where they came from—and asks whether he can listen to music. He plugs in to bossa nova, bobbing his head while three girls laboriously type their names, followed by doting sentiments (in Portuguese) about Carla: "i love aunt carla"; "aunt carla is beautiful."

Bona Espero's girls, outnumbered three to one by boys, rarely smile, even when I train my camera on them; in photos, all look vaguely defiant. When they deign to play with the younger kids, it's time for head games. Nelida, a nine-year-old girl with blunt, squared features and a hopeless crush on Sebastian, notices one morning that eight-year-old Luis has snagged Sebastian's attention. She runs over to Luis and whispers, "Aunt Carla says we are not to speak to the adults." It's a lie, but Luis leaves off, puzzled and chagrined; it's hard to say whether he believes or fears her. His sister, Luisa, at ten, is a self-appointed behavior monitor, endlessly barking orders at her younger brother and three small cousins.

The third girl is Vera, compact and afro'd, three shades darker than all the other children. Ursula tells me she's from one of the local villages founded by fugitive slaves. Over a century later, their descendants still keep to their villages. Vera walks about clutching a platinum blond Barbie doll. Instead of playing with the others, she sits at lunch giggling maniacally for attention. After July's midwinter holiday, Ursula explains, Vera won't return; in the court's view, she's regressed at Bona Espero and had best return to her mother. Sometimes with little warning, the mothers come back for their kids, having persuaded some social worker or other of their fitness to raise the child. And by dinnertime, mother and child are gone.

"Do you ever feel like fighting to keep them?"

Ursula chooses her words. "The mother is sacrosanct," she says reverentially, which I take to mean, "This is not a fight I could win." "We never say a word against their mothers. We hope the kids keep in contact and give their mothers some money when they start earning it. But often they go years with no word from their mothers."

The next morning I lug a suitcase I've brought, full of school supplies, to the dining hall; three girls vie with one another to unzip it. I pick out a piece of red paper, fold it in eight, and trace a paper girl straight out of the fifties: hair in a flip, pointy A-line skirt. The three human girls lean over my snapping scissors in a hush; clearly they've never seen anyone do this. As soon as I unfurl the first octet of dollies, both girls and boys set upon the construction paper, each picking out his or her own color. Luis, first in line, picks blue. I fold the paper and start to draw a girl—"*Ne!*" he shouts in Esperanto, "*Faru knabon, ne knabinon!*" (Make a boy, not a girl!) Twenty-four paper girls and seventy-two paper boys later, I suggest gluing the paper kids together and festooning the hall. No way; each kid clings tightly to his or her paper friends and will not give them up.

All but Rafael, who is sitting quietly, crayoning a smiling face on the round yellow head of each paper *knabo*. Those who notice grab crayons and follow suit. By the time all are drawing faces, Rafael has found, among the scraps, the unmistakable shape of a shield and glues one onto each of the eight boys. A few minutes later, he holds up his work for our admiration: "*Rigardu!*" (Look!) He's proud of his paper phalanx; these boys will stick together, and they are all protected.

He's not always so busy. Sometimes, as the children drift back to the dorm to wash for dinner, Rafael sits alone with his daydreams, petting Samba. When I picture him twenty years from now, I see him working for a software firm, drinking Starbucks, surfing the Net. On his screen, a beagle eating with chopsticks.

*   *   *

Sometimes their names are hard to grasp. There's a vogue for hand-me-down English names—Washington, Wellington; some, like Adenilson, slightly foxed. Ursula says parents pinch names they hear on commercials or telenovelas. She recalls one boy named Armani, another named Sony, and a little pixie named Erlan, after a chocolate bar. When it came time to get Erlan some documents, Ursula changed her name to Tanya. "It's the same number of letters," she explains, as if this clarifies anything. "Nowadays, Tanya has a degree in animal technology and she works for the government. If her name had still been Erlan, then what?"

Then what, indeed. "How many kids live here now," I ask, "as compared to ten years ago?"

Ursula gives me a look of disgust. "People always ask, 'How many kids live here?' We don't breed chickens here." Then, in English: "Quality! not quantity!" Still, the numbers are dramatically lower these days. In 2006, twenty-seven kids lived here; now the number floats between twelve and fifteen. Staffing has become very difficult; young teachers drift away to the cities. And Ursula and Giuseppe, though rugged and energetic, are forty years older than they were when they arrived. Fewer children means fewer conflicts; fewer all-night trips to Brasília to treat a child's snake bite.

"Isn't the average child a lot younger these days?"

"You're right," she says. "In the nineties, we had a lot of thirteen- to fifteen-year-olds. They'd start having sex at home and their parents would ship them off to the 'orphanage.' But it wasn't a solution. We have no walls here; they can just run away—and a couple of them did."

"And if the point is to make them literate, how many of the kids can read and write? Half? A quarter?"

"More than that," Ursula starts to say, then reframes the question. "There are degrees of success. By grade four, they're all literate, which gives them options not open to their parents, who can't make out the sign for the bakery. Then another group make it through grade eight; a smaller group find their way to the end of grade twelve in Alto Paraíso. About twenty are now teachers; others work for the government, for television companies, for the police; they run gas stations, just about anything. About 10 percent go to higher education."

That sounds like a lot, except that in Brazil "higher education" can mean any kind of educational or training course. During my visit, Ursula learns of a bill before the government to drop the motto "Order and Progress" from the Brazilian national flag. Apparently there has not been enough of either to bring the rate of functional literacy above 50 percent. Instead of seeing the bill as a concession of failure, Ursula finds the news cheering. "Revolutionary!" she chirps, since dropping the motto will finally make the flag legible to all.

Before the bus from Alto Paraíso arrives, Ursula teaches geography to six older kids on her veranda. Today they turn to a lesson on their state, Goiás, but once they've all shown they can find it on the map, Ursula changes gears. "It's an unhappy thing to sit around and do nothing!" she tells them, locking each one's gaze, in turn. "What makes people happy is to produce and take initiative! Otherwise, people turn to bad ways." She pauses for effect. "Every night 137 people are killed in São Paulo and Rio. But here in Alto Paraíso there is peace."

These kids know both too little and too much. They don't know how to read a thermometer or type on a laptop. They don't know about Facebook or Wikipedia or trigonometry. They can find Goiás on a map, but not the United States, and some, at eleven or twelve, can barely capture a few consonants during dictation. They do know how to avoid beatings and rape, how to visit someone in jail, how to sleep on a floor, and how to hustle a few *reals* for cane juice. And they know, with varying degrees of competence, Esperanto.

After the kids run off, Ursula invites me to stay for tea. I'm about to comment that most geography lessons don't include murder statistics; instead I say, "I had a strange dream last night." From where, this impulse to tell her my dream?

"I was walking through a parking lot at night and saw our two family cars parked next to each other. As I was walking toward them, they each pulled away in separate directions. I just stood there on the asphalt, in the dark, orphaned."

Shrink-like, she nods her head gravely, indicating for me to go on.

"It's these kids, abandoned by mothers, fathers, grandmothers, aunts . . . so many ways of being orphaned. Now I'm dreaming that *I'm* the orphan."

"Your marriage," she says, gently slipping in the corner piece of the puzzle.

I thought I'd left my marriage, but no; a husband and wife have died, leaving a middle-aged orphan in care of the night.

5. Tia Carla

"Tia Carla" (pronounced "*Chi*a *Car*la") is a petite forty-year-old with a pretty-mom smile, but when disapproval darkens her eyes and dissolves the smile, her grave beauty emerges. To the children, she is all-seeing and all-knowing. She puts them through their daily chores—showering, sweeping their rooms, checking the rice for stones, stacking dishes in the dishwasher—and prepares their breakfast and lunch. Then, promptly at 1:00 p.m., when they've donned their green-and-yellow uniforms and lined up outside the classroom in four neat columns, she miraculously morphs into their schoolteacher, leading them in a daily prayer ("We thank you, God, for our school and our teacher"), and running them through five hours of spelling, grammar, reading, writing, and arithmetic. Weekends, she takes them hiking, and in the evening shows videos and makes them popcorn. At night she sleeps under the same roof, and on their birthdays, she bakes them cakes. To each child, she is like a birthday, precious and rare, and somehow, yours.

Ursula, sitting on her veranda beside a climbing pink rosebush, tells me how Carla came to Bona Espero. Thirty-three years ago, on Ursula's forty-first birthday, a small girl was handed to her through the open window of the Jeep. The child wasted no time to announce that she was hungry.

"'What did you eat today?' I asked. The child: 'Nothing.' 'For breakfast?' I asked. 'Nothing to have for breakfast.' 'For lunch?' "Nothing to have for lunch.' She broke my heart." Ursula imitates the frightened child shaking her head to each question. Her eyes are moist, and I'm not sure whether these are the child's tears or hers.

Back at Bona Espero, Carla clung to Ursula, unwilling to let her last, best chance at survival out of sight. From the start, the child showed a commanding intelligence; she quickly became fluent in Esperanto, traveling with the Grattapaglias to congresses in Brazil and abroad. When it came time for secondary school, she was sent, along with Guido Grattapaglia, to an agricultural high school in Brasília. Among the legends of Bona Espero recorded by Dobrzyński is the story of Carla and the sow. Giuseppe, who had raised the sow from pigletcy, couldn't bear to slaughter it. But seventeen-year-old Carla, barely five feet tall, announced that she had just recently learned how to slaughter a pig. Without further ado, she plunged a butcher's knife into the pig's heart.

Two years later, Carla was one of eighteen teachers in the state accepted for an accelerated, on-the-job training course to earn her teaching certification. Bona Espero paid her tuition. Every Friday the teachers were bused about two hundred miles to Formosa, where they studied all weekend and slept on the floor, six to a room. And twenty years later, thanks to some distance learning, she's about to complete a master's degree in educational psychology.

What else she might have accomplished, had she not become a single mother at twenty-five, is anyone's guess. Pregnant and unmarried, she did the only logical thing: stayed at Bona Espero to raise her son. Nestor is now a fifteen-year-old, slim, smart, and boy-band handsome, who attends the high school in Alto Paraíso. Several afternoons a week, shuttled home on a worker's motorbike, he's Carla's teaching assistant, checking the kids' classwork, keeping them on task. In the evening, when he's not doing physics homework, he puts on Raven-Symoné CDs and dances hip-hop with the kids. On the dance floor, at dinner, on the trail that runs in the shadow of Whale Mountain, Nestor becomes the eldest of fifteen children. If Carla is their world's axis, the dashing Nestor gives it some tilt. Not everyone wants to go to high school in Alto Paraíso and then to university to study journalism. But everyone wants to be Nestor.

* * *

In 1976, Giuseppe, Ursula, and three other Bona Espero teachers began to volunteer, in a sort of teacher tag team, to teach elementary school in the town of Alto Paraíso. Five years later, Giuseppe was refused teacher certification on the ground that he was not a Brazilian citizen. According to Dobrzyński, Giuseppe was asked for proof of military service, to which he replied that he was an Italian citizen; months later, he was asked if he'd voted in the last national election, to which he replied that he was an Italian citizen. Then one day a car pulled up to Bona Espero with commissioners from the Labor Ministry demanding to know where the charcoal furnaces were. They were combing the entire charcoal-producing region to find infractions of the child labor laws. When they were told—and shown—that Bona Espero does not produce charcoal, the inspectors came up with another infraction to report: *the children were rinsing dishes.*

The Grattapaglias knew they were being targeted; how could they teach the core values of family life without expecting children to help with daily chores? This conflict with the authorities had that blend of absurdity, opacity, and menace that is called, in other hemispheres, Kafkaesque. Ursula spent the better part of a day driving to Brasília, where she met with officials in the Labor Ministry. The examiners, she was told, had reported that since Brazilians themselves exploited children, a fortiori the foreigners at Bona Espero must be doing so, too. Furthermore, she was taken to task for having a tiled floor in her house instead of a customary Brazilian sand floor. When Ursula realized that someone had surreptitiously photographed their home and school, she took up pitched battle. They would close the school, she told the official. The kids who lived there could remain, but now Alto Paraíso would have to educate them.

The Labor Ministry quailed and the local board of education, for whom the Grattapaglias had worked unpaid for years, began to back-pedal. But Ursula and Giuseppe held their ground. For three years, the children of Bona Espero were bused to Alto Paraíso at the town's expense, where they were jammed into crowded classrooms. The children took turns sleeping in town, since there weren't enough beds for all; Ursula and Giuseppe took turns chaperoning. During evenings spent at Bona Espero, the children received extra coaching to shore up their deficits in reading, writing, and arithmetic. In 2001, the Grattapaglias reopened the school, but not without a guarantee that it would be accredited and supported as a public school. It is now a pillar of the Alto Paraíso education system, which sends the yellow schoolbus out to the cerrado every day at noon.

6. The Builder

Some cultures have their Eddas and Kalevalas. Bona Espero has Giuseppe's infrastructural sagas, in which he plays the reluctant hero, brandishing his calculator amid four decades of fiascos—and the occasional success.

In the seventies, there was no construction industry in the region, and there was not much need for one. The nearest mason, a notorious alcoholic, lived more than a hundred miles away. Local homes were made with adobe walls, roofed with straw or branches. When it came time to build, Giuseppe's workforce comprised illiterate field hands who picked up work here and there. "I had to take out a meter stick and show them: 'This is a meter,'" he told me. "'This is how you make a straight line.'" To renovate the "white house" in 1978 required building an oven and manufacturing four thousand bricks, which they did with the help of volunteers from Germany, France, and the United States.

"The local men," Giuseppe says, with a rolling laugh that starts in his elbows, moves to his shoulders, and wobbles his head. "Around here live the last free men in the world. They regard work as a biblical curse. When I had to repair the bridge, I hired four workers. Every morning when it was time for work, it would be me and the tractor. One guy's equipment was in the shop. Another had the wrong day. One had a sick family member. And another—he puts out his lower lip and imitates the shrug—"'*my shovel broke.*' There's a catch-all phrase you hear a lot in these parts: 'It's not possible.'"

Funding, except for money garnered through judicious sales of land, invariably flows through Esperantic channels; Ursula says proudly that they never solicit funds. Construction of the epic, multipurpose community hall, which Giuseppe and crew finished in 2006, began with a blind couple, the former president of the Italian Esperanto Federation and his wife. "In 2003," says Ursula, "they arrived with a guide and went about touching everything—the kids, the trees, the fruit—and finally asked, 'What do you need?' I told them: 'A hygienic kitchen and a social hall,' and they raised ten thousand Euros.

"That," says Ursula broadly, "bought the foundation.

"A year later, at a Rotary convention, a Japanese woman approached us and said, 'Can you help us find a home in Brazil?'" The woman turned out to be the head of the Oomoto sect, which has a long history of support for Esperanto; she was accompanied, according to Ursula, by her personal stylist.

"The Oomoto paid for the walls," says Ursula, "and the Germans paid for the roof. It took Giuseppe and the workers nine months to build it." This triumphal conclusion seems to call for a proverb, and she obliges: "Goethe said, 'Whatever you can do or dream you can, begin it.'" Two hours have gone by, and Giuseppe looks eager to move on. He asks whether the interview is finished.

"Not quite," I say. "One more question: What else would you like to build here?" Giuseppe doesn't hesitate. "My last construction project will be a mausoleum to the martyrs of Bona Espero."

7. Plantman

In fact, there already is a tomb at Bona Espero, out between the papaya groves and the water tank: the remains of the founder, Arthur Vellozo, topped by a fifteen-foot-high Leninesque bust of Zamenhof. "Ursula and Giuseppe want to be buried here too," says Paulo, who is giving me a tour of his farm this afternoon, and the story of his life—in English sprinkled with oregano. In his early forties, Paulo had earned a degree in interior design and was living in northern Italy selling snowboards and high-end ski outfits. Then came a creeping sense of unease. "Something was happening; I didn't know what at first. I was living in a world of lies—lying to get money, lying to spend it." Paulo's speech is explosive, his tongue tending toward "caps-lock." " I didn't hear myself," he says, "but I was CRYING OUT against the lies. And here's what happens when you start to live by the truth: you can't tolerate LIES anymore."

For Paulo, the path of truth led to Brazil, to the city of Goiana, to a storefront where he decided to open an Italian restaurant. Three times he tried, and three times failed. "I waited for coincidences, since NOTHING WILL HAPPEN that wasn't meant to happen. And then I met Vitor, a very spiritual person. He CANALIZES energy and he taught me how to send my energy to others." His eyes widen, fixed on mine, and start to redden. Suddenly tears flow, which he wipes away delicately, each with a different finger. "It's KERRRAZY!" he says, "People who feel as I feel are so happy, they are CRYING. I hardly even know what I'm saying when I feel it. I see a person and I feel their need, their suffering, and I just . . . *Ramón!*"

He suddenly hails a field hand several rows away, and Ramón, in a khaki sunhat, straightens up and looks at him, smiling. Paulo mirrors his smile, staring at him intently. They both stare and smile for at least two minutes. It's hard to watch, what with the bugs biting and the sun beating down, but I can't take my eyes off them. The flesh on the back of my neck is crawling. Finally, Paulo breaks the spell, yelling a question in Portuguese over the rows of peppers. Ramón nods, still smiling, and returns to weeding.

"Yes!" says Paulo. "Ramón felt it, he received it. I can send the energy by phone, too, long distance. To Italy there's maybe a five seconds delay? So I send and I count to myself"—he whispers—"one—two—three—four—five, and 'WOW,' they say on the other end, 'WOW, that's KERRRAZY good!' The last time I went to a medium," he adds soberly, "he had to shield his eyes when I came in the room."

I didn't; maybe my eyes have adjusted to his aura.

"So I started reading ancient books: *The Book of the Dead*, the *I Ching*, the *Gitas*; the teachments of Jesus. The REAL ones, not the ones the church sets out for us. Like when Jesus say, 'Drink my blood, eat my meat,' it's mean that God is in all of us. AND WE ARE IN GOD. And evil is just the absence of God. That's all it is."

"Augustine says the same," I begin, but next to the *Tibetan Book of the Dead*, Augustine's a Johnny-come-lately. Paulo shrugs and resumes: "Think about it: our souls have an amazing opportunity here to learn. We go from universe to universe, but here on earth we can take a GIANT LEAP forward. So I'm learning to love my enemy. Because I want to love EVERYBODY. Think about it."

I'm thinking: You don't need Tibetans to learn to love everybody. Ask Hillel. Ask Jesus. For that matter, ask Zamenhof.

"When I knew that I was sent here to put my energy into the ground to feed these children, then I ACT. I come to Ursula and Giuseppe and they say, 'Here's ten hectares, see what you can do.' So I left a great house in Goiana—and a girlfriend who was a model!—to come here and plant. I put my energy into the plants and sometimes they stay quiet, shhhhh, a month, a year, two years, and then—WHOOMP!—POW!—they come up KERRAZY big." It's like talking to a comic book hero, Plantman.

"And I don't get paid; no, I pay Ramón out of my own pocket. If I leave, I leave everything. But who would?" He seems to have in mind his life with Carla and Nestor, with the ten boys for whom he provides a father's lore—how to swim, how to fish, how to make a bow and arrow from bamboo. A father's love.

But no, he's talking about another dimension entirely. "It's just full of souls here, FULL OF SOULS. Even Kubitschek felt it, homing in on this place from his helicopter." In the late 1950s, President Juscelino Kubitschek made good on his motto, "Fifty years of progress in five," by founding the new capital, Brasília. Rumor has it that Kubitschek's helipad, during his forays into Goiás, was on the grounds of Bona Espero. "Think about it," says Paulo.

He leans in and locks my gaze; the moral of the story is at hand. "We are all living in someone's dream."

* * *

Late in the afternoon, when the heat of the day has passed, Paulo and I kneel on opposite sides of a platform full of palm seedlings, transplanting the successes and weeding out the failures. He's been talking about his various careers—interior design, cooking, patrolling for avalanche victims with a GPS ("*beep, beep, beepeepeepeep*"), and I ask how he started farming. The question seems to amuse him. "I knew *nothing* about farming; I just figured it out, like: why isn't this working?" his rubbery face assumes a befuddled expression. "AHH, I'll try this. And this?" He taps his bald pate twice. "AHH, I'll try that."

He begins to rattle off stats: the vegetable field is seventy by eighty meters. He's installed over three kilometers of irrigation pipes. On four hectares, he's planted five hundred-odd fruit trees; around the rest of the property, more than two hundred non-fruit trees. The water tank, filled by water pumped up from the lake, holds ten thousand liters. Last year the garden yielded one ton of tomatoes. Lately, he's grown a dense pasture of mombasa grass, with four distinct quadrants.

He walks me through a large shed he's just built for raising seedlings and storing tractors. It's the kind of shed Nero might have built for his seedlings and tractors; aureate, capacious. He's painted it classic Brazilian colors—sky-blue and ochre—and put in a bathroom "so the gardeners don't have to pee in the fields." Of late, from the bend in the highway, it's the most prominent building you see. Paulo calls it a "laboratory." Ursula calls it "Paulo's palazzo."

Bona Espero runs on two different calendars: Ursula's and Paulo's. The Ursuline calendar refers to epochal events of the past forty years: "the-time-of-the flood"; "the-time-of-the-fire"; "the-time-the-board-of-the-UEA-came-to-Bona-Espero." The Pauline calendar refers to the future: "when-we'll-be-raising-horses"; "when-we'll-be-using-wind-power"; "when-we'll-be-farming-fish." Paulo points to a jagged gash in the chicken wire. "You see that? That's where the *cascavel*—how do you say, rattlesnake?—poked out his head, but we were READY for him." He picks up what looks like a blind person's white stick; at one end is a red plastic loop which, when he tugs the other end, tightens like a noose. "I got him, Ramón cut the wire, and then I took the snake out to the fields." *No animals were harmed in the making of this utopia.*

Suddenly, abruptly, Plantman's face darkens, his brow furrowed. "It's just a matter of time before people wake up. You've seen what's happening: tsunamis, earthquakes, hurricanes. When the energy comes, the first thing it does is to shift the plates. BAM. And you see what's going on in the economy, don't you? Watch CNN: This morning the Dow fell 3 percent, and that's just this morning. A matter of time before EVERYONE FINALLY SEES . . . and they'll all start coming. Here. To Goiás."

He squares his shoulders and faces me. "It's all depend on your faith. You have to be prepared for the energy. Do you have FAITH? Are you PREPARED? Are you ready to leave behind the world of lies?"

I'm not likely to receive the energy, but am I ready to leave behind the world of lies? "I've just left my marriage of thirty years," I say. "If I'm not ready now, I'll never be."

This evening, after walking two miles down the red dirt road, I wave my little clamshell phone high overhead, fishing for texts. Suddenly my phone buzzes, and buzzes again and again. It seems so uncanny, finding messages in the ether. Maybe Paulo's right: *We are all living in someone else's dream.*

8. Sebastian's Mantras

It's not easy making a living as an Esperanto rocker, in Buenos Aires or anywhere. To pick up some income, Sebastian's been working in an amusement park as a Hannibal Lecter impersonator. Hard to think of anyone caging up that boyish, chiseled face, like wasting ozone. When the owner shut down the park in Buenos Aires, Sebastian decamped to the Canary Islands for a few months, where he wrote a novel and some short stories.

"Were they good?" I ask. "Did you like them?"

"*Like* them? I *love* them, I think I am a *genius*. But the publishers did not agree."

The upper-middle-class son of a doctor and a homemaker, Sebastian was educated in a bilingual English-Spanish school in Buenos Aires: it was cosmopolitan, well-appointed, "lots of Jewish kids." He speaks Esperanto whip fast, with the raw, gutted *r*s of native Spanish-speakers, but he's fluent in English, so we mix it up.

These days, he's chanting Sanskrit instead of singing Esperanto, wondering how to make a living at this: mantras for pesos. In the affluent neighborhoods of Buenos Aires, as in Park Slope or Pacific Heights, the ratio of well-heeled women to yoga mats is about one to one. He's planning to record his mantras, then sell his CDs at yoga classes, where he'll perform for donations. Five times a day, while Paulo is "canalizing" energy in the fields, Sebastian repeats one hundred and eight sets of mantras, one for every channel of the body. With a long track record of New Age pursuits, including Gurdjieff groups, Kundalini yoga, and EFT (Emotional Freedom Technique), Sebastian is what my father would have called a "seeker," my mother a *luftmensch.*

When I ask Sebastian if I can hear some of his music, he's aloof. "Sure," he says coolly, "later on, this evening." I'm expecting an invitation to his cabin, but instead, he hands over a thumb drive containing his three Esperanto CDs and 493 other Brazilian songs. That evening I start with Sebastian's ear-candy make-out songs with titles like "Tuj" (Immediately) and "Ador" (Adoration); then the soaring paeans about world peace; finally, thumping techno beats about clones, druids, and penguins. One of his songs, written for rank beginners, is posted on the lernu! website. It's probably the first breakup song ever with no direct objects; it's certainly the sexiest:

> *Jen la suno, jen la luno*
> *Jen du malsamaj astroj*
> *Jen vikingo, jen urbano*
> *Jen la plej malsamaj homoj*
>   *Jen vi kaj mi, akvo kaj oleo*

> Here's the sun, here's the moon,
> Here are two different stars
> Here's a viking, here's a city-guy
> Here are two different people
>   Here are you and me, water and oil

The next evening I hand the thumb drive back to him and invite myself over to his cabin.

"The telenovela isn't over till eight fifteen," he says indifferently.

"So I'll come at eight thirty." His shrug says, "Suit yourself." We're the only two unattached adults for miles around, if you don't count the *ayahuasca* addicts, and I can wait out his telenovela habit.

I do, and for the next two weeks, we spend the evenings together, singing, alone and in harmony, and listening—to Esperanto Desperado, Morphine, Cyndi Lauper, Ravi Shankar. We snack on my dwindling supply of raisins from Target and drink passion-fruit juice from his *miksilo* (blender). Sometimes Samba comes to the door, and Sebastian, in a weird falsetto, cries "*Sambacita!*" and swings the door open. Samba quivers, knowing it's verboten to go inside, but Sebastian coaxes her in and calms her with mantras. We end every evening standing under the night sky amid his pineapple plants, counting shooting stars and laughing giddily.

Then he walks me chastely back to the guesthouse, our flashlights scanning the brush for snakes.

* * *

"Could you see living here, in Bona Espero?"

It's a Wednesday morning, and Sebastian is showing me what's left of the *arbidoj,* five hundred tiny seedlings planted in 2008 during the UN's International Year of Planet Earth. Only half of them took; those that didn't have left dark spaces among the two-foot trees, like missing teeth. "It's beautiful here, and the climate's much too cold for parasites; you'll sooner die of boredom than bacteria. But live here? No. I don't have money and I don't have a woman. Don't misunderstand," he adds quickly. "If I needed a woman to cure me of loneliness, I'd be in a lot of trouble. You can't expect another person to solve your loneliness." The advice hits hard.

"Lately I'm spending a lot of time alone," I say, "since I separated from my husband, and—"

"Where is he, your ex?" he asks.

I'm taken aback. "My ex? No!—He's still my husband."

He wasn't expecting to step on a mine. "Well, *sorry!*" he says, rolling his eyes.

"No, *I'm* sorry, but you're the first person ever to do that, turn my husband into an *ex.* Have you ever been married?"

"No, but maybe I'm ready to get married now," he says drily, "because I don't give a shit about anything."

It's funnier than it would have been a year ago. "Oh, I get it. You're the ideal husband?"

"Well," he says, "maybe I've never been married, but I know one important thing."

"Yeah?"

"Love always pays."

9. Mosaic of the Future

Scratch Ursula's reasonable, world-weary veneer and you'll find a raving *finavenkistino.* "English is John the Baptist for Esperanto," she tells me. "Global English shows how sorely the world needs a common language.

Let's face it, we Esperantists are pioneers, and pioneers are always considered mad. When they invented the electric bulb, people said, 'That's crazy, what will happen to the candles?' When they invented cars, people said, 'That's crazy, what will happen to the horses?' In the nineties someone said, 'Soon you'll be able to send letters by wires,' and people said, 'That's impossible!' Technology is now making it possible for Esperanto to win; all we lack are human minds and spirit. The question is, can people really recognize what progress is? Esperanto is not a philosophy; it is a stone in the mosaic of the future." The awkward chips of white and green on Zamenhof's tomb, the five-pointed star: a mosaic of the future, set by the hand of the past.

One thing about the future of Bona Espero is clear; it does not lie in the hands of the Grattapaglias' sons, who live in Brasília with non-Esperantist wives and children fluent in Portuguese and Italian. What it was like to cart two middle-class Italian teens off to rural Brazil is a complicated story. Ursula has told what she'll tell of it to Dobrzyński: the ordeal of sending her two sons to school fifteen hours away in Brasília, the nightly radio calls to check on them, the monthly drives to see them. The nights she cried, missing them. This much she'll review with me, but no more. "Every family has its drama," she says, rising.

Giuseppe wants the story to end in a major key, more for his sake than for mine. "They admire what we've done here, but they suffered for it. On

Ursula and Giuseppe Grattapaglia, receiving the Medal of Tolerance in Brasília, 2013 [Ursula and Giuseppe Grattapaglia]

balance, it was good. We never had those adolescent quarrels between parents and kids. When we saw them each month, it was joyful. The experience of independence strengthened them. And the opportunities in Brazil are vast. Their friends in Italy have all had to settle for part-time jobs here and there; it's so hard to start a career there. But here everything has been open to them. Take our son the plant geneticist. In Europe there are forty trees, exhaustively studied. Here there are four hundred trees, most of which have never been written about. He has become a world expert on eucalyptus, he runs an institute that pairs industry with scientists to find out—for instance, can you get cellulose from eucalyptus? These kinds of questions.

"And the other, who studied agriculture, then economics, then worked in a bank, then came here and worked in construction for six months—at only twenty-five, he became an economist in the Italian embassy.

"So you see," he says, weighing the air with both hands, "on balance . . ."

It's a phrase my father used to use, when he talked about marriage: *On balance.*

*   *   *

All over rural Brazil, cars are parked at crossroads, waiting for buses. In a few hours, I'm to catch the "Class Bus" line to Brasília, which runs a morning bus and an afternoon bus, but has no schedule to speak of. Giuseppe and Sebastian will drive me the four miles to the highway, and we'll park and wait. "It shouldn't take more than two hours," says Giuseppe. After two hours with no traffic at all, the bus glints in the distance; my last photo is of Sebastian sitting in the middle of the highway in a lotus position.

At breakfast, Nelida and Luisa gave me a tiny notebook they'd made, a few ripped pieces of paper nested into one another. I asked all the kids to autograph it; one by one they signed their names, slowly, carefully. When it was Leandro's turn, he wrote his name and a dark round period, then paused. "May I write my mother's name?" he asked. I nodded and he wrote in cursive, "Dina." Clemente reached for the pen, but Leandro held it tight. "May I write my other mother's name?" he asked, already writing: "Ester."

On the terrace, Ursula gave me the phone number of an Esperantist in Brasília whom she'd commandeered to show me around the city. Giuseppe suddenly walked by from his office. "Just tell me what lies she's been telling you," he joked, "and I'll tell you all the other ones."

"What I want to know, Giuseppe, is this: What can you tell me about Ursula that she would never say about herself?"

He exploded in laughter, clapping his hands. "Well! Ursula!" His head bobbed left and right like that of a punch-drunk boxer. "The thing you need to know about Ursula is that she loves lost causes. Give her a lost cause, and she *throws* her arms around it. She loves everybody."

Her lips set, Ursula nodded, approvingly, and caught my eye: *This is why I married him.*

"And Ursula—what can you tell me about Giuseppe that he'd never say about himself?" She looked him up and down. "Giuseppe," she said, laughing, "is Buddha. Always, always happy."

Buddha smiled beatifically, and said he had an appointment with a machete; the banana groves needed tending before we left.

Once he'd gone, Ursula asked, as if it had just occurred to her, "So what kind of book are you writing?"

"What kind of book?" I was stalling, and she knew it. "It's a hybrid, history and memoir. It's about Zamenhof, his language, his dreams, and the people he entrusted to build Esperanto, then and now. It's about Esperanto as a bridge of words, and all the 'internal ideas' that have crossed it. And it's about my wanderings in *Esperantujo*, the people I've met in Europe, Asia, California, here. . . ." I didn't tell her it's about me, too, though I never meant it to be; about how Esperanto helped me to navigate my middle-aged anguish, to get across what I needed to say. "And the last chapter is about Bona Espero."

She was unsettled. "Bona Espero doesn't need a *whole chapter,*" she admonished, then softened. She took my hands in hers across the table, and tears came to her eyes.

Now I was unsettled; I was the writer, she was my subject. We shouldn't be holding hands. My tears shouldn't come out to meet hers.

Neither of us spoke, but her voice was in my ear—

> . . . *love is the essence of life*
—and Giuseppe's—
> *She loves everybody*
—and Paulo's—

Because I want to love everybody!
—and Sebastian's—
Love always pays.
"Don't worry," I said, "it's about what you're doing here in Bona Espero. It's about love among the androids."

Coda: Justice in Babel

During my travels among Esperantists in Europe, Asia, and Latin America, I've come home to the United States to encounter a few perdurable myths about Esperanto. Sometimes it seems that these myths about Esperanto are more robust than Esperanto itself; three in particular stand out.

The first is the "heyday" myth: Esperanto had its heyday, but isn't it . . . over? Whereas languages may become dead or extinct, this myth assumes that Esperanto was merely a fad, having gone the way of hula hoops, stuffed hummingbirds on ladies' hats, and other caprices of mass culture. This myth creeps up on late-night TV in Stephen Colbert's recurrent references to Esperanto—"the most popular human animal hybrid fantasy franchise ever published in Esperanto"—as a shorthand for absurdity, obscurity, and irrelevance. In fact, Esperanto was never a mass-culture phenomenon, except occasionally as a metaphor.

In the past half century, Esperantists, who are highly self-conscious about language and communication, have tended to strain against the current of mass culture. To those who hold with the "heyday" myth, it makes no impact to point out that Esperanto, in its second century, has a community that extends over six continents and sixty-two countries. To "heydayers," Esperantists are simply people who did not get the memo that Esperanto is over. It never occurs to them to wonder why they are still quick to opine about Esperanto, if it is indubitably a thing of the past.

The second myth is what filmmaker Sam Green calls "the gray jumpsuit" myth: that Esperanto, in its aim for universality, leads us toward a world of uniformity and cultural homogeneity. It's a myth first voiced in the nineteenth century, during the romance of nationalism; voiced again, in a Marxist key, by Gramsci a century later. And it is prevalent in the United States, a country that refuses to put its schoolchildren in uniforms, leaving such gear to those who serve their country (soldiers), their locality (police), or time (prisoners). But one does not see jumpsuits, gray or otherwise, at Esperanto gatherings, where people wear colorful national costumes, celebrate diverse cultures, buy anthologies of national literatures in Esperanto, and take daily lessons in the host country's language.

This, at least, is the current state of affairs; as far as Esperanto's history is concerned, the cultural diversity question is a bit more complicated. Zamenhof, characteristically, espoused different opinions in different contexts, sometimes within a single essay. To the French Academy of Sciences he argued that Esperanto would only strengthen national languages, though in the same text, he wrote, "We confess that however much we knock our head about, we can't understand at all what the detriment for humanity would be if one fine day . . . there no longer exist nations and national languages, but there exist only one all-human family and one all-human language."[1]

Gary Mickle, an American Esperantist living in Germany, has set out to demystify the movement's touted "diversity protection claims." Esperantists, by propounding a counter-mythology to the "gray jumpsuit" myth, have anthropomorphized Esperanto as a gentle, unfailing guardian of rights, a superego that disciplines the unpredictable negotiations between the Esperantic ego and (yes) id. Perhaps; among the proponents of a universal language, there have been worse offenses. That said, since 1970, when the Declaration of Tyresö denounced "linguistic imperialism," the UEA has been strongly in favor of linguistic and cultural diversity. In the 1996 Manifesto of Prague, the UEA pledged to "unshakably" uphold seven objectives: democracy, global education, effective education, multilingualism, language rights, language diversity, and human emancipation.

The manifesto made clear what Esperanto could contribute to language rights activism: a century of experience in managing transnational identity, the creation of durable international networks, and a record of living up to an exacting standard of language equality. Under the presidency of Mark Fettes (who authored the Manifesto of Prague) the UEA has recently formulated a strategic plan dedicating Esperanto to *lingva justeco,* linguistic justice for a global Babel. The *interna ideo,* renovated by and for a new generation, lives on.

The third myth is the utopianism myth: that Esperantists believe in, expect, and labor for the *fina venko,* when the whole world is speaking Esperanto (and, according to the "gray jumpsuit myth," *only* Esperanto). That *finavenkismo* took a fatal blow in the League of Nations debacle in 1921–22 is beyond dispute; six decades later, it was finally buried in the marshlands of Rauma. Zamenhof himself was only intermittently concerned with dreams of a distant, utopian future. On the contrary, his was the future that was, as he said at Boulogne in 1905, already "floating in the air," fluttering "images of a time to come, of a new era."[2] And he entreated Esperantists to seize these images and make them real; to "build into the blue," in the words of philosopher Ernst Bloch.

While Zamenhof could wax rhapsodic about unforeseen technologies for a new century, his idea for changing the world was based on a strong continuity between experience and expectation. As a physician, he knew well that it was in the nature of human beings to change, whether to perish of disease, or to be slowly cured. He sought to change human beings *by literally changing the mind,* shaping the way it perceives, thinks, judges, and makes what it will of the minds of others. Indeed, he may have felt that the process was not entirely different from, say, administering medication for trachoma. Esperanto involved no technological miracles; it was made by hand, with books, paper, and pen, and it would be given life by brains, tongues, and hearts.

These three myths—the "heyday" myth, the "gray jumpsuit" myth, the "utopianism" myth—all bespeak a certainty that Esperanto doesn't matter—*shouldn't* matter—to Americans. Yet somehow the notion that Esperanto doesn't matter seems to matter quite a bit. Americans need to believe these myths because by doing so, they project onto Esperanto their deepest fears: that American culture is consumerist and faddish; that beneath all the diversity fanfare, there is a residual, Tocquevillian conformism; and that to believe that a male, white, slave-holding elite of the eighteenth century gave us our contemporary, multicultural nation is utopian at best and, at worst, delusional. Americans' myths about Esperanto, at bottom, are there to shore up fractured mythologies of America.

There's a fourth myth about Esperanto that needs to be refuted, but this one obtains among Esperantists themselves. The "myth of neutral-

ity" asserts that because Esperanto is neutral regarding politics and religion, it is therefore apolitical. On the face of it, this myth is not hard to
refute, since its very premise is faulty; Esperanto's vaunted neutrality is
only meaningful in the context of both politics and religion. Esperanto
emerged in the Pale of Settlement as an answer (albeit unorthodox) to
the Jewish question; and in the shadow of Dreyfus, Zamenhof (the "Jewish prophet") sacrificed his Jewish-derived Hillelist ethics so that his
language-movement might endure. Moreover, the notion that Zamenhof
was blind to class struggle, most famously espoused by Lanti in the SAT
schism of 1921, is unfounded. On the contrary, Zamenhof's disenchantment with Zionism came about, in part, from his disgust that class struggle was cleaving apart the early settlements in Palestine. Instead of being
blind to class, Zamenhof was clear-sighted enough to recognize that
class identity was inimical to his vision of a *granda rondo familia* of all
humanity.

What Esperantists have never fully recognized is that Zamenhof offered Esperanto not only as a bridge across ethnic divides but also as a
means for bridging political differences. Zamenhof wanted diverse
peoples to talk not only past their differences but also about them. Within
his program for Homaranism, he envisioned multiethnic cities, states,
and continents—indeed, a multiethnic world—using Esperanto for the
sake of negotiating differences. There's a reason why Esperanto could yet
become an exquisite instrument for political dialogue: Esperanto is itself
a dialogue between modernity and tradition. On the one hand, Zamenhof designed it for liberal individuals in search of modernity, progress,
and autonomy; on the other, he designed it to consolidate and unify a
community around timeless concepts of the good: justice, peace, harmony, and fellow-feeling. But unlike most communities bound by traditional values, the Esperantic community shares a future, not a past, and
one must choose to belong to it. Thus, Esperanto does more than balance
the claims of the individual with those of the community; it reconciles
these claims every time a liberal individual freely chooses to belong to the
Esperantic community.

Esperanto is not simply applicable to politics; it is *essentially* political. I realize this is a provocative claim, not least because I've unsettled
Esperantist audiences by making it. But my argument is that Esperanto
dovetails with the contemporary so-called liberal-communitarian debate; "so-called" because the debate has become an ongoing, evolving

dialogue between two camps: proponents of a liberal, rights-bearing self, irrespective of identity (à la John Rawls's "veil of ignorance"), and champions of communities with prerogatives and purposes (à la Michael Sandel's communitarian critique of Rawls). Since the 1980s, each side has challenged the other to assimilate its claims, be they ontological, political, or ethical. In *Politics and Passion: Toward a More Egalitarian Liberalism*, for example, Michael Walzer argues that the "liberal hero, the autonomous individual, choosing his or her memberships, moving freely from group to group in civil society" is a fiction unless we take account of the vast importance of "involuntary association,"[3] or, as Walzer puts it elsewhere, "a radical givenness to our associational life."

> Most of us are born into or find ourselves in what may well be the most important groups to which we belong—the cultural and religious, the national and linguistic communities within which we cultivate not only identity but character and whose values we pass on to our children (without asking them).

What strikes me, after seven years in *Esperantujo,* is that Esperanto bridges the dichotomy between what is "radically given" and what is "freely chosen." Esperanto is not "radically given" to anyone, not even to *denaskuloj,* who are free to take it or leave it. No, Esperanto is radically *chosen.* And to choose a language is to see the world a certain way; to question it a certain way; to assess, criticize, acclaim, or reform it within certain parameters. Esperantists *choose* the givenness that language gives the world. When Walzer demands "a political theory as complicated as our own lives,"[4] he might well be describing the complicated lives of Esperantists.

These days, the center-periphery model in which Esperanto emerged, a model that survived numerous schisms and endured amid empires, great powers, and cold warriors, has given way to new transnational networks located everywhere at once: in cyberspace, if you will. Esperanto, by necessity, is learning the language of cosmopolitanism, which, in the words of sociologist Ulrich Becker, entails "the erosion of clear borders separating markets, states, civilizations, religions, cultures, life-worlds of common people."[5] Like other geographically scattered communities, Esperantists no longer speak of themselves as international; instead, they are cosmopolitans, citizens of a global Babel. The poet Jorge Cama-

cho describes the Esperantists as a *malpopolo*—an unpeople—partaking
of a cosmopolitan, moveable feast.

> [Esperanto is] not about the culture and society of a separate
> people, but about the discontinuous culture and society, or the
> paraculture and parasociety, or the subculture and subsociety, of
> a group of human beings from different peoples, scattered every-
> where on the globe, and who live part of their life in, through,
> and often also for Esperanto.

I worry a little when Esperantists talk like cosmopolitans, and not simply because in Nazi Germany and the Soviet Union Esperantists paid so
dearly for being deemed cosmopolitans. No, I worry because disappointment with cosmopolitanism was one of Zamenhof's chief motives for
inventing Esperanto. As a Jew in the Pale of Settlement, he rejected the cosmopolitan model of Jewishness as "inauthentic." On the contrary, his model
for a modern Jewish identity was a Romantic, Herderian idea of a people
bound by a common language. When Zionism and modern Hebrew
failed that dream, he reshaped it around Hillelism—and Esperanto.

But if Camacho's endlessly morphing *malpopolo* sounds like post-
modern cosmopolitanism, don't be fooled: Camacho remains a quizzical
Herderian. "Esperanto continues to give me something," he writes,
"which I don't find anywhere else: an irrational sense of direct belonging
to the world."[6] That is because conversation, the lifeblood of Esperanto,
is what solders individuals into community. In the words of the philosopher Charles Taylor:

> "Fine weather we're having," I say to my neighbor. Prior to this,
> he was aware of the weather, may have been attending to it; obvi-
> ously I was as well. It was a matter for him, and also for me. What
> the conversation-opener does is make it now a matter for *us*: We
> are attending to it now together. . . .
>
> A conversation is not the coordination of actions of different
> individuals, but a common action in this strong, irreducible
> sense; it is *our* action. It is of a kind with—to take a more obvious
> example—the dance of a group or a couple, or the action of two
> men sawing a log. Opening a conversation is inaugurating a
> common action. . . .

In human terms, we stand on a different footing when we start talking about the weather.[7]

It is the Esperantic conversation, that century-long haphazard culture of chitchat and palaver, that builds a bridge between you and me, turning my action into *ours,* myself into *us.* It provides, in Camacho's phrase, an irrational sense of directly belonging to the world. Which is another way of saying that whatever the historical destiny of Esperanto will be—wherever it ends up on earth, on Mars, or in some other galaxy entirely—it begins in conversation: "Fine weather we're having."

Belan veteron ni ĝuas.

Glossary

═══

Akademio de Esperanto: Academy of Esperanto (formerly, Language Committee)

bela: beautiful

bonvenon: welcome

bonvolu: please

ĉapelo: a circumflex; literally, a hat

civitane (closing in a letter): alternative to *samideane* used by Civito members

Civito: *see* Esperanto Civito

ĉu: interrogative particle; whether; interjection meaning "oh!"

dankon, koran dankon: thank you, heartfelt thank you

denaska: raised speaking Esperanto

denaskulo, denaskuloj (pl): a person/people raised speaking Esperanto

Esperanto: literally, "the Hoping One"

Esperanto Civito: community constituted by the "Pact for the Esperanto Civito"

Esperantujo: the Esperanto community; the diasporic para-nation of Esperanto

fina venko: the "final victory" of Esperanto; *finavenkismo* is the aspiration for same

Fundamento: the sixteen "untouchable" rules governing Esperanto grammar and usage

egaleco: equality

geja: gay

gejofobio: homophobia

ĝis la revido: until we meet again

gravulo: a VIP
ho ve: woe is me (like Yiddish "oy vey")
Ido: literally "offspring," a language derived from Esperanto
interna ideo: inner idea
jida: Yiddish
juda: Jewish
judadivena: of Jewish origin
kabei: to abandon the study of Esperanto
kara lingvo: dear language (e. g. Esperanto)
komencanto: beginner
komitato: committee
konsulo (m), konsulino (f): "consul" or delegate
korelativo: correlative (as in "table of correlatives")
lesbo, lesbanino: a lesbian
"La Espero": "The Hope," by L. L. Zamenhof, the Esperanto anthem
Libera Folio: *Free Page*, an online magazine
Lingvo Internacia: international language, the original name of Esperanto
movado: movement
planlingvo: planned (sometimes called "artificial") language
saluton: hello
samideane (closing in a letter): in the "same idea"; see samideano
samideano/j (m), samideanino/j: fellow Esperantist/s
samseksemulo/samseksemulino: a gay man/woman
sekso: sex
strangulo: weirdo
tabelvorto, tabelvortoj (pl): correlative, correlatives ("tableword/s")
Universala Kongreso: annual worldwide UEA congress
Unua Libro: "First Book," the inaugural 1887 pamphlet
Usono: United States
Usonozo: United States sickness

Acronyms and Abbreviations

═══

ASE: Asocio de Sovietaj Esperantistoj // Association of Soviet Esperantists

BEA (now EBA): Brita Esperanto-Asocio // Esperanto Association of Britain

CED: Centro de Esploro kaj Dokumentado pri Mondaj Lingvaj // Center for Research and Documentation of World Language Problems

ĈEL: Ĉina Esperanto-Ligo // Chinese Esperanto League

CO: Centra Oficejo // Central Office (Rotterdam)

E@I: Edukado@Interreto // Education@Internet

EANA: *Esperanto-Asocio de Nord-Ameriko* // Esperanto Association of North America

ELNA: Esperanto Ligo de Nord Ameriko // Esperanto League for North America (see E-USA)

E-USA: Esperanto USA

ESF: Fondaĵo pri Esperantaj Studoj // Esperantic Studies Foundation

GEA: Germana Esperanto-Asocio // German Esperanto Association

GLAT: Gejoj, Lesbaninoj, Ambaŭseksemuloj, Transgenruloj // LGBT

GLEA: Germana Laborista Esperanto Asocio // German Labor Esperanto Association

HeKo(j): Heroldo Kommuniko(j) // Heroldo Communique(s)

IEL: Internacia Esperanto-Ligo//International Esperanto League

IJK: Internacia Junulara Kongreso // International Youth Congress

IKU: Internacia Kongresa Universitato // International Congress University

JEA: Japana Esperantista Asocio // Japan Esperantist Association

KCE: Kultura Centro de Esperanto // Esperanto Cultural Center (La Chaux-de-Fonds, Switzerland)

KVA: Komisiono por Virina Agado // Commission for Women's Issues

LF-Koop: Literatura Foiro Cooperative

LIBE: Ligo Internacia de Blindaj Esperantistoj // International League of Blind Esperantists

LSG: Ligo de Samseksamaj Geesperantistoj // League of Gay ("Same-Sex-Loving") Esperantists

MEM: Mondpaca Esperantista Movado // Esperanto Movement for World Peace

NASK: Nord-Amerika Somera Kursaro // North American Summer Esperanto Institute

NEM: Neutrala Esperanto Movado // Neutral Esperanto Movement

PIV: Plena Ilustrita Vortaro // *Complete Illustrated Dictionary*

PVZ: Plena Verkaro de Zamenhof // *Complete Works of Zamenhof*

SAT: Sennacieca Asocio Tutmonda // World Anational Association

SEJM: Sovetia Esperanto Junulara Movado // Soviet Esperanto Youth Movement

SEU: Sovetrespublikara Esperantista Unio // Esperanto Union of the USSR

SkE: *Sekso kaj Egaleco* // Sex and Equality

TEJO: Tutmonda Esperantista Junulara Organizo // Worldwide Esperanto Youth Organization

TTT: Tut-Tera Teksaĵo // World Wide Web

UDEV: Unuiĝo de Esperantistaj Virinoj // Union of Esperantist Women

UEA: Universala Esperanto Asocio // Universal Esperanto Association

UK: Universala Kongreso // Universal Congress

VEA: Vjetnama Esperanto-Asocio // Vietnam Esperanto Association

Notes

Introduction

1. Roberto Garvía, *Esperanto and Its Rivals: The Struggle for an International Language* (Philadelphia: University of Pennsylvania Press, 2015), 128.
2. Sidney S. Culbert to David Wolff, 24 Oct. 1989. http://www.panix.com/~dwolff/docs /culbert-methods.html, accessed 9 Feb. 2014. See also Donald J. Harlow to Bob Petry, 16 Mar. 1999. http://listserv.brown.edu/?A2=ind9903C&L=AUXLANG&F=&S= &P=9580, accessed 9 Feb. 2014.
3. Mike Lewis, "Quirky Linguist Loved Life, and Ruth for 70 years," *Seattle Post-Intelligencer*, 15 Nov. 2003.

Part I: The Dream of a Universal Language

1. Umberto Eco, *The Search for the Perfect Language,* trans. James Fentress (Oxford, UK: Blackwell, 1997), passim.
2. Rhodri Lewis, *Language, Mind and Nature: Artificial Languages in England from Bacon to Locke* (Cambridge, UK: Cambridge University Press, 2007), 170.
3. John Locke, *An Essay Concerning Human Understanding* (New York: Collins, 1964), 262.
4. Ibid., 292, 302, 302–3.
5. Ibid., 261.
6. Robert Darnton, "What Was Revolutionary About the French Revolution?" *New York Review of Books,* 19 Jan. 1989, 35: 21, 22, http://www.nybooks.com/articles/archives /1989/jan/19/what-was-revolutionary-about-the-french-revolution/?insrc=toc, accessed 14 Mar. 2012.
7. George Steiner, *After Babel: Aspects of Language and Translation* (Oxford, UK: Oxford University Press, 1977), 82.
8. Garvía, *Esperanto and Its Rivals,* 64.
9. Giacomo Leopardi, letter of 23 Aug. 1823, quoted in Eco, *Search,* 303.
10. Andrew Large, *The Artificial Language Movement* (Oxford, UK: Blackwell, 1985), 51.
11. "Volapük in Danger," *New York Times,* 11 Dec. 1887, 4.
12. Large, *Artificial Language,* 68.

13. Donald Harlow, "How to Build a Language," http://donh.best.vwh.net/Esperanto/EBook/chap03.html#volapuk, accessed 19 Jan. 2010.

14. Garvía, *Esperanto and Its Rivals*, 26.

15. Ibid., 31.

16. W. J. Clark, *International Language: Past, Present and Future* (London: J. M. Dent, 1907), 95, http://babel.hathitrust.org/cgi/pt?id=nyp.33433082185384;view=1up;seq=111, accessed 19 Jan. 2010.

17. L. L. Zamenhof to N[ikolai] Borovko, 189[6], *Originala Verkaro*, ed. Joh. Dietterle (Leipzig: Ferdinand Hirt, 1929) [trans. from Russian to Esperanto], 418.

18. Johan Derks, "How 'International' Is Your Word?" *Fiat Lingua,* http://fiatlingua.org/wp-content/uploads/2012/11/fl-00000F-00.pdf, accessed 12 Feb. 2014.

19. Ludovic Lazarus Zamenhof, *Doctor Esperanto's International Language*, trans. R. H. Geoghegan, ed. Gene Keys, 1889, Part II, http://www.genekeys.com/Dr_Esperanto.html, accessed 13 Feb. 2014.

20. L. L. Zamenhof to Borovko, 189[6], *Originala Verkaro*, 421.

Part II: Doktoro Esperanto and the Shadow People

1. L. L. Zamenhof to [Alfred] Michaux, 21 Feb. 1905, in *Mi Estas Homo,* ed. Aleksander Korĵenkov (Kaliningrad: Sezono, 2006), 100.

2. L. L. Zamenhof to Borovko, 189[6], in *Originala Verkaro*, ed. Joh. Dietterle (Leipzig: Ferdinand Hirt, 1929), 422.

3. Aleksander Korĵenkov, "Mark Fabianoviĉ Zamenhof, Instituisto en Ŝtataj Lernejoj," *Ondo de Esperanto* 216 (2012): 4. For a list of M. F. Zamenhof's publications, see N. Z. Maimon, *La Kaŝita Vivo de Zamenhof* (Tokyo: Japana Esperanto-Instituto, 1978), 146.

4. Korĵenkov, "Mark Fabianoviĉ Zamenhof," 5.

5. Ibid., 5.

6. Ivan T. Berend, *History Derailed: Central and Eastern Europe in the Long Nineteenth Century* (Berkeley: University of California Press, 2003), 188.

7. Maimon, *La Kaŝita Vivo*, 144.

8. Ibid., 33.

9. Aleksander Korĵenkov, "Vera Trezoro de Oficista Saĝo: La Varsovia Cenzuristo M. F. Zamenhof," *La Ondo de Esperanto* 186 (2010): 13-14.

10. Quoted in Marjorie Boulton, *Zamenhof: Creator of Esperanto,* trans. Boulton (London: Routledge and Kegan Paul, 1960), 6.

11. Berend, *History Derailed*, 57.

12. Johann Gottfried Herder, *Reflections,* quoted in Jeffrey Veidlinger, *Jewish Public Culture in the Late Russian Empire* (Bloomington: Indiana University Press, 2009), 114.

13. Steiner, *After Babel*, 81.

14. Aleksander Korĵenkov, *Homarano* (Kaunas: Sezono, 2009), 62.

15. L. L. Zamenhof to Borovko, 189[6], *Originala Verkaro*, 420.

16. "Esperanto and Jewish Ideals," *Jewish Chronicle,* 6 Sep. 1907, 17.

17. Korĵenkov, *Homarano,* 285, n33.

18. Ibid., 46.

19. Christer Kiselman, "La Evoluo de la Pensado de Zamenhof pri Religioj kaj la Rolo de Lingvoj," *Religiaj kaj filozofiaj ideoj de Zamenhof: Kultura kaj Socia Fono,* ed. Christer Kiselman (Rotterdam: Universala Esperanto-Asocio, 2010), 45, http://www2.math.uu.se/~kiselman/bjalistokoueak.pdf, accessed 7 Jan. 2014.

20. Maimon, *La Kaŝita Vivo*, 99.

21. "Esperanto and Jewish Ideals," 17.

22. Dovid Katz, *Words on Fire: The Unfinished Story of Yiddish* (New York: Basic Books, 2004), 200.
23. Ibid., 304.
24. L. L. Zamenhof to BILU members, 18 Nov. 1883, *Mi Estas Homo,* 27–28.
25. L. L. Zamenhof, *Doctor Esperanto's International Language,* Part I, http://www .genekeyes.com/Dr_Esperanto.html, accessed 9 Jan. 2015.
26. David Richardson, *Shamrocks on the Tanana: Richard Geoghegan's Alaska* (Snowqualmie, WA: Cheechako Books, 2009), 13.
27. Korĵenkov, *Homarano,* 83.
28. Humphrey Tonkin, "*Hamlet* in Esperanto," unpublished paper, 3, http://uhaweb .hartford.edu/tonkin/pdfs/HamletInEsperanto.pdf, accessed 12 Feb. 2014.
29. Peter G. Forster, *The Esperanto Movement* (The Hague: Mouton, 1982), 60.
30. Korĵenkov, *Homarano,* 104.
31. L. L. Zamenhof to [Alfred] Michaux, 21 Feb. 1905, *Mi Estas Homo,* 105.
32. Korĵenkov, *Homarano,* 91.
33. L. L. Zamenhof to [Alfred] Michaux, 21 Feb. 1905, *Mi Estas Homo,* 105.
34. Korĵenkov, *Homarano,* 111.
35. Wim Jansen, "Summary in English," *Woordvolgorde in het Esperanto: Normen, Taalgebruik en Universalia* (Utrecht: Lot, 2007), 275, http://www.lotpublications.nl /publish/articles/002492/bookpart.pdf, accessed 12 Feb. 2014.
36. Korĵenkov, *Homarano,* 99.
37. Ibid.
38. Ibid., 102.
39. Boulton, *Zamenhof,* 57.
40. L. L. Zamenhof, "Introduction," *Doctor Esperanto's International Language,* http://www .genekeyes.com/Dr_Esperanto.html, accessed 9 Jan. 2015.
41. Tonkin, "*Hamlet* in Esperanto," 7.
42. Ibid., 9.
43. Garvía, *Esperanto and Its Rivals,* 76.
44. Ibid., 79.
45. L. L. Zamenhof to William Heller, 30 Jun. 1914, *Mi Estas Homo,* 217–18.
46. Paul Mendes-Flohr and Jehuda Reinharz, *The Jew in the Modern World,* 2nd ed. (New York: Oxford University Press, 1995), 542.
47. L. L. Zamenhof, "Hilelismo," *Mi Estas Homo,* 43.
48. Ibid., 62.
49. Ibid., 44.
50. Ibid., 46, n1.
51. Ibid., 61.
52. Ibid., 69.
53. Andrew Wernick, *August Comte and the Religion of Humanity* (Cambridge, UK: Cambridge University Press, 2001), 21.
54. L. L. Zamenhof, "Hilelismo," *Mi Estas Homo,* 73.
55. Ibid., 78–79.
56. Ibid., 81, 82.
57. L. L. Zamenhof to [Abram] Kofman, 15 (28) May 1901, *Mi Estas Homo,* 97.
58. "Esperanto and Jewish Ideals," 17.
59. Korĵenkov, *Homarano,* 60.
60. Forster, *The Esperanto Movement,* 75.
61. Ibid., 76.
62. Korĵenkov, *Homarano,* 126.

63. Ibid., 164.

64. L. L. Zamenhof to [Émile] Javal, 8 Jan. 1906, *Mi Estas Homo*, 127.

65. L. L. Zamenhof to [Alfred] Michaux, 21 Feb. 1905, *Mi Estas Homo*, 99.

66. Korĵenkov, *Homarano*, 168.

67. Korĵenkov, ed., *Mi Estas Homo*, 263; thanks to Roberto Garvía for pointing this out.

68. Quoted in Forster, *The Esperanto Movement*, 82.

69. Quoted in Korĵenkov, *Homarano*, 236.

70. "Esperanto and Jewish Ideals," 17.

71. L. L. Zamenhof to [Alfred] Michaux, 21 Feb. 1905, *Mi Estas Homo*, 100.

72. Quoted in Boulton, *Zamenhof*, trans. Boulton, 79.

73. Quoted in Korĵenkov, *Homarano*, 179.

74. Ibid., 180.

75. Korĵenkov, *Homarano*, 301, n 19.

76. Garvía, *Esperanto and Its Rivals*, 25.

77. Forster, *The Esperanto Movement*, 75.

78. Émile Javal to L. L. Zamenhof, 15 Oct., 1905, Ludovikito [Ito Kanzi]. *Postrikolto de Ludovikaĵoj*, 197, quoted in Árpád Rátkai, "Lazar Markoviĉ Zamenhof kaj la Zamenhof-Falsaĵaro," *Esperantologio* 2009, 5–6, http://www.vortaro.hu/lmz.pdf, accessed 2 Dec. 2012.

79. Boulton, *Zamenhof*, 78.

80. Korĵenkov, *Homarano*, 184.

81. Quoted in Forster, *The Esperanto Movement*, trans. Forster, 94.

82. Kiselman, "La Evoluo," 53.

83. Sarah Abrevyava Stein, *Making Jews Modern* (Bloomington: Indiana University Press, 2006), 213.

84. Korĵenkov, *Mi Estas Homo*, 169.

85. Quoted in Kiselman, "La Evoluo," 53.

86. Quoted in Forster, *The Esperanto Movement*, trans. Forster, 101.

87. Garvía, *Esperanto and Its Rivals*, 103–28.

88. Korĵenkov, *Homarano*, 214.

89. Émile Javal to L. L. Zamenhof, Dec. 1905, quoted in Forster, *The Esperanto Movement*, trans. Forster, 118.

90. Forster, *The Esperanto Movement*, 114–15.

91. Ibid., 116–17.

92. Ibid., 122.

93. L. L. Zamenhof to Hippolyte Sebert, 27 Oct. 1907, quoted in Boulton, *Zamenhof*, trans. Boulton, 126.

94. Quoted in Forster, *The Esperanto Movement*, trans. Forster, 123.

95. L. L. Zamenhof, "Cirkulera Letero al Ĉiuj Esperantistoj," *Originala Verkaro*, 448.

96. Forster, *The Esperanto Movement*, 130.

97. Ibid., 131.

98. Quoted in Forster, *The Esperanto Movement*, 133.

99. Michael D. Gordin, *Scientific Babel: How Science Was Done Before and After Global English* (Chicago: University of Chicago Press, 2015), 149.

100. Quoted in Boulton, *Zamenhof*, trans. Boulton, 138.

101. Boulton, *Zamenhof*, 190.

102. Forster, *The Esperanto Movement*, 154.

103. Ibid., 156.

104. Quoted in ibid.

105. L. L. Zamenhof to Local Congress Committee, 14 Feb.1912, *Mi Estas Homo*, 199.
106. L. L. Zamenhof, "La Respondo de D-ro Zamenhof," *Die Wahrheit* 29 Oct. 1912, trans. Doron Modan (Yiddish to Esperanto), *Mi Estas Homo*, 246–47.
107. Quoted in Maimon, *La Kaŝita Vivo*, 109–10.
108. Quoted in Korĵenkov, *Homarano*, 256.
109. Ibid.
110. L. L. Zamenhof, "Protesto," 16 Jul. 1914, *Mi Estas Homo*, 221.
111. Quoted in Korĵenkov, *Homarano*, 258.
112. Boulton, *Zamenhof*, 187.
113. Ibid., 188–89.
114. Ibid., 187.
115. Quoted in Korĵenkov, *Homarano*, 261.
116. Hector Hodler, quoted in L. L. Zamenhof, "Super," quoted in Forster, *The Esperanto Movement*, trans. Forster, 160–61.
117. Quoted in Korĵenkov, *Homarano*, 266–67.
118. Ibid., 266.
119. Ibid., 263.
120. Ibid., 223.
121. Ibid., 268.

Part III: The Heretic, the Priestess, and the Invisible Empire

1. "First Esperanto School in the United States," *Amerika Esperantisto* 39 no. 1 (1927): 3.
2. E. Borsboom, *Vivo de Lanti* (Paris: SAT, 1976), 23.
3. E. Lanti [Eugène Adam], *For la Neŭtralismon* (Beauville: SAT, 1991), 10.
4. Ibid., 11.
5. Borsboom, *Vivo*, 26.
6. Quoted in Borsboom, *Vivo*, 25.
7. Lanty [Lanti], "Tri Semajnoj," *Sennacieca Revuo* 4 no. 4 (1923), 4.
8. Quoted in Borsboom, *Vivo*, 25.
9. Lanty [Lanti], "Tri Semajnoj," *Sennacieca Revuo* 4 no. 2 (1922), 2.
10. Ibid., 10.
11. Quoted in Dante Germino, *Gramsci: Architect of a New Politics* (Baton Rouge: Louisiana State University Press, 1990), 28.
12. Forster, *The Esperanto Movement*, 202.
13. Quoted in Ulrich Lins, *La Danĝera Lingvo* (Moscow: Progreso, 1990), 212.
14. Ibid., 218.
15. Ibid., 219, 225.
16. Ibid., 235.
17. Ibid., 246.
18. Borsboom, *Vivo*, 111, 112.
19. Gordon Bowker, *George Orwell* (Boston: Little, Brown, 2003), 7.
20. Borsboom, *Vivo*, 71.
21. Bowker, *George Orwell*, 106.
22. D. J. Taylor, *Orwell: The Life* (London: Chatto & Windus, 2003), 96.
23. Bowker, *George Orwell*, 106.
24. Ibid., 191.
25. E. Lanti to S-ro R. K., Aug. 1933, *Leteroj de E. Lanti* (Laroque: SAT, 1987), 74.
26. E. Lanti, "Absolutismo," *El Verkoj de E. Lanti* [vol. 1] (Paris: SAT, 1991), 58.
27. E. Lanti, "Herezaĵo," *El Verkoj de Lanti* [vol. 1], 85–86.

28. George Orwell, "Politics and the English Language" *Horizon* 13 no. 76 (1946): 258, http://www.unz.org/Pub/Horizon-1946apr?View=PDF.
29. Borsboom, *Vivo,* 142.
30. Lanti, "Absolutismo," 61.
31. Ulrich Lins, *Utila Estas Aligo* (Rotterdam: Universala Esperanto-Asocio, 2008), 68.
32. Carolyn N. Biltoft, "Speaking the Peace: Language, World Politics and the League of Nations, 1918–1935" (Ph.D. diss., Princeton University, 2010), 91, 91, 106.
33. *New York Times,* Oct. 2, 1921, in Ulrich Becker, ed. *Esperanto in the New York Times 1887–1922* (New York: Mondial, 2010), 229.
34. Biltoft, "Speaking the Peace," 97.
35. Forster, *The Esperanto Movement,* 175.
36. Biltoft, "Speaking the Peace," 106–7.
37. Roxanne Panchasi, *Future Tense: The Culture of Anticipation in France Between the Wars* (Ithaca, NY: Cornell University Press, 2009), 154.
38. Biltoft, "Speaking the Peace," 104.
39. Forster, *The Esperanto Movement,* 177.
40. Edmond Privat, *Aventuroj de Pioniro* (La Laguna: J. Régulo, 1963), 31, 129.
41. Biltoft, "Speaking the Peace," 99.
42. Forster, *The Esperanto Movement,* 183.
43. George Cox, *A Grammar and Commentary of the International Language Esperanto* (London: British Esperanto Association 1906), vii–viii.
44. "Herbert F. Höveler," http://eo.wikipedia.org/wiki/Herbert_F._Höveler, accessed 10 Apr. 2010.
45. Ibid.
46. Ibid.
47. F. W. Hamann, "The Progress of Esperanto Since the World War," *Modern Language Journal* 12 no. 7 (1928): 550.
48. Ibid., 552.
49. David K. Jordan, *Being Colloquial in Esperanto* (Lanham, MD: University Press of America, 1992), 105–8.
50. Michael T. Kaufman, *Soros: The Life and Times of a Messianic Billionaire* (New York: Knopf, 2002), Kindle edition.
51. Geoffrey Sutton, *Concise Encyclopedia of the Original Literature of Esperanto, 1887–2007* (New York: Mondial, 2008), 27, 74.
52. Forster, *The Esperanto Movement,* 180.
53. Quoted in Michael North, *Reading 1922: A Return to the Scene of the Modern* (Oxford, UK: Oxford University Press, 1999), 16.
54. North, *Reading 1922,* 157.
55. Otto Neurath, "From Hieroglyphics to Isotype," trans. Marie Neurath, in *Future Books* 3 (1946): 96.
56. Phil Patton, "Neurath, Bliss and the Language of the Pictogram," AIGA, http://www.aiga.org/neurath-bliss-and-the-language-of-the-pictogram/p3website, accessed 15 Apr. 2010.
57. "Educator Describes 'Picture Esperanto,'" *New York Times,* 10 Jan. 1933, 25.
58. Jill Lepore, *A Is for American: Letters and Other Characters in the Newly United States* (New York: Vintage, 2002), 190, 28.
59. *Chicago Commerce,* 6 Oct. 1916, 29.
60. William Harmon, *A History of the Esperanto League for North America, Inc.* (El Cerrito, CA: ELNA, 2002), 6.
61. Richardson, *Shamrocks on the Tanana,* 129, 195.

62. "Esperantists Raise Flag," *New York Times*, 21 Jul. 1908, in Becker, *Esperanto*, 81.

63. G. W. Wishard, "From Readers: A Consideration of the Merits of the Language Called Esperanto," *New York Times*, 11 Jun. 1904, in Becker, *Esperanto*, 31.

64. William A. Lewis, "Views of Readers," *New York Times*, 8 Aug. 1908, in Becker, *Esperanto*, 91.

65. "Mr. Alden's Views," *New York Times*, 15 Aug. 1902, in Becker, *Esperanto*, 24.

66. "Mr. Alden's Views," *New York Times*, 28 May 1904, in Becker, *Esperanto*, 29.

67. "Mr. Alden's Views," *New York Times*, 5 Nov. 1904, in Becker, *Esperanto*, 37.

68. "Views of Readers," *New York Times*, 4 Jul. 1908, in Becker, *Esperanto*, 72, 72.

69. "Socialists and Esperantists," *New York Times*, 27 Aug. 1907, in Becker, *Esperanto*, 57.

70. L. L. Zamenhof, "What Is Esperanto?" *North American Review* 184 no. 606 (1907): 20, 21.

71. Ibid., 20–21.

72. James Duff Law, *Here and There in Two Hemispheres* (Lancaster, PA: Home, 1906), 111.

73. L. L. Zamenhof, "What Is Esperanto," 15–16.

74. Ibid., 21.

75. "There Are Flaws in Esperanto," *New York Times*, 29 Dec. 1907, in Becker, *Esperanto*, 62.

76. James G. Ravin, "Albert Einstein and His Mentor Max Talmey," *Documenta Ophthalmologica* 94 (1997): 1–17.

77. "Gloro," *Time*, 5 Apr. 1937, http://ial.wikia.com/wiki/Arulo, accessed 13 Feb. 2014.

78. "New York 'Esperanto' Society," *Amerika Esperantisto* 4 no. 6 (1909): 142.

79. Ibid., 144.

80. "Electronic Wonders Show at Garden," *New York Times*, 4 Oct. 1908, in Becker, *Esperanto*, 114.

81. "Esperanto for Clayworkers," *Brick*, 1 Mar. 1908, in Ralph Dumain, "The Autodidact Project," http://www.autodidactproject.org/esperanto2010/baker-clay.html, accessed 9 Nov. 2009.

82. "Esperanto Tried at Normal College," *New York Times*, 3 Dec. 1907, in Becker, *Esperanto*, 61.

83. "Former Service Man Shot Dead by Nurse," *New York Times*, 4 Jun. 1922, in Becker, *Esperanto*, 23.

84. Boulton, *Zamenhof*, 153.

85. Ibid., 154.

86. "Esperantists in Session Today," *Baltimore American*, 15 Aug. 1910, 7.

87. "Address of Dr. Zamenhof," *Amerika Esperantisto* 8 no. 3 (1910): 46.

88. *New York Times*, 13 Aug. 1910, in Becker, *Esperanto*, 138.

89. *New York Times*, 13 Aug. 1910, in Becker, *Esperanto*, 139.

90. "Umpires Speak Esperanto," *New York Times*, 19 Aug. 1910, in Becker, *Esperanto*, 144.

91. "Esperantists at Church," *New York Times*, 15 Aug. 1910, in Becker, *Esperanto*, 141.

92. "Cornell and Esperanto," *Cornell Alumni News*, 26 Jun. 1912, 451.

93. "He Condemns Esperanto," *New York Times*, 31 Dec. 1908, in Becker, *Esperanto*, 125.

94. "The Case of Esperanto: George Macloskie," *North American Review* 183 no. 604 (1906): 1150.

95. "The Esperantist's Effort," *The New York Times*, 17 Mar. 1912, in Becker, *Esperanto*, 172.

96. [Statement of] Richard Bartholdt, "Esperanto: Hearings Before the Committee on Education . . . on House Resolution 415" (Washington, D.C.: Government Printing Office, 1914), http://www.gutenberg.org/files/16432/16432-h/16432-h.htm, accessed 9 Feb. 2014.

97. [Statement of] A. Christen, "Esperanto: Hearings Before the Committee on Education . . . on House Resolution 415" (Washington, D.C.: Government Printing Office, 1914), http://www.gutenberg.org/files/16432/16432-h/16432-h.htm, accessed 9 Feb. 2014.

98. 1910 Census, US Census Bureau, http://www.censusrecords.com/content/1910_census.

99. [Statement of] A. Christen, "Esperanto," np.

100. "District of Columbia—Race and Hisptanic Origin: 1800 to 1990," U.S. Census Bureau, http://www.census.gov/population/www/documentation/twps0056/tab23.pdf.

101. Ralph Dumain, "William Pickens (1881–1954)," *The Autodidact Project,* http://www.autodidactproject.org/esperanto2010/pickens-whoswho.html, accessed 5 Jun. 2011.

102. William Pickens, *The Heir of Slaves: An Autobiography* (Boston: Pilgrim Press, 1911), 122, http://www.autodidactproject.org/esperanto2010/pickens-whoswho.html, accessed 5 Jun. 2011.

103. Quoted in "The Progress of Esperanto," *North American Revew* 184 no. 607 (1907): 224.

104. William Pickens, "Esperanto, The New International Lanaguage," *The Voice of the Negro* 8 no. 4 (1906): 259, 260, 262.

105. R. B. Stuart, "Four Generations: The Historical Footprints of the Pickens Family," Hamptons Online, http://www.hamptons.com/Lifestyle//People-in-Focus/1808/Four-Generations-The-Historical-Footprints-of.html?articleID=1808#.UfGFAKx2nBg, accessed 5 Jun. 2011.

106. Pickens, "Esperanto, The New International Language," 260.

107. Sho Konishi, *Anarchist Modernity: Cooperatism and Japanese-Russian Intellectual Relations in Modern Japan* (Cambridge, MA: Harvard University Asia Center, 2013), 12.

108. Steven J. Erickson and Alan Hockley, *The Treaty of Portsmouth and Its Legacies* (Hanover, NH: University Press of New England, 2008), 100.

109. Ibid., 95.

110. Ibid., 96, 97.

111. Ulrich Lins, "Esperanto as Language and Idea in China and Japan," *Interlinguistics* 32 no. 1 (2008): 49, DOI 10.1075/lplp.32.1.05lin.

112. Hou Zhiping, ed., *Konciza Historio de la Ĉina Esperanto-Movado* (Beijing: Nova Stelo, 2004), 11.

113. Ibid., 12.

114. Ibid. 4–5; trans. assistance from H. Tonkin.

115. Lins, *La Danĝera Lingvo,* 171–72.

116. Quoted in Sutton, *Concise Encyclopedia,* 107.

117. Ibid., 108.

118. Konishi, *Anarchist Modernity,* 287.

119. Sutton, *Concise Encylopedia,* 108.

120. Gotelind Müller and Gregor Benton, "Esperanto," in Gregor Benton, *Chinese Migrants and Internationlalism: Forgotten Histories, 1917–1945* (London: Routledge, 2007), 292.

121. Ibid., 109.

122. Sutton, *Concise Encyclopedia,* 111.

123. Hitosi Gotoo, "Esperanto Inter la Japana kaj Korea Popoloj: Ooyama Tokio kaj lia Tempo," *La Revuo Orienta,* Dec. 2011, www.sal.tohoku.ac.jp/~gothit/historio/ooyama.html, accessed 20 Mar. 2015.

124. Ibid.

125. Zhiping, *Konciza Historio,* 21.

126. Ibid., 35.
127. Müller, "Esperanto," 113.
128. Ibid., 12.
129. Ibid., 11.
130. Zhiping, *Konciza Historio*, 60.
131. Gotelind Müller, "Hasegawa Teru alias Verda Majo (1912–1947): A Japanese Woman Esperantist in the Chinese Anti-Japanese War of Resistance" (Heidelberg: University of Heidelberg, 2013), 13.
132. Zhiping, *Konciza Historio*, 60.
133. Müller, "Hasegawa Teru," 13.
134. David Poulson, "A Happy Ending," in *A Whisper From a Hurricane: The Story of Verda Majo*, http://www.suite101.com/articles.cfm.esperanto, accessed 1 Oct. 2011.
135. Zhiping, *Konciza Historio*, 27.
136. Lins, *La Dangera Lingvo*, 106.
137. Forster, *The Esperanto Movement*, 220.
138. Lins, *La Dangera Lingvo*, 99, 97–98.
139. Adolf Hitler, *Mein Kampf* (excerpt), in Anson Rabinbach and Sander Gilman, *The Third Reich Sourcebook* (Berkeley: University of California Press, 2013), 190.
140. Lins, *La Dangera Lingvo*, 93, 94.
141. Richard Evans, *The Third Reich at War* (London: Penguin, 2008), 171.
142. Lins, *La Dangera Lingvo*, 107.
143. Ibid., 110, 111.
144. Ibid., 124–25.
145. Ibid., 127.
146. *Esperanto Revuo*, no. 10 (Oct. 1934): 161.
147. "Nia Misio," *Esperanto Revuo*, no. 12 (Dec. 1934): 3, 2.
148. Zofia Banet-Fornalowa, *La Familio Zamenhof* (La Chaux-de-Fonds: Kooperativo de Literatura Foiro, 2000), 73.
149. Ibid., 75.
150. Wendy Heller, *Lidia: Life of Lidia Zamenhof, Daughter of Esperanto* (Oxford, UK: George Ronald, 1985) 59.
151. Ibid., 39.
152. Ibid., 71.
153. Ibid., 38.
154. Ibid., 39.
155. Ibid., 77.
156. Ibid., 86.
157. Quoted in Susannah Heschel, "German-Jewish Scholarship on Islam as a Tool for De-Orientalizing Judaism," *New German Critique*, no.117 (2012): 101.
158. Banet-Fornalowa, *La Familio Zamenhof*, 81.
159. Ibid.
160. Quoted in Heller, *Lidia*, 143, 144.
161. Ibid., 145.
162. Ibid., 163, 164–65.
163. Ibid., 168, 178.
164. Ibid., 181.
165. Ibid., 158.
166. Ibid., 181, 158, 181.
167. Ibid., 183.

168. Ibid., 190.

169. Ibid., 206, 209.

170. Lins, *La Danĝera Lingvo*, 299, 301, 284.

171. Ibid., 395.

172. Ibid., 384.

173. Borsboom, *Vivo*, 155.

174. Eileen Shaughnessy to Nora Myles, 3 or 10 Nov. 1936, in George Orwell, *Orwell: A Life in Letters*, ed. Peter Davison (London: Harvill Secker, 2010), 66.

175. Borsboom, *Vivo*, passim, for the account of Lanti's final years.

176. Heller, *Lidia*, 224, 226, 224.

177. Ibid., 227.

178. Roman Dobrzyński, *La Zamenhof-Strato* (Varpas: Kaunas, 2005), 25.

179. Lins, *La Danĝera Lingvo*, 124.

180. Ibid.

181. Dobrzyński, *La Zamenhof-Strato*, 50.

182. Josef Šemer, "La Lastaj Tagoj de Lidja Zamenhof," *Israela Esperantisto* 113 (1993): 2.

183. Shoghi Effendi, "Lydia Zamenhof," *Messages to America*, http://www.gutenberg.org/files/19277/19277-h/19277-h.html#toc216, accessed 21 Aug. 2013.

Part IV: Esperanto in a Global Babel

1. "La Malneutrala, 'Neutraleco,'" *La Suda Stelo* 6 no. 2 (1937): 9.

2. "Biografiaj Notoj," in Carlo Minnaja, ed., *Eseoj Memore al Ivo Lapenna* (Denmark: Internacia Scienca Instituto Ivo Lapenna, 2001), 15.

3. Ibid., 60.

4. Lins, *Utila Estas Aliĝo: Tra la Unua Jarcento de UEA* (Rotterdam: Universala Esperanto-Asocio, 2008), 80.

5. "La Malneutrala, 'Neutraleco,'" 9, 9–10.

6. Ibid., 82.

7. Forster, *The Esperanto Movement*, 233.

8. "Membronombroj de UEA," http://eo.wikipedia.org/wiki/Membronombroj_de_UEA, accessed 15 Feb. 2014.

9. Forster, *The Esperanto Movement*, 235.

10. Birthe Lapenna, "Ivo Lapenna kaj la Internacia Lingvo," in Minnaja, *Eseoj*, 26.

11. Carlo Minnaja, "Konscio," and Gunther Becker, "Ivo Lapenna kaj la Lingvoj," in Minnaja, *Eseoj*, 77, 203.

12. Donald J. Harlow, "History in Fine," *The Esperanto Book* (1995): 34, http://donh.best.vwh.net/Esperanto/EBook/chap07.html, accessed 8 Feb. 2014.

13. Humphrey Tonkin, *Lingvo kaj Popolo: Actualaj Problemoj de la Esperanto-Movado* (Rotterdam: Universala Esperanto-Asocio, 2006), 77.

14. Forster, *The Esperanto Movement*, 241.

15. Ibid., 79.

16. "Boxes of Esperanto Stuff from Connors," *Esperanto USA*, http://www.esperanto-usa.org/en/content/boxes-esperanto-stuff-connors, accessed 4 Nov. 2012.

17. *Amerika Esperantisto* 68 nos. 1–2 (1954): 6.

18. William R. Harmon, "ELNA and EANA: Founding and Unfounding," in *A History of the Esperanto League for North America*, trans. David Richardson, 41.

19. *Amerika Esperantisto* 64 nos. 3–4 (1950): 54.

20. *Amerika Esperantisto* 65 nos. 9–10 (1951): 77, 82.

21. "Polish Refugee Literally Talked Himself to Life," *Los Angeles Times*, 18 Oct. 1953, 23.

22. *Amerika Esperantisto* 67 nos. 9–10 (1953): 65.

23. *Amerika Esperantisto* 68 nos. 5–6 (1954): 53.

24. *Esperanto: The Aggressor Language*, FM 30-101-1 (Washington, D.C.: Department of the Army, 1962), 2.

25. *The Big Picture: Aggressor*, National Archives and Records Administration, ARC Identifier 2569631 / Local Identifier 111-TV-362, https://archive.org/details/gov.archives .arc.2569631, accessed 1 Dec. 2011.

26. *Esperanto: The Aggressor Language*, 216.

27. Harmon, *A History*, 54.

28. *Amerika Esperantisto* 67 nos. 7–8 (1953): 55.

29. Harmon, *A History*, 54.

30. Ibid., 42, 43.

31. Lins, *Utila Estas Aligo*, 89.

32. *Amerika Esperantisto* 70 nos. 5–6 (1956): 75, 80.

33. Lins, *Utilo Estas Aligo*, 92.

34. Tatiana Hart to Esther Schor, email, 3 Jul. 2011.

35. Lins, *Utila Estas Aligo*, 94.

36. Ibid., 96.

37. Forster, *The Esperanto Movement*, 245.

38. Ivo Lapenna, *Hamburgo en Retrospektivo: Dokumentoj kaj Materialoj pri la Kontraŭneŭtraleca Politika Konspiro en Universala Esperanto-Asocio*, 2nd ed. (Copenhagen: Horizonto, 1977), 35.

39. Quoted in Minnaja, "STELO, TEJO kaj Ivo Lapenna dum la generacia Ŝanĝo," in Minnaja, *Eseoj*, 99.

40. Lins, *Utila Estas Aligo*, 97, 97.

41. Ibid., 98.

42. Lapenna, *Hamburgo en Retrospektivo*, 93.

43. Ibid., 94.

44. Humphrey Tonkin interview, 27 Aug. 2007.

45. Lapenna, *Hamburgo en Retrospektivo*, 98.

46. Tony Judt, *Postwar: A History of Europe Since 1945* (New York: Penguin, 2005), 192.

47. Humphrey Tonkin interview, 17 Oct. 2010.

48. "Paca Kunekzistado kun la Ŝtato," "'Kio ne estas Malpermesita, Tio estas Permisita'— Sovetia Esperanto-Movado en Kvazaŭ Sekreta Misio," *Spegulo*, Autumn 2008, http:// e-novosti.info/forumo/viewtopic.php?t=5124, accessed 4 Mar. 2015. See also Mikaelo Bronŝtejn, *Legendoj pri SEJM* (Moscow: Rusia Esperanta Unio, 2006), passim.

49. Dina Newman interview, 28 May 2009.

50. "La 'Juda Demando,'" "'Kio ne estas Malpermesita.'" Ibid.

51. "Many Voices, One World: Towards a New More Just and Efficient World Information and Communication Order: Report by the International [MacBride] Commission for the Study of Communication Problems (London: Kogan Page, 1981), 273. http:// unesdoc.unesco.org/images/0004/000400/040066eb.pdf.

52. James Traub, *The Best Intentions: Kofi Annan and the UN in the Era of American World Power* (New York: Farrar Straus and Giroux, 2006), 21–22.

53. "Al Niaj Legantinoj," *Virina Bulteno* no. 1, [3] Jun. 1911, 1.

54. C.-L. De Ferrer, "Konsiloj al niaj Koleginoj," *Virina Bulteno* no. 2, Jan. 1912 [20 Dec. 1911], 3.

55. "Egaleco de Salajroj," *Virina Bulteno* no. 1, [3] Jun. 1911, 2.

56. "La Laboro de la Virinoj," *Virina Bulteno* no. 3, [15] Apr. 1912, 1.

57. E. Herzog, "Indianaj Stataj Oficinistoj," *Virina Bulteno* no. 3, [15] Apr. 1912, 1.

58. Marie Henkel, "Elekto de Profesio por Niaj Filinoj," *Virina Bulteno* no.2, Jan. 1912 [20 Dec. 1911], 1.

59. Roksano [Jeanne Flourens], "Moda Kroniko," *Virina Bulteno* no. 1, [3] Jun. 1911, 3.

60. Reine Rippe, "Feminismo," *Sennacieca Revuo* 46 no. 5 (1924): 15.

61. Garvía, *Esperanto and Its Rivals,* pp. 96–97.

62. *Esperanto,* 25 (1929): 176.

63. Lins, *La Danĝera Lingvo,* 107.

64. *Esperanto,* 29 (1933): 151.

65. *Sekso kaj Egaleco* no. 4 Oct (1980)15–16.

66. Anna [Brennan] Löwenstein, "*Sekso Kaj Egaleco*: Feminisme Remerori," *Femina* no. 13 (2008): 14.

67. Ibid., 15.

68. *Sekso kaj Egaleco* no. 1 (1980): 10.

69. Anna Löwenstein, "Diskriminacio Kontraŭ Virinoj," *Kongresa Libro* 65a Universala Kongreso (Stockholm: Loka Kongresa Komitato, 1980), 43.

70. *Sekso kaj Egaleco* no. 5 (1981): 23.

71. *Sekso kaj Egaleco* no. 16 (1988): 8–9.

72. *Sekso kaj Egaleco* no. 1 (1980): 11.

73. *Sekso kaj Egaleco* no. 3 (1980): 5.

74. Ibid., 8.

75. *Sekso kaj Egaleco* no. 4 (1980): 7, 8, 9.

76. Ibid., 11.

77. *Sekso kaj Egaleco* no. 11 (1985): 18, 18–19.

78. Ibid., 6.

79. *Sekso kaj Egaleco* no. 16 (1988): 1.

80. Eliza Kehlet interview, 20 Dec. 2013.

81. *Sekso kaj Egaleco* no.15 (1987): 1, 3.

82. *Sekso kaj Egaleco* no. 3 (1980), 6.

83. "Inaŭgura Parolado de D-ro John C. Wells," *Esperanto* 73 (1980): 146.

84. "Geja Jubileo Forgesita en Havano," *Libera Folio,* 26 Aug. 2010, http://www.liberafolio .org/2010/geja-jubileo-forgesita-en-havano, accessed 23 Dec. 2013.

85. Ibid.

86. http://esperanto.org/Ondo/H-raumo.htm, accessed 12 Apr. 2015.

87. L. L. Zamenhof to [Abram] Kofman, 28 May 1901, *Mi Estas Homo,* 97.

88. Humphrey Tonkin, "Ideoj Kiuj Restas Freŝaj," *Kongresa Libro* 72a Universala Kongreso de Esperanto (Rotterdam, Universala Esperanto-Asocio, 1987), 18.

89. http://www.esperantio.net/index.php?id=15#chIIart11, accessed 12 Apr. 2015.

90. Maria Rafaela Uruenja, "Esperanta Civito kaj Internacia Juro," http://www.eventoj .hu/steb/juro/civito-kaj-juro.htm, accessed 25 May 2014.

91. Ibid.

92. Detlev Blanke, "Pri Raŭmismo," 15 Jun. 2000, http://www.helsinki.fi/~jslindst/bja -diskuto.html, accessed 22 Feb. 2011.

93. http://www.esperantarespubliko.blogspot.com/, accessed 1 Feb. 2014.

94. Robert Phillipson, *Linguistic Imperialism* (Oxford, UK: Oxford University Press, 2003), 11.

95. 2014 Q4 world average: 42.4 percent without access to the internet, "World Internet Penetration Rates," http://www.internetworldstats.com/stats.htm, accessed 29 June. 2015.

96. https://eo.wikipedia.org/wiki/Vikipedio, accessed 5 Jul. 2015.

97. http://www.ikso.net/en/pri_ecxei/index.php, accessed 12 Dec. 2013.

98. Kalle Kniivilä, "Baldaŭ Kvarona Jarcento," http://www.glasnost.se/2007/baldau -kvarona-jarcento/, accessed 2 Feb. 2014.

99. Kalle Kniivilä to Esther Schor, email, 24 Jan. 2014.

100. Ibid.

101. *Libera Folio*, 24 Apr. 2008, http://www.liberafolio.org/2008/epchtibeto/, accessed 30 Oct. 2013.

102. Renato Corsetti, "Ŝanĝiĝo de la Vortaro en Kreolaj Lingvoj," in Detlev Blanke and Ulrich Lins, eds., *La Arto Labori Kune* (Rotterdam: Universala Esperanto-Asocio, 2010), 381.

103. Ibid., 373.

Coda

1. Quoted in Korĵenko, *Homarano*, 128.

2. Boulton, *Zamenhof*, trans. Boulton, 79.

3. Michael Walzer, *Politics and Passion: Toward a More Egalitarian Liberalism* (New Haven, CT: Yale University Press, 2004), 3.

4. Ibid., 7, 10, 140.

5. Quoted by Humphrey Tonkin and Mark Fettes, "Esperantic Studies and Language Management in a Globalized World" presentation, "Multidisciplinary Approaches in Language Policy and Planning," University of Calgary, 5 Sep. 2013.

6. Jorge Camacho, "La Esperanta Malpopolo," in Blanke, *La Arto Labori Kune*, 522, 524, 526.

7. Charles Taylor, "Cross-Purposes: The Liberal-Communitarian Debate," in Derek Matravers and Jon Pike, *Debates in Contemporary Political Philosophy: An Anthology* (New York: Routledge, 2003), 199–200.

Selected Bibliography

========

General Sources

Auld, William, ed. *Esperanta Antologio: Poemoj 1887–1981*. Rotterdam: Universala Esperanto-Asocio, 1984. [Esperanto]

Banet-Fornalowa, Zofia. *La Familio Zamenhof*. La Chaux-de-Fonds, Switzerland: Kooperativo de Literatura Foiro, 2001. [Esperanto]

Boulton, Marjorie. *Zamenhof: Creator of Esperanto*. London: Routledge and Kegan Paul, 1960.

Eichholz, Rüdiger and Vilma Sindona Eichholz. *Esperanto in the Modern World: Studies and Articles on Language Problems, the Right to Communicate, and the International Language (1959–1982)*. 2nd ed. Bailieboro, Ont.: Esperanto Press, 1982.

Forster, Peter G. *The Esperanto Movement*. The Hague: Mouton, 1982.

Harlow, Donald. "How to Build a Language." http://donh.best.vwh.net/Esperanto/EBook/chap03.html#volapuk.

Janton, Pierre. *Esperanto: Language, Literature and Community*. Ed. Humphrey Tonkin. Albany: State University of New York Press, 1993.

Korĵenkov, Aleksander. *Homarano*. Kaunas, Lithuania: Sezono, 2009. [Esperanto]

Lapenna, Ivo. *Esperanto en Perspektivo: Faktoj kaj Analizoj pri la Internacia Lingvo*. Rotterdam: Universala Esperanto-Asocio, 1974. [Esperanto]

Mazower, Mark. *Governing the World: The History of an Idea, 1815 to the Present*. New York: Penguin, 2012.

Privat, Edmond. *Vivo de Zamenhof*. Ed. Ulrich Lins. Rotterdam: Universala Esperanto Asocio, 2007. [Esperanto]

Richardson, David. *Esperanto: Learning and Using the International Language*. Eastsound, Wash.: Esperanto League for North America, 1988.

Tonkin, Humphrey. *Esperanto, Interlinguistics, and Planned Language*. Lanham, Md.: University Press of America, 1997.

Zamenhof, Ludovic Lazarus. *Doctor Esperanto's International Language*. Trans. R. H. Geoghegan; ed. Gene Keys. (n.p.: 1889). http://www.genekeyes.com/Dr_Esperanto.html.

Zamenhof, Ludovik Lazarus. *Leteroj de L. L. Zamenhof*. Ed. Gaston Waringhien. 2 vols. Paris: SAT, 1948. [Esperanto]

Zamenhof, L.-L. *Mi Estas Homo*. Ed. Aleksander Korĵenkov. Kaliningrad, Russia: Sezono, 2006. [Esperanto]

Zamenhof, L. L. *Originala Verkaro*. Ed. Johannes Dietterle. Leipzig: Ferdinand Hirt, 1929. [Esperanto]

Part I: The Dream of a Universal Language

Darnton, Robert. "What Was Revolutionary about the French Revolution?" *New York Review of Books*. January 19, 1989.

Eco, Umberto. *The Search for the Perfect Language*. Trans. James Fentress. Oxford, UK: Blackwell, 1997.

Large, Andrew. *The Artificial Language Movement*. Oxford, UK: Blackwell, 1985.

Lewis, Rhodri. *Language, Mind and Nature: Artificial Languages in England from Bacon to Locke*. Cambridge, UK: Cambridge University Press, 2007.

Locke, John. *An Essay Concerning Human Understanding*. New York: Collins, 1964.

Okrent, Arika. *In the Land of Invented Languages: Esperanto Rock Stars, Klingon Poets, Loglan Lovers, and the Mad Dreamers Who Tried to Build a Perfect Language*. New York: Spiegel and Grau, 2009.

Steiner, George. *After Babel: Aspects of Language and Translation*. Oxford, UK: Oxford University Press, 1977.

Stillman, Robert E. *The New Philosophy and Universal Languages in Seventeenth-Century England: Bacon, Hobbes, and Wilkins*. Lewisburg, Pa.: Bucknell University Press, 1995.

Tonkin, Humphrey. "Hamlet in Esperanto." Unpublished paper. http://uhaweb.hartford.edu/tonkin/pdfs/HamletInEsperanto.pdf.

Tonkin, Humphrey. "The Semantics of Invention: Translation into Esperanto." In *The Translator as Mediator of Cultures*. Ed. Humphrey Tonkin and Maria Esposito Frank, 169–90. Amsterdam: John Benjamins, 2010.

Waringhien, Gaston. *Lingvo kaj Vivo: Esperantologiaj Eseoj*. Rotterdam: Universala Esperanto-Asocio, 1989. [Esperanto]

Part II: Doktoro Esperanto and the Shadow People

Berend, Ivan T. *History Derailed: Central and Eastern Europe in the Long Nineteenth Century*. Berkeley: University of California Press, 2003.

Dobrzyński, Roman. *La Zamenhof-Strato*. Kaunas, Lithuania: Varpas, 2005. [Esperanto]

"Esperanto and Jewish Ideals." *Jewish Chronicle*, 6 Sept. 1907.

Fettes, Mark. "'*Esenco kaj estonteco'—jubilea rerigardo*." http://www.lingviko.net/db/14_Fettes.htm [Esperanto]

Fettes, Mark. "*Studoj pri interlingvistiko: Festlibro omaĝe al la 60a jariĝo de Detlev Blanke*. Sabine Fielder and Liu Hatiao, eds. Dobřichovice (Prague): Kava-Pech, 2001. [Esperanto and German]

Garvía, Roberto. "Religion and Aritficial Languages at the Turn of the Twentieth Century: Ostwald and Zamenhof." *Language Problems and Language Planning* 37, no. 1 (2013): 47–70.

Gitelman, Zvi. *A Century of Ambivalence: The Jews of Russia and the Soviet Union, 1881 to the Present*. 2nd ed. Bloomington: Indiana University Press, 2001.

Gordin, Michael D. *Scientific Babel*. Chicago: University of Chicago Press, 2015.

Jannsen, Wim. "Summary in English," *Woordvolgorde in het Esperanto: Normen, Taalgebruik en Universalia*. Utrecht: Lot, 2007. http://www.lotpublications.nl/publish/articles/002492/bookpart.pdf.

Katz, Dovid. *Words on Fire: The Unfinished Story of Yiddish*. New York: Basic Books, 2004.

Kiselman, Christer, ed. *Religiaj kaj Filozofiaj Ideoj de Zamenhof: Kultura kaj Socia Fono*, 41–63. Rotterdam: Universala Esperanto-Asocio 2010. http://www2.math.uu.se /~kiselman/bjalistokoueak.pdf. [Esperanto]

Kolker, Boris. "Lasta Artikolo de L. L. Zamenhof pri Judaj Temoj." *Israela Esperantisto* 14 (2004). http://donh.best.vwh.net/Esperanto/zamen.html. [Esperanto]

Korjenkov, Aleksander. "Mark Fabianoviĉ Zamenhof, Instrituisto en Ŝtataj Lernejoj." *Ondo de Esperanto* 216 (2012): 3–6. [Esperanto]

Korjenkov, Aleksander. "Vera Trezoro de Oficista Saĝo: La Varsovia Cenzuristo M. F. Zamenhof." *La Ondo de Esperanto* 186 (2010): 10–15. [Esperanto]

Maimon, N. Z. *La Kaŝita Vivo de Zamenhof.* Tokyo: Japana Esperanto-Instituto, 1978. [Esperanto]

Margalit, Avishai. "Fraternity," *Vrij Nederland,* 21 Dec. 2005. http://www.vn.nl/Standaard -Media-Pagina/Fraternity.htm.

Mendes-Flohr, Paul and Jehuda Reinharz. *The Jew in the Modern World.* 2nd ed. New York: Oxford University Press, 1995.

Kück, Andreas. "Pri la Libro 'Oficialaj Lingvoelementoj de Esperanto' (OLEO)." http:// www.akueck.de/oleo.htm. [Esperanto]

"Oficialaj Informoj 12, 4 May 2009, Listo de Rekomendataj Landnomoj," http://akademio -de-esperanto.org/decidoj/landnomoj/listo_de_rekomendataj_landnomoj/. [Esperanto]

Richardson, David. *Shamrocks on the Tanana: Richard Geoghegan's Alaska.* Snowqualmie, Wash.: Cheechako Books, 2009.

Romaniuk, Zbigniew, and Tomasz Wiśniewski. *Ĉio Komeniĉiĝis ĉe la Verda: Pri Ludoviko Zamenhof, lia Familio kaj la Komenco de Esperanto.* Trans. from Polish, Przemyslaw Wierzbowski. Łódź, Poland: Ksiezy Młyn, 2009. [Esperanto]

Stein, Sarah Abrevyava. *Making Jews Modern.* Bloomington: Indiana University Press, 2006.

Veidlinger, Jeffrey. *Jewish Public Culture in the Late Russian Empire.* Bloomington: Indiana University Press, 2009.

Wernick, Andrew. *August Comte and the Religion of Humanity.* Cambridge, UK: Cambridge University Press, 2001.

Zamenhof, L. L. *Fundamenta Krestomatio de la Lingvo Esperanto.* 18th ed. Ed. G. Waringhien. Rotterdam: Universala Esperanto-Asocio, 1992. [Esperanto]

Zamenhof, L. L. "Respondo 47, Oficiala Gazeto III," *Lingvaj Respondoj.* Ed. Gaston Waringhien, 1911. http://eo.wikipedia.org/wiki/Landnomoj_en_Esperanto#Fontindikoj _kaj_piednotoj. [Esperanto]

Part III: The Heretic, The Priestess, and the Invisible Empire

Becker, Ulrich, ed. *Esperanto in The New York Times (1887–1922).* New York: Mondial, 2010.

Biltoft, Carolyn N. "Speaking the Peace: Language, World Politics and the League of Nations, 1918–1935." Ph.D. diss., Princeton University, 2010.

Borsboom, E. *Vivo de Lanti.* Paris: SAT, 1976. [Esperanto]

Bowker, Gordon. *George Orwell.* Boston: Little, Brown, 2004.

Drawter, Isaj. *Lidja Zamenhof: Vivo kaj Agado.* La Laguna: Stafeto, 1980. [Esperanto]

Dumain, Ralph. "William Pickens (1881–1954)." The Autodidact Project, http://www .autodidactproject.org/esperanto2010/pickens-whoswho.html.

Esselstrom, Erik. "The Life and Memory of Hasegawa Teru: Contextualizing Human Rights, Trans/Nationalism, and the Antiwar Movement in Modern Japan." *Radical History Review,* no. 101 (2008): 145–159. DOI 10.1215/01636545-2007-042.

Falk, Julia S. *Women, Language and Linguistics: Three American Stories from the First Half of the Twentieth Century.* London: Routledge, 1999.

Germino, Dante. *Gramsci: Architect of a New Politics.* Baton Rouge: Louisiana State University Press, 1990.

Goes, Heidi. *Afero de Espero: Konciza Historio de la Esperanto-Movado en Afriko.* Bydgoszcz, Poland: Universala Esperanto-Asocio, 2007. [Esperanto]

Gotoo, Hitosi. "Esperanto Inter la Japana kaj Korea Popoloj: Ooyama Tokio kaj lia Tempo." *La Revuo Orienta,* Dec. 2011, www.sal.tohoku.ac.jp/~gothit/historio/ooyama.html. [Esperanto]

Harmon, William. *A History of the Esperanto League for North America, Inc.* El Cerrito, Calif.: ELNA, 2002.

Heller, Wendy. *Lidia: The Life of Lidia Zamenhof, Daughter of Esperanto.* Oxford, UK: George Ronald, 1985.

Hutton, Christopher. *Linguistics and the Third Reich: Mother-Tongue Fascism, Race, and the Science of Language.* London: Routledge, 1999.

Ives, Peter. *Gramsci's Politics of Language: Engaging the Bakhtin Circle and the Frankfurt School.* Toronto: University of Toronto Press, 2004.

Konishi, Sho. *Anarchist Modernity: Cooperatism and Japanese-Russian Intellectual Relations in Modern Japan.* Cambridge, MA: Harvard University Asia Center, 2013.

Lanti, E. [Eugène Adam]. *Leteroj de E. Lanti.* Paris: SAT, 1940. [Esperanto]

Lanti, E. [Eugène Adam]. *For la Neutralismon.* Beauville, France: SAT, 1991. [Esperanto]

Lanty, E. [Eugène Adam]. "Tri Semajnoj en Rusio." *Sennacieca Revuo* 4 (1922–23). [Esperanto]

Lepore, Jill. *A Is for American: Letters and Other Characters in the Newly United States.* New York: Vintage, 2002.

Lins, Ulrich. "Esperanto as Language and Idea in China and Japan," *Interlinguistics* 32 no. 1 (2008): 47–60. DOI 10.1075/lplp.32.1.05lin.

Lins, Ulrich. *La Danĝera Lingvo.* Moscow: Progreso, 1990. [Esperanto]

Lins, Ulrich. *Utila Estas Aliĝo: Tra la Unua Jarcento de UEA.* Rotterdam: Universala Esperanto-Asocio, 2008. [Esperanto]

North, Michael. *Reading 1922: A Return to the Scene of the Modern.* Oxford, UK: Oxford University Press, 1999.

Mendelsohn, Ezra. *The Jews of East Central Europe Between the World Wars.* Bloomington: Indiana University Press, 1983.

Müller, Gotelind. *Hasegawa Teru alias Verda Majo (1912–1947): A Japanese Woman Esperantist in the Chinese Anti-Japanese War of Resistance.* Heidelberg: University of Heidelberg, 2013.

Müller, Gotelind and Gregor Benton. "Esperanto." In Gregor Benton, *Chinese Migrants and Internationalism: Forgotten Histories, 1917–1945,* 92–114. London: Routledge, 2007.

Neurath, Otto. "From Hieroglyphics to Isotype." Trans. from German, Marie Neurath. *Future Books* 3 (1946): 93–100.

Panchasi, Roxanne. *Future Tense: The Culture of Anticipation in France Between the Wars.* Ithaca, N. Y.: Cornell University Press, 2009.

Pickens, William. "Esperanto, The New International Language." *The Voice of the Negro* 8 no. 4 (1906): 258–62.

Privat, Edmond. *Aventuroj de Pioniro.* La Laguna: J. Régulo, 1963. [Esperanto]

Ŝemer, Josef. "La Lastaj Tagoj de Lidja Zamenhof." *Israela Esperantisto* no. 113 (1993): 1–3. [Esperanto]

Taylor, D. J. *Orwell: The Life.* London: Chatto & Windus, 2003.

Vossoughian, Nader. *Otto Neurath: The Language of the Global Polis*. Rotterdam: NAi, 2008.

Zamenhof, L. L. "What Is Esperanto?" *North American Review* 184, no. 606 (1907): 15–21. http://www.jstor.org/stable/25105745.

Zhiping, Hou, ed. *Konciza Historio de la Ĉina Esperanto-Movado*. Beijing: Nova Stelo, 2004. [Esperanto and Chinese]

Part IV: Esperanto in a Global Babel

Blanke, Detlev and Ulrich Lins, eds. *La Arto Labori Kune*. Rotterdam: Universala Esperanto-Asocio, 2010. [Esperanto]

Bloch, Ernst. *The Principle of Hope*. Trans. Neville Plaice, Stephen Plaice, and Paul Knight. Vol. 1. Cambridge, Mass.: MIT Press, 1986.

Bronŝtejn, Mikaelo. *Legendoj pri SEJM*. Moscow: Rusia Esperanta Unio, 2006. [Esperanto]

Camacho, Jorge. *La Liturgio de l'Foiro* (2007). http://www.gutenberg.org/files/23586/23586-h /23586-h.htm. [Esperanto]

Camacho, Jorge. *La Majstro kaj Martinelli* (2008). http://www.gutenberg.org/files/27593 /27593-h/27593-h.htm. [Esperanto]

Coupland, Nikolas, ed. *The Handbook of Language and Globalization*. Oxford, UK: Wiley-Blackwell, 2010.

Dobrzyński, Roman. *Bona Espero: Idealo kaj Realo*. Martin: Stano Marček, 2008. [Esperanto]

Esperanto: The Aggressor Language, FM 30-101-1. Washington, D.C.: Department of the Army, 1962.

Judt, Tony. *Postwar: A History of Europe Since 1945*. New York: Penguin, 2005.

Koselleck, Reinhart. *Futures Past: On the Semantics of Historical Time*. New York: Columbia University Press, 2004.

Künzli, Andreas, Boris Kolker, and Anatolo Gonĉarov. "'Kio ne estas Malpermesita, Tio estas Permisita'—Sovetia Esperanto-Movado en Kvazaŭ Sekreta Misio." *Spegulo* (Autumn 2008): 134–57. http://e-novosti.info/forumo/viewtopic.php?t=5124. [Esperanto]

Kymlicka, Will, and Alan Patten, eds. "Introduction." *Language Rights and Political Theory*. Oxford, UK: Oxford University Press, 2003, 1–51.

Lapenna, Ivo. *Elektitaj Paroladoj kaj Prelegoj*. 2nd ed. Rotterdam: Universala Esperanto-Asocio, 2009. [Esperanto]

Lapenna, Ivo. *Hamburgo en Retrospektivo: Dokumentoj kaj Materialoj pri la Kontraŭneŭtraleca Politika Konspiro en Universala Esperanto-Asocio*. 2nd ed. Copenhagen: Horizonto, 1977. [Esperanto]

Lindstedt, Jouko. "La Manifesto de Raŭmo: Historia Endkonduko—kaj Elkonduko." http://www.helsinki.fi/~jslindst/raumo-jl.html. [Esperanto]

Lins, Ulrich. *Utila Estas Aliĝo: Tra la Unua Jarcento de UEA*. Rotterdam: Universala Esperanto-Asocio, 2008. [Esperanto]

Löwenstein, Anna. "*Sekso Kaj Egaleco*: Feminisme Remerori." *Femina* no. 13 (2008): 14–16. [Esperanto]

Minnaja, Carlo, ed. *Eseoj Memore al Ivo Lapenna*. Denmark: Internacia Scienca Instituto Ivo Lapenna, 2001. [Esperanto]

Pabst, Bernhard. "Marie Hankel (1844–1929), Esperanto-Dichterin, Organisatorin, Feministin." Bonn: self-published, 2002. http://www.familienforschung-pabst.de /EspBiographien/EspBiogr/Hankel.pdf. [German]

Phillipson, Robert. *Linguistic Imperialism*. Oxford, UK: Oxford University Press, 2003.

Sekso kaj Egaleco (1979–1988). http://www.gazetejo.org/node/419. [Esperanto]

Silfer, Giorgio [Valerio Ari]. "Kion Signifas Raumismo." *La Ondo de Esperanto* no. 5 (1999): 55. http://esperanto.org/Ondo/H-silf55.htm. [Esperanto]

Taylor, Charles. "Cross-Purposes: The Liberal-Communitarian Debate." In *Debates in Contemporary Political Philosophy: An Anthology.* Ed. Derek Matravers and Jon Pike, 195–212. New York: Routledge, 2003.

Tonkin, Humphrey. "'Generale Parolante':—Lapenna kiel gvidanto kaj oponanto." *Beletra Almanako* 8 (June 2010): 103–13. [Esperanto]

Tonkin, Humphrey. "Ideoj Kiuj Restas Freŝaj." *Kongresa Libro, 72a Universala Kongreso de Esperanto,* 16–22. Rotterdam, Universala Esperanto-Asocio, 1987. [Esperanto]

Tonkin, Humphrey. *Lingvo kaj Popolo: Aktualaj Problemoj de la Esperanto-Movado.* Rotterdam: Universala Esperanto-Asocio, 2006. [Esperanto]

Tonkin, Humphrey and Mark Fettes. "Esperantic Studies and Language Management in a Globalized World." Presentation. "Multidisciplinary Approaches in Language Policy and Planning," University of Calgary, 5 Sep. 2013.

Urueña, Maria Rafaela. "Esperanta Civito kaj Internacia Juro." http://www.eventoj.hu/steb/juro/civito-kaj-juro.htm. [Esperanto]

Acknowledgments

═══

For gifting the world with Esperanto, my abiding gratitude to Ludovik Lazarus Zamenhof.

I want to thank the dedicated Rob Moerbeek at the Biblioteko Hektor Hodler in Rotterdam and the hospitable staff at the UEA Central Office: Osmo Buller, Roy McCoy, Ionel Onet, Stanka Starcevik, Clay Magalhães, Francisco Veuthey, and Tobiasz Kaźmierski. Mark Fettes and Veronika Poór, in their respective roles as president and general director of the UEA, have done everything possible to encourage me. The staff of the Österreichische Nationalbibliothek in Vienna, especially Herbert Mayer, kindly assisted my research, as did the staffs of the New York Public Library and the Firestone Library at Princeton University, with particular thanks to John Logan, David Jenkins, and Karin Trainer. A welcome grant from the Esperantic Studies Foundation inaugurated the Macaulay Esperanto Fellowship; thanks also to Dean Ann Kirschner for her enthusiasm and to Bill Maxey for his innovative five-borough teaching.

My footnotes don't adequately acknowledge the scholarship of several important Esperantologists, including Ulrich Becker, Detlev Blanke, Roman Dobrzyński, Ralph Dumain, William R. Harmon, David Jordan, Christer Kiselman, Aleksander Korĵenkov, the late N. Z. Maimon, Geoffrey Sutton, John Wells, Bertilo Wennergren, and especially Ulrich Lins. For their contributions to my research, I'm grateful to Desaix Anderson, Carolyn Biltoft, Julia Falk, Roberto Garvía, Michael Gordin, Tatiana Hart, Susannah

Heschel, Sarah Horowitz, Stan Katz, Mark Mazower, Arika Okrent, Rachel Price, Jeffrey Veidlinger, and Michael Walzer.

It's a privilege to be part of an open-minded community of humanists at Princeton University. Dean David Dobkin generously supported my travel; Carol Rigolot and the Council for the Humanities provided an Old Dominion Fellowship. Michael Wood, Claudia Johnson, and Bill Gleason, past and present chairs of the Department of English, have provided both moral and financial support; many thanks to the department's dedicated staff. Portions of this book have been presented at Princeton to the Society of Fellows, the Old Dominion Fellowship, and the Program in Translation and Intercultural Communication, deftly chaired by David Bellos. I am also grateful to Brian Horovitz, Nancy Sinkoff, Jonathan Wilson, Nora Gerard, and the conference committee of the Association for Jewish Studies for inviting me to present my work at Tulane, Rutgers, Tufts, the National Yiddish Book Center, and the 2014 and 2015 AJS Conferences, respectively. My colleagues at NASSR warmly received a wayward romanticist's presentations on the concept of universal language.

In 2007 Alana Newhouse, ever on the cutting edge, was the first to publish an excerpt from this book in the *Forward*. My writing here has also benefited from several other distinguished editors: Leon Wieseltier (formerly) at the *New Republic*; Jonathan Freedman at *Michigan Quarterly Review*; Jackson Lears at *Raritan*; and Nancy Sherman at *Pakn Treger*.

My Virgil in *Esperantujo* has been the wise and generous Humphrey Tonkin. Humphrey has shared his time, wit, deep knowledge of all things Esperantic, skills as a translator, and love of literature. When there is a judgment call, I call on him. His inspiring friendship and counsel have made all the difference.

For their hospitality and camaraderie, I'm grateful to Renato Corsetti and Anna Löwenstein, Alejandro Cossavella, Birke Dockhorn, Jane Edwards, Ursula and Giuseppe Grattapaglia, Anatoly and Irina Ionesov, Lee Miller, and José Antonio Vergara. Amri Wandel, guide extraordinaire, helped me avoid falling to my death in Nahal Darga, in four languages. To *samideano* Hans Adriaanse, for explaining everything, *koran dankon*. Filmmaker Sam Green, with his documentary *The Universal Language* (2011), has enabled us all to see Esperanto with fresh eyes.

I cannot personally thank the thousands of Esperantists with whom I've shared congresses and gatherings—even mojitos and salsa lessons—

over the past decade. But this book is the richer for my conversations with the following: Steven Brewer, Neil Blonstein, Mikael Bronŝtejn, Alberto Calienes, Betty Chatterjee, Michael Cuddy, Stephen Cybulski, Probal Dasgupta, Ellen Eddy, István Ertl, Giti Ferdosnia, Ada and Igor Ferreira de Sousa and Riccardo Biaggi, Allan Fineberg, Hoss Firooznia, Normand Fleury and Zdravka Metz, Donald Gasper, Marielle Giraud, Ronald Glossop, Kenneth Goldberg, Geoffrey Greatrex, Przemek Grzybowski, Alperen Güman, Ueli Haenni, Jerzy Handzlik, Lucy Harmon, Juliano Hernández Angulo, Bill Harris, Eliza Kehlet, Simmon Keith, Kalle Kniivilä, Anna Lászay, Juan Lazaro Besada, E. James Lieberman, Lai Ty Hai Ly, Perla Martinelli, Maria Lourdes Martinez, Rafael Mateos, Jed Meltzer, Doron Modan, Shai Mor, Dina Newman, Nam Ngo, Murat Ozdizdar, Fernando Paredes, Nguyen Thu Quynh, Tsvi Sadan, Keyhan Sayadpour, Giorgio Silfer, Konuralp Sunal, Brandon Sowers, Spomenka Stimec, Indu Thalapia, Hiroki Usui, Arnold Victor, Julie Winberg, Brittany Young, Tom Yuval, Can Zamur, the *NASKanoj* of 2008, the children of Bona Espero, and the talented CUNY students in the Macaulay Esperanto Fellowship. In losing Don Harlow, Yosi Shemer, Esti Sebban, and Dori Vallon-Wheeler, *Esperantujo* has lost several great souls. They are much missed.

Steve Wasserman believed in this book from the start, and I will be forever grateful for his wise counsel and deep reading. Metropolitan Books, led by Sara Bershtel and Riva Hocherman, has been an excellent home for this project about a wandering, universal language. Riva Hocherman taught me how to sculpt this elephant, helping me to chip away everything that isn't elephant. Every page of this book has benefited from her good sense, sage advice, and empathic reading. I can't imagine having an editor with a more profound or nuanced understanding of language, nationhood, Judaism, Zionism, universalism—in short, everything that matters most in this book, and for this (and her patience) I am eternally grateful. Thanks also to Metropolitan's excellent team, including Grigory Tovbis, Molly Bloom, Emily Kobel, Alison Klooster, Pat Eisemann, and Meryl Sussman Levavi.

I'd like to think that because *Bridge of Words* survived the ordeals of my past decade, including two hurricanes, a burglary, divorce, and in 2013 the deaths of two beloved people, it now embarks on its public life tempered and durable. For their "silken ties of love and thought," for being my "supporting central cedar pole," I thank my family. Daniel, Jordan, and Susannah lovingly consoled me, boosted my spirits, and bore with my travel schedule; Jordy even wears the Esperanto T-shirts I gave him. For their home-team cheers and much else, I thank Joshua, Lori, Noemi, Shayna, and Rafaella; Gideon, Shara, and Sandy; Laura; Walter and Elyssa; Bert and Karen; Sherri; Bob and Lily; and Dan M., Rachael, and Christa. Walter Greenblatt, aside from providing exemplary co-parenting and enduring friendship, helped me mull over what sort of book this might someday be during a chilly walk around Mountain Lakes: "for this relief, much thanks." My late father, Joseph M. Schor, was an inspiration and a source of quiet strength; I miss him greatly. For caring for him with loving kindness, thanks to Marilyn Rillera, Eljay Mundin, and Teresita Ilar. Dean Drummond left me his passion for life, his transcendent music, and his loving family: Aleta, Rick, Adrian, and Gabriel; Ilana, Sharon, Micah, and Ella; Barry, Iis, Julian, and Gita; Booker, Ruby, and Marie.

My thanks to the many friends and colleagues who lent me the succor and fortitude to see this book to completion: Patti Hart, Laura Nash, Adrienne Sirken, Sally Goldfarb, Joe Straus, Michael Straus-Goldfarb, Martha (Marni) Sandweiss, Maayan Dauber, Susanne Hand, Melissa Lane, Andrew Lovett, Linda Bosniak, Andrew Bush, Sandie Rabinowitz, Deborah Hertz, Joanne Wolfe, Irwin Keller, Galit Gottlieb, David Gottlieb, Robbie Burnstine, Andrea and Steve Maikowski, Cathy and Russ Molloy, Margie and Steve Barrett, Janine and Chris Martin, Anne Barrett Doyle, Andrew Solomon, Rosanna Warren, Joel Cohen, Herbert Marks, Michael Greenberg, Leonard and Ellen Milberg, Harvey Kliman and Sandy Stein, Jeff Knapp and Dori Hale, Jonathan Wilson, Deborah Nord, Philip Nord, Maria DiBattista, Susan Stewart, Jill Dolan, Stacy Wolf, Nigel Smith, Jeff Dolven, Sarah Rivett, Susan Wolfson, Sean Wilentz, Bruno Carvalho, Colin Dayan, Ken Gross, Michael Gorra, Ilan Stavans, Liora Halperin, and Dorothea Von Moltke. My dear and trusted interlocutor Jonathan Rosen got it before I did, as he so often does.

For the joy of his company and the delight of his art, my love and gratitude to Dan Schlesinger, whom I recognized in profile.

ESTHER SCHOR
Princeton, 2016

Index

About the Author

ESTHER SCHOR is the author of *Emma Lazarus*, which received a 2006 National Jewish Book Award, and *Bearing the Dead: The British Culture of Mourning from the Enlightenment to Victoria*. A poet and essayist, she has published two volumes of poems, *Strange Nursery: New and Selected Poems* and *The Hills of Holland*, as well as a memoir, *My Last J-Date*. Her essays and reviews have appeared in *The New York Times Book Review*, *The Times Literary Supplement*, the *New Republic*, *Tablet*, the *Jewish Review of Books*, and *The Forward*, among other publications. A professor of English at Princeton University, Schor lives in Princeton, New Jersey.